Modern Critical Views

Modern Critical Views

Modern Critical Views

HENRY JAMES

Edited and with an introduction by
Harold Bloom
Sterling Professor of the Humanities
Yale University

CHELSEA HOUSE PUBLISHERS
New York ◊ Philadelphia

Printed and bound in the United States of America

3 5 7 9 8 6 4

∞ The paper used in this publication meets the minimum
requirements of the American National Standard for Permanence
of Paper for Printed Library Materials, Z39.48–1984.

Library of Congress Cataloging-in-Publication Data
Henry James.
  (Modern critical views)
  Bibliography: p.
  Includes index.
  1. James, Henry, 1843–1916—Criticism and
interpretation. I. Bloom, Harold. II. Series.
PS2124.H43 1987   813'.4   86–24444
ISBN 0–87754–696–7 (alk. paper)

Contents

Editor's Note

This book brings together what I judge to be the best criticism yet written on the work of Henry James, the foremost American novelist. The critical essays are reprinted here in the chronological order of their original publication. I am grateful to Marijke Rijsberman, Henry Finder, and Susan Laity for their erudition and judgment in helping me to edit this volume.

My introduction first discusses James's relation to Emerson and his tradition, and then centers upon *The Portrait of a Lady* and Isabel Archer as a representation (and critique) of Emersonian Self-Reliance. The chronological sequence of criticism begins with Francis Fergusson's investigation of James's idea of dramatic form, and the part that idea played in James's only literary failure: his career as a dramatist.

Richard Poirier, still the best of Jamesian critics, reads the early novels *The American* and *Washington Square* for their comic sense of James's complex fate as the central American novelist. *The Golden Bowl,* James's late masterpiece, is interpreted by Laurence Bedwell Holland as a crisis of transformation in which James himself becomes morally implicated, even as he labors to bring forth both a sense of evil and a possibility of redemption from the fictive marriages that he has created.

"Daisy Miller" is read by Carol Ohmann as a drama of changing authorial intentions on James's part, while Tony Tanner analyzes *The Ambassadors* in terms of Strether's stance at a crucial moment in the novel. Two enigmatic and masterly novellas, "The Turn of the Screw" and "The Beast in the Jungle," are interpreted, by Juliet McMaster and Elisabeth Hansot respectively, as fables of Jamesian temporality, at once visionary and frightfully actual.

David Howard, meditating on *The Bostonians*, finds the novel to be both a generous and a sardonic Jamesian investigation of the American past in relation to American character and personality, of both North and South. Centering upon the Parisian episode of *The Tragic Muse,* D. J. Gordon and

John Stokes discuss James's dilemma in connecting the public and the artistic lives. In the context of *The American, The Awkward Age,* and *The Sense of the Past,* Robert L. Caserio illuminates *The Wings of the Dove* as an intricate instance of James's narrative art at its most strenuously advanced. *The Wings of the Dove* also figures in Martin Price's essay, as does *The Ambassadors,* but Price's principal emphasis is upon *The Awkward Age,* which he explicates brilliantly as a parable of Jamesian moral imagination.

The Spoils of Poynton and *What Maisie Knew* are studied by Carren O. Kaston as fables of the dialectical balance in James of the contraries of imagination and desire, in a nice juxtaposition with the preceding essay by Deborah Esch, which reads "The Jolly Corner" as an ironic reversal of James's usual choice of imagination over the labyrinths of desire. Mark Seltzer in some sense addresses the same dialectic in his reading of *The Princess Casamassima,* which he sees as an immense but worked-through and rigorous continuity between "seeing, knowing, and exercising power."

In the concluding essay of this book, the Portuguese critic Maria Irene Ramalho de Sousa Santos provides a superb commentary upon the tragic freedom that Isabel Archer attains by her dark choice of returning to her impossible marriage with Osmond. That investigation of choice as a shadowed, late version of American Self-Reliance returns us to my introduction, with its similar sense of Isabel's troubled relationship to Emerson's American dream of somehow bringing together, in a new and radical unity, our empirical and ontological selves.

Introduction

The intense critical admirers of Henry James go so far as to call him the major American writer, or even the most accomplished novelist in the English language. The first assertion neglects only Walt Whitman, while the second partly evades the marvelous sequence that moves from Samuel Richardson's *Clarissa* through Jane Austen on to George Eliot, and the alternative tradition that goes from Fielding through Dickens to Joyce. James is certainly the crucial American novelist, and in his best works the true peer of Austen and George Eliot. His precursor, Hawthorne, is more than fulfilled in the splendors of *The Portrait of a Lady* and *The Wings of the Dove*, giant descendants of *The Marble Faun*, while the rival American novelists—Melville, Mark Twain, Dreiser, Faulkner—survive comparison with James only by being so totally unlike him. Unlikeness makes Faulkner—particularly in his great phase—a true if momentary rival, and perhaps if you are to find a non-Jamesian sense of sustained power in the American novel, you need to seek out our curious antithetical tradition that moves between *Moby-Dick* and its darker descendants: *As I Lay Dying, Miss Lonelyhearts, The Crying of Lot 49*. The normative consciousness of our prose fiction, first prophesied by *The Scarlet Letter*, was forged by Henry James, whose spirit lingers not only in palpable disciples like Edith Wharton in *The Age of Innocence* and Willa Cather in her superb *A Lost Lady*, but more subtly (because merged with Joseph Conrad's aura) in novelists as various as Fitzgerald, Hemingway, and Warren. It seems clear that the relation of James to American prose fiction is precisely analogous to Whitman's relation to our poetry; each is, in his own sphere, what Emerson prophesied as the Central Man who would come and change all things forever, in a celebration of the American Newness.

The irony of James's central position among our novelists is palpable,

1

since, like the much smaller figure of T. S. Eliot later on, James abandoned his nation and eventually became a British subject, after having been born a citizen in Emerson's America. But it is a useful commonplace of criticism that James remained the most American of novelists, not less peculiarly nationalistic in *The Ambassadors* than he had been in "Daisy Miller" and *The American*. James, a subtle if at times perverse literary critic, understood very well what we continue to learn and relearn; an American writer can be Emersonian or anti-Emersonian, but even a negative stance towards Emerson always leads back again to his formulation of the post-Christian American religion of *Self*-Reliance. Overt Emersonians like Thoreau, Whitman, and Frost are no more pervaded by the Sage of Concord than are anti-Emersonians like Hawthorne, Melville, and Eliot. Perhaps the most haunted are those writers who evade Emerson, yet never leave his dialectical ambiance, a group that includes Emily Dickinson, Henry James, and Wallace Stevens.

Emerson was for Henry James something of a family tradition, though that in itself hardly accounts for the plain failure of very nearly everything that the novelist wrote about the essayist. James invariably resorts to a tone of ironic indulgence on the subject of Emerson, which is hardly appropriate to the American prophet of Power, Fate, Illusion, and Wealth. I suggest that James unknowingly mixed Emerson up with the sage's good friend Henry James, Sr., whom we dismiss as a Swedenborgian, but who might better be characterized as an American Gnostic speculator, in Emerson's mode, though closer in eminence to, say, Bronson Alcott than to the author of *The Conduct of Life*.

The sane and sacred Emerson was a master of evasions, particularly when disciples became too pressing, whether upon personal or spiritual matters. The senior Henry James is remembered now for having fathered Henry, William, and Alice, and also for his famous outburst against Emerson, whom he admired on the other side of idolatry: "O you man without a handle!"

The junior Henry James, overtly celebrating Emerson, nevertheless remarked: "It is hardly too much, or too little, to say of Emerson's writings in general that they were not composed at all." "Composed" is the crucial word there, and makes me remember a beautiful moment in Stevens's "The Poems of Our Climate":

> There would still remain the never-resting mind,
> So that one would want to escape, come back
> To what had been so long composed.

Emerson's mind, never merely restless, indeed was never-resting, as was the mind of every member of the James family. The writings of Emerson, not composed at all, constantly come back to what had been so long composed, to what his admirer Nietzsche called the primordial poem of mankind, the fiction that we have knocked together and called our cosmos. James was far too subtle not to have known this. He chose not to know it, because he needed a provincial Emerson even as he needed a provincial Hawthorne, just as he needed a New England that never was: simple, gentle, and isolated, even a little childlike.

The days when T. S. Eliot could wonder why Henry James had not carved up R. W. Emerson seem safely past, but we ought to remember Eliot's odd complaint about James as critic: "Even in handling men whom he could, one supposes, have carved joint from joint—Emerson or Norton—his touch is uncertain; there is a desire to be generous, a political motive, an admission (in dealing with American writers) that under the circumstances this was the best possible, or that it has fine qualities." Aside from appearing to rank Emerson with Charles Eliot Norton (which is comparable to ranking Freud with Bernard Berenson), this unamiable judgment reduces Emerson, who was and is merely the mind of America, to the stature of a figure who might, at most, warrant the condescension of James (and of Eliot). The cultural polemic involved is obvious, and indeed obsessive, in Eliot, but though pleasanter in James is really no more acceptable:

> Of the three periods into which his life divides itself, the first was (as in the case of most men) that of movement, experiment and selection—that of effort too and painful probation. Emerson had his message, but he was a good while looking for his form—the form which, as he himself would have said, he never completely found and of which it was rather characteristic of him that his later years (with their growing refusal to give him the *word*), wishing to attack him in his most vulnerable point, where his tenure was least complete, had in some degree the effect of despoiling him. It all sounds rather bare and stern, Mr. Cabot's account of his youth and early manhood, and we get an impression of a terrible paucity of alternatives. If he would be neither a farmer nor a trader he could "teach school"; that was the main resource and a part of the general educative process of the young New Englander who proposed to devote himself to the things of the mind. There was an advantage in the nudity, however, which was that, in Emerson's case at least, the things of the mind did get themselves admirably well considered. If it be his great distinction and his special sign that he had a more vivid conception

of the moral life than any one else, it is probably not fanciful to say that he owed it in part to the limited way in which he saw our capacity for living illustrated. The plain, God-fearing, practical society which surrounded him was not fertile in variations: it had great intelligence and energy, but it moved altogether in the straightforward direction. On three occasions later—three journeys to Europe—he was introduced to a more complicated world; but his spirit, his moral taste, as it were, abode always within the undecorated walls of his youth. There he could dwell with that ripe unconsciousness of evil which is one of the most beautiful signs by which we know him. His early writings are full of quaint animadversion upon the vices of the place and time, but there is something charmingly vague, light and general in the arraignment. Almost the worst he can say is that these vices are negative and that his fellow-townsmen are not heroic. We feel that his first impressions were gathered in a community from which misery and extravagance, and either extreme, of any sort, were equally absent. What the life of New England fifty years ago offered to the observer was the common lot, in a kind of achromatic picture, without particular intensifications. It was from this table of the usual, the merely typical joys and sorrows that he proceeded to generalise—a fact that accounts in some degree for a certain inadequacy and thinness in his enumerations. But it helps to account also for his direct, intimate vision of the soul itself—not in its emotions, its contortions and perversions, but in its passive, exposed, yet healthy form. He knows the nature of man and the long tradition of its dangers; but we feel that whereas he can put his finger on the remedies, lying for the most part, as they do, in the deep recesses of virtue, of the spirit, he has only a kind of hearsay, uninformed acquaintance with the disorders. It would require some ingenuity, the reader may say too much, to trace closely this correspondence between his genius and the frugal, dutiful, happy but decidedly lean Boston of the past, where there was a great deal of will but very little fulcrum—like a ministry without an opposition.

The genius itself it seems to me impossible to contest—I mean the genius for seeing character as a real and supreme thing. Other writers have arrived at a more complete expression: Wordsworth and Goethe, for instance, give one a sense of having found their form, whereas with Emerson we never lose the sense that he is still seeking it. But no one has had so steady and constant, and above all so natural, a vision of what we require and what we are capable of in the way of aspiration and independence. With Emerson it is ever the special capacity for moral experience—always that and only that. We have the impression, somehow, that life had never bribed him to look at anything but the soul; and indeed in the world in which he grew up and lived the bribes and lures, the beguilements and prizes, were few. He was in an admirable position for showing, what he constantly endeavoured to show, that the prize was within. Any one who in New England at that time could do that was sure of success, of listeners and sympathy: most of all, of course, when it was a question of doing it with such a divine persuasiveness. Moreover, the way in which Emerson did it added to the charm—by word of mouth, face to face, with a rare, irresistible voice and a beautiful mild, modest authority. If Mr. Arnold is struck with the limited degree in which he was a man of letters I suppose it is because he is more struck with his having been, as it were, a man of lectures. But the lecture surely was never more purged of its grossness—the quality in it that suggests a strong light and a big brush—than as it issued from Emerson's lips; so far from being a vulgarisation, it was simply the esoteric made audible, and instead of treating the few as the many, after the usual fashion of gentlemen on platforms, he treated the many as the few. There was probably no other society at that time in which he would have got so many persons to understand that; for we think the better of his audience as we read him, and wonder where else people would have had so much moral attention to give. It is to be remembered however that during the winter of 1847–48, on the occasion of his second visit to England, he found many listeners in London and in provincial cities. Mr. Cabot's volumes are full of evidence of the satisfactions he offered, the delights and revelations he may be said to have promised, to a race which had to seek its entertainment, its rewards and consolations, almost exclusively in the moral world. But his own writings are fuller still; we find an instance almost wherever we open them.

It is astonishing to me that James judged Emerson's "great distinction" and "special sign" to be "that he had a more vivid conception of the moral life than any one else," unless "the moral life" has an altogether Jamesian meaning. I would rather say that the great distinction and special sign of James's fiction is that it represents a more vivid conception of the moral life than even Jane Austen or George Eliot could convey to us. Emerson is not much more concerned with morals than he is with manners; his subjects are power, freedom, and fate. As for "that ripe unconsciousness of evil" that James found in Emerson, I have not been able to find it myself, after reading Emerson almost daily for the last twenty years, and I am reminded of Yeats's late essay on Shelley's *Prometheus Unbound,* in which Yeats declares that his skeptical and passionate precursor, great poet that he certainly was, necessarily lacked the Vision of Evil. The necessity in both strong misreadings, James's and Yeats's, was to clear more space for themselves.

Jealous as I am for Emerson, I can recognize that no critic has matched James in seeing and saying what Emerson's strongest virtue is: "But no one has had so steady and constant, and above all so natural, a vision of what we require and what we are capable of in the way of aspiration and independence." No one, that is, except Henry James, for that surely is the quest of Isabel Archer towards her own quite Emersonian vision of aspiration and independence. "The moral world" is James's phrase and James's emphasis. Emerson's own emphasis, I suspect, was considerably more pragmatic than that of James. When James returned to America in 1904 on a visit, after twenty years of self-exile, he went back to Concord and recorded his impressions in *The American Scene*:

> It is odd, and it is also exquisite, that these witnessing ways
> should be the last ground on which we feel moved to ponderation
> of the "Concord school"—to use, I admit, a futile expression; or
> rather, I should doubtless say, it *would* be odd if there were not
> inevitably something absolute in the fact of Emerson's all but
> lifelong connection with them. We may smile a little as we "drag
> in" Weimar, but I confess myself, for my part, much more sat
> isfied than not by our happy equivalent, "in American money,"
> for Goethe and Schiller. The money is a potful in the second case
> as in the first, and if Goethe, in the one, represents the gold and
> Schiller the silver, I find (and quite putting aside any bimetallic
> prejudice) the same good relation in the other between Emerson
> and Thoreau. I open Emerson for the same benefit for which I
> open Goethe, the sense of moving in large intellectual space, and
> that of the gush, here and there, out of the rock, of the crystalline
> cupful, in wisdom and poetry, in Wahrheit and Dichtung; and
> whatever I open Thoreau for (I needn't take space here for the

good reasons) I open him oftener than I open Schiller. Which comes back to our feeling that the rarity of Emerson's genius, which has made him so, for the attentive peoples, the first, and the one really rare, American spirit in letters, couldn't have spent his career in a charming woody, watery place, for so long socially and typically and, above all, interestingly homogeneous, without an effect as of the communication to it of something ineffaceable. It was during his long span his immediate concrete, sufficient world; it gave him his nearest vision of life, and he drew half his images, we recognize, from the revolution of its seasons and the play of its manners. I don't speak of the other half, which he drew from elsewhere. It is admirably, to-day, as if we were still seeing these things *in* those images, which stir the air like birds, dim in the eventide, coming home to nest. If one had reached a "time of life" one had thereby at least heard him lecture; and not a russet leaf fell for me, while I was there, but fell with an Emersonian drop.

That is a beautiful study of the nostalgias and tells us, *contra* T. S. Eliot, what James's relation to Emerson actually was. We know how much that is essential in William James was quarried out of Emerson, particularly from the essay "Experience," which gave birth to Pragmatism. Henry James was not less indebted to Emerson than William James was. *The Portrait of a Lady* is hardly an Emersonian novel; perhaps *The Scarlet Letter* actually is closer to that. Yet Isabel Archer is Emerson's daughter, just as Lambert Strether is Emerson's heir. The Emersonian aura also lingers on even in the ghostly tales of Henry James.

II

Isabel Archer may be the fictional heroine above all others with whom modern literary intellectuals are certain to fall in love. That sounds funny, yet is intended quite seriously. That Henry James himself was in love with her is palpable. Critics and biographers frequently associate her with Minny Temple, James's beloved cousin, who had died at the age of twenty-four. That James was deeply in love with Minny Temple we may doubt, but if he ever was in love with any woman, it was with her, and with her representation in the heroine of *The Portrait of a Lady*.

Leon Edel makes the interesting (and disquieting) suggestion that Isabel is a portrait not only of Minny but of James himself:

The allusion to her "flame-like spirit" suggests that Isabel is an image of James's long-dead cousin Minny Temple, whom he would describe in the same way. But if Isabel, with her eager imagination and intellectual shortcomings, has something of Minny in her make-up, she has much of Henry himself. He endows her with the background of his own Albany childhood, and when he sends her to Europe and makes her into an heiress, he places her in a predicament similar to his own. James was hardly an "heir"; but his pen had won him a measure of the freedom which others possess through wealth. In posing the questions: what would Isabel do with her new-found privileges? where would she turn? how behave? he was seeking answers to the transcendentalism of Concord: his novel is a critique of American "self-reliance."

A much more sophisticated analysis of the problematical ways in which James's masterpiece is a critique of Emerson is provided by Richard Poirier in *The Comic Sense of Henry James* (1960):

This connection between James and Emerson is worth attention because, as it has already been shown, the idealistic and romantic attitudes towards experience which are to be found in Emerson's essays are observable as well in the whole body of significant American fiction from Melville and Hawthorne to Faulkner. The relationship between James and Emerson is important within the larger fact that both of them subscribe to attitudes which are discernibly American, regardless of whether the literature derives from New England, New York, the South, or the West. It has often been said that Isabel Archer is an imitation of George Eliot's Dorothea Brooke, but it is apparent from all the novels of James which have no resemblance to *Middlemarch,* and from their Emersonian echoes, that *The Portrait of a Lady* could have brought the theme of aspiration to the point it does without the help of George Eliot.

Poirier's important formulation seems to me the necessary beginning of critical wisdom concerning *The Portrait of a Lady.* As Poirier observes, the novel's severest irony "is the degree to which Osmond is a mock version of the transcendentalist," which makes it not surprising that "Isabel, whose mental processes are authentically Emersonian, should see an image of herself in the man she marries." I would add to Poirier's point that Osmond is as much a mock version of the Paterian aesthete as he is of the Emersonian transcendentalist, which is again appropriate, since Isabel is both an authentic Emersonian and a true Paterian consciousness. Her blindness as to Osmond's true nature, a blindness not cleared away until too late, may be taken as James's implicit judgment that Emerson and Pater alike had no true vision of evil, but that would make James too much a forerunner of T. S. Eliot and too little an heir of George Eliot, to whom his affinities are far more profound. It makes little sense to say that Dorothea Brooke in *Middlemarch* falls into her initial dreadful marriage because her Wordsworthian idealism cannot accommodate reality, and even less sense to believe that Isabel Archer is a victim either of Emersonian aspiration or of Paterian sensibility.

Whatever James took Emersonian self-reliance to be, we can recognize in Isabel her own version of Emerson's post-Christian American religion, with its grand style of aspiration, that seems to center for James's Lady in the Sage of Concord's most dangerous admonition:

> Life only avails, not the having lived. Power ceases in the instant
> of repose; it resides in the moment of transition from a past to
> a new state, in the shooting of the gulf, in the darting to an aim.
> ("Self-Reliance")

Isabel declines to be one of the secondary women, which means that she rejects European history. As a believer in self-reliance, she quests after a knowing in which she herself will be known. Does her quest fail as massively as the disaster of her marriage to Osmond would seem to indicate? Poirier, reading the novel as Jamesian comedy, gives a complex answer, which informs me without altogether persuading me. Is Isabel's what Emerson called a great defeat, necessarily unacceptable to Americans because we demand victory? Is James somehow more Virgilian than Emersonian? In Poirier's judgment, as I interpret it, James is both, because Isabel ends as that sublimely unlikely compound ghost, a Virgilian Emersonian:

> James had a very tenuous and unorganized sense of the connection between sexual psychology, on the one hand, and, on the other, the desire for freedom and death. He had a very clear and conscious idea, however, about the relationship between freedom and death, and it is that which comes through to us from the final chapters. What Caspar offers her in the garden is an old call to action and freedom: "The world is all before us." While the intensity of her reaction to Caspar deserves the closest attention,

the reasons for her refusal to go away with him need no explanation. She is simply not deeply enough in love with him nor has she ever been. When she hurries away from him, however, she is also escaping his call to leave the "garden" of her dreams now that, like Eden after the fall, it has become a place of desolation. The Miltonic echo in his plea is unmistakably placed there. The same line occurs much earlier in the novel when Isabel sees her relatives off for America. Having done her duty by these figures out of her past, and in possession of what seems unhampered independence, she walks away from the station into the London fog: "The world lay all before her—she could do whatever she chose." In James's use of the phraseology of *Paradise Lost* ("The world lay all before them, where to choose/Their place of rest. . . ."), there is not only a Miltonic sadness, but also an irony derived from the fact that neither Isabel nor Caspar is free to choose anything. His life is in useless bondage to his love for her, while hers is dedicated to its errors. And there is nothing in her act which holds the promise, as does Adam and Eve's, of eventual happiness through suffering, even though Ralph assures her that there is. Her action is absolutely within the logic of her Emersonian idealism, so much so that the logic takes its vengeance. In effect she tells the reader, to borrow from "The Transcendentalist," that "you think me the child of my circumstances: I make my circumstance,"—including, one might add, "my own misery." It is of no importance to her that, in fact, she has been so calculatingly deceived by other people that it is preposterous to assume all the responsibility for her own past. To admit this would be finally to subscribe to Madame Merle's view that the "self" is determined, in part, by "an envelope of circumstances" that one does not always create. Isabel's action at the end is fully consistent with everything she does earlier. Now, however, she asserts her idealism of self not in innocence but in full knowledge of the world. For that reason, freedom, which was the condition of self-creation, becomes a form of indifference to the fact that returning to Rome will, as Caspar admonishes, cost her her life.

The overt anti-Emersonianism of Madame Merle's view of the self, noted both by Philip Rahv and by Poirier, seems to me an involuntary or repressed allusion on James's part. Yet I read the novel's conclusion a touch more hopefully than Poirier does. Caspar Goodwood is hardly the answer, any more than Warburton was, and James himself labored to make certain that Ralph Touchett could not be the answer either. Since Isabel fuses Minny Temple and James himself, no marriage could be the answer, and the male otherness of Goodwood only drives Isabel back to the house of death. When James revised the novel for the New York edition, his emphasis upon both Isabel's possibilities for freedom and the severe limitations set by context and fate upon that freedom became obsessive, particularly in regard to Isabel's hovering dread of the erotic threat to her inward liberty. The "disagreeably strong push, a kind of hardness of presence, in his way of rising before her," clearly dismisses the revised Goodwood as a distasteful phallic phenomenon, and so unacceptable to Isabel, who finds, however absurdly, in the repellant Osmond "a future at a high level of consciousness of the beautiful." Anthony J. Mazzella, in his close study of the novel's revisions, finds in "the new Isabel" a more remarkable consciousness, both of freedom and of vulnerability, than was possessed by the original Isabel. This is surely equivalent to the difference between the Emerson of "Self-Reliance" and the dark necessitarian of *The Conduct of Life,* so that we move from the sage who insisted that "the only sin is limitation" to the theoretician of "Power" who warns us that "nothing is got for nothing," and that this is the true law of Compensation.

It cannot be accidental that Isabel's psychosexual vulnerabilities are so like James's own (so far as we are able to tell) and that her apotropaic gestures are essentially his also. Leon Edel wisely avoids any overt characterization of the Master's ineluctable modalities of sexual evasiveness, which have been speculated on so bizarrely by others, with suppositions as remarkable as Hemingway's, who jauntily persuaded Scott Fitzgerald that their greatest American precursor had been physically impotent. In *The Sun Also Rises,* the castrating wound of Jake Barnes is related to James's catastrophe, fantasied both as a bicycle- and a horse-riding accident. Crazy as this was, it is no weirder than the notion even Edel plays with, which is that Henry James never could resolve his homoerotic attachment to his brother William, scarcely less eminent as philosopher and psychologist than Henry was as a novelist.

I suspect that Henry James in his psychosexual orientation resembled Walt Whitman more strongly than he did anyone else in literary history. Like Whitman, his desires were essentially homoerotic, and, again like Whitman, he appears to have evaded any merely actual fulfillment of those desires. The distrust of human sexuality in both writers is immense, though the truly esoteric and hermetic Whitman proclaimed his ostensible passions for men, women, the soul, and the United States in a deliberately misleading sexual rhetoric, while the oddly less esoteric Master subtly swerved away from any explicitly sexual diction. A close reader of *Song of Myself* comes to realize that Whitman's poetry, and perhaps Whitman himself, were auto-erotic, while the student of James eventually knows that James and his fiction seem to lack the "narcissistic scar" that Freud saw as marking all of us, being a memento of our first failure in love, the loss of our parent of the sex opposite to ours to our parent of the same sex as ours. Whatever his authentic relation to George Eliot and to Trollope, to Hawthorne and to Emerson, James also seems not to have needed to restitute a wounded narcissism as an author. His striking originality as a novelist, nearly akin to Whitman's as a poet, has a still obscure but vital relation to his warding-off of mere sexuality. Just as Whitman is an erotic rather than a sexual poet, since he crosses sex with death, so James is an intensely erotic novelist, while largely eschewing direct representations of the sexual.

Isabel's eros, being transcendental, is not crucified by the failure of her marriage, since her Jamesian desire remains for her own aspiring self and not for any outward companion. Moral readings of *The Portrait of a Lady* seem to me always to fail, because inherited systems of morality—Christian or humanistic—are irrelevant to Isabel's Emersonian self, as they are to Whitman and to James. Distinguished readers always go wrong on this. I think of the novelist Graham Greene, who remarked that James's ruling passion, in the *Portrait* as elsewhere, was the idea of treachery, or of the moral philosopher Dorothea Krook, who criticizes Isabel for "fatal aestheticism." Madame Merle's treachery, though it has its interest, remains peripheral to Isabel's fate, and James himself is far more tainted with a "fatal aestheticism" than Isabel or Emerson are. Searching for a tragic flaw in Isabel always leads to the banal discovery that, like Emerson, she supposedly lacks that grand New Critical, neo-Christian, T. S. Eliotic virtue—a Vision of Evil. But Isabel is the heroine of the American, post-Christian version of the Protestant will; she is the heiress of all the ages, and so inherits from the great sequence of Clarissa Harlowe, Elizabeth Bennet, Emma Woodhouse, and Dorothea Brooke. What matters is the integrity of her will. For her, love entails her conferring of esteem upon others, and accepting back from them only her own authentic self-esteem. Her will declines the Freudian cosmos of mourning and melancholia. No shadow of the object can fall upon her ego. Consider the great scene between her and Goodwood, a scene more visionary than melodramatic, that effectively ends the inward aspect of the novel. Goodwood has echoed Milton: "The world's all before us—and the world's very big," a truth that Isabel knows better than does her perpetually frustrated suitor:

Isabel gave a long murmur, like a creature in pain; it was as if he were pressing something that hurt her. "The world's very small," she said at random; she had an immense desire to appear to resist. She said it at random, to hear herself say something; but it was not what she meant. The world, in truth, had never seemed so large; it seemed to open out, all round her, to take the form of a mighty sea, where she floated in fathomless waters. She had wanted help, and here was help; it had come in a rushing torrent. I know not whether she believed everything he said; but she believed just then that to let him take her in his arms would be the next best thing to her dying. This belief, for a moment, was a kind of rapture, in which she felt herself sink and sink. In the movement she seemed to beat with her feet, in order to catch herself, to feel something to rest on.

"Ah, be mine as I'm yours!" she heard her companion cry. He had suddenly given up argument, and his voice seemed to come, harsh and terrible, through a confusion of vaguer sounds.

This however, of course, was but a subjective fact, as the metaphysicians say; the confusion, the noise of waters, all the rest of it, were in her own swimming head. In an instant she became aware of this. "Do me the greatest kindness of all," she panted. "I beseech you to go away!"

"Ah, don't say that. Don't kill me!" he cried.

She clasped her hands; her eyes were streaming with tears. "As you love me, as you pity me, leave me alone!"

He glared at her a moment through the dusk, and the next instant she felt his arms about her and his lips on her own lips. His kiss was like white lightning, a flash that spread, and spread again, and stayed; and it was extraordinarily as if, while she took it, she felt each thing in his hard manhood that had least pleased her, each aggressive fact of his face, his figure, his presence, justified of its intense identity and made one with this act of possession. So had she heard of those wrecked and under water following a train of images before they sink. But when darkness returned she was free. She never looked about her; she only darted from the spot. There were lights in the windows of the house; they shone far across the lawn. In an extraordinarily short time—for the distance was considerable—she had moved through the darkness (for she saw nothing) and reached the door. Here only she paused. She looked all about her; she listened a little; then

she put her hand on the latch. She had not known where to turn;
but she knew now. There was a very straight path.

What Isabel's straight path will lead her to is the renewed Emersonian
realization that she herself is her own alternative. More than the noise of
waters is in her own swimming head. The erotic imagery of this superb
encounter is oceanic, but more in the mode of Whitman's maternal, deathly
ocean than in what Freud deprecated as "the oceanic sense" of mystical
illusion. A mighty sea, fathomless waters, a rushing torrent, and most of all,
those wrecked and under water following a train of images before they sink—
these figures can be read from at least two radically different perspectives,
both Whitmanian enough. One would oppose the waters to Isabel as the
eros of otherness that she rejects, but the other would offer the waters as
emblem of a world centered upon Isabel, in evidence that she had made her
circumstances, and so chose to accept them, the world of Wallace Stevens's
"Tea at the Palaz of Hoon":

What was the sea whose tide swept through me there?

Out of my mind the golden ointment rained,
And my ears made the blowing hymns they heard.
I was myself the compass of that sea:

I was the world in which I walked, and what I saw
Or heard or felt came not but from myself;
And there I found myself more truly and more strange.

This is a hymn of self-reliance, and the chanter could be Whitman, or
Emerson, or Pater (adding strangeness to beauty in quest of the Romantic).
Or she could be Isabel Archer, not at the close of the novel, but beyond, in
that resumed difficult marriage with Osmond, whom she no longer loves,
and who no longer loves her. But she herself will be the compass of that sea.

FRANCIS FERGUSSON

James's Idea of Dramatic Form

It has often been pointed out that James's attempt to write for the theatre marks an important turning point in his career. He had behind him a certain success as a writer of fiction, but this success had begun to wane. He felt that his aims as an artist were becoming clearer, but that his public was losing interest. After his experience with the theatre he returned to the novel. But at the moment of writing his plays he could not see what form his work was to take, and he seems to have considered the possibility at least that it would be drama. He had followed the theatre all his life, and was aware that his fiction approached the form and texture of drama. He envied Dumas and Labiche their secure possession of a stage, an audience, a "theatre."

But the theatre he had to write for was the British theatre of the eighties. The well-made play of the Scribe tradition, lightened and sweetened to suit the taste of the theatregoers of Victorian London, held the stage. Drama was understood as a plot or machine for holding the attention of an audience for two hours, and then releasing it in a good humor. The great Sarcey wrote, "The audience is the necessary and inevitable condition to which dramatic art must accommodate its means. . . . From this simple fact we derive all the laws of the theatre without a single exception." When James set out to write his comedies he put the problem to himself in exactly these terms: to accept that audience and learn to obey the laws derived from its habits and its taste. "The mixture," he wrote, "was to be stirred to the tune of perpetual motion

From *The Kenyon Review 5*, no. 1 (Autumn 1943). © 1943 by Kenyon College.

and served, under pain of being rejected with disgust, with the time-honored bread-sauce of the happy ending."

This narrow and cynical conception of drama is of course "true" as far as it goes. It is a necessary condition of drama that it hold an audience. Yet on this basis we have no clue to the distinction between various dramatic genres, or even between drama and other devices for entertaining an audience in a theatre. The notion goes back, I think, to the seventeenth century, when all the arts addressed themselves to a comparatively small and homogeneous society, the embodiment of all values and the arbiter of taste. The neoclassic theorists in their reading of Aristotle failed to notice the distinction between *mythos* and *praxis,* plot and action; they did not digest the Aristotelian notion of drama as the imitation of an action by means of plot. This left them without an explicit theory of the substance of drama, and hence with a purely mechanical and empirical idea of its form. They assumed that serious drama was substantially the conflict between love and honor, or passion and reason, or desire and duty. Subsequent generations of theatregoers were to lose their interest in this theme, but not their demand for entertainment. We have seen the tyranny of the consumer become as absolute in drama as in advertising, and the playwright study his trade in the same spirit as the layout man and copy-writer.

James found no difficulty in learning the tricks of this trade, and he turned out four plays which are mechanically as neatly put together as one could wish. All four are perpetually agitated comedies, parlor games, the stakes "love" and money. At the beginning of each we are shown the characters paired off in a certain arrangement which is not quite satisfactory; by the end they have effected a shift into a new and happier pattern. The suspense, the speed of the story, and the succession of clear and stagey situations never flag for a moment. James had solved the problem which he as craftsman had set himself. But it was easy for him, as it is for us, to see why the experiment was not a success. It was not satisfactory to him because the nature of the form ruled out in advance any subject he would have been interested in trying to dramatize. He could only take a minor idea, he says, which, with the habit of small natures, proved thankless. It is too evident that he disliked his characters and that the happy ending offended his taste. This must all have been as puzzling and unsatisfactory to his audience as it was to him.

When he wrote the preface to the published plays he speculated a little ruefully about what the plays might have been. He thought that the tone of farce might have carried them off if the audience had not so inexorably demanded the "bland air of the little domestic fairy tale." In spite of his attempts at good nature, his plays do approximate now and then a cold, hard Jonsonian type of farce, based on flat external caricature, and boldly absurd situations—a form in which the mechanical ticking of the plot is part of the basic vision. I think it possible that if one produced a James play now in the costume of the eighties one might bring out this farce. Perhaps an audience would even accept it as a satirical picture of a society now safely remote.

He abandoned the stage, but without thinking that the drama or even the theatre lacked the resources he required. It was rather that particular form of drama and that particular theatre which baffled and thwarted him. As he turned away from the theatre he wrote, "Give me an hour, just an hour; Dumas and Augier never lacked it, and it makes all the difference; and with it I shan't fear to tackle the infinite." It was about this time too that he wrote the article on Coquelin which contains the following fine description of that actor's art:

> M. Coquelin's progress through this long and elaborate part, all of fine shades and pointed particulars, all resting on the keenest observation as well as appealing to it, resembles the method of the psychological novelist who (when he is in as complete possession of his form as M. Coquelin of *his*) builds up a character, in his supposedly uncanny process, by touch added to touch, line to line, illustration to illustration, and with a vision of his personage breathing steadily before him.

II

When James embarked upon his last group of novels and his critical prefaces he was free to tackle the subject which really interested him. It was in the effort to "dramatize" this subject that he made his great discoveries in dramatic form and technique. It is true that by rejecting the theatre as he found it he also rejected some of the limitations which any theatre imposes upon drama: the strict time limits, and the obligation to maintain a certain rhythmic tension in the face of that impatient crowd of Sarcey's. He clearly luxuriates in this freedom, multiplying his discriminations, taking his time, putting out of patience a large group of readers who accuse him of verbosity and hair-splitting. His novels are not literally dramas. I am not even sure that the phrase "described dramas" is very accurate for them. Yet both the texture of the writing and the large outlines of the form are truly dramatic. And I wish to suggest that his ideas of form and of techniques of presentation throw at least as much light upon drama as upon fiction.

The critical prefaces have been carefully studied by Joseph Warren Beach, Percy Lubbock, R. P. Blackmur, and others with whose work I am less familiar. Thanks to their work many of James's technical notions have become generally available. In the following notes I have taken some of the ideas, and indicated how they might be applied to drama, and what basic conceptions of dramatic form they constitute.

"Picture and Scene"

Percy Lubbock makes much of the distinction between "picture" and "scene" which James mentions several times in his prefaces. He writes,

> It is the method of picture-making that enables a novelist to cover his great spaces of life and quantities of experience so much greater than any that can be brought within the acts of a play. . . . The limitation of drama is as obvious as its peculiar power. It is clear that if we wish to see an abundance and multitude of life we shall find it more readily and summarily by looking for an hour into a memory, a consciousness, than by merely watching the present events of an hour, however crowded. . . . But it needs a mind to create that vista.

A novelist may and often does break down and tell all, while a writer for the stage never can. In this sense the novelist commands a resource not available to the dramatist. But this resource, so conceived, James disdained. He felt how easily it degenerated into mere formless loquacity. He preferred to dramatize the picture too, by viewing it through a consciousness different from his own, that of a character in the drama. The method is that of the dramatist, and if you look at a drama which contains "great spaces of life and quantities of experience" you can see the dramatist employing it. Behind the chief characters in *Antony and Cleopatra, Troilus and Cressida, King Lear,* these great spaces extend, because the characters are aware of them. In the two hours of playing time of *Ghosts* Ibsen makes us feel many years of Mrs. Alving's life and experience by making the characters in their various ways feel them. Mr. Lubbock's analysis suffers throughout from his failure to understand the nature and scope of the stage medium. The actors are not there only to illustrate for us the facts of the story, but through their make-believe to create an imagined world for the eye of the mind to dwell upon. Good dramatic writing, like good acting, owes much of its quality to the establishment of these imagined perspectives behind and beyond the little figures on the boards.

The Fine Intelligence as "Reflector" and as Compositional Center

James almost invariably used a fine intelligence to give us the clue to the other characters and to the issues and values of his dramas. It had to be a fine intelligence if it was to perceive what James wanted his audience to perceive through it, yet it could not be James himself, for then James would have been telling us *about* his subject instead of presenting it to us directly. The problem and the solution both belong to drama, and good drama is full of Jamesian "reflectors." Enobarbus in *Antony and Cleopatra* is one. In the first three acts he interprets Antony and Cleopatra for us. We come to depend on him for the clue even when we have the chief characters in the flesh before us. This function is very clear in scene 13 of act 3, when Cleopatra receives Caesar's emissary and Antony has him whipped. Enobarbus not only shows us what to think of Antony and Cleopatra at various moments, he also sums up the impression of the whole scene for us several times and at the end. It is not too much to say that the scene is composed and pulled together for us in Enobarbus' consciousness of it. Shakespeare thus uses Enobarbus both as "reflector" and as "compositional center" for this scene.

These notions of the reflector, and of the fine intelligence as the center of composition, are as useful in the analysis of Chekhov's or Congreve's plays as in the analysis of Shakespeare's. The practitioners of "well-made" drama, who usually conceive their subjects in terms of a single narrative line or a monolinear argument, the demonstration of a thesis, do not need the notion of the reflector. Any dramatist who conceives his subject in the round, capable of being looked at from various angles, needs and uses these devices. But it was James who defined them clearly.

Situations as Lamps or Reflectors

James describes the structure of *The Awkward Age* as follows:

> I drew on a sheet of paper . . . the neat figure of a circle consisting of a number of small rounds disposed at equal distance about a central object. The central object was my situation, my subject in itself to which the thing would owe its title, and the small rounds represented so many distinct lamps, as I liked to call them, the function of each of which would be to light with all due intensity one of its aspects. . . . Each of my "lamps" would be the light of a single "social occasion" in the history and intercourse of the characters concerned and would bring out to the full the latent color of the scene in question and cause it to illustrate, to the last drop, its bearing on my theme.

In this passage the Jamesian conception of the "round" subject is very clear. He thinks of it as a metaphysical or moral entity rather than as a sequence of events. It is, I think, an Action in Aristotle's sense of the word. The distinction between plot and action thus reappears in James's analysis of form, and he is then able to think of the story, or plot or arrangement of incidents as a means to an end: the end of revealing the Action which is the subject of the play.

He points out that the "occasions" which make up *The Awkward Age* are in effect the acts of a play. They are very much like the acts of a Chekhov play. The reviewers of Chekhov have not yet seen that his plays are composed, not as stories, in which the chief point of interest is to find out "what happened," but as a series of social occasions each of which throws its light upon the central subject. *The Cherry Orchard,* for instance, has a minimum of story in this sense, but a maximum of subject. The first act is the occasion of the return of Mme. Ranevsky's party to the Cherry Orchard; the second, a dilatory gathering on a warm evening; the third a rather hysterical party; the fourth, the departure of Ranevsky and her family. Each of these occasions illumines a facet of the subject, or action, "to possess the Cherry Orchard." By the time we are through we have seen this action from various angles and on various levels; and the completing of this vision, rather than the overt event which ends the little thread of story, completes for us the play.

There is of course no contradiction between the use of an intelligence as reflector and the use of the situation as reflector. The intelligent character reflects the occasion, and the occasion throws its light upon the central subject.

Jamesian Suspense

Though the story is never the main interest in James's late works, they are very carefully composed in the dimension of time, having a beginning, a development, and an end in temporal succession. As Joseph Warren Beach points out, this order is that of the reader's developing awareness of the subject. We are finding out, not what happened, but what the true values in the situation are. And this process of discovery is itself dramatized. Sometimes it is dramatized for us in the growing awareness of the fine intelligence at the center of the composition. Very often the development of the investigation is controlled by switching from one intelligence to another. And in addition we are led from one social occasion or scene to another, whose succession (as well as their relation to the central subject) is significant.

If you once grant at all the interest of the subject, the investigation becomes a very intense and exciting project. Mr. Beach aptly compares this suspense to that of a well-planned detective story, which is an investigation on another level. But for some reason Mr. Beach seems to doubt that it is "dramatic."

There are many familiar dramas in which this type of suspense (once James has made us aware of it) may be demonstrated. It is very instructive, for example, to notice how in *Hamlet* our sense of the evil in Denmark is made to develop as we feel it now from the point of view of the soldiers, now from the point of view of the King, now from the point of view of Polonius, and now from the point of view of Hamlet himself. Perhaps the clearest example is *Oedipus the King.* This drama is primarily an investigation; and though it has the swift movement and the "plot interest" of the mystery story, it is also an investigation of the moral and metaphysical realities of Oedipus' situation. These interest the chorus even more deeply than the question, Who killed Laius?

James's Subject as a Static Composition

When we have taken, in succession, the points of view of the various "reflectors," when we have seen the central intelligence, on various "occasions," complete its investigation, the drama is over, and the subject is revealed as a static composition. In *The Golden Bowl,* for instance, Maggie Verver is gradually revealed as the central intelligence. She understands, at length, herself and all the other characters in relation to the issues and the values of the action they have been through—she gets at last the "truth" of their situation. In her awareness and then in the mind's eye of the reader the whole comes to rest, and is perceived as motionless, like the composed canvas of a painter.

Mr. Beach has described the composition of James's later novels in terms like these. He concludes that James's subject is essentially plastic rather than narrative or dramatic. He thinks that the narrative movement is lost in these later novels; and though he feels that they are full of the sense of "dramatic struggle" he cannot quite explain to himself how, granted the static subject, drama can still be there. I should prefer to say that the late novels are narrative *and* dramatic *and* plastic. The heresy would be to insist on one aspect of their form to the exclusion of the others.

As for the painter, he also may compose with a temporal succession of perceptions in mind; he also has ways of guiding the eye of the spectator from element to element to the final "stasis of aesthetic pleasure."

The notion of drama as a static composition is not popular with modern writers on the subject. Yet in what other terms are we to describe the full-stop, the final rest, with which a completely achieved drama ends? This moment or this aspect corresponds to the epiphany in Greek drama. In Euripides the epiphany is characteristically presented in plastic terms—an arrangement of properties and corpses, with a visible *deus ex machina*. In Sophocles, though there may be a significant grouping of the characters, in tableau form, at the end, the final synthesis is made in the mind of the chorus as it at last "sees the truth."

III

It is easy to see, after the event, why James never found a public stage for his drama. The first answer is of course that the established and recognized public stage was too limited and too hard to crack. If you then go on to study the drama in his best novels, you see that this drama, by its very nature, postulates an audience which doesn't exist, so to speak, in public; and that it is founded upon James's anomalous and unique traditionalism, which is also far removed from the public consciousness.

James's drama is that of a fine, perceptive spirit which endeavors to secure for itself the best that the world has to offer: "Life," at its sharpest point of intensity and awareness. This fine spirit is always dispossessed, even disembodied. There is usually some circumstance to explain its having been deprived of life—an American upbringing, poverty, a fatal but hidden disease. Some of James's critics have tried to explain this deprivation in Freudian terms, as the result of some disturbance in James's own emotional life. It is true that James keeps sexual passion at the periphery of his consciousness; but his drama is no more disembodied sexually than it is in a number of other ways. His attitude to sex may be a symptom rather than a cause, and one can believe that if he had had a place and a name, "sex" also would have been added unto him. However that may be, his fine spirits exist almost exclusively on the plane of moral awareness and activity.

To "register" at all, they require therefore a stage, a setting, a "theatre" which is based upon and embodies their awareness. James's fine spirits are usually American, but he hypostatizes the setting as "Europe," as a drawing room, like Shaw's secure, feeling eternal (so that even the Shavian bandits drink tea at five)—but unlike Shaw's the epitome of culture and the heir of the ages. Its architectural setting, its costume and its custom, its taboos and its hierarchies, all of its forms, embody the values the Jamesian Americans are seeking, and above all the value of concrete embodiment itself. For James's people, who must exist on what he called the "high plane," are extremely worldly, pagan, moral, and irreligious. The values they seek are traditional, but a tradition which no longer informed a society would be of no use to them whatever.

This drama is "dramatic" enough, even stagey, and James always felt it to be so. It is not subjective or private, being in the tradition of European moralists since the Greeks. But it is difficult to make its elements visible to a modern audience.

I have remarked that Chekhov was no more interested than James in the monolinear story or thesis, but saw his subject in the round; and that he evolved a form with many close analogies to James's. He also assumed a society—or rather (the distinction is important) found one—and stuck close to it. He was in this the physician rather than the moralist; he took the people, the themes, and the situations he found around him. The material of his art was what his audience was already prepared to recognize, whereas a large part of James's ingenuity is spent in making the elements of his composition visible at all. Chekhov's people are perhaps more lost than James's, but being lost in the flesh and the feelings, they are not lost to public view. If James had known Chekhov he would probably have felt that he had "lapsed to passivity from the high plane."

James did know Ibsen's plays, and was among the first in London to recognize his mastery as a dramatist. The plays of Ibsen's naturalistic period start, like James's own comedies, with Scribe, and it is possible to read them as social theses or as well-constructed stories. But his plays are composed on a deeper level also. He is neither sociologist nor entertainer, but, like James, a moralist. James recognized this also, but with mixed feelings. In Ibsen's plays, he wrote, "the lamp of the spirit burns as in tasteless parlors with the flame practically exposed." He may have been remembering the America he left, which must have been similar in many ways to Ibsen's Norway. James could no more accept Ibsen's Norway as real and ultimate than he could the America of the seventies. Ibsen's characters are not trying to realize a life of the spirit in any sort of traditional cultivated society; it is doubtful whether, in their gloomy quests, they envision the possibility of *any* "life," and certainly they are unaware of a traditional wisdom that could have anything to say to them. James complains that Ibsen's dramas always end at the point where the true interest and the true comedy of things should begin. And I think one can see that if Rosmer and Rebecca, for example, had married under the eyes of a group of interested and intelligent friends, instead of jumping into the millrace together, a truly "bristling" Jamesian subject would have resulted. But at the same moment Ibsen would have lost his audience. The plays which do end on such a note, *The Lady from the Sea, Little Eyolf,* are still the least esteemed of all Ibsen's dramas.

Did James ever think that British society actually provided the setting and the awareness he needed? Probably not; certainly not for long—his early letters seem to show that clearly. He willingly admitted that his people were too intelligent and too gifted to be probable. Their ideal social intercourse was derived from James's experience of society, but eventually became almost independent of it. He seems to have been moving toward an unrealistic theatrical convention, based on the rules and the tensions of politeness; the kind of convention which makes possible a Bérénice, a Hippolyte, an Alceste, a Millamant. Such a "stage" was a fundamental postulate of his inner life and of his art, and even in the semi-retirement of his last period he continued to live up to its ghostly urbanity and agility. It is this which makes his prose so entirely unlike that of Proust or Virginia Woolf. Though he left society, he clung to its values; and while Proust recorded the dissolution of the moral being, James, with his shadow-boxing, kept in excellent trim.

The drama that James knew did not survive the last war. The most interesting writers for the stage between 1918 and 1939—among whom I should include Yeats, Eliot, Cocteau, Obey, Lorca—start completely afresh. The influences of the Moscow Art Theatre, the Ballet, and the Music Hall, combine to produce a new conception of the theatrical medium. Not only nineteenth-century naturalism, but most European drama back through the seventeenth century, is explicitly rejected in favor of medieval farce, Greek tragedy, peasant rituals and entertainments. The new dramatists are likely to be interested in religion, in myth, and in types of symbolism designed to reach a popular audience. Most of them would I think approve of Cocteau's description of *poésie de théâtre* as like the cordage of a ship—a composition of large coarse elements easily perceptible at a distance. Their estrangement from the audience of before the war—if indeed it still exists—is complete. They neither ask for the support of the carriage trade, nor try, like James, to build a notion of the ideal cultivated spectator into their theatrical forms. The traditions and the symbols they like antedate the founding of the drawing-room.

It is not yet clear whether this strategy is any less desperate than James's. The vision they get of a drama speaking directly to the population in simple, ancient, fundamental terms, is perhaps a flattering illusion, like that of the mythical drowning man who sees his whole life before him at the moment of going under for the last time. Paris in the twenties is already far away, and we see now some of the dangers in the new line. One needs, I think, to place against Cocteau's theatrical virtuosity, and Eliot's abstract theological framework, and Lorca's luxuriant popular imagery, the Jamesian and classic conception of an Action, seen in the round, seen from many angles. James paid dearly for his position above the battle, but he found there some curiously universal technical concepts, useful in contexts he never dreamed of; and a conception of dramatic form which we still need if we are to see the drama of his time and ours in the right perspective.

RICHARD POIRIER

The American *and* Washington Square:
The Comic Sense

In James's own response to Paris there is an intensely felt differentiation
between its admirable but highly constricting emphasis on social and literary
techniques and, opposing this, those more humanly inclusive and aspiring
qualities which he found in Turgenev and in himself. This differentiation is
apparent everywhere in *The American,* but most clearly in the almost allegorical rigidity with which James places his characters in relationship to one
another. It is extremely important to notice, however, that he initially assigns
certain values to characters mostly through the verbal comedy with which
he introduces them. James's comedy in his introductory descriptions of a
character's personal appearance accomplishes two almost contradictory
things: it emphasizes the representational significance of a character, but, at
the same time, it prevents us, by making us laugh, from being immediately
moralistic in our reactions. This is quite different from, say, the allegorical
tendencies in Trollope. In *Barchester Towers* Trollope engages our interest
in a very limited social issue by making us, through his descriptions of
character, partisans of the "good" side. He does so, however, with little of
the modifying and complicating comedy one finds in James. Indeed, part of
the pleasure in Trollope is in the ease with which we can have an uncom-
plicated antipathy: Harding, we are told, "did not hate the chaplain as the
archdeacon did, and as we do." In *The American,* old Madame de Bellegarde
and her son Urbain, whose names make us wonder if James was not forgetting

From *The Comic Sense of Henry James: A Study of the Early Novels.* © 1960, 1967
by Richard Poirier. Oxford University Press, 1967.

himself when [in *Partial Portraits*] he accused Trollope of being primitively satiric for calling one of his characters Quiverful, are both placed in static moral positions from the moment we meet them. But James's stylistic ingenuity in describing them makes us take pleasure in those very features of their characterizations which, as the plot will reveal, are actually poisonous. Comedy is thereby a means of temporarily suspending our desire to make moral generalizations. In a way, this use of verbal surface is an imitation, in James's art, of manners in Parisian society. By using his literary art to take us in, as it were, James makes it less likely that we will misunderstand how easily Newman is deceived by social art. Like Newman, we later see that in allowing ourselves to be entertained we had missed seeing enough.

When James dislikes a character in *The American* he does so with verbal flamboyance, particularly in his revisions of the novel, and with a colourful and hyperbolic abuse. As I have been saying, he thereby deflects those responses of disapproval which the point of the description would seem to allow. A similar use of language in characterization is what induces us in American frontier literature to admire the scoundrels, like Johnson J. Hooper's Simon Suggs, or, in Dickens, to be sometimes delighted by the characters who most appal us. Mr. H. R. Hays, if his comments on satire in the late novels are any indication, would call this "cheating by way of technique," by which he means that James tries to hide his "shaky values" by trickery. Such a view of the matter could only be held along with an extremely naïve conception of fiction. Dramatic literature exists only because it does "cheat," as philosophy does not. It does not "reveal" attitudes to us or affirm values, it makes us *experience* certain kinds of action by making us respond to certain kinds of language. And above all it is meant to entertain us. Fiction makes us feel, if anything, the necessity of moral uncertainty when confronted with a dramatic imitation of life. This is particularly apparent if one responds to the comedy in an action. A comic description substantially lessens, though it does not remove, the tendency towards moral strictures. The reason for this is that comedy is in itself an evidence that the object or the person being dealt with is under control. There is less worry about a villain when he is the object of a jest. This may explain why in the revisions of his novels James tends to increase and heighten the comedy which he imposes on those he does not like. Having securely tied them down some years earlier, he proceeds to decorate his victims for our entertainment. Consider, for example, the initial descriptions of Tristram. In the first edition he is said to be

> corpulent and rosy, and though his countenance, which was or-
> namented with a beautiful flaxen beard, carefully divided in the

middle and brushed outward at the sides, was not remarkable for intensity of expression, he looked like a person who would willingly shake hands with any one.

[he] was a rather degenerate mortal. . . . People said he was sociable, but this was as much a matter of course as for a dipped sponge to expand.

After the final revision, Tristram is

large, smooth, and pink, with the air of a successfully potted plant, and though his countenance, ornamented with a beautiful flaxen beard carefully divided in the middle and brushed outward at the sides, was not remarkable for intensity of expression, it was exclusive only in the degree of an open door of an hotel—it would have been closed to the undesirable.

[He] had somehow found means to be degenerate without the iridescence of decay. People said he was very sociable, but this was as much a matter of course as for a dipped sponge to expand.

The comparisons in this description are extravagant, especially in the revisions, where the changes may be regarded as indicating a clarification by exaggeration of what James originally implies. The revision does not suggest that James intended to change the substance of what he had originally written, but only that he wanted to intensify the comic response which is elicited by both versions. Each of them emphasizes the absurdity and vulgarity of Tristram's sociability. Indeed, part of Tristram's significance in the novel is in the way he lets us discriminate about the otherwise highly valued quality of responsiveness and openness. The metaphors, particularly in the revised form, have in common the suggestion of unintelligent absorption of whatever is offered: he is compared to a "plant," the "open door of an hotel," and a "sponge." His sense of what is "undesirable" is, like that of the objects to which he is compared, determined not by intelligence but by the most simpleminded and predetermined discrimination.

The analysis of the meaning of these comic metaphors is as tiresome, even, perhaps, as unconvincing, as the analysis of most jokes. To admit this is a way of stressing the point that in the act of reading, in experiencing these passages with proper attention and excitement, we do not very seriously acknowledge the significance which analysis allows us to see in these metaphors. We do not, and James does not want us to do so. Conceiving of a metaphor as having two parts, one of which is the picture that entertains and the other the significance that instructs, we can say that James wants us to laugh at the first rather than be solemnly concerned with the second. The significance is inescapably suggested when we look for it, particularly after the dramatic action has encouraged us to a retrospective analysis. But it is important to admit that it is retrospective. By the end of the novel our amusement at the picture has exhausted itself, and we are left with the bare meaning in its full dramatic force—Tristram's tiresome social coarseness. All the flabby promiscuity of his incomprehending mind comes out with comic outrageousness in his final remarks to Newman after Claire has been irrevocably lost:

> If I express myself strongly it is all because I love you so much; and from that point of view I may say I should as soon have thought of making up to that piece of pale high-mindedness as I should have thought of making up to the Obelisk in the Place de la Concorde.

The picture in the metaphors I have been discussing is comic to the point of slap-stick. Even the rhythm of the sentences in which the metaphors occur is that of a man who is not worried about scoundrels and who enjoys keeping them in line for us by making them look foolish. Only later are the implications of the metaphors brought into focus by the dramatic action.

The relationship between dramatic action and metaphorical patterns in this novel is, therefore, a delicate one. To analyse a metaphor at a given moment in the novel, to assign it a significance in some metaphorical pattern garnered from the novel as a whole, and then to claim as a result that the experience of that particular moment is the same as the significance heaped upon the metaphor is too pervasive a practice in literary criticism to need illustration. It is a result of such analytical procedure that comedy in James has been ignored. It has been ignored by critics who ask not "what is it like to be reading this" but "what does this mean," and by "mean" they customarily have in mind something like the content usually and properly associated with non-dramatic discourse, philosophy, or sociological psychology. In talking about comedy, it is necessary to stress that in dramatic literature the primary concern of literary criticism is the *way* we apprehend the meaning, our experience of it rather than the meaning itself, abstractly considered. *The American* is in many ways both shrill and superficial in its handling of character and in the exclusion of moral and psychological complications from the kind of life which it organizes. It is saved from being wholly superficial not by its philosophical meanings but by the way in which we are allowed to apprehend them. It is made into an experience that mature readers can appreciate by its comedy, and this will become more apparent in a further discussion of its metaphors and their dramatic function.

The basic dramatic conflict is, essentially, between Newman's way of looking at life and Madame de Bellegarde's. The nature of the conflict, as well as the partisanship of James, is apparent in the descriptions of personal appearance. These descriptions are, first of all, invariably comic, though they differ as to the kind of comedy, and, second, they all involve metaphors either of seclusion, for the Bellegardes, or hospitality, for Newman and his allies. The thematic expression of things that are "fixed" and "free" has already been discussed as a basic feature of James's comedy. At this point in James it is not merely a principle behind his characterizations, as in *Roderick Hudson*. It is also an explicit part of his comic vocabulary. In *The American,* as I observed previously, the notion of "free" and "fixed" characters is expressed largely in terms of openness and enclosure, of largeness and expansion as against smallness and contraction. Madame de Bellegarde's mouth is first described as a

> conservative orifice, a little pair of lips at once plump and pinched, that looked, when closed, as if they could not open wider than to swallow a gooseberry or to emit an "Oh, dear, no!"

And although the figure of Urbain is described as noble and majestic, he is said to have "small opaque eyes," and in the revised edition his "thin smile" is made into the comic picture of "a smile that affected [Newman] as the scraping of a match that doesn't light." In his habit of walking up and down the room he is compared to "a sentinel at the door of some smooth-fronted citadel of the proprieties." Similarly, their house in Paris has a face "as impassive and as suggestive of the concentration of privacy within as the blank walls of Eastern seraglios—it answered to Newman's conception of a convent." There are many such comparisons in the novel, all of them in sharp contrast to the impression we are given of Newman, who, in the first page, is lounging "with legs out-stretched" in the spacious Salon Carré of the Louvre. Unlike the Bellegardes, he confidently offers to let the world "go ahead and try me," a phrase of which he is extremely fond. He can wittily remark to Tristram, who selected Newman's rooms with an eye to the latter's social standing, that "I didn't know I 'stood' socially at all—I thought I only sat around informally—rather sprawling than anything else." Such images, when they have to do with Newman, are like those which help characterize the good Americans in *The Ambassadors,* where Maria Gostrey describes her expatriate countrymen by the humorously deprecating remark: "We're abysmal—but may we never be less so!"

The calculation with which James discriminates between characters in terms of "open" and "closed" sensibilities, and the way in which these discriminations are made initially by his metaphorical descriptions of appearance, is apparent in the introductions of Claire and Valentin. Both share this quality of "openness," of "general hospitality to the chances of life," which characterizes the hero in the first scene of the novel. They are, as it were, imprisoned Americans, and Newman tries literally to set them both free. James's comedy in describing them is unlike that in his descriptions of the older Bellegardes. Comedy in this instance is not satiric, and it is not meant to make us laugh. But like James's satiric comedy it has its source in highly energetic verbal exaggeration. The metaphors are periphrastic, and there is a delight in their extreme inventiveness and oddity. Akin to this sort of comedy is the comic pleasure, even sometimes the laughter, produced by any display of exorbitant human dexterity. There is a kind of gay sportiveness in the metaphors by which James expresses his pleasure in Claire and Valentin. In his descriptions of Tristram and the older Bellegardes, the extravagance of metaphor absorbs morally serious implications in comic absurdity. Similarly, when James likes a character in this novel his hyperboles tend to take us beyond discriminations about him and into a pleasurable idealization. In these instances, as in the satiric characterizations, James's revisions indicate that he enjoyed extemporizing on distinguishing features which he had essentially created in the first edition. As an example, Claire's grey eyes in the first edition are said to be "gentle and intelligent," and they become in the final revision "like a brace of deputed and garlanded maidens waiting with a compliment at the gate of a city." Such a change once again puts a stress through metaphor on "hospitality," the repeatedly emphasized characteristic of the "American" figures in the novel. Later, Claire's openness, her capacity for experience, is contrasted explicitly with her mother's stultifying completeness of character in a metaphor which makes it plain that, for Newman, Claire is a kind of American:

> Madame de Cintré's face had, to Newman's eye, a range of expression as delightfully vast as the wind-streaked, cloud-flecked distance on a Western prairie. But her mother's white, intense, respectable countenance, with its formal gaze, and its circumscribed smile, suggested a document signed and sealed; a thing of parchment, ink, and ruled lines.

Valentin is also associated with America in the hero's mind because Newman thinks it a shame that his friend's movements should be confined to the intertwining streets of Paris "when over there in America one's promenade was a continent," and he tries to arrange things so that Valentin will have an American future as surely as Claire will. As Newman sees him, he resembles his sister

> not in feature, but in the expression of his clear bright eyes, completely void of introspection, and in the way he smiled. The great point of his face was that it was intensely alive—frankly, ardently, gallantly alive. The look of it was like a bell, of which the handle might have been in the young man's soul: at a touch of the handle it rang with a loud, silver sound. There was something in his quick, light brown eye which assured you that he was not economising his consciousness. He was not living in a corner of it to spare the furniture of the rest. He was squarely encamped in the centre and he was keeping open house.

This passage and others like it illustrate a quality in James which is customarily ignored. Everyone knows that he is delicately complex in what he says, but it is seldom observed that we are led to respond to the refinements of his sensibility by very loud and broad verbal effects. It can be said of his language, particularly of his images, what he himself said of the "vibration" which he felt from a meeting with George Eliot:

> It was doubtless even excessive in proportion to its cause—yet in what else but that consisted the force and the use of vibrations? It was by their excess that one knew them for such, as one for that matter only knew things in general worth knowing.

The excessiveness in James's style, particularly in his images, is in part expressive of that melodramatic inclination which many, especially Mr. Leo B. Levy and Mr. Jacques Barzun, have noticed. It has not been noticed, however, that this same excessiveness tends to satirize the melodrama it creates, as in *Roderick Hudson,* or that its effect on the evaluation of character in *The American,* even when its final implications are most serious, is, in our immediate response, largely comic. While Mr. Dupee is essentially correct in observing that James's "remarkable metaphors" proliferate in the period of the 1890s, it should be observed that the tendency and very often the practice begins in the novels of the seventies. It is hard to forget Fleda's response in *The Spoils of Poynton* to one of Mrs. Gareth's speeches about Owen, "as if it had been the shake of a tambourine borne toward her from a gypsy dancer." But it should also be remembered that in the first edition of *Roderick Hudson* Mr. Leavenworth's face "bore a certain resemblance to a large parlor with a very florid carpet, but no pictures on the walls." Such images, and those which either occur in the first edition of *The American* or are implicitly there ready to be coined in the revision, spring from a very diverse literary tradition.

Miss Constance Rourke's account [in *American Humor*] of the literary traditions available to James at the time of *The American* is well known and highly respected. It involves, however, a number of rather surprising errors. She remarks, for example, that James's originality resides partly in his showing "that defeat had become at last an essential part of the national portraiture," where "triumph had hitherto been the appointed destiny." All of Melville, Hawthorne, and the best of Twain is, by this proposition, disregarded. Furthermore, it is apparent from what has been said so far about James's involvement in the literary world of Paris and London that it is unnecessary and unprofitable to look for the sources of his literary expression wholly in American literature. Miss Rourke explains his comedy as if it were indebted mostly to popular American humour and some of its raciness to the spectacular displays put on by Barnum. I am not questioning the fact that James was aware of the literary enormities practised by writers in his native idiom. But awareness is no guarantee that he was substantially influenced by them. His knowledge of frontier idiom is apparent in a review of *Marian Rooke,* where he accuses Henry D. Sedley of "using a form of the traditional Sam Slick dialect, in which all the humorous quaintness is omitted and all the extravagent coarseness is retained." And he explains Newman's ability to "top" Valentin's anecdotes by the fact that

> Newman had sat with Western humorists in knots, round cast-iron stoves, and seen "tall" stories grow taller without toppling over, and his own imagination had learned the trick of piling up consistent wonders.

Given what we know about James's taste and reading, however, it is likely that he was influenced more by Dickens than by American popular humour in his creation of highly imaginative images. There is also a good chance that he learned a lot about descriptive exaggeration from Swift. In 1874, reviewing a novel by J. W. de Forest, he quotes an example of what he considers "color laid on not exactly with a camel's-hair brush":

> his pulpy pink face wore an air of abiding perplexity which rivalled that of his Dundrearyish friend Ironman. At times it seemed as if his large watery features would decompose entirely

with irresolution, and come to resemble a strawberry-ice which has been exposed to too high a temperature.

(Honest John Vane)

Of this James remarks that

The author's touch, in this and similar cases, has more energy than delicacy, and even the energy aims rather wild. Did Mr. de Forest refresh his memory of Swift before writing the adventures of John Vane? He would have been reminded that though the great master of political satire is often coarse and ferocious, he is still oftener keenly ingenious.

James himself is "keenly ingenious" in the manner of Swift. As applied to Swift, the term means, for one thing, that *Gulliver's Travels* may be read as a fanciful and amusing children's book or as a serious allegory. Ideally, it is read as both simultaneously. Essentially the same kind of ingenuity is apparent in the workings of James's metaphors. The *point* of what he says in a particular figure comes to life after we have been entertained by it. He is more like Swift and less like Dickens in this particular use of language, because there always is a point behind the entertainment offered by his hyperbole. I have already commented on the effect of this in the working out of the plot of *The American* and in the control of our reactions to characters until that plot evolves. The profit of James's technique—of inviting us more to the enjoyment at a given point of the excessiveness of his descriptions than to solemnity about their significance—is clear enough when we think of Madame de Bellegarde and her friends.

While we recognize their malevolence from the moment they appear, we do not know whether to take it as part of a comedy of manners or as a portent of disaster. Both possibilities are there in the language, the first in the picture of the metaphors which we "get" as we read along; the second, in the significance of the metaphors which we fully grasp only when the action is completed. If it is to be a comedy of manners, the novel will be about the achievement of romantic ambition; if it is to be a tragedy of manners, to borrow a phrase from Mr. Frederick C. Crews, it will be about the futility of ambition. The progress of the novel is from the one to the other, which is to say that the novel moves from comic emphasis on the entertaining aspects of the metaphors to seriously melodramatic emphasis on their portentous significance. The function of James's comedy is to keep us in suspense much of the time as to which of these outcomes is the more likely. Looked at another way, the novel is about the conflict between the predominance of the pleasant images about openness and the threatening images about enclosure. The images of contraction and withdrawal which invest every description of the Bellegarde family and their properties lend an almost warlike quality to Newman's desire "to expand, without bothering about it—without shiftless timidity on one side, or loquacious eagerness on the other—to the full compass of what he would have called a 'pleasant' experience." In doing so within the Bellegarde family, Newman provides what Valentin tells him at the outset will be an "entertaining" spectacle. We can now turn to that—to the comedy in the novel which depends less on James's metaphors than on dialogue and dramatic confrontation.

The comic scenes and dialogue in the novel result in large part from the dramatic conflict between Newman's self-confident frankness and the adroit and devious sophistication of the Bellegardes, or, to repeat the terms, between "open" and "closed" social behaviour. Much of the comedy and, through it, some of the most attractive expressions of Newman's character occur because he is too spontaneously and innately superior to be able to recognize the evidences in social conduct of contrived and devious nastiness. When Valentin tells him that his inability to recognize aristocratic social superiority will make his attempts to win Claire "something of a spectacle," he replies, ironically, that "it *is* a pity that I don't understand you. I shall lose some very good jokes." At the outset, the "spectacle" reveals the capacity of the Bellegardes for witty and pointed conversation, and even when their perfidy is most apparent, near the end of the novel, the irony and sarcasm in which they and their friends indulge remains highly polished and controlled.

The even tone of comic social discourse in the novel, even though there is a progressive intensification of feeling behind it, suggests a number of things. In the first place it illustrates in the French characters the beguiling artfulness of persistent social custom and manner. Newman admires this in Madame de Bellegarde even as James admired the technique of Flaubert, though he found the substance wanting. When Newman confronts her with evidence that she is a murderer, she merely gives a small cough, "a piece of dissimulation which struck Newman as really heroic," and which brings from her less impressive elder son the question, "Dear mother, does this stuff amuse you so much?" In the second place, the consistency of social poise in the Bellegardes and their circle, with its attendant conversational witticisms, has almost the same effect on the reader as the use of comic metaphors. It keeps us from feeling certain that we really do know what is going on behind it. The discrepancy between manners and reality in the social action of the novel is like the discrepancy between the comic suggestions in

James's descriptions of Madame de Bellegarde and the dangerous realities behind them. Thus, the comedy which comes from dramatic dialogue contributes as much as the comedy in the metaphors to putting us off, as it were, and to making what finally does happen into a "mystery" which is only less surprising to us than to Newman. In illustration of this, there are three scenes involving witty social discourse which reward attention. They occur roughly at the beginning, the middle, and the end of the novel, and there is little variation between the first and the third, even though the conditions of the action have radically changed.

The first of these scenes occurs when Valentin introduces Newman to his mother, his brother, and his sister-in-law. For us, as for Newman, the centre of interest is the old Marquise, Madame de Bellegarde. Newman has been warned by Valentin not to expect to purchase her favour by being funny: "Take warning by me," he cautions his friend, "she never laughs." The effect of her constraining influence is apparent less on Valentin, whom she considers Newman's *amuseur,* than on her older and favourite son Urbain. "He is much better than this one," she tells Newman, "but he will not amuse you." The fact that neither Urbain nor his mother is very responsive to other people's humour no more prevents them from being comic themselves than it prevents Jaggers in *Great Expectations,* a man who never laughs. However, their humour is of a particular kind. Notably in the case of Urbain, the characteristic wit accepted in the Bellegarde household has the taint of being the product of punctiliously learned, but slightly defensive, high social manner. He and his mother object especially to the comic tone of Valentin. For them, he is a kind of "lord of misrule" because he can so freely and pointedly adopt what Santayana defines as the "comic mask—the irresponsible, complete, extreme expression of each moment."

Madame de Bellegarde's objection to spontaneous and free comedy finds expression in her own considerable wittiness. Indeed, she uses comedy in defence of the fixity of her position, and she satirically "bristles," as James might say, to fend off the comic improvisations by which Valentin and Newman display their different kinds of irreverence for her social posturing. The meeting between Newman and Madame de Bellegarde is therefore a contrast of the comic attitudes which are characteristic of the two types of characters that have been discussed, the "fixed" or "closed" characters and the "free" or "open" ones. The result of the meeting is a social victory for the Bellegardes and a moral victory for Newman. She effectively keeps him in place, but, compared with his expansive good nature and his impressive indifference to making fun of himself, which is a sign of his considerable strength, her self-assured witticisms are stagy and theatrical. It is as if she were addressing not this particular man but a version of him which she might have found in a bad satiric novel, a "literary" version of the untutored man of business who is something even odder, an American.

Some of Madame de Bellegarde's wit is the effect of a pretended vagueness, by which she implies that she cannot really believe in Newman's reality:

> "You are an American?" she said presently. "I have seen several Americans."
>
> "There are several in Paris," said Newman jocosely.
>
> "Oh, really?" said Madame de Bellegarde. "It was in England I saw these, or somewhere else; not in Paris. I think it must have been in the Pyrenees, many years ago. I am told your ladies are very pretty. One of these ladies was very pretty! such a wonderful complexion! She presented me a note of introduction from some one—I forget whom—and she sent with it a note of her own. I kept her letter a long while afterwards, it was so strangely expressed. I used to know some of the phrases by heart. But I have forgotten them now, it is so many years ago. Since then I have seen no more Americans. I think my daughter-in-law has; she is a great gadabout, she sees every one."

Madame de Bellegarde is certain of only one thing: that she could not have met an American in Paris, the same Paris where for James the literary people were not *accueillants*. For the rest she is very uncertain: "I think," "I am told," "I used to know," "I have forgotten." This is very different from her customary idiom, especially from the way she talks later in the scene when Newman expresses his desire to marry her daughter. She responds to this proposition with impressive brevity, by merely shaking her head and pronouncing a soft "no," while to his reminder that he is very rich she simply articulates "how rich?"

Madame de Bellegarde is a worthy opponent for a man who has seen a free-fight in Arkansas. She is a woman of formidable personal force and intelligence, and her vagueness in this conversation, like all her gestures, is a calculated effort to make people feel her powerful self-sufficiency. She means to suggest to Newman the extraordinary peculiarity, so far as she is concerned, of anyone's being an American, and she also means to suggest that the peculiarity is of no interest to her. It is simply not an imaginable part of her world. Americans, so the rhythm and substance of her comment implies, are hard to remember because no civilised society (she saw her last American in the mountains of the Pyrenees) has anything that resembles them. By the time she is finished with her references to "these," "your women," and "strangely expressed," Americans have become anthropological specimens. She thereby lends weight to the later suppositions of her friends that in his courtship of her daughter Newman is the "beast" in a re-enactment of "Beauty and the Beast." Newman's willing participation in the comedy, his "jocosity," defeats the implication that he is a barbarian, though his humour is slightly barbaric when measured against the brilliant dramatic skill of Madame de Bellegarde. Her talk is evidence of highly developed cultivation, even though it is put to the uses here of an imperturbable and polished bitchery. It is a social version of that "technical" skill which James admired in French literature.

In the conversation just discussed James manifests in his use of dialogue the same intention which he shows in his use of comic metaphors. Because we enjoy Madame de Bellegarde and because James contrives to make us find her entertaining, we tend to suspend moral disapproval of the way she treats Newman. To appreciate the value of this scene largely as entertainment is to have that "want of 'moral reaction'" of which Newman himself is accused by Babcock. Babcock, who anticipates the Wentworths in *The Europeans,* and is treated with an equally tender satire, cannot bear what he considers Newman's "gross intellectual hospitality." Just such hospitality lets us, no less than Newman, enjoy Madame de Bellegarde in spite of our suspicions about her ultimate culpability. She is marvellously clever and entertaining at the same time that she is making insinuations which are to be the very justifications for her ultimate rejection of the hero.

This brings us to a point of some importance. Comedy as it is being used here has the function of forestalling our concerns about the morality of characters, conceived of as individuals, while it stimulates our interest in them as representatives of certain kinds of social conduct. The psychology of Madame de Bellegarde is no less superficially created than that of the other characters in *The American.* But this does not mean that her status, her embodiment of a social type, is to be experienced with anything less than a complex variety of reactions. We might say that we think less of her than of the rôle she plays, and that our admiration results from the highly intelligent comedy which she creates. She is not meeting a man named Newman, she is playing a part in the social *occasion* of meeting an American millionaire. James's comedy as well as her own draws attention to her social as distinguished from her psychological identity. Our interest is engaged more by her manners, which seem to have the weight of a whole society behind them, than by any of her more personal eccentricities. We are made willing to be morally deferential because such a scene as this is presented less as a dramatic meeting which is significant for the individuals involved than as a show-piece put on to illustrate their permanent social differentiations. It is not unlike watching a morality play, wholly secularized and then presented as a musical comedy.

Despite the satire to which Newman is submitted by Madame de Belle-garde's remarks, and despite his inability to grasp fully the abusiveness of her wit, Newman emerges from this conversation and from the one that follows it in this scene even more of an idealized American than before. This may seem odd on the face of it, since if, as James puts it in *The Lesson of Balzac,* we "accept the color of the air" with which "the author suffuses his picture," we must accept James's own high estimation of witty conversation. We admire Newman, as a result, not because he is impressive in his own salon, but because he is impressive in the Bellegardes'. The fact that we are asked to appreciate Madame de Bellegarde necessarily disposes us to respect relatively supple responses to conversational ragging. That Newman emerges unscathed is partly to be ascribed, ironically, to his incomprehension. His own self-expression is never warped by a mean-minded suspiciousness that he is being insulted. As a result he appears to be indifferent in a grandly aristocratic way. He interprets all of the carefully contrived jibes as pleasant and even silly jokes.

In the scene being discussed, then, both Newman and the Bellegardes have their most attractive capacities fully engaged. The result, as the scene nears its conclusion, is one of the most charming conversations in the novel. Newman has just indiscreetly remarked to this family of unemployed aris-tocrats that he is sometimes conscious of having too much time on his hands. He is unfortunately not proficient in literature, he tells them, and he is ac-customed in any case to daily business activity: "I began to earn my living when I was almost a baby." And he adds, without any intentional sarcasm, that "elegant leisure comes hard." This speech is followed by an understand-able and profound silence, after which the conversation continues:

> "You began to earn your living when you were a mere baby?" said the marquise.
>
> "Hardly more—a small boy."
>
> "You say you are not fond of books," said M. de Bellegarde; "but you must do yourself the justice to remember that your studies were interrupted early."
>
> "That is very true; on my tenth birthday I stopped going to school. I thought it was a grand way to keep it. But I picked up some information afterwards," said Newman reassuringly.
>
> "You have some sisters?" asked Madame de Bellegarde.

"Yes, two sisters. Splendid women!"

"I hope that for them the hardships of life commenced less early."

"They married very early, if you call that a hardship, as girls do in our Western country. One of them is married to the owner of the largest india-rubber house in the West."

"Ah, you make houses also of india-rubber?" inquired the marquise.

"You can stretch them as your family increases," said young Madame de Bellegarde, who was muffling herself in a long white shawl.

Newman indulged in a burst of hilarity, and explained that the house in which his brother-in-law lived was a large wooden structure, but that he manufactured and sold india-rubber on a colossal scale.

Newman's "burst of hilarity" is not ours. He laughs at what he takes to be the Marquise's European gullibility about the wonders of the American West, or at least that is a way of taking his unnecessary explanation that the houses are wooden. We, on the other hand, laugh at the sophisticated play of mind, the vaudevillian inventiveness by which the Bellegardes not unpleasantly make fun of him. Nor is the fun entirely without point on James's part, when we notice that the dramatic conflict is adroitly characterized within the terms of the metaphor of "open" and "closed" by the juxtaposition of the expanding American rubber house with the "muffled" daughter-in-law of the Marquise.

While we see in the comedy the essential and profound differences between Newman and the Bellegardes, he sees only those differences which might be explained away. The reader's view of social differentiations is, thereby, essentially Valentin's. He is a partisan of Newman, but with a clear sense of the comedy of his position. Even though in temperament he is similar to Newman, he first calls on him, because, given their backgrounds, they are "too different to quarrel." At first he will not take his desire to marry Claire seriously. "You are not noble, for instance," he remarks, to which Newman exclaims, "The devil I am not!" In finally agreeing to further his friend's cause, he is expressing as much positive aversion for his mother and brother as fondness for the American intruder. His motive is partly in the anticipation of the amusement he will find in observing the encounters between people who are so abrasively dissimilar. In this respect he is like Mrs. Tristram who, in first suggesting the match, did so, she rather cruelly admits at the end,

out of "curiosity" as to "whether such a marriage could actually take place."
Both Mrs. Tristram and Valentin have a strong sense of personal futility, of
the waste of their own lives, which tends to make them want to experiment
with the lives of other people.

Even for those who are most anxious to help him, therefore, Newman
is, as it were, on stage when he confronts the heads of the Bellegarde family
and their friends. All his friends are more aware than he is of what is going
on. Being a part of the world of sophistication to which we, through James's
style, are given an entrance, they support Newman but want also to see if
he will measure up to the test. The test is met in such scenes as this first
meeting with the Bellegarde family. In the next meeting to be considered,
the issues of the confrontation are more sharply apparent than in the first.
But if the wit is slightly more sarcastic it is only because Newman, with the
aid of Valentin, has to deal with Urbain, a son much less clever and self-
assured than his mother. For the most part, the general tenor of the social
comedy remains essentially what it was in the first scene, despite the fact
that Newman would like to get beyond mannered talk and into plain speech.

In this meeting Newman is told that the Bellegardes will allow Claire
to listen to his proposals. Only Valentin, Newman, and Urbain are present,
with Valentin acting as a comic *raisonneur*. During their conversation, he
continually translates Urbain's snobbish insinuations into language plain
enough to expose their potential vulgarity. This naturally infuriates the elder
brother, since to indicate the necessity for clarification, as Valentin does, is
to grant that Newman is justified in being confused by the mystique of social
"differences." It is to suggest that the elaborate manners of the Bellegardes
do not necessarily express any objective reality. To put the matter generally,
if we do not accept the validity of a claim to superiority, then all expressions
of it become comic. This is especially true when a person's unjustified confidence is so smug as to make him assured that everyone will naturally
recognize his superiority. With such presumption to status comes the comic
illusion that it need only be *suggested* to be realized, and that the proof of
one's security of position lies in the very indirection of high social manners.
To those who do not allow the claim in the first place the manners seem
foolishly affected.

This is roughly what Fielding has in mind in *Joseph Andrews* when he
observes that "the only source of the true Ridiculous (as it seems to me) is
affectation," and that the causes of affectation are either vanity or hypocrisy.
Both of these emerge during this scene as particular characteristics of Urbain,
but they are revealed to us not by Newman but by Valentin. He is aware, as
Newman could not be, of what aristocracy could mean and has meant in his

ancient family. More to the point, he is also aware that Urbain's willingness to accommodate Newman is a matter of very cold and vulgar reality, the desire, in this old but impoverished family, for a fortune. As the conversation begins Valentin tells Newman that at the family conference in which his proposal to Claire was discussed:

> My mother and the marquis sat at a table covered with green cloth; my sister-in-law and I were on a bench against the wall. It was like a committee at the Corps Législatif. We were called up, one after the other, to testify. We spoke of you very handsomely. Madame de Bellegarde said that if she had not been told who you were, she would have taken you for a duke—an American duke, the Duke of California. I said that I could warrant you grateful for the smallest favors—modest, humble, unassuming. I was sure that you would know your own place, always, and never give us occasion to remind you of certain differences. After all, you couldn't help it if you were not a duke. There were none in your country; but if there had been, it was certain that, smart and active as you are, you would have got the pick of the titles. At this point I was ordered to sit down, but I think I made an impression in your favor.

The comedy in this speech derives from its extravagant unreality. In addition, the casual rationality of Valentin's tone makes the absurdities he is describing even more ridiculous, the consequence of a comic technique which owes something to Swift's *A Modest Proposal*. In the dialogue which follows, Urbain's manner of speech presumes, with quite uncalculated comic results, to give reality to the unreal pretentiousness of attitude already parodied by Valentin:

> "The novelty has not quite worn away, I confess," the marquis went on; "perhaps it never will, entirely. But possibly that is not altogether to be regretted," and he gave his thin smile again. "It may be that the time has come when we should make some concession to novelty. There have been no novelties in our house for a great many years. I made the observation to my mother, and she did me the honor to admit it was worthy of attention."
>
> "My dear brother," interrupted Valentin, "is not your memory just here leading you the least bit astray? Our mother is, I may say, distinguished for her small respect for abstract reasoning. Are you very sure that she replied to your striking proposition

in the gracious manner you describe? You know how terribly incisive she is sometimes. Didn't she, rather, do you the honor to say, 'A fiddlestick for your phrases! There are better reasons than that'?"

"Other reasons were discussed," said the marquis, without looking at Valentin, but with an audible tremor in his voice; "some of them possibly were better. We are conservative, Mr. Newman, but we are not also bigots. We judged the matter liberally. We have no doubt that everything will be comfortable."

. . . "Comfortable?" [Newman] said, with a sort of grim flatness of intonation. "Why shouldn't we be comfortable? If you are not, it will be your own fault; I have everything to make *me* so."

"My brother means that with the lapse of time you may get used to the change"—and Valentin paused to light another cigarette.

"What change?" asked Newman in the same tone.

"Urbain," said Valentin, very gravely, "I am afraid that Mr. Newman does not quite realize the change. We ought to insist upon that."

"My brother goes too far," said M. de Bellegarde. "It is his fatal want of tact again."

Valentin plays the part in this, as in other scenes, of the wise clown; as Urbain says in the revised edition, he has "no nice sense of what shouldn't be said." By his irony he indicates that he sees the asininity of Urbain's attempt to patronize Newman, and that he realizes, too, that Newman's inability even to imagine what Urbain is talking about prevents him from sufficiently discomfiting his adversary. The comedy in the earlier scene involved a series of jokes by which Newman was characterized by the Bellegardes as almost anthropologically peculiar. He was, for them, unreal. The comedy in this scene is similarly based on a conception of Newman's originality, the "difference" with which Urbain and his mother must try to be "comfortable." But Valentin's irony reveals that the unreality is in the pretensions of Urbain and not in Newman. Newman does not understand what Urbain is talking about, and the reader is encouraged by Valentin's comic renditions at least to pretend not to understand it either.

There is a sense in which Urbain's absurdity puts us off as much as it does Newman. It is not yet apparent that Urbain and his mother take their pretensions with a fateful seriousness. If Newman fails to recognize the portentousness of their manners, out of his sublime self-assurance that they cannot in any way affect the fate of a healthy and strong-willed man, so do we fail of a similar recognition, out of the assurance, given by the comedy, that Newman and Valentin can sufficiently control even the ugliest manifestations of Urbain and his mother. The comedy has the function of giving us a false sense of security in Newman's success. As a result, the reader of the novel reacts pretty much as Newman does when he hears from Claire, in the presence of Urbain and Madame de Bellegarde, that she must give him up: "This sort of thing can't be, you know. A man can't be used in this fashion."

The barrier between Newman and the Bellegardes cannot be removed by verbal explanations. They cannot possibly tell one another about the nature of the difference between them. The Bellegardes are impervious not only to the force of Newman's eloquence but even to the threat that he will expose them to public shame, using the document supplied by the old family maid, Mrs. Bread. Newman himself becomes aware of this when, confronting them with the evidence that Madame de Bellegarde murdered her husband, he finds her so inexpressively defiant. When he visits the Duchess, whom he met at his engagement party, with the intention of telling his secrets, he comes for the first time to understand just what Madame de Bellegarde's impenetrableness can rely on as a positive strength. While the whole atmosphere of the novel becomes darkened, and even as the plot moves towards the ultimate defeat of Newman's hopes, we are given in this scene with the Duchess an example of urbane and mannered comedy, a dramatic presentation of the elegant social play to which Newman at the beginning of the novel was exposed in his first meeting with the Bellegardes. This is James's way of pointing out the undisturbed continuity of poise which Newman cannot disrupt and which does not even allow him the opportunity to try.

Newman's inability to complete his errand results partly from his refusal to take cheap and immediate advantage, a characteristic of him revealed early, in the anecdote of his refusing to make a substantial profit on a man who had at one time subjected him to a calculated meanness. It is equally important, however, that the dramatic movement of the scene and the quality of the Duchess's social discourse actually give him no chance to tell his story even if he should finally decide to do so. Before his visit gets under way it is interrupted by the arrival of the Prince, who is described with the comic grotesqueness that customarily invests characters who do not contribute to the success of James's heroes:

> The Prince was a short, stout man, with a head disproportionately large. He had a dusky complexion and a bushy eyebrow, beneath which his eye wore a fixed and somewhat defiant expression; he seemed to be challenging you to insinuate that he was top-heavy.

There is a good deal of animus in the introduction of the Prince, and more so when James changes the phrase "he was top-heavy" to "he might be hydrocephalic." The vitality in the portraiture seems the more curious when we consider that the Prince has a place in the novel only in this scene, a matter of no more than two pages. When he is announced, the Duchess asks Newman to remain. The Prince is a bore, so she claims, and she desires his visit to be short. We are surprised, therefore, when her conversation with him takes the amusing and even delightful turn that it does. The Duchess, a woman of extraordinary theatrical corpulence—she earlier reminded New- man of the "Fat Lady at a fair"—begins her talk with the Prince by a description of the "sentimental vicissitudes of the Princess X," and this leads

> to a discussion of the heart history of Florentine nobility in gen-
> eral; the duchess had spent five weeks in Florence and had gath-
> ered much information on the subject. This was merged, in turn,
> in an examination of the Italian heart *per se*. The duchess took
> a brilliantly heterodox view—thought it the least susceptible or-
> gan of its kind that she had ever encountered, related examples
> of its want of susceptibility, and at last declared that for her the
> Italians were a people of ice. The Prince became flame to refute
> her, and his visit really proved charming.

We are entertained by this exactly at the point when our hero is most exasperated. This odd state of affairs can be explained by observing once again that James's social comedy at the expense of the Parisians depends upon our not taking them seriously as individuals. They are grotesque rep- resentations of people we expect to find only in the theatre, and the scene itself is managed as if it were an entr'acte. They intend that their subject of conversation should be unreal in the sense that neither is responsible for more than the sheer pleasure of contriving playful and pleasurable dialogue. To make the matter even more comically theatrical, James shows both of them as physical freaks, so that the romantic nature of their remarks is, in its intensity, both theoretical and amusingly artificial. Though no point is made of it in the language of this scene, the dramatic circumstances of the novel let us imagine that Newman's sense of exclusion at the loss of Claire is especially painful at this moment in that the discussion of love and passion assumes a world in which these things are frivolously public and very much a matter of delightful flamboyance. It is not surprising, in view of this, that Newman takes no part in the talk, that he "was naturally out of the con- versation." This experience gives him more of a clue to the impossibility of his position—he leaves almost immediately for England—than has any of his encounters with Madame de Bellegarde or Urbain:

> The duchess help him—that cold, stout, soft, artificial woman help him?—she who in the last twenty minutes had built up between them a wall of polite conversation in which she evidently flattered herself that he would never find a gate.

A combination of pleasure and distaste emanates from the handling of this and the earlier scenes. Such were James's feelings about the society which he creates in the novel and about the Paris which he knew while writing it. The expression of this is in the kinds of comedy that have been observed, both in metaphorical uses of language and in comic dialogue. This comedy is at the same time committed to the defence of Newman because it shows that the social environment in which he is active has sufficient charm and attractiveness to deceive us as well as him. It can be said, as a consequence, that comedy tends in all of its uses to idealize the hero.

The attractiveness which is given to Madame de Bellegarde by her witty social adeptness is, by the end, like the outside of those little vases, already mentioned, to which James compares French literature written after 1848, "skillfully moulded and chiselled," but hiding from view the "unclean things" that are inside. The conversation between the Prince and the Duchess excludes Newman as by a "wall of polite conversation" through which he cannot find a gate, and it suggests how the grotesque circumscription, which has entrapped Claire and which keeps Newman from saving her, arches out from the Bellegarde family to encompass the whole society of which they are a part, connecting even with the wall of the convent behind which Claire has for ever disappeared. Her retreat into the Carmelites is a public confirmation, of which her brother does not approve, that behind the ever tightening "closeness" of her family and their society is the reality of death instead of life, of death posing as life. The metaphorical suggestions of this from the earlier part of the novel are confirmed by the dramatic action and by the progressive exclusion of Newman from those conversations in which artificiality of manner serves as well as any physical barrier to make him feel the futility of his efforts. His vigil outside the house of the Carmelites in which Claire has begun her life of silence and abnegation is described in a way that implies that the place is a symbol for a whole society. The language gathers up the metaphors which have characterized that society since the beginning of the novel and finally ratifies their full significance:

Newman found himself in a part of Paris which he knew little—

a region of convents and prisons, of streets bordered by long dead walls and traversed by few wayfarers. At the intersection of two of these streets stood the house of the Carmelites—a dull, plain edifice, with a high shouldered blank wall all round it. From without Newman could see its upper windows, its steep roof and its chimneys. But these things revealed no symptoms of human life; the place looked dumb, deaf, inanimate. The pale, dead, discoloured wall stretched beneath it, far down the empty side street—a vista without a human figure.

Newman's plans for Claire had been imagined by him and by James in terms quite unlike this. When Newman first proposes, James remarks that Claire has the "air of a woman who has stepped across the frontier of friendship and, looking around her, finds the region vast," and when she seems oppressed by melancholy family secrets Newman reflects that "what he offered her was, in fact, above all things a vast, sunny immunity from the need of having any."

The brutal sharpness of contrast in the images of hope and futility, of imagination and deadness indicate something of critical importance about the organization of this novel. Because of the combination of elaborate manners on the part of the Bellegardes with Newman's preternaturally healthy lack of suspiciousness, the revelation of their treachery comes with an unannounced dramatic shock. What had been comedy of manners suddenly becomes a melodrama in which all the excesses of expression naturally accruing to it are to be taken not comically but as an adequate response to the nature of things. This does not mean that no humour is involved in the melodrama, but that there is no satiric humour. James subscribes to Newman's violent and enraged feelings by agreeing with him that the betrayal of the Bellegardes is nothing that he could have anticipated and nothing that makes realistic sense. The question for criticism is whether in representing this James does not reveal weaknesses in his plot and his characterization.

The plot of *The American* turns on a mystery, on the refusal of Claire de Cintré to marry Christopher Newman. She cannot explain to him how this has happened, and she does not seem to understand it herself: "It's like a religion. There's a curse upon the house. I don't know what—I don't know why—don't ask me." The novel does not allow us to feel any less shocked than Newman by Claire's inconstancy. When he expresses his reaction to it, he does so in terms that might well serve the literary critic in assessing the movement of the plot: "It was too strange and too mocking to be real; it was like a page torn out of a romance, with no context in his own experience." It has very little context, for that matter, in the experience offered by the novel. There is nothing in what has been given about the characters to explain the extraordinary choice of the Bellegardes.

Claire, for example, barely exists at all outside the schematization in which she plays the part of a European whose qualities are innately American. During most of the conversations at the Bellegardes' she says nothing, and what we know about her comes from the descriptions in which James puts an emphasis on the suggestive openness of her facial expressions. The characterizations of Urbain and Madame de Bellegarde are fuller, but there, too, the details are largely absorbed into representational definition. The making of this definition is mostly comic, the comedy carrying the implication not only that Newman cannot appreciate what the Bellegardes stand for but also that there is something vile behind their high manners. The corruption, when it is finally revealed, involves the fact that several years earlier Madame de Bellegarde's unscrupulous determination to make a profitable marriage for her daughter impelled her to murder her own husband. To discover also that their manners include such extraordinary idealism that they must forbid Claire to marry an American millionaire is, therefore, to feel more than a little cheated. It is, of course, possible to imagine characters who are capable of such apparently paradoxical action, but James does not give body to them in this novel, and it is his rather than our job to do so. He is, as we have seen, committed, for purposes of social satire, to exactly the opposite kind of character.

In James's Preface to *The American*, written some thirty years after the first publication of the novel, he sees it as a weakness that he does not definitely place the clue to Claire's conduct in the hands of the reader, and that he fails to account for the proposition that the Bellegardes would obviously prefer Newman's fortunes to the seclusion of their only daughter in a Carmelite convent. The assumption behind James's criticism is that a clue *could* have been given, that the plot and the characterization might have taken the direction that they do, and that an explanation might somehow have been added. But given the kinds of characterization that are found in *The American*, it would not have been possible, short of writing quite another kind of novel, to have provided such explanations. Neither in the characterizations of individual members of the Bellegarde family, none of whom is given a complicated psychology, nor in the society which they are made to represent is there provision for the impractical renunciation of the Bellegardes at the end. Renunciation, a term reserved for the selfless reactions of James's heroes, is a proper way to describe the rejection of Newman by these villains. It is a completely profitless act unless measured by standards of romantic idealism, and these are not the standards, it need hardly be said, which have motivated the Bellegardes at any point. Their renunciation is not entirely in the tradition of Jamesian heroes, of course, since, while acting as they do, they break a solemn vow, and in that they are treacherous. Only the treachery itself is not surprising. It would have been predictable if they had forced Claire to give up Newman in order that she might marry Lord Deepmere. An act of cynical self-interest, disguised as a desire to have Claire marry in her own class, would be wholly in character. Precisely for that reason it is incomprehensible that their treachery should be at the service of intangible social principles which they easily violated by allowing the engagement in the first place.

The comedy in the novel depends to a considerable extent on the fact that behind the social manners of the Bellegardes there exists not the positive prejudices of an aristocratic coterie but an eye for the main chance and an old-world capacity to scheme in order to achieve it. The rejection of Newman involves the assertion of ideals for which practical sacrifices must be made, and this is not the kind of thing which could unfold from character as this novel has created it in the Bellegardes. One cannot feel in *The American,* to paraphrase what James remarks of good fiction in general, that character is the determination of incident and incident is the illustration of character. Once the characters are "placed" in the categories which allow for James's satire, there is nothing that can be called development in characterization. Instead of it there is only a dramatic intensification of the differences between the categories. This intensification is expressed mostly through modulations in James's satire on the pretensions of the Bellegardes. It is not related in any way to a dramatization of a change of heart, developing with the action, by which the Bellegardes are moved to reject Newman. There is no drama-tization of this, there is merely the announcement that it has occurred.

The flatness of characterization, which allows for the comic descriptions and comic dramatic dialogue in the novel, prevents James from dramatizing the moral and psychological complications involved in his plot. This is evident in the characterization not only of the Bellegardes, who cause the compli-cation, but also of Newman, who stimulates them to act as they do. There are times, in fact, when James's treatment of Newman indicates that he may have been trying to give the novel more satisfying coherence than it has.

This is to say that there are suggestions here and there of the hero's legitimately objectionable qualities. Had these been developed, the comedy would have been more subtly discriminating than it is and his rejection by the Bellegardes would have been at least understandable as a reaction to things in him which the reader had also recognized. James's seeming reservations about Newman can be summed up by saying that he is a man without imagination. In his simplistic view of Europe he is to be distinguished from Isabel Archer or from Roderick Hudson. It could not be said of either of these, as it is of Newman, that the complex Parisian world "neither inflamed his imagination nor irritated his curiosity." His coarseness of observation is made part of his charm, however, as when, in the opening scene, he admires the painting of the marriage feast at Cana by Paul Veronese because "it satisfied his conception, which was ambitious, of what a splendid banquet should be." On the other hand, there are a few instances where it is less clear that James means us to see Newman's potential vulgarity in so favourable a light. He tells us, for example, that Newman "had already begun to value the world's admiration of Madame de Cintré, as adding to the prospective glory of possession," and, even more ambiguous, he gives Newman the remark that while he should like his wife to interpret him to the world, he is worried that "when the instrument was so perfect it seemed to interpose too much between you and the genius that used it." Had the implications of such passages been developed in any dramatically coherent way, they would have allowed for a closer relationship in the novel between character and the development of plot. Though the action of the Bellegardes might still be called a "mystery" or an expression of a kind of "religion," it would at least be apparent that something considerable in Newman had provoked them to it.

But whatever qualifications are made about Newman are localized ones scattered here and there. What seem to be personal defects are transmuted into delightfully natural characteristics, so that responses which might be taken as simple-minded become instead an evidence of the healthy and boyish American incapacity to take social hierarchy as seriously as it asks to be taken. Consider, for example, James's observation about Urbain's reaction to Newman. It points with a good deal of suggestiveness to the effect on the Bellegardes of Newman's lack of imagination. As usual, however, the suggestions are dissolved by satiric jibes in the hero's favour:

> His tranquil unsuspectingness of the relativity of his own place
> in the social scale was probably irritating to M. de Bellegarde,
> who saw himself reflected in the mind of his potential brother-
> in-law in a crude and colorless form, unpleasantly dissimilar to
> the impressive image projected upon his own intellectual mirror.

Newman cannot conceive of any values but his own, and he is not joking when, in response to Claire's accusation that he is only using Valentin for amusement and "would not like to resemble him," he replies: "I shouldn't like to resemble anyone." The ground is laid, a piece here and a piece there, for a conflict between the Bellegardes and Newman which would involve definitions of personality and of social value less superficial than those we discover in *The American*. The novel rests instead on other grounds, those defined and for the most part limited by the conception of character and experience discussed under the rubric "open" and "closed." As a result, the novel does not encourage any qualifications to Newman's expression of dismay at the loss of Claire, even though the terms of his expression blatantly contradict those others which I have been adducing:

> "Why should you object to me so—what's the matter with me? I can't hurt you, I wouldn't if I could. I'm the most unobjectionable fellow in the world. What if I am a commercial person? What under the sun do you mean? A commercial person? I will be any sort of a person you want."

It could be argued that this speech is dramatically effective in showing how Newman misconceives the effect he makes on people dedicated to social proprieties, and it could also be said that for this reason it is proper that there should be a contradiction between James's feelings about Newman's unimaginativeness and Newman's willingness to imagine himself into any rôle that is needed. But James is only sporadically critical of Newman's incapacity to place himself in the position of other people. James's failure ever to qualify the touching and seductive eloquence of his speeches, the reiteration that the reasons for his rejection cannot but be unreasonable, and the satiric insistence on the superficiality of the Bellegardes—these elements in the novel do not suggest that we are to make any discriminations against Newman's evaluation of himself. The weight of idealized characterization very nearly obliterates the kind of potential qualification to which I have been pointing. Being the open-minded, generous-spirited American, he need be respectful only of the ideal of his own good-humoured prosperity, and such an ideal not only can overlook social standards at all alien to it but even differentiations of a technical order, like foreign languages. Though a knowledge of these is not customarily given a man merely because he is a fine fellow, James tells us that Newman

> found his way in foreign cities by divination, his memory was excellent when once his attention had been at all cordially given, and he emerged from dialogues in foreign tongues, of which he had, formally, not understood a word, in full possession of the particular fact that he had desired to ascertain.

Why indeed *should* the Bellegardes find such a man objectionable? It is no wonder that the social comedy in the novel invariably involves the exposure of different kinds of European unreality, either their inventive and charmingly absurd talk about rubber houses and Dukes of California or, later, the unreal and self-parodying social exclusiveness of Urbain.

The comedy at the end, once all the social machinations have been exhausted, shows the effects of having the plot turn upon a motive for the Bellegardes which to Newman, and to us, does not grow out of the dramatization of conduct and character earlier in the novel. The comedy becomes macabre. It registers Newman's sense of the irrationality of experience, and his recognition, when Valentin's failure is placed within the context of his own, that the very nature of things is in all likelihood perversely fateful. Violence and futility dominate not only the conclusion of Newman's relationship with Claire but also of Valentin's affair with Noémie. These two plots are carefully synchronized to suggest the presence in quite different lives of seemingly unnatural calamity. Valentin remarks to Newman of himself and Noémie that "it's a striking contrast to your noble and virtuous attachment—a vile contrast!"

James's attempt to put the two romances in juxtaposition is unmistakable: the news of Noémie's being "launched" as a courtesan is announced in the same chapter with the news of Newman's engagement; Valentin observes that "her ideal has been satisfied" at a time when Newman is most exultant about his own good fortune; at the end of chapter 12 Valentin leaves for Geneva and the duel in which Noémie's fickleness has involved him, and chapter 13 witnesses Claire's departure from Paris on orders from her mother; Newman hears almost simultaneously that his engagement has been broken and that Valentin has been wounded; and, finally, he witnesses Valentin's funeral in the same chapter in which he is told that Claire is going to a living death in the convent. The advantage of making such a series of close parallels between apparently contrasting relationships is described adequately enough by James himself in a review of *Middlemarch*. He there comments on the "balanced contrast between the two histories of Lydgate and Dorothea":

> Each is a tale of matrimonial infelicity, but the conditions in each
> are so different and the circumstances so broadly opposed that
> the mind passes from one to the other with the supreme sense of
> vastness and variety of human life, under aspects apparently sim-
> ilar, which it belongs only to the greatest novels to produce.

The two plots in *The American* do not, of course, take place "under

aspects apparently similar," but except for that James's remark on George
Eliot helps us to see what he was about in his own novel. The relationship
between the two plots might be conceptualized by thinking of Newman as
defeated by the forces of restriction and seclusion, while Valentin is defeated
by what James in another review once referred to as the "irregular society
in France that has become so extensive and aggressive." Noémie represents
social freedom gone astray—a "free spirit," as she is called in the revised
version. But while she is outside the social exclusiveness of Parisian high
society, her position is one conventionally established for its convenience.
This is Valentin's excuse for her to the sometimes disgusted Newman. Her
profession plays almost as much a part in the world of manners as the social
cultism of the Bellegardes. Both Newman and Valentin are defeated by corrupt manifestations of a firmly established social order, and it is therefore
dramatically right that the one should die simultaneously with the death of
the other's hopes. Duelling, which kills Valentin, is a mystery to Newman
just as are the social customs which deprive him of Claire, and both are
founded upon history and tradition. Newman's violence of expression in the
last eight chapters of the novel is caused by his discovery that neither his
healthy decisiveness nor his practical good sense can do anything about the
mysterious forces which seem to determine his destiny as well as Valentin's.
As he sits with his dying friend, he thinks of his own plight in a way which
could as easily refer to either of them:

> What had happened to him seemed to have, in its violence and
> audacity, the force of a real calamity—the strength and insolence
> of Destiny herself. It was unnatural and monstrous, and he had
> no arms against it.

Newman's sense of the unreality of the disasters which occur at the end
of the novel is the basis for much of the comedy which we find there. The
general nature of it may be illustrated by the reaction of Mrs. Bread to
Newman's melodramatic speech about his suffering and his intention to
destroy her employers. Newman tells her:

> "I want to bring them down—down, down, down! I want to
> turn the tables upon them—I want to mortify them as they mor-
> tified me. They took me up into a high place and made me stand
> there for all the world to see me, and then they stole behind me
> and pushed me into this bottomless pit, where I lie howling and
> gnashing my teeth! I made a fool of myself before all their friends;
> but I shall make something worse of them."

"Something worse," he continues, might include the hanging of Madame de Bellegarde. At this point Mrs. Bread expresses the innocently concerned reaction that "it would break up the family most terribly, sir!"

The comedy in this exchange results from the reminder of the distance between common experience and Newman's. This is accomplished, in part, by the use of the stock phraseology of ordinary domestic trouble. Mrs. Bread does not intend to be funny—she is as good, and about as interesting, as good bread. But her remark is comic because it represents the ridiculous inappropriateness to Newman's feelings of ordinary statements and the language that goes with them. His is the language of an archangel expelled from heaven, from the "high place" which Valentin refers to early in the novel, and hers is of some uncomprehending spinster lady into whose prim garden he has fallen. The Satanic comparison is appropriate enough, given James's language, and is made more so as we watch Newman proceed, with devilish clairvoyance into the nature of her pride, to seduce Mrs. Bread into betraying her employers. To do so he tries to infuse into her complaints some of the intensity of his own, especially in the final version of the novel. Mrs. Bread recounts, for example, that when Madame de Bellegarde suspected her of having an affair with her husband "she said that if I'd sit in her children's school room I should do well for a penwiper! When things have come to that I don't think I need stand on ceremony." To this Newman rejoicingly exclaims, "I never heard of anything so vicious! Go on, Mrs. Bread."

The comedy as the novel progresses changes from jokes about ordinary social matters, made by highly imaginative uses of language, to jokes about extraordinary experiences, such as Newman's rejection, made by juxtaposing them with relatively flat and habitual uses of language. Comedy of this latter kind occurs in James when an aspect of reality totally different from the one which we are momentarily accepting interjects itself. Such comedy can be truly called philosophical, and it has versions which include the final scene of Chaplin's *City Lights,* when a flower-pot falls on the head of the comic hero as he tearfully takes a flower from the blinded heroine, as well as the last scene of *King Lear,* in the peculiar effectiveness of Lear's remarking just before he dies, "Pray you undo this button. Thank you, sir." Such comedy is to be found not only in Newman's interview with Mrs. Bread and the subsequent scenes in which he deals with Urbain, but also in the death scene of Valentin. In attendance, aside from Newman, is Valentin's aptly named friend M. Grosjoyaux and another, M. Ledoux, who remarks, after Valentin has received the last rites, that hope for his recovery is mistaken kindness, since "when a man has taken such excellent measures for his salvation as our dear friend did last evening, it seems almost a pity he should put it in peril again by returning to the world." Valentin, in an echo of Mercutio, expresses a movingly courageous and comic view of his own death when, to Newman's "And how are you getting on?" he replies "Oh, I'm getting off! They have quite settled that; haven't they?" The concluding chapters have much of this odd gaiety, some of it coming directly from James, as in his paraphrase of Newman's feelings about Claire's decision to enter the Carmelites: "How could she fail to perceive that his house would be much the most comfortable sort of convent?" The highly comic scene with the Duchess and the Prince occurs even after this, at a point when Newman has completely given up hope.

There is nothing extraordinary about the use of comedy at the culmination of a series of distressing and very uncomic actions. Under such circumstances the kind of comedy involved in Valentin's remark on his death is a way of reminding oneself that existence goes on beyond the periphery of one's own disaster. It is a way of affirming that though your situation is killing you, you still have the capacity to recognize that life is going on outside it. Comedy in these circumstances is a form of courage and vanity. This explains why the wit of Madame de Bellegarde when Newman confronts her with his evidence makes him admit to a grudging admiration for her "magnificent pluck."

James's comedy in *The American* usually multiplies the versions in which the object in front of him can exist. It reminds us of other aspects of the experience with which he is dealing, of the multiplicity of possible responses even to events so calamitous that they seem to predetermine the way we are to react to them. A somewhat peculiar illustration is in the remark of Madame Urbain to Newman just after his frustrating visit to the Carmelite convent: "Poor Claire—in a white shroud and a big brown cloak! That's the *toilette* of the Carmelites, you know. Well, she was always fond of long, loose things." That we can find this funny under the circumstances in which it is said testifies to the liberality of mind which James's comedy can induce. Because of this, he might have made his characterizations more complex than they are, and have thereby avoided the problem in the plot which he himself recognizes in the Preface.

None the less, the courage and largeness of view implied in this use of comedy does anticipate Newman's final reaction to the shocking incoherence of his experience. By burning the evidence with which he might ruin the Bellegardes, he proves his superiority to them and affirms that exalted view of the possibilities of human conduct which he and James found wanting in an uncongenial Parisian world. James, by his comedy, defies Fate no less than Newman does by his conduct. In neither case is there a willing submission to conventional assumptions about human reactions, either to the claims of old civilization or even, where reaction is more apparently predetermined, to social treachery and personal disaster. In *The American,* the heroics of Newman's final action and of James's art are one.

That characters can be given a public solidity without the evocation of their place within a traditionally mannered society or even within a nationality is apparent in *Washington Square.* While he was writing it for the *Cornhill Magazine,* James was highly conscious of the fact that by using only American characters, and by setting the scene of their actions almost wholly in the still developing city of New York, he was deprived of certain resources which he had found useful in the novels before *Confidence.* He complains to Howells that it is a "poorish story—the writing of which made me feel acutely the want of 'paraphernalia.'" His feeling is expressed more generally in the same letter, when he argues against Howells' contention that an American novelist is as well provided for in his native country as is his English or French counterpart:

> I sympathize even less with your protest against the idea that it takes an old civilization to set a novelist in motion—a proposition that seems to me so true as to be a truism. It is on manners, customs, usages, habits, forms, upon all things matured and established, that a novelist lives—they are the very stuff his work is made of; and in saying that in the absence of those "dreary and worn-out paraphernalia" which I enumerate as being wanting in American society, "we have simply the whole of human life left," you beg (to my sense) the question. I should say we had just so much less of it as these same "paraphernalia" represent, and I think they represent an enormous quantity of it.

The last sentence might serve to confirm the point of the allegory in *The Europeans* by which, in my reading of the novel, the exclusion of Eugenia from the Wentworths' is a dramatic image of the incapacity of the New England ethos to include highly civilized artistic expression. But Eugenia was more than "manners, customs, usages, forms," and in citing these as necessary requirements of the novelist, the "very stuff his work is made of," James is somewhat sentimentalizing his case. Eugenia was, above all, a theatrical person, and to the conventions not merely of the theatre but of what we might call our mythic imagination, a novelist can always appeal for a body of customs and assumptions which are relevant even to the most un-

developed society. This is too often forgotten, particularly by the literary
branch of the Southern Agrarians, while from all sides there is the repeated
assertion, grim and vague, that great novels depend upon a society in which
tradition is a living thing. While this may be true, it should not be construed
to mean, as it usually is, that the society itself has to be traditional. A group
of backwoodsmen from every corner of the country can gather together and
give quite a lively image of "manners" and "form." They can share innumerable "customs, usages, habits" which depend entirely upon an intuitive
theatrical sense. By this I mean that everybody somewhere along the line
develops in his imagination a picture of typical or even mythic figures—the
"bad" woman with a heart of gold, the clever city man and the shrewd
farmer. Literary tradition is as much a matter of a writer's almost unconscious sense of these as it is of his conscious imitation of other works. James
in particular has a very intuitive sense of theatricality and of the conventional
typologies. The very outrageousness in his naming of characters, such as
Henrietta Stackpole and Fanny Assingham, is a way of catering to our desire
not to believe in the living reality of fictional characters. It is central to my
argument that James is almost always anxious to assure himself that a character is not a person, but that he is much larger than any person could be.
Only by being so can he absorb the fullest analysis and the toughest, most
wild-swinging efforts of James's comedy.

In terms of what has just been said, it is possible to see how *Washington
Square* can be a novel in which there is great substantiality of character and
extremely effective comedy without any recourse to the sort of "old civilization" referred to in James's letter. To put it briefly, *Washington Square* is
in its basic situation a melodramatic fairy-tale, complete with characters who
have archetypes in everyone's most rudimentary literary experience and imagination. There is no need to have read Balzac's *Eugénie Grandet* to be aware
of literary analogues if we consult our memories of Cruel Father, Motherless
Daughter, Handsome Lover, and Fairy God-Mother, in this case an aunt.
James's transposition of these elements from the Old to the New World
makes them stand out with even sharper and larger clarity. He himself indicates an awareness of the value of such a procedure when, referring to his
first conception of *The American,* he recalls:

> I doubtless even then felt that the conception of Paris as the
> consecrated scene of rash infatuations and bold bad treacheries
> belongs, in the Anglo-Saxon imagination, to the infancy of art.
> The right renovation of any such theme as that would place it in
> Boston or at Cleveland, at Hartford or at Utica—give it some
> local connection in which we had not already had so much of it.

James effectively accomplishes this "renovation" in *Washington Square,* giving it that strength and thickness of surface upon which he can expend the full force of his imagination. This is a case, much like *The Europeans,* where the public status of the characters permits James the greatest freedom in going to work on their private identities. The difference between the two novels is that the public status of characters in *Washington Square* depends not at all on their social place or nationality, and is wholly a matter of their similarity to stock characters in stage melodrama and the fairy tale.

James compels our attention precisely because his dramatization of character and situation modifies and even reverses the suppositions which their public and conventionalized reputations encourage. This is why a recognition of James's comedy, invariably overlooked in the mole-like search for buried philosophical treasure, is indispensable to any understanding of his achievement. In an extended use of the terms, "comedy" and "dramatization" become almost interchangeable in James: both describe the vital art of turning the anticipated into the unexpected response. These novels do not allow us to presume that certain actions, such as the exploitation of a sweet-natured but awkward young woman, carry with them a predetermined moral attitude. Given this as a subject-matter, a novel can be pleasantly comic or severely depressing or what the author will, depending entirely on the evocations of his language. Not to acknowledge this in a reading of *Washington Square* is to fall into an account of it as controvertible as Mr. Jacques Barzun's, first printed in 1943 in an otherwise valuable essay, "Henry James, Melodramatist." His opinion of the novel is reaffirmed by a very recent reprinting of his article in *The Energies of Art,* and I make such an issue of it only because Mr. Barzun *seems* to be saying exactly what I have said about the situation and characters in the novel:

> The wickedness of being cold, of deliberately sacrificing others to one's lusts, of taking advantage of another through legal or social or emotional privilege, obsesses James. *Washington Square* is an unparalleled example, in which Dr. Sloper's remark to his daughter, "You will do what you like," is as terrifying as the crack of a whip. And its force is derived from the essentially melodramatic situation of a motherless daughter victimised by a subservient aunt and a selfish father—a being for whom the melodramatic epithet of "fiend in human form" is no longer sayable but still just.

The opening sentence comes close to saying what this chapter has perhaps repeated too often, that James is acutely conscious of "experimentation" in human relationships, and the rest of the statements give an impression of *Washington Square* not unlike the one which I have briefly sketched. Nonetheless, it should be apparent from my general argument that I would find Mr. Barzun's account seriously misleading. Mr. Barzun sees what James is saying, but he gives no indication that he has experienced the way in which it is said. While it is true that James is obsessed with the idea of one human being taking emotional advantage of another, it is not true that he is obsessed with the "wickedness" of this. There is no "wickedness" in any of the novels I am discussing, with the exception of *The American,* which presents one of the few instances in James of characters about whom it is possible to be morally unequivocal. In considering James's preoccupation with relationships in which one character victimizes another, it is well to remember that very often, even in the extreme case of Osmond, the victimizer is also something of a victim.

We are made most aware of this when trying to find the source of some of James's comic sense. To notice the comedy in James is to participate in a highly impersonal and morally sophisticated rendering of experience. In narrating *The Bostonians,* for instance, he is too urbanely civilized to neglect the possibilities for comedy even in situations as melodramatically evil as those Mr. Barzun describes. What follows from this is a modification of the inexpensive moral judgments that melodrama customarily invites. James's conception of evil is closer to Shakespeare than to Webster, a writer who could only conceive of it melodramatically. It seems to me unlikely that Mr. Barzun could have responded to James's scrupulous weighing of emotional involvement and still be able to observe that for Dr. Sloper "the melodramatic epithet of 'fiend in human form' is no longer sayable but still just." If it is no longer "sayable," then it cannot be "just," now or ever, and it is specifically such humane creations as the moral atmosphere of James's novels that have made such epithets not only unsayable but meaningless.

The issue may be rephrased by saying that the comedy to which we are asked to respond in the novel and the nature of the judgments on conduct which is implied in it, put us in a mood which can only be called contemplative. How indeed does it happen that a man as brilliant and witty as Dr. Sloper, with whose appreciations James himself is associated for the first half of the novel, can become by the end so brutal and uncomprehending? To take him throughout simply as a melodramatic figure is to ignore the fact that before the terrible scene on the Alps his ironic observation of experience is, with some slight modification, James's own. James encourages us to feel this by giving a consistently melodramatic view of Dr. Sloper only to the foolishly romantic Mrs. Penniman. "She has got such an artificial mind," as

Mrs. Almond very rightly puts it. What James calls her "foolish indirectness and obliquity of character" is the subject of some of Dr. Sloper's comic abuse. This takes the form, when he accuses her of giving Townsend the run of the house, of his *pretending* to be fiendish, sarcastically exaggerating her silly impressions of him and playing, with an ironic contempt, upon her coarse sensationalism:

> She was tasting the sweets of concealment; she had taken up the line of mystery. "She would be enchanted to be able to prove to herself that she is persecuted," said the Doctor; and when at last he questioned her, he was sure she would contrive to extract from his words a pretext for this belief. "Be so good as to let me know what is going on in the house," he said to her, in a tone which, under the circumstances, he himself deemed genial.
>
> "Going on, Austin?" Mrs. Penniman exclaimed. "Why I am sure I don't know. I believe that last night the old gray cat had kittens."
>
> "At her age?" said the Doctor. "The idea is startling—almost shocking. Be so good as to see that they are all drowned. But what else has happened?"
>
> "Ah, the dear little kittens!" cried Mrs. Penniman. "I wouldn't have them drowned for the world!"
>
> Her brother puffed his cigar a few moments in silence. "Your sympathy with kittens, Lavinia," he presently resumed, "arises from a feline element in your own character."
>
> "Cats are very graceful, and very clean," said Mrs. Penniman, smiling.
>
> "And very stealthy. You are the embodiment both of grace and of neatness; but you are wanting in frankness."
>
> "You certainly are not, dear brother."
>
> "I don't pretend to be graceful, though I try to be neat. Why haven't you let me know that Mr. Morris Townsend is coming to the house four times a week?"

The comedy in this passage is in the tradition of literary anti-feminism, of the situation in which the reasonable and assertive male intentionally sets out to shock the giddy imaginations of the women who surround him. The scenes between Fielding's Squire Western and his sister are funny partly for this reason. Sloper is exasperated, like the Squire, by being constantly in a household full of women but having no wife, so that none of his sense of their inferiority is softened or made more tolerable by romantic feeling. This is particularly true in Sloper's case, since the premature death of his beautiful wife is an irremediable sorrow, and "save when he fell in love with Catherine Harrington, he had never been dazzled, indeed, by any feminine character-istics whatever." A man of this sort, who has at the same time generously tolerated the company of Aunt Lavinia long after her usefulness has ended, is not likely to feel put upon by a litter of kittens, and we can take what he says about them less seriously than she does. The contrast in their patterns of speech, with her humourless and literal responses and his witty habit of picking up her language and turning it sarcastically against her, suggests that Dr. Sloper's only alternatives are to address her as he does, with the enjoy-ment of using her as an object of wit, or to address her not at all.

James is actually more sarcastic than Sloper about Lavinia's habit of melodramatization. There is a recurrent snigger in his references to her as a "woman of imagination," and in derisive explanations of her conduct, such as the fact that "she was very fond of kissing people's foreheads; it was an involuntary expression of sympathy with the intellectual part." The satire in her characterization has an important consequence: it means that her view of Catherine's situation absorbs most of its potential melodrama and projects it comically:

> She had a vision of this ceremony [a marriage of Catherine and Townsend] being performed in some subterranean chapel—sub-terranean chapels in New York were not frequent, but Mrs. Pen-niman's imagination was not chilled by trifles—and of the guilty couple—she liked to think of poor Catherine and her suitor as the guilty couple—being shuffled away in a fast-whirling vehicle to some obscure lodging in the suburbs, where she would pay them (in a thick veil) clandestine visits; where they would endure a period of romantic privation; and where ultimately, after she should have been their earthly providence, their intercessor, their advocate, and their medium of communication with the world, they would be reconciled to her brother in an artistic tableau, in which she herself would be somehow the central figure.

Because of such comedy as this, directed against melodramatic feeling about Catherine's plight, the actual melodramatic horror of the scene in the Alps, the turning-point in the movement of the novel, has a thoroughly brutal impact. We know on the basis of what precedes it that if comedy could legitimately afford any relief to the experience, James would have been aware of it. There is no hint of parody, however, even though the scene is full of stock sensationalism: it is set among "hard-featured rocks and glowing sky," and before he actually deserts her by hurrying on ahead, Dr. Sloper, looking at Catherine with "eyes that had kept the light of the flashing snow summits," asks, "should you like to be left in such a place as this, to starve?" Because Dr. Sloper has enough of James's own humorous awareness of fraudulently romantic self-expression, his own intensities at this moment seem to arise from a compelling emotional necessity. The scene marks the point in the novel where Dr. Sloper's way of expressing himself about Catherine begins to diverge most radically from James's. By tracing the progress of that divergence we see how James's identification with Sloper's ironic manner in the first half of the novel gives way to a criticism of it. This will serve to indicate something about James's own feelings at this point in his career about the proper comic use of the characters whose destinies he controls.

Dr. Sloper represents that half of James which is interested in the "fixed" externality of people, in their type, as I have been calling it, and the nature of his irony is an indication of this. Sloper is, indeed, like Zola's novelist in that, as James tells us, he has, as physician, "passed his life in estimating people (it was part of the medical trade), and in nineteen cases out of twenty he was right." "I am helped," he tells Mrs. Montgomery, "by a habit I have of dividing people into classes, into types." This habit applies very specifically to Catherine: he suspects from the first that she is "commonplace" and when she "had become a young lady grown he regarded the matter as settled." Here, as in most matters, he is right, and the novel does nothing to convince us until after the trip to Europe that Catherine is not stolid, tedious, and dully sweet. In this, James and Sloper are in essential agreement. Naturally, James's sentiments cannot ever appear to be exactly the same as the Doctor's. As the narrator he can, first of all, make sympathetic statements about Catherine which her father can only indirectly reveal through his actions and conversation, while, so far as adversely critical remarks are concerned, we naturally feel that they are less cruel said behind her back, as it were, by James, than to her face by her father. But these matters are simply a part of the necessary difference between the kinds of personal revelation possible to the author, and those that can be made by a character in a novel which is omnisciently narrated.

Taking this into account, it is still evident that the comedy in James's introductory remarks about Catherine has the tone of Sloper's irony. Our approval of James's tone necessarily disposes us, though with slight trepidation, to admire the Doctor's. A good indication that James intends this is in his juxtaposition of his own and Dr. Sloper's comments on Catherine's dress. Every reader of the novel will remember the scene at Mrs. Almond's dance when Sloper finds himself face to face with his daughter and, after seeing that her red satin gown is both too expensive and too mature for a woman her age, greets her with the question, "Is it possible that this magnificent person is my child?" His irony in the subsequent conversation is extremely unkind, especially as used on so helpless and uncomprehending a target, and yet it has its source in the same attitude towards Catherine which we find some pages earlier in James's own account of her taste in clothing:

> When it had been duly impressed upon her that she was a young lady—it was a good while before she could believe it—she suddenly developed a lively taste for dress: a lively taste is quite the expression to use. I feel as if I ought to write it very small, her judgment in this matter was by no means infallible; it was liable to confusions and embarrassments. Her great indulgence of it was really the desire of a rather inarticulate nature to manifest itself; she sought to be eloquent in her garments, and to make up for her diffidence of speech by the fine frankness of costume. But if she expressed herself in her clothes, it is certain that people were not to blame for not thinking her a witty person.

The passage indulges in a touch of unironic compassion, but so does Dr. Sloper on many occasions, as when, at another party of Mrs. Almond's, her embarrassment at being seen by her father in conversation with Townsend is so obvious that "the doctor felt, indeed, so sorry for her that he turned away, to spare her the sense of being watched." Generally, however, James's comedy in the early chapters is like Dr. Sloper's: that of a highly witty man who would refuse to be intimidated, by sentimental reasons, from enjoying the comic possibilities of Catherine's deportment. Indeed, before her affair with Townsend becomes passionate enough to reveal the hidden depths of her character, she offers little else to an agile mind than a subject for ironic pleasantries. Otherwise, the vocabulary for one's reaction exhausts itself with the remark that after all "she's a very harmless young woman."

Dr. Sloper uses her for his own entertainment in the way James uses characters whom he comically "fixes" in order that his jibes will never seem to do an injustice to the human potentiality for improvement. "Decidedly," he observes to himself, "my daughter is not brilliant." Sloper's irony is a way of testing his conclusions by seeing just how passive and unresponsive she is, and he is so certain that he has her figured out that if she does resist it is not an indication of her promise but merely a "surprise," which entertains him the more. The word "entertainment" is used by every character in the novel and by Sloper himself to describe his treatment of his daughter. And even after he has decided that she is capable of determined opposition to him, he remarks to Mrs. Almond that "I wanted to see if she really would stick. But, good Lord, one's curiosity is satisfied! I see she is capable of it, and now she can let go." He cannot conceive of her acting out of a private motive of which he is unaware. So far as he is concerned, she can only have a kind of public function, in the sense that he is her audience and everything she does is of necessity designed not for her needs but for his expectations. She exists for his pleasure or she does not exist at all. The threat of disowning her in the Alps is a confirmation of what I am suggesting: a Catherine whose feelings he can no longer take ironically would indeed not be the same Catherine who is his daughter.

There is an extraordinary pathos in the scene in the Alps, however, which tinges all of Sloper's ironies and cruelties. He doesn't dare believe in the potentialities of his daughter. His capacity for love has been destroyed by the failure of all the other potentialities he believed in—the death of a wife he adored in giving birth to Catherine, and the death of his son at the age of three, "a boy of extraordinary promise." The irony of his fate is more injurious than any he concocts, when, in the very process of losing the last of his family, he begins to sense potentialities in her for which he had given up hope. If she is not superficial, if she really does "matter," as James would say, then he is fated to be deprived of her by the logic of his whole life, and his wit is a way of assuring himself that while everything worth while may be taken by death, Catherine, at least, will not be lost by anyone's falling in love, with her. If his judgments had the arrogance of imperturbable self-sufficiency, and if his ironic cruelties derived from an assured independence of the need to be loved, then he would hardly have to call on Morris Townsend's aunt to be told, "Don't let her marry him!" The comfort he derives from this is not that he is right about Townsend, but that he is right about Catherine; that he need not fear that he has failed to see in her more than a disinterested man might.

His need to view her as he does and the nature of his attention, once he has decided that she is commonplace, is deftly indicated in the fact that we first see him addressing her about her clothing, and later, even after the effects upon her of her passion, finding her "about as intelligent as the bundle of shawls." He can only comprehend the surface of her character because he wants to believe that the rest of it is a settled matter. To express this in terms which indicate the nature of Sloper's similarity to James, we can say that he chooses to depend upon her "fixity," just as James depends on the character of the Bellegardes, on any of his "fools and fixed constituencies," on Catherine herself, for that matter, for almost half the novel. The difference between Sloper and James is that Sloper will not permit himself to see the possibilities of Catherine's "freedom," her capacity for defying any theories which he may have about her. He does not allow her a chance to dramatize the as yet unrealized qualities of her nature.

James's ironic voice and Sloper's are never, to repeat, exactly the same because in the latter there is always a taint of direct cruelty, but they begin to separate entirely at about the point when Catherine and her father leave for Europe. The change occurs not because Catherine becomes more pitiable but because she becomes less so. She becomes interesting. This is seldom noticed in criticism of the novel, which prefers to focus on her as a pathetic cipher, explaining, usually with some of the patronizing charity of Miss Mary McCarthy, that "in James there is a delicate tenderness toward Catherine that is the courtesy extended to all inanimate and inarticulate creatures" and that to mistreat her is a "crass insensitiveness on man's part to life of a lower order." This account, however plausible, yet requires the answer that when Catherine is essentially lifeless she is subjected to James's very nimble wit. It is as if he were trying to coerce her into life. Somehow, the circumstances of her birth, involving the death of her mother and the subsequent bitterness of her father, combined with her own frightened quiescence, give one the somewhat poetic impression that she is a child still-born. When she becomes, in fact, a woman, there is a distinctly noticeable change in James's tone. On her return from Europe, even Mrs. Penniman notices a difference: that her appearance has improved, "she looked rather handsome," and that there is a disturbing authority, especially for Aunt Lavinia, in her manner and speech. Catherine's way of addressing her aunt gives James an opportunity for some delightfully malicious pleasure:

> Mrs. Penniman was not used, in any discussion, to seeing the war carried into her own country—possibly because the enemy generally had doubts of finding subsistence there. To her own consciousness, the flowery fields of her reason had rarely been ravaged by a hostile force. It was perhaps on this account that in defending them she was majestic rather than agile.

James's comic appetite, it should be clear from this, has not flagged at this point in the novel. All its energy is simply directed away from Catherine. By loving Townsend, she has achieved, as James beautifully phrases it, "the clairvoyance of her passion." This is what gives her the confidence to judge Aunt Lavinia "finally and without appeal," to feel "absolved" of the duty to justify her intentions to her father, now that she values herself enough to recognize a note of contempt in his voice, and to speak even to Townsend with impressive personal power when he plans a trip to New Orleans without her:

> "When persons are going to be married they oughtn't to think so much about business. You shouldn't think about cotton; you should think about me. You can go to New Orleans some other time—there will always be plenty of cotton. It isn't the moment to choose—we have waited too long already."

Having had no object for her love until the age of twenty, save her father, and having been unable to express even that except through shy evasions in her dealings with him, Catherine finds in Townsend someone who makes her feel worthy of giving love and of demanding it. When this happens her father's irony, despite the rightness of his diagnoses, becomes unworthy of both of them. He is unwilling to see that the reason for her passivity in Europe is not her childish modesty or her customary unassertiveness, but evidence, instead, of romantic preoccupation, of what James calls her "undiverted heart." His wit becomes a mockery of her for even pretending, as he sees it, that she is a woman in love. As he passes her window on the day of Townsend's final departure, "he stopped a moment on the bottom of the white steps, and gravely, with an air of exaggerated courtesy, lifted his hat to her." He does not know that Townsend has left her, but, even worse, perhaps, he simply assumes that to her the masculine gestures of formal deference are of necessity a caricature. When he does know that the affair is finished, though he is for ever in the ironic position—this man who prides himself on being "always right"—of not knowing how it ended, he has a final moment of revengeful "entertainment" in asking Catherine:

> "How does he take his dismissal?"
> "I don't know!" said Catherine, less ingeniously than she had hitherto spoken.
> "You mean you don't care? You are rather cruel, after encouraging him and playing with him for so long!"
> The Doctor had his revenge, after all.

Dr. Sloper's irony at the beginning of the novel was that of a disappointed but brilliantly witty man dealing with the pathetic and clumsy simplicity of his daughter. His irony involved the imposition of worldly knowledge upon a person who acted in almost total ignorance of it. By the end, his irony is that of a man who can deal with complications in his daughter's experience and her unpredicted emotional growth only by maintaining a view of them which is cruelly and sarcastically simple.

His brilliance of mind functions almost wholly along the lines of Zola's novelist, who might as well be an experimental physician. He admits to "dividing people into classes, into types," and he assures Mrs. Montgomery that "I may easily be mistaken about your brother as an individual, but his type is written on his whole person." Again, he reveals an interesting habit of speaking of the exteriors of the people he is analysing, and his sureness about Townsend is really not an intuition about his personality so much as a conclusion based on a knowledge of environment. That is the point, perhaps, of the title of the novel and most certainly of the descriptions in it of New York. Although for Mr. Dupee these passages provide "an atmosphere and no more," they actually serve the important function of making us recognize the fantastic development of a great city in which everyone is both literally and metaphorically moving uptown. In view of this no young man of any worth could possibly be impoverished or out of a position. James's descriptions of the city, along with his characterization of Townsend's successful cousin Arthur, who is marrying Sloper's niece and planning to move every three or four years "because the city's growing so quick—you've got to keep up with it," effectively suggest to us, even before it is confirmed, that Townsend is a ne'er-do-well. Sloper himself married an heiress and moved into what was then the embodiment of "the last results of architectural science" in Washington Square, but he was also at the time a successful physician. He can see clearly into the character of Morris Townsend because he knows how such a man might respond to the social and economic environment of New York; Sloper has been a combination, as it were, of Morris Townsend, the fortune-hunter, and Arthur Townsend, the energetic man of affairs. To be right about Morris requires exactly the talent of which Sloper boasts: a knowledge of types and of their response to external circumstance.

Thus his mind works well enough on all the world which surrounds Catherine, and we admire his perceptions of her place in it just so long as that world seems more substantial than anything going on inside her. In the environment of polite New York society, she is the type of ordinary, soft, and simple-minded girl and, having so decided, he perceives her in her external relationships with considerable intelligence and wit. But while he sees all round her he never bothers to take another look inside. For that reason, James, who at the beginning was himself addicted to a view of Catherine which lent itself to social comedy, disengages his view from Sloper's just as soon as Catherine reveals the movements of inner life. She becomes a "free" character for James and remains a "fixed" one for her father.

All of his passion, when she stays true to Townsend even after the trip to Europe, is expended not in an analysis of her feeling but in elaborate colorations of the situation. He can even suggest that she hopes he will die:

> "Your engagement will have one delightful effect upon you; it will make you extremely impatient for that event."
>
> Catherine stood staring, and the Doctor enjoyed the point he had made. It came to Catherine with the force—or rather with the vague impressiveness—of a logical axiom which it was not her province to controvert; and yet, though it was a scientific truth, she felt wholly unable to accept it.

Sloper's wit in these remarks is that of a man who is not addressing himself to a person he knows but to a situation in which he contrives to place her. Roughly, it is the sort of comedy we found in *The American,* when Madame de Bellegarde speaks to Newman as if she were engaging in a theatrical skit designed to show how great ladies deal with visiting barbarians. Her talk is not meant to take his individuality into account any more than Sloper's has any possible relevance to Catherine as a particular human being. When he talks to her in this way he is dealing with her once again as a "type," assuming that a girl in her situation would wish her father dead. James's achievement in the characterization of Dr. Sloper has its most brilliant manifestation when, in such speeches as these, we discover that the Doctor's sensibility has become, at least tangentially, like Aunt Lavinia's. She is predominantly the person who creates situations without regard for the fact that, given the people with whom she is dealing, the situations are absurd. Just as Sloper's irony becomes brutal as the novel nears its crisis, so her silliness becomes vicious, notably in her insinuation that the Doctor murdered his wife and son and will also kill Catherine:

> "Whatever you have done, stop doing it; that's all I wish."
>
> "Don't you wish also by chance to murder your child?" Mrs. Penniman inquired.
>
> "On the contrary, I wish to make her live and be happy."
>
> "You will kill her; she passed a dreadful night."
>
> "She won't die of one dreadful night, nor of a dozen. Remember that I am a distinguished physician."
>
> Mrs. Penniman hesitated a moment. Then she risked her retort. "Your being a distinguished physician has not prevented you from already losing *two members* of your family!"
>
> She had risked it, but her brother gave her such a terribly in-

cisive look—a look so like a surgeon's lancet—that she was frightened at her courage. And he answered her, in words that corresponded to the look: "It may not prevent me, either, from losing the society of still another."

The control of tone in the Doctor's very impressive rejoinder effectively suggests his superiority to Lavinia in intellectual and temperamental energy. He becomes increasingly like her, however, in that his language indicates a bias against obvious reality and in favour of its most outrageous possibilities. Since his habits of mind will not allow him to understand Catherine, all he can do is speculate about the theoretical possibilities of her situation in the abstract. In doing so he, no less than Lavinia, creates rôles for her which she is simply not large enough to fill, though he speaks to her as if she were. In this lies the explanation for the cumulative brutality in the comic dialogue.

We can say, in conclusion, that it is best not to think of this novel as a melodrama, but to observe that in response to the experience which it includes Dr. Sloper becomes a melodramatist and James does not. The development of his character is from scientist to melodramatist. *Washington Square* is a masterpiece if for no other reason than its making us *feel* the closeness of these two ways of manipulating life. The scientific attitude, with its presumptions about the predictability of a course of events, necessarily leads to melodrama when human beings refuse to imitate the logical hypotheses which are imposed upon them. Thus, *Washington Square* recapitulates the connection, noticed in every novel we have considered, between melodramatic expression and the discovery of the unpredictable.

Melodrama is the voice of the scientific mind when its theories have been defied by facts, when it is raised in a very illogical protest against the freedom of what it had assumed it had fixed. To apply this proposition to such various novels as *The American* and *Washington Square* requires only that its terms be given a legitimate latitude. In doing so it can be said that scientific logic and what is often called specifically American innocence can be almost synonymous. There is little difference between a belief in the inevitability of progress and a faith in the efficacy of scientific experiment. In Faulkner, the greatest American novelist to follow James, there is indeed a kind of fusion in the figure of Thomas Sutpen, from *Absalom, Absalom!*, of Christopher Newman, the innocent, and Dr. Sloper, the scientist. Sutpen's trouble is

that innocence which believed that the ingredients of morality were like the ingredients of pie or cake and once you had measured them and balanced them and mixed them and put them into the oven it was all finished and nothing but pie or cake could come out.

Simply because he believed in the necessary virtue of logic and of a "design" for living in which other people could be used, Sutpen calls forth the outraged response of those whose own private needs he violates. To this he can only respond with a plaintive and still innocent bewilderment about what he calls "a maelstrom of unpredictable and unreasoning human beings." *Absalom, Absalom!* is a novel which absorbs and evaluates a highly melodramatic content, and just as Sutpen, the calculating man, deserves to be associated with the exorbitantly emotional Rosa Coldfield, so Sloper belongs in a class not merely with Lavinia but with Mrs. Light of *Roderick Hudson*. They are an improbable combination only superficially; essentially they really do belong together. Each calculates the future and tries to control the fate of a daughter, and each reacts in the same way when the daughter refuses her assignment.

Washington Square differs from *Roderick Hudson* and *The American*, however, in that its melodrama is significant more to the psychological than to the moral life of its characters. Melodramatic style in the speeches of Dr. Sloper is not satirized, as it is in Mrs. Light, nor is it to be commended, as in the case of Newman, where it is a complaint that freedom to determine one's destiny is itself in the grip of historically dignified powers of restriction and emotional impoverishment. In *Washington Square,* in *Confidence,* and in the proposal scene of *The Europeans,* melodrama directs our attention towards psychological complications in those characters whose reactions create it. The vocabulary of science and experimentation which is found in each of these novels places the problem of unpredictability not in Fate or in history but within the human personality and the self-delusions it contrives.

To see this is to care more for the problem of Dr. Sloper than for the chance to call him a fiend or a villain. As I pointed out at the beginning, all the circumstances of the novel are in the convention of a melodramatic fairy-tale. But the novel itself is a literary achievement in so far as it exceeds the expectations initially aroused by its given circumstances. Sloper is corrupted precisely because he believes in them with an accelerating desperation. In escaping from this, James is detached from the Doctor's ever-heightening ironic tone, and he leaves him at last to the ineffectual torment of his own sense of humour. Thus, in its dramatic development, *Washington Square* confirms the very nature of its own literary achievement; it shows us the melodramatic direction which was open to it but which James declined. Once again, the experience dramatized within the novel is a version of James's own artistic experience in writing it, particularly as this relates to the creation and uses of character.

LAURENCE BEDWELL HOLLAND

The Crisis of Transformation:
The Golden Bowl

The image of society presented in *The Golden Bowl* is built on the pair of fictive marriages, projected first and then achieved, and the strange family they institute, which are central to both the form and the import of the novel because they are made symbolic not only of marriages in actual life but of other social institutions and processes which are fused with them. Yet the fusion of these other social patterns with the marriages is so complete that the marriages acquire a heightened significance in their own right. They are at once the stage for the drama and part of the drama itself, and *The Golden Bowl* not only acknowledges the importance of the institutions of marriage and the family in the culture it represents by holding so sharp a focus on them but helps create those institutions in their modern form by imposing on them burdensome functions beyond their customary capacity and infusing them with the power to sustain them. James's novel devotes its full power simultaneously to sanctioning the institution of marriage as a convention and to challenging its given conventional status, exposing the flaw in the "ghastly form," demanding of the "magnificent form" and of the partners in it the full redeeming intimacy of intense passion, a willed fidelity within the tightened bond, an authentic commitment to the communion it affords and to the larger community of purpose it can make possible. Terrors and cruelties are revealed within the form, easy convenience and profitable usage, the façade of decorum as well as the sustaining form of passion, the mere mask

From *The Expense of Vision: Essays on the Craft of Henry James.* © 1964, 1982 by Faith Mackey Holland. Princeton University Press, 1964.

as well as the speaking form of love or the abysmal passion Maggie comes to know. The perilous mixture of weakness, convenience, utilitarian usage, a flawed harmony, and a community of devotion which the form affords is characteristic of the society in its larger dimensions which *The Golden Bowl* helps to mold, with the result that "the marriages" (as James intended to entitle the novel until recalling that he had already used that title) are at once part of the novel's subject and, like the bowl itself, a containing metaphor for its social vision.

The plans for the Prince's marriage that occupy his thoughts in the opening chapter harbor an historical drama of larger proportions in which Adam Verver, his prospective father-in-law, holds, to begin with, a more important role than the Prince's fiancée. The handsome Prince seems an architectural façade to Adam, and the enigmatic millionaire seems shielded in the "flawless freshness of [his] white waistcoat" by the mysterious "great white curtain" which the Prince associates with the fate of Poe's Gordon Pym, with the American imagination and "the state of mind" of his new American friends. Both are revealed in the contours of the social roles and historic missions which first characterize them.

Restless and unoccupied after the recent exertions which have brought the "capture" of Maggie, the Prince stands looking at a heap of objects in a shop window that seem the "loot" accumulated by the "insolence of the Empire." Latent in his career are combined precisely the predatory "insolence" and, in larger measure, the massive power of an established "empire" which he associates with the modern London that has replaced the older "*Imperium*" of his native Rome. The older empire seems to be recovered in memory by the sight of modern Bond Street. If he seems strikingly unoccupied and place-less in relation to this imperium, as he does in relation to the wedding arrangements made in his behalf (the "inspired harmony" reached by the Ververs' lawyers and "his own man of business"), he is nevertheless ready to make a place for himself in the new life being prepared for him. His traditional past still receives his respect—indeed, his habit of simply receiving its inherited benefits, including the attentions of some twenty women, links him to traditional aristocratic customs and he looks forward to resurrecting his past with Adam Verver's money, excavating the family estates now buried by a "cloud of mortgages" as "thick" as the ashes from Vesuvius.

Yet he knows that his traditional security has lapsed into the mere momentum of its past vigor and that he has at least a tenuous claim to a place in the imperium of the present: his familiar name, "Amerigo," which associates him, as Fanny Assingham puts it, with the "pushing" adventurer who followed after Columbus and managed to become at least "'name-father'" to the new land. If his efforts are less inventive and aggressive than luckily opportunistic, he is nevertheless aware of the limitations of his past and regards his marriage as the quest "for some new history that should, so far as possible, contradict, and even if need be flatly dishonour, the old." His family archives include the deeds of some men of good character and the "crimes" and "follies" of others, but his past has become singularly ineffective and he cannot simply inherit it: "If what had come to him wouldn't do he must *make* something different," and the "material for the making," he recognizes, "had to be Mr. Verver's millions." The crucial difference between the Prince's history and Adam's is that the Italian's is a record of money spent and gone while the American's is a current account of cash available for spending, the veritable bath of fluid wealth in which Adam has soaked his future son-in-law, with Maggie adding drops of "good faith," "innocence," and "imagination." The financial arrangements in connection with his marriage have scarcely invoked "the principle of reciprocity," but the Prince hopes to move closer at least to that enviable equilibrium: having mastered the English language for its utility in all but the most intimate transactions, he is now as his marriage approaches "practising his American"; Amerigo practices it so as "to converse properly, on equal terms as it were, with Mr. Verver."

The drama of *The Golden Bowl* rests in large part on the tensions created by Adam Verver's money and the other values associated with the American character. Together they constitute a language which the others are induced to speak, and the drama's irony arises from the fact that the language of the new imperium does provide an effective medium of communication but threatens to rule out, by its very power and fluency, the "reciprocity" the Prince aspires to, the shared relationship he seeks, the veritable equality which communion in the new language might afford.

The language, the "manner," the power and the system of morals which operate alike with the swift efficiency of a machine, and the enigmatic whiteness which the Prince associates with the American character are in volume 1 embodied chiefly in Adam Verver, who dominates the Prince's attention at the start almost as thoroughly as he proves later to dominate his daughter's. The Prince, whose crystal form Adam gilds and appreciates, is to Adam "an object of beauty, an object of price," in the art collection with which Adam plans to endow the museum he is building in American City, the community which he has adopted as home in his native state. Adam's "apprehensive passion" is appreciative, whether in matters of business or of taste, and James's diction in Book Third places Adam precisely on the threshold of the creative imagination. His "'peak in Darien,'" comparable to that of Cortez in Keats's sonnet, was the transforming discovery of "the affinity of Genius, or at least of Taste, with something in himself," the discovery that he was "equal somehow with the great seers . . . and he didn't after all perhaps dangle so far below the great producers and creators." He is the "financial 'backer'" rather than "stage manager" or "author of the play," but he is associated intimately with the "grasping imagination" and with the exercise of power to which Professor Edel has drawn attention in James's own ambitions.

In Adam's case, "acquisition of one sort" has proved "a perfect preliminary to acquisition of another," and he has learned to enjoy the pursuit just as he had learned to like in business the "calculation and imaginative gambling all for themselves," the combination of exploitation and luck, "the creation of 'interests' that were the extinction of other interests, the livid vulgarity . . . of getting in, or getting out, first." The "insolence" of empire which is, at the most, quiescent in the Prince and safely established in Britain's shops has been more powerful in Adam. His ambition to become a "Patron of Art" is presented as involving release from his first marriage, breaches in decorum, a challenge to established authority. His first wife, with her uninformed tastes for the merely decorative, was alien to the ambitions he discovered on a trip to Europe after her death; no decent or "real lady," it occurred to him later, could have been a "companion of Cortez," and while the new ambitions of the "plain American citizen" appear to himself as the imperial vision of Cortez, they appear also as the "'cheek' of the young man who approaches the boss without credentials" or acquires a friend by accosting a stranger on the street.

His particular "real friend, in all the business," is his own self in its new role as Patron, a self which he discovers by intruding without a formal introduction; knocking at the door of its "private house," and admitted only after humiliating delay, he stands "twirling his hat, as an embarrassed stranger," or, "trying his keys, as a thief at night." The freedom to *see* which he asserts is the result of the bold determination figured in the comparisons he makes between himself and two popes, earlier and inferior patrons who neglected Michelangelo. And the museum he plans for American City is not simply the product of earlier ages, the "Golden Isles" which he has been able to "rifle"; it is "positively civilization condensed, . . . a house on a rock . . . from whose open doors and windows, open to grateful, to thirsty millions, the higher, the highest knowledge would shine out to bless the land."

Adam Verver's embarrassment in connection with the memory of his first wife, his temporary rebuff at the house of his aspirations, and the pride he takes later in the possession of a grandson, point ahead to Faulkner's Thomas Sutpen and his design for a community and a dynasty in *Absalom, Absalom!*, but Adam Verver in contrast to Faulkner's protagonist has had exceptionally good luck; he is a strikingly successful, fortunate, and amiable magnate whose "years of darkness had been needed to render possible the years of light" in his marital life as well as in his business affairs, and James's analysis accords to Adam the dignity of a complex, essentially mysterious, integrity. The density of the figure derives from its puzzling mixture of affability, compressed imaginative power, and insolence, his insolence being the assertively proud exertions of an entrepreneur whose enterprise works independently of older customs and decorum. The novel acknowledges that "amiability" is often helpful if not the very "principle of large accumulations," but the novel probes unsuccessfully for the link in Adam's case between so "insolent" a concentration in business matters and so sociable a temperament in all other affairs. That "variety of imagination" on which "amiability" depends is "fatal, in the world of affairs," unless, as in Adam's case, it is "so disciplined as not to be distinguished from monotony"; Adam Verver has for several decades been "inscrutably monotonous" behind the "iridescent cloud" of his native American manner, the "soft looseness" which displays few folds but has nevertheless a "quality unmistakable."

Both screened and expressed by that manner is the "special genius" of the American businessman, a "spark of fire" shining in Adam Verver's "inward vagueness as a lamp before a shrine twinkles in the dark perspective of a church." Fanned by youthful vigor and the good fortune of being an American—the encouragement given by "example and opportunity" in the New World—his "genius" has converted his mind into "a strange workshop of fortune," a "mysterious" though plain and "almost anonymous" factory which enclosed, at the height of his business activities, "a miraculous white-heat." This power is joined with the "perfection of machinery" it has produced and with the "acquisitive power engendered and applied," but it is enclosed in the virtually "anonymous" and child-like manner which Adam displays at the opening of Book Second, when he indulges in a rare moment of privacy in the billiard room but feels ashamed of his concern for his own "personal advantage" and acknowledges it with "confessing eyes." His manner shows that he is playing at "depravity" for the "amusement" of it, knowing that his moments alone are doomed to be short because of the demands upon him (which he welcomes) and the power which almost despite himself he communicates to others. An "impersonal whiteness" is a screen for which his "vision sometimes ached" in the face of the "many-coloured human appeal" of social intercourse—and the novel's first detailed treatment of Adam shows him seeking that refuge in a retreat through the "tortuous corridors" of Fawns.

But the power of his money is inescapable and is augmented by the awe in which people hold it—by the "attribution of power" beyond what he may otherwise have, which others, reading the symbolism of his cash, infer that he *must* have as a virtually "infinite agent." Together they have an effect and constitute a burden which he cannot pretend to escape, for he has made himself vulnerable to social demands: his manner reveals the amiable *accessibility* of one American archetype, the individual longing for a community. His youthful eyes make it impossible to tell whether "they most carried their possessor's vision out or most opened themselves to your own." In their watchful gaze other persons are drawn toward possible communion, whether with Adam himself or with others, "moving about, for possible community, opportunity, the sight of you scarce knew what," either "before" or "behind" the focus of Adam Verver's attention. It is precisely that kind of attention that *The Golden Bowl* fixes in turn on Adam Verver at the opening of Book Second, following his retreat through the "tortuous corridors" only to infringe on his "achieved isolation," envying his sense of "having the world to one's self " and aiming to "share this world," subjecting him to its possessive scrutiny but rendering that scrutiny "tender indeed almost to compassion."

The novel's intrusion on Adam's privacy simply anticipates the social demands from which he had taken flight, which are the efforts represented by the Mrs. Rance who pursues him into the billiard room at Fawns, the efforts to get him remarried. By the time the routinely determined efforts of womankind have been replaced by Maggie's own, and such available spouses as the Misses Kitty and Dotty Lutch have been replaced by the beautiful Charlotte Stant, *The Golden Bowl* has projected the form which it tries at once to challenge and to redeem: the "arrangement," the "pagoda," the funny form in which marriage as a constituted convention, familial affection of father and daughter, the business transactions entailed in the purchase of a work of art and an expanding imperialism, and an affair of sexual passion are interdependent, each relation contingent on the others for both the opportunity and the sanction to develop. All are or soon become monstrous: the conventional marriages become hollow if convenient shells; the familial affection becomes instituted incest; the business transactions become merely acquisitive instead of productive as Adam's "workshop of fortune" had been when operating at its earlier "miraculous white-heat"; the affair of passion culminates in an adulterous betrayal. But these distortions do not simply express the perversions that each relation has become; they express also the power and validity which each is in some measure acknowledged to have, the heightened pressure of energy and form which each acquires in interaction with the others, and the double pressure which James exerted in the effort to preserve "his form with closeness" while at the same time infusing the novel with an energy which "strains, or tends to burst, with a latent extravagance, its mould."

The first half of the novel—including the chapters which culminate in Adam's marriage and those which culminate in Charlotte's and the Prince's assignation in Gloucester—is informed by all these pressures and by James's willingness (a combination of desire and resignation) to incur in the arena of his fiction the risks of his art and the sacrifice it enacts. Adam's courtship of Charlotte, and the renewal of her affair with the Prince, are part of James's effort to construct a novel that will both accede to the conditions of his world and celebrate them while challenging them in the attempt to redeem them. Adam's marriage and Charlotte's assignation tax the flaw in the golden bowl and prepare for the incident later when it will be broken on the marble floor; but they also prepare for, and thus help to create, the possibility that it may be salvaged and filled with love. Each of the relations, the marriage and the affair, is a flawed bowl which images a sought perfection.

The institution of marriage which the Prince recommends blandly to Charlotte early in the novel (she should "marry some capital fellow") is the social relation which, in his eyes, most reveals people to each other and is acknowledged by Charlotte to be succinctly "the condition" on which a place in her world depends since she declines the position of a "shopgirl" or "old maid." Marriage, she declares to Adam, would give her "an existence" and "a motive outside of myself." But the marriage arranged for her is as much a part of the world of shops as Maggie's marriage, whereby the enterprising Prince captured his bride and Adam Verver bought a precious title for his collection. Compensation for Charlotte's sacrifice of the Prince is what Fanny Assingham wants a "good" marriage to bring her, as well as protection for the previously arranged marriage of Charlotte's lover to Maggie. Moreover, Maggie recommends marriage for Adam specifically as compensation for the loss of his daughter; Maggie's leaving his house, where she had been virtually "married" to him, has thrust him on the "market." And when Maggie persuades Adam to invite Charlotte for a visit, she does so as an act of beneficence and as an opportunity to put Charlotte's talents to use in the new program of entertaining which Fanny has urged on her diffident American friends; Maggie will both help Charlotte and use her, though she will "admire her still more than I used her."

Convenience, compensation, aesthetic mastery, and the careful negotiations of a tactful bargain characterize Adam's courtship and Charlotte's acceptance, and both the utility and the bargain in the beginning serve chiefly Adam's and Maggie's affection for each other. Having agreed that Charlotte's talents should not be "wasted," Adam finds himself liking what Maggie and Fanny tell him about her, "almost as if her portrait, by some eminent hand, were going on, so that he watched it grow under the multiplication of touches." He finds her "a domestic resource," meeting her often in his grand-child's nursery when she fills Maggie's place during Maggie's trip to Italy with the Prince. Adam has at least "an inkling" that he is, "as a taster of life, economically constructed" and that he has the odd habit of applying "the same measure of value" to "new human acquisitions" such as Charlotte as he does to "old Persian carpets," Oriental tiles, or Luini paintings. And James presents this "aesthetic principle" in Adam as something dangerously illicit but as yet contained safely within the tidy confines of Adam's domestic self and within the control of his bookkeeping. Though one of the "profane altar-fires," it feeds exclusively on "the idea (followed by appropriation) of plastic beauty," not spreading to consume the rest of the "spiritual furni-ture" of Adam's mind as it does "in so many cases." It has not "raised the smallest scandal in his economy at large," though Adam's aesthetic power is in the dubious position of lucky "bachelors or other gentlemen of pleasure who so manage their entertainment of compromising company that even the austerest housekeeper . . . never feels obliged to give warning."

The telling consideration for Adam, finally, is moral and aesthetic as well as compactly economical: by marrying Charlotte he will serve Maggie, playing along with her fancy that he is younger than his forty-seven years and convincing her that by marrying she has not "forsaken" him. The "whole call of his future to him, as a father" lights the landscape at Fawns (as it does the entire novel) as if by "some strange midnight sun," giving it "a spoken pretension to beauty" and the "inordinate size" of an "hallucina-tion." The aim to serve Maggie falls in "beautifully" with the prospect of his marriage, and for Charlotte to serve likewise will be "the proper direc-tion" for Charlotte's "leisure" to take.

The marriage which Adam proposes to Charlotte, with Maggie's tacit encouragement, is well within the range of Adam's aesthetic and moral econ-omy, as are the terms of Charlotte's acceptance. The occasion which brings Adam to the point of a proposal is his trip with Charlotte to Brighton to inspect the Damascene tiles which he has heard are in the possession of Mr. Gutermann-Seuss. The negotiations constitute a ceremony which precipitates and illuminates his decision to propose marriage. He girds himself for both the marriage proposal and the negotiations for the tiles, and Charlotte's sharing the trip with him not only quickens his affection but opens up new vistas for his future exploits as a buyer and connoisseur. With her enviable appreciation of "type"—even, as the Prince has noticed, when it appears in "cabmen" and "faces at hucksters' stalls" in the vast London democracy— she leads Adam to relish the distinctive Semitic features of the numerous Gutermann-Seusses and to anticipate new delights in his future bargain hunts. She had seemed earlier to the Prince to match his "notion, perhaps not wholly correct, of a muse," and now her "free range of observation," her habit of registering "almost any 'funny impression,'" renders for James as well as for the reader and Adam the postures and accents of the "fat, ear-ringed aunts," the "glossy, cockneyfied . . . uncles," and the eleven "gradu-ated offspring" of Mr. Gutermann-Seuss, the swarming family who surround the purchasers as if gathered "for some anniversary gregariously and reli-giously kept." Adam reflects that Charlotte's taste for the "funny" would in the future alter his "customary hunt for the possible prize, the inquisitive play of his accepted monomania" and make of it a "somewhat more bois-terously refreshing . . . sport." For the transaction proper, Charlotte and Adam are led into a private chamber, but afterward they rejoin the family and Adam is "merged in the elated circle formed by Charlotte's free response to the collective caress of all the shining eyes," and they share "heavy cake and port wine" in a ceremony which gives "their transaction," as Charlotte notices, "the touch of some mystic rite of old Jewry."

So solemnized and celebrated, the transaction is one of the most complex events in the novel since it founds his proposal of marriage on an act which is both a commercial transaction and a ceremony, which the proposal itself consummates but also supersedes. On the way to the Gutermann-Seuss's Adam considers his "majestic scheme" of securing happiness for himself, Maggie, and Charlotte as carefully as if he held "a glazed picture in its right relation to the light." He first associates his intention with the volatile young heroes in fiction who pour out the language of love in enviable soliloquies; in the abstract diction assigned him by James, Adam speaks enviously of the sheer power to "speak." Yet he distinguishes his "scheme" from theirs, since they pursue the feverishly impetuous "path of passion properly so called"; Adam feels that his plan to marry is "a thing of less joy than a passion" but that it might nevertheless "have the essential property" and "dignity" of "providing for more contingencies." Marriage as he envisions it is a substi-tute for the difficulties and deviousness encountered on "the path of passion properly so called," and it gains its more lasting utility at the cost of passion.

Correspondingly, when with Charlotte and Mr. Gutermann-Seuss dur-ing the transaction, Adam finds that his experience is different, though different not from transactions in fiction but from those in comparable "bourgeois back parlours" when he has "pried and prowled," risking "the very bloom of honour." On those typical occasions he lingered over inspecting the purchase, enjoyed the "criticism" of the treasure, the bargaining ("what was called discussion") and thought predominantly of "his acquisition and the figure of his cheque." Now, by contrast, he finds that the transaction proceeds swiftly in silence because his attention is engrossed by Charlotte's presence; the "predominance of Charlotte's very person" makes the deferment of talk about the purchased tiles as pleasant "as some joy promised a lover by his mistress, or as a big bridal bouquet held patiently behind her." The tiles are perfect—"scarcely more meant to be breathed upon . . . than the cheek of royalty"—but the monied American Patron with the simple insolence of empire buys them in a transaction which for the first time in his career is as "fine as the perfection perceived" in the regal treasure he buys; and the swift perfection of his decision is owing to Charlotte's presence and his accelerating intention to propose to her. It is in view of "the relation of intimacy with him . . .which she had accepted" by virtue of being present with him and, particularly, hearing the stipulated "sum"—as a consequence, that is, of Adam's "having exposed her" to the "hard business-light" of the chamber where they negotiate "with the treasure and its master"—that Adam carries through his proposal. James declares that, "fabulous as this truth may sound," Adam finds in the experience they have shared the grounds for proposing to Charlotte, either as an obligation incurred by affection or as a penalty for transgression: it is "a sentimental link, an obligation of delicacy" or it is "perhaps one of the penalties of its opposite," that is, a penalty for compromising her.

The episode is crucial for James's fable because it reveals in a fantastic light indeed the faults of the marriage arranged for Adam and Charlotte while also providing the basis for according their marriage any stature at all as a moral and intimate form. Their intimacy during the transaction is exaggerated if not created in Adam's anticipations, for the implications of Charlotte's silent presence remained undefined except insofar as they are anticipated hopefully by Adam. But the occasion brings into new focus both the earlier affair of Charlotte and the Prince and the episode in the Bloomsbury shop.

The earlier affair had been an affair of passion without contractual or commercial considerations, though the Prince's appreciation of Charlotte's charms is possessive and his willingness to take them or leave them is condescending. Their affair was an emotional and sexual involvement which was stronger on Charlotte's part but one which could be abruptly terminated on grounds which the Assinghams and the reader must hypothesize. The trans-action at Brighton, by contrast, is a stunning and appalling amalgam of intimacy and commerce, with Adam breathing more intimately on the cheek of the tiles he buys than on Charlotte and sacrificing appreciative pleasures to the efficiency of his purchase, and with Charlotte indifferently taking part, then responding freely to the "collective caress of all the shining eyes" of the Gutermann-Seusses. The incident is made to seem decidedly more illicit than the affairs of the fictional gallants which Adam contrasts to his own because it is distinctly void of the "passion properly so called" which theirs, like Amerigo's and Charlotte's, may claim.

Yet the scene presents paradoxically at the same time the image of a relation intimately engaged in and publicly sanctioned by a ceremony, and if it lacks the "joy" presumably known to the Prince and Charlotte, this ceremony nevertheless, like familiar engagement and wedding ceremonies in western culture, sanctions a marriage which is not yet consummated as a marriage or fully achieved: it does not celebrate a marriage already accomplished but one which it provides for and helps create. Though Adam's and Charlotte's relation during the negotiations lacks the passion of love, it has the sanction of ceremony and it is closer to a shared communion than the business deals which Adam has known to the peril of his honor in other parlors.

Moreover, it is closer to intimacy than were the Prince and Charlotte on the telling occasion when they found the bowl in Bloomsbury. Then they talked in their familiar Italian, but the Prince left the shop, leaving Charlotte to negotiate alone with "their entertainer." Now Charlotte remains with Adam in the parlor where they are together closeted with the tiles and their "master." Her silent presence inspires Adam not only to his suspiciously speedy efficiency but to the "perfection" of his purchase and then removes his mind from the tiles to talk with Charlotte about them, the lover's gift or "bridal bouquet" he anticipates enjoying. In other words, she inspires the transformation of an ordinary business negotiation into a more intimate transaction than Adam has ever known, stimulating Adam to imagine the incident, at least, as an affair, with Charlotte as his intimate partner. At the same time, she leads him to give precedence, over the business deal and the beautiful tiles, to her. In the context of the novel the two are compromised by the incident yet bound closer by a certain measure of affection and in-terest, and the incident moreover joins them by anticipation in the imagined or prospective form of union in marriage. And Adam, unlike the Prince in his affair in Rome, finds in the event at Brighton the grounds of an obligation to propose marriage, as he proceeds instantly to do.

The fantastic scene is powerful because of the many pressures it exerts which contribute to the *funny form* of James's novel. It makes of the fictive courtship and marriage of Adam and Charlotte inside the novel a contorted image of numerous actualities which either do or might exist outside it, all the more contorted an image for the range of its relevance and the variety within the conjunction it forges: conventional marriage as a domestic, sexual, and commercial convenience, deliberately chosen by the partners but subordinating marital to familial and occupational concerns; the traffic of prostitution; the transformation of an ordinary acquisitive enterprise in the realms of business and of taste into a more discriminating, intimate, and viable experience.

Within the novel, the fictive marriage is a promising though perilously flawed form which virtually demands that it be either violated or reconstituted in the name of passion, a terrifyingly brittle vessel to sustain the burden of advantages, kindnesses, and other expectations intended for it and the pressure of needs and impulses which may threaten it from without. The fictive marriage subjects the actualities of the institution to an appallingly intense light while embodying also the promise or ideal communion of the form: yet the promise itself is flawed and must be recast in the crucible of experience. When the action of book 2 culminates in Charlotte's agreement to marry and the messages of approval which Maggie and the Prince (with what amount to their "caressing eyes") send on to Paris, the dialogue and the telegrams simply complete the odd arrangement already provided for in the exotic "back parlour" at Brighton.

In discussing the proposal, Adam and Charlotte display a mixture of candor and of intentions unexplored or undisclosed, contingencies anticipated, dismissed, or veiled. They bargain tactfully, and Charlotte warns that he may learn later or perhaps never know the unpleasant things about her; she asks him to consider that she might "get what I want for less" than marriage to him would entail and that he might express his kindness in some other way, and warns that his wife might be his daughter's rival for his affection. Adam encourages her to "make something" or get some advantage from his affection for her, and, to reassure her concern for Maggie, admits that he is marrying in part to relieve Maggie of the fear that she has "forsaken" him. Though Charlotte questions whether this idea is "quite enough to marry me for," she concedes that the plan is "beautiful" and that Adam has "certainly worked it out!" She must suppress a sudden "small cry" when Adam suggests that they join Maggie and the Prince in Paris to seek their approval, so keen is her excitement and anxiety at the prospect of being often near the Prince, but she agrees to await Maggie's approval.

Adam's "majestic scheme" hinges on Charlotte's accession to his insistence that his "luck" is nothing without Charlotte to complete his good fortune and "make me right," and it hinges too on the approval of his daughter and son-in-law. Maggie's telegram of congratulations lacks her usual "grace" as Charlotte sees it in being addressed to Adam alone, and Adam mistakenly thinks that the second telegram, to Charlotte, is also from Maggie and thanks his daughter for in effect giving him his wife. But under the odd circumstances James has contrived, Charlotte tells Adam succinctly "I'll give you what you ask," and the novel's "majestic scheme" is given the sanction of this crucial incident. The second telegram, drawn from the "cartridge-box" of a uniformed messenger as he approaches the "stronghold of the concierge," is addressed to Charlotte alone and is not from the daughter but from the son-in-law. And the telegram, which Adam in his confidence feels no need to read when Charlotte offers it to him, is one which might prevent the marriage if Adam knew its contents but which secures Charlotte's consent. When the message is later divulged, it completes the fascinating though terrifying grotesque design on which the novel is founded. James puts the opening phrase in the Prince's original French (the language he had once intimated was the "most apt" for "discriminations . . . of the invidious kind"), then translates the rest into the Jamesian English which Amerigo speaks perfectly: "*À la guerre comme à la guerre then. . . . We must lead our lives as we see them; but I am charmed with your courage and almost surprised at my own!*"

Even two years later Charlotte cannot resolve with certainty the ambiguities of the treasured telegram. She wonders whether the Prince, in giving his more than perfunctory consent, was indicating that he felt "secure" in resisting the temptation which her proximity would present or "seasoned" in welcoming it, or whether he had the courage simply to face the increased strain on his conduct which her marriage would entail. But the telegram defines the "moral energy," as James had called it in "The Art of Fiction," which is required of his art, and of Charlotte and Amerigo, by the fantastic arrangement which James's "scheme" (the "sacrament of execution" which "marries" form and substance), along with the motives of characters and the habits, conditions, and goals of their society, together have produced.

Within two years, the arrangements have produced the "crisis" which Charlotte is prepared to enjoy at the opening of book 3, a crisis which challenges not only the marital and familial lives of the chief participants but the exceedingly fortunate society which their interlocked marriages represent. The marriages not only facilitate but institutionalize the dangerously close though authentically tender affection of Adam and his daughter and grand-child, while institutionalizing also, in an accepted and even familial form, the charged companionship of Charlotte and the Prince, renewing the passion they have known. The marriages singly and together become in fact a mockery of the form; they are a mere convenience, serving the almost indolent domesticity of the wealthy father and daughter (whose disappearance from society at large into the limbo of their affluence and familial intimacy is dramatized by the novel's focus on the experience of Charlotte and Amerigo and the Assinghams), and sustaining the fruitless public rituals when the Prince and Charlotte appear together on formal occasions. When Charlotte is first seen by the reader after her marriage, at the Ambassador's reception, the flaws in the original arrangement have already come more vividly to light, but Charlotte and the Prince are not the only ones who have threatened the marriages and the possible communion which, along with the possible debasements, they might afford.

In his use of Charlotte and the Prince as centers of attention James presents the deterioration of the marriages through the eyes of characters whose opportunism and passivity have contributed to the crisis but who also suffer from it and are in part its victims. Adam's career as a Patron has (for all we hear about it) virtually ceased, and since the birth of the Principino, he and Maggie have retired within the debilitating ease of the marriages. Adam has thought proudly of Maggie and the Prince as an image of "marriage demonstrated" beyond the experience of his own first marriage, particularly since the birth of their male child, and his affections have become monopolized by his daughter in her familial role as wife and mother and by his grandson. The novel presents this affection as an out-and-out usurpation of the Prince's position as father and husband.

Both the attitudes which *distinguish* Adam's feeling for his grandson from his feeling toward art and those which *connect* the two, contribute to his displacement of the Prince. Adam insists that a painting resemble the master who is thought to have produced it, but he does not judge other matters by their "looks," and "so far as he was not taking life as a collector, he was taking it . . . as a grandfather." Yet if the Principino's features display any claim of Amerigo's to his paternity, Adam ignores them, and while he thinks the boy more "precious" than other "small pieces he had handled," he can "manipulate and dandle," "toss and catch again" the infant with what prove to be possessive hands. In what the novel wryly brands an odd twist to the "old story," Maggie and Adam have "converted the precious creature into a link" not between parents but between "a mamma and a grandpapa," and readers are asked to see the boy as "a hapless half-orphan, with the place of immediate male parent swept bare and open to the next nearest sympathy." The child is cloistered at Fawns in chambers as guarded as the nursery in "a royal palace," yet even in the case of the royal Prince his "absence" is preferred; he must enjoy the child when Adam's priority allows a merely "auxiliary admiration" and must accept wonderingly the American's characteristic surrender to the young and Adam's "impunity of appropriation."

Adam's companionship with Maggie likewise has relegated the Prince to the periphery of their family circle, leaving it to Fanny Assingham to amuse him (as she is left to amuse callers) while Maggie and Adam converse apart in a tête-à-tête of their own, a situation that has become more outlandish after Adam's and Charlotte's marriage. And while Charlotte's disdainful irony in explaining the situation to an appalled Fanny Assingham at the Ambassador's reception is a clear sign that Charlotte and the Prince are contemplating doing something about their plight, the irony does not discredit Charlotte's assertions but highlights glaringly the abnormalities of the situation and the crisis in which she determines to act.

A slight indisposition has kept Adam from the reception, Charlotte explains, and he had insisted that both Maggie and Charlotte go to the party with the Prince; Maggie has suddenly left before even entering the reception rooms to return to her father, and consequently Charlotte and the Prince are there alone; the father and daughter doubtless are enjoying a "little frugal picnic," a "little party at home." Their separation after Adam's marriage has simply increased their desire to be together, and since they now no longer literally live together Maggie arranges for visits; they virtually pay calls on each other and engage in "make-believe renewals of their old life." Though the two couples live in separate households, Adam and Maggie now have "more contact and more intimacy" than before. The affectionate and wealthy father and daughter have in effect "placed" both Charlotte and Amerigo on the edges of their routines, if not of their affections, and one should, "as they say . . . know one's place." In sum, Charlotte's husband treats her as being "of less importance to him than some other woman," despite her efforts to "make him capable of a greater" affection than what Fanny calls his "natural interest in his daughter."

The Prince, on the same occasion, brings out the effect on all of them of Maggie's and Adam's wealth and good nature, which is namely to bring to bear, as the Prince had noticed early, astonishing amounts of "American good faith" and to afford, for themselves at least, "innocent pleasures, pleasures without penalties"; the "absence of prejudice backed by the presence of money" suggests the open high confidence, and the power which implements and protects it, that the Ververs display. At the Ambassador's reception, the Prince points out that he as well as Charlotte is "in Mr. Verver's boat," which floats at all, as Fanny understands, only because his "father-in-law's great fortune" has provided "the element" in which he "could pecuniarily float." Whatever the motives of the characters to begin with, and whatever their motives become, the Verver money, affluence, and trusting kindness toward others have a tangible impact, both corrosive and creative, on the action.

With their solicitude for each other, Adam and Maggie are able to spend hours and evenings together (there are quarters at the Ververs' house for Maggie and the baby when they stay over), while encouraging Charlotte and Amerigo to find companionship with each other and indeed using them to represent the two families in social affairs. Charlotte cannot escape the responsibility she shares by claiming that the "doing" has *all* been the Ververs' and that "it's all a matter of what they've done *to* us," nor is the Prince exonerated by simply noting that they themselves have been more than passive in accepting the Ververs' beneficence and the marriages. But James's "language of exaggeration" (like Kate's in *The Wings of the Dove*) does define a real pressure which bears down on Charlotte and the Prince in declaring that "no more extraordinary decree had ever been launched against such victims than this of forcing them against their will into a relation of mutual close contact that they had done everything to avoid."

And the Prince reveals more than his own negligent and shrewd deference to Adam's power ("treating him" as he and Charlotte do with the deference due "a Pope, a King, a President . . . or just a beautiful Author") when he wonders at the connection between Adam's familial affections and his banking affairs: Adam governs the Prince's relation to Maggie as he does "everything else," relieving him of "all anxiety about his married life in the same manner in which he relieved him on the score of his bank-account." The Prince is amused rather than irritated by the situation which leaves him still on the circumference of his new family, but he perceives that Adam's strangely close relation with his daughter has "the same deep intimacy as the commercial, the financial association founded, far down, on a community of interest." Like "capitalists and bankers," "illustrious collectors," "American fathers," and Americans generally, the Ververs do each other favors and do him the favor of the "treat" he is enjoying "at his father-in-law's expense."

The "treat" is the fluent "ease" which is "guaranteed" him in his marriage, but it brings with it the situation which leaves him literally jobless (as Bob Assingham emphasizes) and with no office other than those of father and husband, and with nothing in *these* roles to do. The Ververs in their marriages stifle the imagination; the "dagger" and poisoned cup imply admittedly old-fashioned plots, but the Americans rule out any comparable service "worthy" of a truly "personal relation"; they rule out any intriguing responsibility, any "charming charge," any genuinely interesting burden to assume in tribute to "confidence deeply reposed." The Prince's situation is the "dreary little crisis" which he considers, just after ruminating on the Ververs' money, in the empty drawing room of his own house and begins to pace "again and again the stretch of polished floor," to discover in a moment that Charlotte, having found Maggie in charge and safely occupied in Adam's household, has come in private to visit her stepson-in-law and former lover.

It is the "bore of comfort," as Lord Warburton called it in *The Portrait of a Lady,* as well as good fortune's protecting ease, which helps produce the crisis for the marriages, but Charlotte seeks excitement in the life that with their help and consent has been arranged for all of them. She relishes the opportunity at the Ambassador's reception to be seen, "in truth crowned," in the Prince's company, "exposed" and "a bit brazen" but stunning, and convinced, like Gilbert Osmond, that "materials to work with had been all she required and that there were none too precious for her to understand and use." And there is mounting evidence that she and Amerigo may begin, as Fanny thinks, "*really* treating their subject" in intimacy and "finding it much more interesting." Yet Charlotte finds it boring to spend hours sight-seeing alone, and equally dull to perform, as "part of one's contract," the "duties of a remunerated office" as formal hostess for both households, putting up with the "arid social sands" which seem to her astute eye the forged coins in the "debased currency" which their lives have become.

A "debased currency" is an apt metaphor for the adulterations which characterize the domestic lives of Adam and Maggie, innocent and benign but relaxed and withdrawn in the perfunctory routines of their familial lives, and it is apt also for those adulterations that permeate the society surrounding them which is epitomized by the party around Easter at Matcham, a reincarnation of Newmarch in *The Sacred Fount* where Charlotte and the Prince plan their assignation. Maggie and Adam decline the invitation to Lord and Lady Castledean's house party, but Amerigo and Charlotte attend. And the Prince reveals for James, within the tawdry though glittering textures of the life around him, the rudiments of social intercourse which become the matrix for both the imminent betrayal and the imminent redemption in James's drama. At Matcham, as at Newmarch, people are brought into an arranged though shifting scene which stirs with change, creating the prospect of "possible new combinations" and "the quickened play" of sheer "propinquity," even if it produces no more than the assignation which Lady Castledean will arrange, once her titled husband returns to town, with the "sleek," "civil," white-collared Mr. Blint.

The Matcham world is more practiced in sociability on the grand scale than the Ververs', and it displays no trace of familial concerns; but in crucial ways, which the abstract diction and extravagant oddity of James's form bring to light, it fosters the notably relaxed tolerance and risks the specifically comfortable freedom which Adam and Maggie encourage in their spouses and which, in an utterly different but equally risky version, they display in their own strange intimacy. The "happy boldness" with which the Prince and Charlotte, and others at Matcham, mingle together and accept it as simply "funny" is precisely that "eccentricity of associated freedom" which in a different version characterizes Maggie and Adam also. Matcham has simply done *to* the conscience in a cruel way what Maggie and Adam unintentionally have done *with* it in their benign manner: they have isolated it and rendered it safely ineffectual in its subservience to bland good faith in their own proprieties and the services others perform for them. Matcham keeps the conscience at hand as a harmless and useful seamstress, a "snubbed" but docile "poor relation . . . for whose tacit and abstemious presence, never betrayed by the rattle of her rusty machine, a room in the attic and a place at the side-table were decently usual."

In the world of Matcham, Amerigo's innermost self stands half outside or half hidden by its rites, while the "good people who had, in the night of time, unanimously invented them . . . still, in the prolonged afternoon of their good faith, unanimously, even if a trifle automatically, practised them." The "complacency" and "seated solidity" leave the Prince "puzzled as to the element of staleness in all the freshness and of the freshness in all the staleness, of innocence in the guilt and of guilt in the innocence," the mixture by which the "enquiring mind" is so "sharply challenged." The Prince's actions themselves remain rather "automatic," but the more courageous Charlotte finds a way within those drab rituals to renew her love with the Prince, and the re-emergence of their passion is at once the final debasement of the form their lives have taken and a challenge to it which provides the half-furtive, half-bold basis for its redemption.

The "congruity" of Charlotte's visiting Amerigo in private at Portland Place which strikes him as almost an act of "violence," the "harmony" of her "breaking into" his vision, is incorrect but nonetheless consonant not only with his increasing desire but with the negligent good faith of the Ververs and the design of the novel whose marriages have sanctioned and even plotted the deepening association of the two, and the developing affair is presented with all the taut ambivalence of its strange morality and its dubious beauty. For the marriages have produced an almost "ideal perfection" of "freedom," a measure of license which is not only shielded but actually created by the interlocking marriages which facilitate their relation, and the Prince feels "the sense of the past" so intensely "revived" when Charlotte suddenly appears that "the future" is joined with their past passion "in a long embrace of arms and lips." As he and Charlotte try again "the old feelings" and compare the pathos of Charlotte's childless marriage to the strange intensity with which Maggie and Adam "adore together" Amerigo's son, Charlotte insists that they must, like Adam and Maggie, "act in concert"—have faith indeed, the Prince adds, "as we trust the saints in glory" and as "fortunately . . . we can." They can oblige Maggie and Adam while converting their companionship into intimacy, shielding it from observation and shielding Adam and Maggie from knowing it; they can, as the Prince sees later, so guard their "intimacy" with the "vigilance of 'care' " as never to expose it and never "consciously to wound" the feelings of husband or wife. Then they join, "grasping and grasped," in an embrace which converts the delight of "response" into the "pressure" of more intense desire and "with a violence that had sighed itself the next moment to the longest and deepest of stillnesses they passionately sealed their pledge."

This intensely sensuous passion is illicit when judged by the moral codes of their society, though that society's affluence encourages it and its behavior sanctions it, but their renewal of their past love has a dignity which the perfunctory professions and habits of their world (notably Lady Castledean and Mr. Blint) do not display. And their love brings to a crisis the passion which the novel must control but which it must also with envy and terror bring into play to infuse in turn the forms which threaten passion. Charlotte provides the initiative and the train schedule for their afternoon at the inn in Gloucester, but the Prince recognizes the strange opportunity that is presented him, the occasion which calls for the combination of abandon and responsible decision which Charlotte and he finally display. The sun-lit day before him seems "a great picture, from the hand of a genius, presented to him as a prime ornament for his collection"—as if he, like Adam, were enjoying "his absolutely appointed and enhanced possession of it." He expects as usual in his "commerce" with women that his books will show a "balance in his favor," and the "sense of beauty" which he shares with James is stirred by the opportunity prepared for him by the vague permissiveness of Maggie and the calculations of Charlotte—by what, in sum, the novel has provided for and calls his "remarkable fortune."

As he watches the other men (excepting Mr. Blint) leave to return to their occupations, each a "lubricated item of the great social political ad-

ministrative *engrenage*," he recognizes that for Maggie's "convenience" he
has lost the respect of these people (and probably the reader) by relinquishing
any role as provider, prince, father, or husband: he has relinquished "his real
situation in the world," and welcomes the chance to do something "quite
beautiful and . . . harmonious, something wholly his own." The opportunity
looms before him like a "precious pearl" in Charlotte, with her traveling
jacket and her timetable, in the beckoning cathedral towers of lustrous
"Glo'ster, Glo'ster, Glo'ster" and the "tomb of some old king" that Charlotte
vaguely recalls, the tomb of Edward II, the deposed king who was betrayed
by his wife and then wrongly murdered, whose grave became a shrine for
visitors bringing rich gifts to the cathedral. The opportunity shines forth too
in the radiant day at Easter time which is "a great gold cup that we must
somehow drain." Amerigo is, to his calculated advantage, simply "taking
. . . what had been given him," and Charlotte reminds him of her earlier
offer of "the gilded crystal bowl in the little Bloomsbury shop," the "beautiful one, the real one, that I offered you so long ago and that you wouldn't
have." The Prince does recall the "treacherous cracked thing" that she had
wanted to "palm off on me" and the "little swindling Jew . . . who backed
you up," scorning any imperfections in its harmony for himself and leaving
it to Charlotte to "risk" them while he takes a more complacent view of
their good fortune.

Their afternoon in Gloucester is never rendered in the novel, but Charlotte's consciously arranged offer, and the Prince's eager exploitation of it,
project in anticipation a more fully achieved relation, a more intensely intimate passion, and a greater strength of commitment than anything yet rendered in the novel, including Adam's and Maggie's tender and terrifyingly
close regard for each other and for Maggie's son, though these are vividly
enough suggested through the minds of Maggie and Adam and through
Charlotte's and the Prince's wonder at them. And the scene at Matcham
which prepares for the lovers' reunion exceeds in impact the other scenes
which come closest to matching it in power, the scenes in the Bloomsbury
shop and in Brighton and Paris which bring the action of the earlier sections
to tentative, preparatory resolutions. These scenes, each given prominence
in the novel's structure, establish the context and rhythm which define Charlotte's and Amerigo's reunion at once as a tentative or partial consummation
of the novel's design and a betrayal of its aims. Charlotte's and the Prince's
affair of passion, and Maggie and Adam's relation, are given the same status
in the novel: that of a strained and contorted fusion of what is authentic,
normative, and good with what is false, perverted, and evil. And both re-

lations give the measure of the other and in their antagonism create the pressure for the remaking of the marriages and the reforming of the love contained within them. Charlotte now finally offers the Prince the flawed bowl she had not bought, and it may now be possessed and filled with the conscious enjoyment of the passion they will drain from the cup.

But if the metaphor of the cracked and gilded bowl which Charlotte invokes defines the prospect of a more intimate communion in passion, it defines with equal clarity another perspective: the golden bowl remains in Bloomsbury still unpurchased, and what Charlotte offers and the Prince delightedly takes is a treacherous substitute for the wedding gift she did not buy for Maggie and the gift she could not offer to a lover who will not deign to consider receiving it from her. Their reunion, while it is not at all what Adam would knowingly sanction, is in strange keeping with Charlotte's agreement "to give what you ask" and with Adam's behavior since, asking for very little and relegating Charlotte to her serviceable "place" while closeting his affections principally with Maggie and her son. Yet the furtive affair with the Prince is a betrayal of the confidence Charlotte had encouraged at Brighton, and it exploits the trust which she and Amerigo have encouraged in Adam since, as well as being a betrayal of the partnership he had imagined sharing with her in buying the tiles and sharing the cake and wine afterward with the admiring family of Mr. Gutermann-Seuss. The effect of Charlotte's and the Prince's strange daring is an action which creates the evil of the betrayal they perpetrate yet creates also the promise of redeeming passion, and James's art is implicated in both the evil and the promise of redemption by the crisis to which his fictive marriages have given form.

The challenge of that crisis to the marriages and to the form of James's novel is dramatized in the last chapters of the first volume when the Assinghams confront it, with terror and compassion, from within the communion of their own intimate embrace. They confront it in the way the reader must—namely, by imagining it—and they begin already for James, within the achieved form of the first volume, to salvage the situation and redeem the promise of *The Golden Bowl*. James's narrative strategy in these chapters is the epitome of the form of the entire novel, for instead of rendering the reunion in Gloucester he gives the imaginings of the Assinghams which anticipate it and then project beyond it the prospect of a denouement. Without the grounds for picturing the towers of Gloucester at Easter time or the " 'tomb of some old king' " which James has given the reader's imagination, they sketch in and prepare for the sacrificial drama which Maggie and the others enact in the second volume, imagining in their desperation that "Charlotte and the Prince must be saved—so far as consistently speaking of them as still safe might save them," and beginning, with the absolute idiocy which is imaged in their name and which Maggie will bring to perfection, to project the faith and sustain the illusion which gild the bowl so as to join in the process of transforming it.

CAROL OHMANN

"Daisy Miller":
A Study of Changing Intentions

Henry James's most popular nouvelle seems to have owed its initial prominence as much to the controversy it provoked as to the artistry it displayed.
"Daisy Miller" caused a bitter dispute in the customarily urbane dining room
of Mrs. Lynn Linton; it gave American writers of etiquette a satisfying opportunity to chastise native mothers and daughters (Daisy should have had
a chaperone; dear reader, take heed); it brought Henry James himself, while
he sat in the confines of a Venetian gondola, a round scolding from a highly
articulate woman of the cosmopolitan world. The causes of argument, of
course, were the character of James's heroine and the judgment her creator
made of her. In late Victorian eyes, Daisy was likely to be either wholly
innocent or guilty; James, either all for her or against her.

Today, Daisy's notoriety attends her only in her fictional world. We take
her now as one of our familiars; we invoke her, in the assurance that she
will come and be recognized, as an American figure both vital and prototypical. Thus Ihab Hassan, for example, joins her in his *Radical Innocence*
with Twain's Huck Finn and Crane's Henry Fleming, and notes that all three
are young protagonists faced with "the first existential ordeal, crisis, or
encounter with experience." Taking Daisy with appreciation and without
alarm, we also reread her character and reevaluate her moral status. We seem
to meet James's sophistication with our own, by agreeing on a mixed interpretation of Daisy: she is literally innocent, but she is also ignorant and

From *American Literature* 36, no. 1 (March 1964). © 1964 by Duke University
Press.

incautious. Or, as F. W. Dupee writes, and his view meets with considerable agreement elsewhere in our criticism, "[Daisy] does what she likes because she hardly knows what else to do. Her will is at once strong and weak by reason of the very indistinctness of her general aims."

Our near consensus of opinion on "Daisy Miller" seems to me largely correct. I certainly do not want to dismiss it, although I do wish to elaborate upon it and ground it in Jamesian text and method. At the same time, however, I wish to suggest that our very judiciousness is supported by only part of James's nouvelle and that other parts, certain scenes in Rome, really call for franker and more intense alignments of both sympathy and judgment. In a sense, the early and extreme reactions to Daisy were adequate responses to James's creation. Whether black or white, these responses did at least perceive that the final issue of the nouvelle was a matter of total commitment. In short, I think James began writing with one attitude toward his heroine and concluded with a second and different attitude toward her.

I

James begins his nouvelle by building a dramatic, and largely comic, contrast between two ways of responding to experience—a contrast at once suggested by the first-person narrator in the opening paragraph:

> in the month of June, American travellers are extremely numer-
> ous; it may be said, indeed, that Vevey assumes at this period
> some of the characteristics of an American watering-place. There
> are sights and sounds which evoke a vision, an echo, of Newport
> and Saratoga. There is a flitting hither and thither of "stylish"
> young girls, a rustling of muslin flounces, a rattle of dance-music
> in the morning hours, a sound of high-pitched voices at all times.
> You receive an impression of these things at the excellent inn of
> the "Trois Couronnes," and are transported in fancy to the Ocean
> House or to Congress Hall. But at the "Trois Couronnes," it
> must be added, there are other features that are much at variance
> with these suggestions: neat German waiters, who look like sec-
> retaries of legation; Russian princesses sitting in the garden; little
> Polish boys walking about, held by the hand, with their governors.
>> (This quotation, and unless otherwise noted every one
>> subsequent, appears in the original version, "Daisy
>> Miller: A Study," *Cornhill Magazine* 37 (June 1878):
>> 678–698, and 38 (July 1878): 44–67).

The carefree exuberance, the noisy frivolity, of the American visitors is set against the quiet formality and restraint of the Europeans, who hold even their little boys in check.

James repeats his opening contrast in virtually every piece of dialogue that follows. While the hero Frederick Winterbourne is an American by birth, he has lived "a long time" in Geneva, the "little metropolis of Calvinism," the "dark old city at the other end of the lake." And Winterbourne's mode of speech suggests the extent to which he has become Europeanized. In Vevey, he finds himself "at liberty," on a little holiday from Geneva. He takes a daring plunge into experience; with no more than a very casual introduction from her little brother Randolph, he speaks to Daisy Miller. "This little boy and I have made acquaintance," he says. Daisy glances at him and turns away. In a moment Winterbourne tries again. "Are you going to Italy?" he asks. Daisy says, "Yes, sir," and no more. "Are you—a—going over the Simplon?" Winterbourne continues. Shortly afterwards, as Daisy continues to ignore him, Winterbourne "risk[s] an observation upon the beauty of the view." Winterbourne's feelings of "liberty" and of "risk" and, later, of "audacity" become ironic in conjunction with his speech. For all his holiday spirit, his language is studiously formal, his opening conversational bits, unimaginative and conventional.

In opposition to Winterbourne, Daisy often speaks in the language of extravagant, if unoriginal, enthusiasm. In her opinion, Europe is "perfectly sweet. . . . She had ever so many intimate friends that had been there ever so many times. . . . she had had ever so many dresses and things from Paris." She wants to go to the Castle of Chillon "dreadfully." Or, unlike Winterbourne again, Daisy speaks in an idiom that is homely and matter-of-fact. When Winterbourne asks, "Your brother is not interested in ancient monuments?" she rejects his formal phrasing and says simply, "[Randolph] says he don't care much about old castles."

For all their differences, Winterbourne and Daisy may still be capable of *rapprochement*. Toward the end of part 1, Daisy teases Winterbourne out of his formality and makes him, for a moment, speak her language—makes him, for a moment, express himself enthusiastically. "Do, then, let me give you a row," Winterbourne says. Daisy replies, "It's quite lovely, the way you say that!" And Winterbourne answers, "It will be still more lovely to do it." Winterbourne is, and Daisy notices this, a "mixture." He is not quite, or at least not yet, thoroughly Europeanized.

Winterbourne may be influenced by Daisy, but he is also subject to the sway of his aunt. Mrs. Costello is a woman of few words. When Winterbourne asks her, in Vevey, if she has observed Mrs. Miller, Daisy, and Randolph, she raps out the reply: "Oh, yes, I have observed them. Seen them—heard them—and kept out of their way." Epigram is Mrs. Costello's favorite way of speaking and perfectly expresses the inflexibility of her approach to experience. Her principles of value have long been set—she need only apply them. Whatever is vulgar, whatever is improper, she condemns out of hand, and shuns. Sage and spokesman of the American set abroad, she guards a *style* of life and reveals its furthest limit of permissible emotion by exclaiming, "I am an old woman, but I am not too old—thank Heaven—to be shocked!"

The opening, then, and indeed the chief focus of "Daisy Miller" is a comic portrayal of different ways of living, different manners. In the social settings with which they are identified, in the ways they speak, as well as in what they say, the various characters range themselves along an axis that runs from the natural to the cultivated, from the exuberant to the restrained.

In the conflict between Geneva and Schenectady, there is, I think, little doubt of the direction James gives our sympathies. Presented with the collision between the artificial and the natural, the restrained and the free, we side emotionally with Daisy. We sympathize with Winterbourne, too, to the extent that he seems capable of coming "alive" and to the extent that he speaks up in favor of Daisy to Mrs. Costello in Vevey and, later, in Rome, to Mrs. Costello and also to Mrs. Walker, another American who has lived in Geneva. For the rest, however, our emotional alliance with Winterbourne is disturbed or interrupted by his Genevan penchant for criticism. At his first meeting with Daisy in Vevey, Winterbourne mentally accuses her—"very forgivingly—of a want of finish." But when Daisy blithely announces that she has always had "a great deal of gentlemen's society," Winterbourne is more alarmed. He wonders if he must accuse her of "actual or potential *inconduite,* as they said at Geneva."

In Rome, although Winterbourne defends Daisy to the American colony publicly, he is, privately, increasingly shocked by her friendship with the "third-rate" Italian Giovanelli. Her walks with Giovanelli, her rides with Giovanelli, her tête-à-têtes in her own drawing room with Giovanelli—all worry Winterbourne. He imitates Mrs. Walker in scolding Daisy. And so he removes himself farther and farther from her. When he finally comes upon her with Giovanelli in the Colosseum at night, he thinks that she has certainly compromised herself. And he is relieved. For his personal feelings for Daisy have gradually been overwhelmed by his intellectual involvement in the problem of Daisy. He is relieved and "exhilarated" that the "riddle" has suddenly become "easy to read." He promptly judges Daisy by her manners—as Mrs. Costello and Mrs. Walker have already done—and condemns her.

"What a clever little reprobate she was," he thinks, "and how smartly she played at injured innocence!"

He learns otherwise too late. He knows, for a moment at the end of the nouvelle, that he has made a mistake; he knows he has wronged Daisy because he has stayed too long abroad, has become too rigid in his values. Yet his knowledge does not change him. The authorial voice concludes the tale by mocking Winterbourne's return to the narrow social code of restraint and prejudice:

> Nevertheless, he went back to live at Geneva, whence there con-
> tinue to come the most contradictory accounts of his motives of
> sojourn: a report that he is "studying" hard—an intimation that
> he is much interested in a very clever foreign lady.

Like so many Jamesian heroes, Winterbourne has lost the capacity for love, and he has lost the opportunity to come to life.

As Winterbourne judges Daisy, judges her unfairly, and completes her expulsion from the American set in Rome, our sympathy for her naturally increases. But I think James does not—save through a certain pattern of symbolic imagery to which I wish to return in a moment—guide us to any such simple intellectual alignment with his American heroine.

Daisy's sensibility has very obvious limitations, limitations we hear very clearly in the statement that Europe is "perfectly sweet." Daisy is more intensely alive than anyone else we meet in Vevey or Rome. But James hints from time to time at a possible richness of aesthetic experience that is beyond Daisy's capabilities—a richness that would include an appreciation of the artificial, or the cultivated, not as it is represented by the mores of Geneva but by the "splendid chants and organ-tones" of St. Peter's and by the "superb portrait of Innocent X. by Velasquez."

And Daisy has other limitations. The members of the American community abroad are very much aware of one another's existence. True, they use their mutual awareness to no good purpose—they are watchbirds watching one another for vulgarity, for any possible lapse from propriety. But Daisy's social awareness is so primitive as scarcely to exist. At Rome, in the Colosseum, Winterbourne's imagination cannot stretch to include the notion of unsophisticated innocence. But neither can Daisy's imagination stretch to include the idea that manners really matter to those who practice them. She never realizes the consternation she causes in Rome. "I don't believe it," she says to Winterbourne. "They are only pretending to be shocked." Her blindness to the nature of the American colony is equalled by her blindness to

Winterbourne and Giovanelli as individuals. While Winterbourne fails to "read" her "riddle" rightly, she fails to "read" his. She feels his disapproval in Rome, but she is not aware of his affection for her. Neither does she reveal any adequate perception of her impact on Giovanelli. To Daisy, going about with Mr. Giovanelli is very good fun. Giovanelli's feelings, we learn at the end, have been much more seriously involved.

James therefore hands a really favorable intellectual judgment to neither Geneva nor Schenectady. He gives his full approval neither to the manners of restraint nor to those of freedom. His irony touches Daisy as well as the Europeanized Americans. And the accumulation of his specific ironies hints at an ideal of freedom and of vitality and also of aesthetic and social awareness that is nowhere fully exemplified in the nouvelle. To be from Schenectady, to be from the new world, is to be free from the restrictions of Geneva. But merely to be free is not enough.

II

Such, then, in some detail are the Jamesian dynamics of social contrast that give us our prudent estimate of Daisy—a heroine innocent and exuberant and free, but also unreflective and insensible of the world around her. But, as I have already suggested, this estimate does not receive support from the whole of the story. To begin with, prudence leads straight to the conclusion that Daisy dies as a result of social indiscretion. What began as a comedy of manners, ends in the pathos, if not the tragedy, of a lonely Roman deathbed and burial. And there is, it seems to me, in this progress from the Trois Couronnes to the Protestant cemetery a change in tone so pronounced, a breach in cause and appropriate effect so wide, as to amount to a puzzling disruption of James's artistry.

To be sure, James tries to make Daisy's death inevitable, and to make it so within, as it were, the boundaries of his comedy of manners. Early in part 2, at Mrs. Walker's late one afternoon, Daisy remarks that she is going to take a walk on the Pincian Hill with Giovanelli. Mrs. Walker tries to dissuade her from the impropriety—a walk at such a time in such a place with such a dubious companion. It isn't "safe," Mrs. Walker says, while Mrs. Miller adds, "You'll get the fever as sure as you live." And Daisy herself, as she walks towards the Pincian Hill with Winterbourne, alludes to the fever: "We are going to stay [in Rome] all winter—if we don't die of the fever; and I guess we'll stay then."

With these remarks, James foreshadows Daisy's death, and links her fate with her carelessness of the manners of restraint. But these preparations do not successfully solve his difficulties either of tone or of cause and effect. They croak disaster far too loudly, far too obviously, and, still, the punishment no more fits the crime than it does in a typical cautionary tale.

In part 1, James has already used the words "natural," "uncultivated," and "fresh" to describe his heroine. And in the choice of the name, Daisy, he may have suggested her simplicity and her spontaneous beauty. In part 2, just after the opening scene at Mrs. Walker's, James follows up the implications of these epithets—"natural," "uncultivated," "fresh"—and of the name Daisy and gives them a somewhat different significance.

In Rome, after Winterbourne has been taken up in Mrs. Walker's carriage and set down again, he sees Daisy with Giovanelli in a natural setting—a setting that James describes in brilliant and expansive terms. Daisy and Giovanelli are in the Pincian Garden overlooking the Villa Borghese:

> They evidently saw no one; they were too deeply occupied with each other. When they reached the low garden-wall they stood a moment looking off at the great flat-topped pine-clusters of the Villa Borghese; then Giovanelli seated himself, familiarly, upon the broad ledge of the wall. The western sun in the opposite sky sent out a brilliant shaft through a couple of cloud-bars, whereupon Daisy's companion took her parasol out of her hands and opened it. She came a little nearer and he held the parasol over her; then, still holding it, he let it rest upon her shoulder, so that both of their heads were hidden from Winterbourne. This young man lingered a moment, then he began to walk. But he walked—not towards the couple with the parasol; towards the residence of his aunt, Mrs. Costello.

This scene links Daisy with the natural world, and links her with that world more closely than any other scene James has so far given us. And it suggests that the distance between Winterbourne and Daisy is greater even than the distance that separates artificial from natural manners, greater than the distance that separates restraint from free self-expression.

That suggestion becomes a certainty on the Palatine Hill:

> A few days after his brief interview with her mother, [Winterbourne] encountered her in that beautiful abode of flowering desolation known as the Palace of the Cæsars. The early Roman spring had filled the air with bloom and perfume, and the rugged surface of the Palatine was muffled with tender verdure. Daisy was strolling along the top of one of those great mounds of ruin

that are embanked with mossy marble and paved with monu-
mental inscriptions. It seemed to him that Rome had never been
so lovely as just then. He stood looking off at the enchanting
harmony of line and colour that remotely encircles the city, inhaling the softly humid odours and feeling the freshness of the
year and the antiquity of the place reaffirm themselves in mysterious interfusion. It seemed to him also that Daisy had never
looked so pretty; but this had been an observation of his whenever
he met her. Giovanelli was at her side, and Giovanelli, too, wore
an aspect of even unwonted brilliancy.

Here Daisy is not identified with a particular society, as she was with the
gay American visitors by the lakeside and in the garden of Vevey, but simply
and wholly with the natural world, which has its own eternal and beautiful
rhythms. Birth is followed by death, and death is followed again by birth.
And the beauty of the natural world—the world to which Daisy belongs—
is supreme. Rome has never been so lovely as when its relics are "muffled
with tender verdure." The monuments of men, the achievements of civilization, are most beautiful when they are swept again into the round of
natural process. At the moment, Daisy seems to share the natural world, as
she did in the Pincian Garden, with Giovanelli. But at the end of the nouvelle
that "subtle Roman" is quite aware of Daisy's distance even from himself.
He knew, beforehand, that the Colosseum would not be for him, as it was
for Daisy, a "fatal place." "For myself," he says to Winterbourne, "I had no
fear."

Once Daisy is identified with the world of nature, we see that she is
subject to its laws of process. Her very beauty becomes a reminder of her
mortality. So the scene on the Palatine (unlike the scenes at Mrs. Walker's
and on the way to the Pincian Hill) does prepare us effectively for Daisy's
burial in the Protestant cemetery; it does convince us that her death is inevitable.

III

Yet James's use of his symbolic natural imagery is at once a gain and a
loss. If it solves, almost at the eleventh hour, certain difficulties of tone and
of cause and effect regarding Daisy's death, it also leaves us with some
permanent breaks in the nouvelle's unity of structure. If Daisy is translated
or transfigured in the end into a purely natural ideal of beauty and vitality
and innocence, then what relevance has that ideal to Schenectady, or to

Geneva? If Daisy's death is "fated," does it matter at all what Winterbourne does? And what sort of agent is Giovanelli? Or can we even call him an agent? Hasn't James made inconsequent by the end of his tale, the dramatic conflict—the conflict between two kinds of manners—that he set up in the beginning? The contrast in manners seems to suggest, to hold up as an ideal, a certain way of responding to life. This ideal would combine freedom and vitality with a sophisticated awareness of culture and society. Yet the symbolic imagery of the Palatine Hill seems to elevate natural freedom and vitality and innocence into an ideal so moving, so compelling, that all other considerations pale beside it. Or, if I rephrase my questions about Schenectady and Geneva, Winterbourne and Giovanelli, and answer them in terms of James's creative experience, they come to this: James began writing "Daisy Miller" as a comedy of manners and finished it as a symbolic presentation of a metaphysical ideal. He began by criticizing Daisy in certain ways and ended simply by praising her.

James's friend in the Venetian gondola was, at least in a general way, aware of his transfiguration of Daisy. And James records her opinion—in effect her scolding—in his preface to the New York edition of his nouvelle:

> [Daisy's] only fault is touchingly to have transmuted so sorry a type [as the uncultivated American girl] and to have, by a poetic artifice, not only led our judgement of it astray, but made *any* judgement quite impossible. . . . You *know* you quite falsified, by the turn you gave it, the thing you had begun with having in mind, the thing you had had, to satiety, the chance of 'observing': your pretty perversion of it, or your unprincipled mystification of our sense of it, does it really too much honour.

James virtually accepts his friend's criticism. Elsewhere in the preface, speaking in his own voice, he says that, when his nouvelle was first published, the full title ran: "Daisy Miller: A Study." Now, for the New York edition, he subtracts the apposition "in view of the simple truth, which ought from the first to have been apparent to me, that my little exhibition is made to no degree whatever in critical but, quite inordinately and extravagantly, in poetical terms." It appears, then, that James's natural symbolic imagery and his translation of his heroine into a metaphysical figure were unconscious developments. Only after he wrote his nouvelle did James himself discover and acknowledge his own "poetical terms."

Once he had discovered those "terms," he chose to emphasize them, not only in his preface, but also in his text for the New York edition. Viola R. Dunbar has already noted that in a number of places in the final version of

"Daisy Miller" James eases his criticism of Daisy and bears down more heavily on the Europeanized Americans. Briefly, he places more stress on Daisy's beauty and innocence, and he associates her more frequently with nature, and more pointedly. At the same time, he gives more asperity to the judgments of Winterbourne and Mrs. Costello and Mrs. Walker. And it is interesting to note as well that James inserts very early in part 1 at least two suggestions of Daisy's final transfiguration. She looks at Winterbourne "with lovely remoteness"; she strikes him as a "charming apparition."

These revisions, though, are occasional and do not essentially change "Daisy Miller." In the New York edition, as well as in the original version, it remains a narrative of imperfect unity, a work that shows unmistakable signs of shifting authorial intention and attitude. And yet, as I have already suggested, James's idealization of his heroine is a matter of gain as well as loss. It resolves certain problems about Daisy's death. More importantly, it adds to the emotional appeal of the second part of the nouvelle. In other words, even if James may have lost something in intellectual consistency by introducing the poetry of Daisy, even if he does to some extent throw away his original comedy of manners, his symbolic natural imagery nonetheless intensifies our response to his story. Again, I return to the articulate lady in the gondola: "As anything charming or touching always to that extent justifies itself, we after a fashion forgive and understand you."

The ideal of a purely natural vitality and freedom and innocence is a strongly, and persistently, attractive ideal. It is attractive, especially, to American writers, and in one variation or another we have, of course, met it before—in Melville, for example, in Hawthorne, in Fitzgerald, in Faulkner. We take James's Daisy Miller, rightly, as prototypical. My purpose here has been to suggest that her relationship to certain major areas of our American experience is even more various than we may previously have thought.

TONY TANNER

The Watcher from the Balcony:
The Ambassadors

Condemned the human particle "over here" was to live, *on whatever*
terms, in thickness—instead of being free, comparatively, or as I at
once ruefully and exquisitely found myself, only to feel and think in it.
Ruefully because there were clearly a thousand contacts and sensa-
tions, of the strong direct order, that one lost by not so living; exqui-
sitely because of the equal number of immunities and independences,
blest independences of perception and judgment, blest liberties of range
for the intellectual adventure, that accrued by the same stroke.
                                        —HENRY JAMES, *The Middle Years*

In his account of his own growth and development contained in his *Autobiography* (by *Autobiography* I mean: *A Small Boy and Others, Notes of a
Son and Brother,* and "The Middle Years"), James projects an image of a
consciousness which, as it grows richer and more subtly responsive, is at the
same time increasingly excluded from direct participation in life. He talks of
his "foreseen and foredoomed detachment" at the same time as he describes
himself as being "gorged with wonders." He seems to become a consciousness without a context. For example: "I lived and wriggled, floundered and
failed, lost the clue of everything but a general lucid consciousness . . . which
I clutched with a sense of its value." It was this that compensated for his
feeling of being "cut off from any degree of direct performance." He remains
what he feels himself to be as a small boy—"a vague outsider." There is, of
course, some pathos in this sense of growing exclusion, but more interesting

From *Critical Quarterly* 8, no. 1 (Spring 1966). © 1966 by Tony Tanner.

is a discernible ambivalence in his attitude to life itself, an ambivalence manifest in such descriptions of himself as "all wondering and all fearing." It
would seem that, from the start, mixed in with his awe at the boundless
wonder of life was an inner fear at its potential dangers and terrors. A fear
not of this or that threat or the potential malevolence of people, but simply
a pervasive sense of the danger inherent in experience as such. James appears,
that is, as an appreciative but apprehensive spectator, and it was just such
an ambivalence of attitude that he was to make the subject of one of his
greatest novels, the one he himself most liked—*The Ambassadors.*

Before turning to that novel, it is worth glancing at some earlier works
which offer clear evidence of this ambivalence. Take a very early story like
"A Passionate Pilgrim." The American hero, Clement Searle, is sick from
the start. He laments the empty inadequacies of his American education and
comes to England for an experience of a fuller life. Here he meets with some
disillusion (some of the characters are treacherous), but the important thing
is the manner of his death. "He was becoming more and more a disembodied
observer and critic; the shell of sense, growing daily thinner and now transparent, transmitted the tremor of his quickened faculty." He dies, really,
from an excess of rich impressions which the frail vessel of his hyper-sensitive
consciousness could not contain. The wondering observer is killed by the
sudden onset of too much material. So, from the start, we see that typically
Jamesian combination of an enraptured yearning for experience of life and
a deeper feeling that life itself is fatal to handle. Another early story, "The
Madonna of the Future" tells of an American artist living in Europe. He
also complains of lack of material in America: "We are the disinherited of
art. . . . We are excluded from the magic circle. The soil of American perception is a poor little barren, artificial deposit. . . . We poor aspirants must
live in perpetual exile." He dreams of painting one great picture (rather as
James dreamed of writing the great American novel), but in fact he dies in
squalor, his canvas still quite blank. Again, the new wealth of experience he
thought so fruitful has proved, instead, to be fatal. James's first full length
novel, *Roderick Hudson,* is also about a young artist, panting for more
material and opportunity than America offers, who is sent to Europe where
he is at first wonderfully stimulated by the new wealth of experience, then
betrayed by it. He dies—another victim of sheer life. In his later introduction
James made an interesting point about this book. In effect he says that the
main fault of the novel is that it shows Hudson as disintegrating improbably
quickly. His collapse is indeed amazingly rapid and James, in his old age
comments: "I felt how many more ups and downs, how many more adventures and complications my young man would have had to know, how much

more experience it would have taken, in short either to make him go under or to make him triumph." James's criticism is acute and correct. From the standpoint of credibility Hudson does capitulate improbably quickly to his European stimuli. But I think this reveals something very interesting about James's own fears at the time. Himself a young aspiring American artist in Europe, he could not stay away from Europe, because of the dazzling range and density of real material it offered. But another part of him seems also to have felt, or dreaded, that the slightest real involvement with this rich stuff of life would prove fatal. The rapidity of Hudson's decline is, I think, the measure of James's own unconscious apprehensions.

But James also mentions something even more interesting in this introduction. He says that the real centre of interest in the novel is "in Rowland Mallett's consciousness . . . and the drama is the very drama of that consciousness." The important thing about Mallett (who is Hudson's patron) is that "what happened to him was above all to feel certain things happening to others." His experience of life, thus, is indirect. The onlooker, not the participator. And James intends that the main drama should be, not the external decline of Hudson, but the internal involved consciousness of Mallett. He is immensely interested in everything; he helps, he watches, he feels, he inquires, he cares. But he himself does not get involved in the treacherous flux of experience. From this novel alone it would be possible to trace the development of two main figures in James's novel. The person who does get involved in experience, often fatally—this would include figures as remote as Daisy Miller and Milly Theale. And then the passive spectator who does not have an external physical destiny in the same way but who wonders about what happens to other people. For this figure the main adventure is his (or her) own musing, appreciating, evaluating consciousness. But he stays out of the mess of life. This non-participating watcher may be an actual artist, or more generally someone who seems somehow bound to brood apart over the wonders and mysteries of life. Maisie is one such figure, the unnamed narrator of *The Sacred Fount* another. There are many of these detached narrators in James's work, figures who hover around the edges of the story without ever quite getting seriously involved in the action. There is an interesting one in "Madame de Mauves" who almost, but not quite, becomes passionately involved with one of the characters in the story he is telling. And in thinking of this one moment of near-involvement he makes a revealing comment. "Why should his first—his last—glimpse of positive happiness be so indissolubly linked with renunciation." But if he has to renounce marital and sensual pleasure, it is nevertheless he who watches and assesses and who most sensitively understands what is going on. He is an incipient artist, in fact. A figure—one of many—who anticipates the profounder study of Louis Lambert Strether.

I am suggesting, perhaps too crudely, that from the start James can be seen exploring his own dual attitude to the great sea of life (I use the image in order to stress how often James uses "water" imagery in his analyses of peoples' experience). It was beguiling but bedeviling: without it one starved; in it one drowned. The two instincts are endlessly at work in his novels—shaping the material, providing the drama, finding the meanings. Involvement and detachment; impassioned eager participation, enlightened and cautious renunciation; a strong attraction to the dusky richness and vivid risks of actual life, a holding back in the interests of internal appreciation and subjective comprehension. Above all, a deep conviction that art must feed on life—the sheer stuff which gives data for perception, which embroils the feelings and provokes the understanding, which nourishes consciousness. *And,* a vague undefined apprehension that the stuff of life could be a quick poison, that it might kill the artist before providing the art, that it was dangerous to touch. This I think is why James often reverted to the image of the artist as a man looking out of a window—looking down, from a lonely security, into the vitality and confusion of the streets. To quote only the most famous example, from his definition of the House of Fiction: at each window of that House "stands a figure with a pair of eyes, or at least with a field glass, which forms, again and again, for observation, a unique instrument, insuring to the person making use of it an impression distinct from every other." This stress on the stance of the "posted presence of the watcher" suggests what certain Jamesian characters come to feel: namely, that it is indispensable to see life, but perhaps not advisable to go down and embrace it; indeed, that if one is to learn to look at life properly it is *essential* to renounce the privileges, as well as the threats, of participation.

It is in *The Ambassadors* that James, for the first time, makes the consciousness of the onlooker figure the central focus of a major novel. Describing his initial conception of Strether James wrote: "He would have issued, our rueful worthy, from the very heart of New England" and "he had come to Paris in some state of mind which was literally undergoing, as a result of new and unexpected assaults and infusions, a change from hour to hour." It is a recurring Jamesian theme: a person confronting new facts with an old vision and being worried because the vision will not adequately account for the facts. Thus, James goes on, "the false position for him . . . was obviously to have presented himself at the gate of that boundless menagerie primed with a moral scheme of the most approved pattern which was yet framed to break down on any approach to vivid facts." The book, then, is to be about an approved moral scheme challenged by confusing vivid facts, and the consequent attempt to find a new adequate scheme, a more inclusive vision which can contain the new range of facts even if it loses its old approval. The drama is to be "the drama of discrimination." The first sentence of the book refers to Strether asking a question, and the book is a long adventure of subtle inquiry, the testing of assumptions, the weighing of claims. How excessively narrow and life-denying is the New England conscience; what is fine and what is fraudulent in the rich aggregation of life's possibilities which Paris represents? The book is, as James says, about a revolution of consciousness in Strether; a revolution which has nothing to do with any carnal temptations offered by Paris but rather its power to stimulate the sensitive and appreciative imagination. It is also a testing of Strether—for he has to submit to the labyrinthine ordeal which other Jamesian characters have suffered before him, an ordeal of darkness and confusion in which the old lights fail and new ones are not immediately forthcoming. In that darkness the abandoned consciousness must generate its own illumination. Thus James on Strether: "he was to be thrown forward, rather, thrown quite with violence, upon his lifelong trick of intense reflexion: which friendly test indeed was to bring him out, through winding passages, through alternations of darkness and light, very much *in* Paris, but with the surrounding scene itself a minor matter, a mere symbol for more things than had been dreamt of in the philosophy of Woollett." And the result would be, says James, still describing how he conceived the novel, that Strether's "whole analytic faculty would be led such a wonderful dance." It is that dance of consciousness which this book, with all of James's most supple, patient sensitivity, tries to enact and disclose. (In connection with this it is worth stressing that all the violence of the book—all the dangers and woundings and fightings—is internal. There is probably more violent imagery in this novel than in any other by James, but it is used to describe feelings, thoughts, reactions, apprehensions—never deeds. To specify: the imagery shows people nearly drowning in heavy seas, engaged on battlefields, struggling in savage jungles. Floods, shipwrecks, rescues are common; animals prowl around; people advance and retreat as in war, they plant flags on gained territory, they flourish bayonets. There are falls, floorings, even broken noses. People stick nails in other people, let fly with arrows, and in general are much given to drawing blood. As well, there is much talk of treasure, even of pirates. But it all refers to internal events and exchanges: in the outer world there is nothing more violent than Sarah Pocock raising her morally outraged voice to Strether. Therefore we must feel with James that there are deadly combats, flounderings, even murders which never ruffle the social surface; that there are cruelties and quarrelings, victimisations and bleedings which all take place in the invisible arenas of consciousness. We must accept this or find his novels, particularly his later ones, absurd.)

So the book is, at its simplest, about the convulsion of values in a complex man. "He came out to do what he could, but everything is altered for him by the fact that nothing, damn it, is as simple as his scheme." The richness of the book is to show the gradual modifications and alterations of vision, the confusions, readjustments, and expansions of consciousness, undergone by a man who starts with a simple moral scheme and is confronted by novel vivid facts which do not, damn it, fit into that scheme. The alternatives are—to renounce the vivid facts (as the other ambassadors in the book do), or take the risk of trying to develop a more comprehensive scheme and vision which can accommodate and respect them. Strether takes that risk. And in this connection it is worth noting his name—Louis Lambert. As Quentin Anderson has pointed out, this is the hero of a novel by Balzac which bears an interesting resemblance to James's novel. In Balzac's novel, Lambert is a theorist who is writing a metaphysical treatise. He is utterly absorbed in his transcendental speculations until one day he has a sudden rush of passion at the sight of a woman in a theatre during a visit to Paris. He returns to the provinces and arranges to marry a Jewish heiress. But before the marriage he goes mad. The narrator conjectures that his madness may well be the result of a sudden "transition from pure idealism to the most intense sensualism." James's story too touches on a theme as perennial as the conflicting claims of the ideal and the real, morality and appearances, the transcendental and the sensual. James himself had used the theme before. For example in the comparatively crude parable "Benvolio," in which a young artist is alternately drawn to a studious retiring ascetic woman called Scholastica, and a rich ripe social figure called the Countess. Scholastica is pure New England transcendentalism, and the Countess, of course, is good old sensual Europe. An amiable and slight tale. But similarly in *The Ambassadors* one could say that Strether is shown transferring his allegiances from the coldly moral New England Mrs. Newsome to the finely social European Mme de Vionnet. It is the subtlety of exploration, not the root theme, which is new in this book.

The action is Strether's "process of vision" and in this action although physical deeds are not of the first importance, concrete settings and environments most certainly are. To detail the significance of all the streets, houses, gardens, galleries, etc., would occupy a disproportionate amount of space; so to simplify the general point I would like to suggest that we can regard Strether's progress in Europe as an ascent to a balcony. When he first goes to visit Chad's house he lingers on the opposite side of the street looking *up* at the balcony on the third floor. One of his first feelings "was that the balcony in question didn't somehow show as a convenience easy to surrender." That is, he feels from the start that once one has a balcony it must be difficult to abandon it. The significance of this emerges later. At this point he is still down in the street looking *up*, then he sees a young man leaning on the rail "looking at the life below." The house itself, Chad's house, is revealing in a way we should note. It is "high broad clear . . . admirably built" and the windows "took all the March sun." Chad too is well built, and he too is a great one for basking in other peoples' warmth. The house is "aided by the presence of ornament" and seems very well-bred—exactly as Chad has become under the tuition of Mme de Vionnet. Strether pausing before the house is indeed Strether pausing before the whole question of what he will do about Chad, though he does not know it yet. And the important thing is that, then and there, he is most drawn to the image of the young man and his "surrender to the balcony." "The balcony, the distinguished front, testified suddenly, for Strether's fancy, to something that was up and up; they placed the whole case materially, and as by an admirable image, on a level that he found himself at the end of another moment rejoicing to think he might reach." More cogently, "a perched privacy appeared to him the last of luxuries." Chad is absent from the house (just as the real Chad is not to be found behind the misleading "distinguished front" he has acquired in Europe), but Strether later admits that he had "nevertheless gone up, and gone up." The reiteration gives a special emphasis to the ascent which is made to seem at once protracted, laborious, and significant. It is the first of many staircases that Strether is to climb; his progress is characteristically upwards. Towards the end of Book Eleven, shortly before Strether discovers about the illicit relationship of Chad and Mme de Vionnet, he goes again to call on Chad—who again is not in his house. This time Strether goes directly to the balcony and spends a long time looking out over the whole suggestive mass of the city at night. In one of James's more significant phrases "Strether found himself in possession as he had never yet been." Visual possession, possession from above. A possession which is also generous and grateful—non-exploitative. "He spent a long time on the balcony; he hung over it as he had seen little Bilham hang the day of his first approach." He is now looking *down*: he has achieved his "perched privacy." It is up there that he has one of his long meditations, thinking of his lost youth, regretting that his life has been all too little "an affair of the senses," thinking about the precious freedom to enjoy which he has only so recently come to appreciate. "It was in the outside air as well as within; it was in the long watch, from the balcony, in the summer night, of the wide late life of Paris." (The second half of that sentence seems to me beautifully and appropriately cadenced; the syntax which both delays, and contains, the whole meaning, is something of a paradigm for the movement of the novel as a whole.) Strether has not, of course, purchased an actual building with a balcony; he is seen appreciating an opportunity which the ever-absent Chad has disdained. The scene is a visible analogue to a certain new perspective, a new mode of vision gained.

To support my contention that the balcony has a profound iconographic significance for James I want to bring together some revealing passages from his *Autobiography*. Very early on, after revealingly referring to the general life around them as "deep waters" ("However, any breasting of those deep waters must be but in the form for me of an occasional dip"), James says "our general medium of life in the situation I speak of was such as to make a large defensive verandah, which seems to have very stoutly and completely surrounded us, play more or less the part of a raft of rescue in too high a tide." The "defensive verandah" from which he could survey, without entering, the dangerous flood. A very apt image for a writer whose most constant image for experience was "water." A later passage provides a more direct autobiographical gloss on the scenes in *The Ambassadors* I have cited. I must quote at some length. James is recalling "the intensity of a fond apprehension of Paris, a few days later, from the balcony of an hotel that hung, through the soft summer night, over the Rue de la Paix."

> I hung over the balcony, and doubtless with my brothers and sister, though I recover what I felt as so much relation and response to the larger, the largest appeal only, that of the whole perfect Parisianism I seemed to myself always to have possessed mentally . . . and that now filled out its frame or case for me from every lighted window, up and down, as if each of these had been, for strength of sense, a word in some immortal quotation, the very breath of civilised lips."

He feels in some strange way that he had always anticipated and expected such a scene:

> I had had before me from far back a picture . . . and here was every touch in it repeated with a charm. Had I ever till then known what a charm *was?*—a large, a local, a social charm, leaving out that of a few individuals. It was at all events, this mystery, one's property—that of one's mind; and so, once for all,

> I helped myself to it from my balcony and tucked it away. It counted all immensely for practice in taking in.

The wondering mind taking "possession" of Paris from a balcony—precisely the significance of the scene in *The Ambassadors*. Again, in describing another place where they stayed in Paris, James defines it as the sort of setting exactly suited to someone with his ambivalent attitude to life. It "hung, at no great height, over the Avenue des Champs-Elysées; hung, that is, from the vantage of its own considerable terrace, surmounted as the parapet of the latter was with iron railings rising sufficiently to protect the place for familiar use and covert contemplation . . . and yet not to the point of fencing out life." A protected place of contemplation from which he can see life, but where life cannot reach him. Another time he recalls waking up and adopting once more this significant position. "I had slipped from my so cushioned sleep . . . to hang, from the balcony of our quatrième . . . over that Place du Palais Royal and up against that sculptured and storied façade of the new Louvre which seemed to me then to represent, in its strength, the capacity and chiselled rim of some such potent vivifying cup as it might have been given us, under a happier arrangement, to taste now in its fulness and with a braver sense for it." It is in this passage that James, using one of his many gustatory images, describes himself storing up "treasures of impression that might be gnawed, in seasons or places of want, like winter pears or a squirrel's hoard of nuts," in general acquiring a "weight of consciousness." And he returns again to that intoxicating moment "as one stood up on the high balcony to the great insolence of the Louvre and to all the history, all the glory again and all the imposed applause, not to say worship, and not to speak of the implied inferiority, on the part of everything else, that it represented." James does not learn very much actual history in his travels; rather he surveys, and wonders over, rich suggestive panoramas, inhaling atmospheres rather than mastering facts. Not the past, but "the sense of the past." He seems always to have been more interested in extensions of consciousness than accretions to memory. In his work, the watchers from the balcony (this includes Maisie as well as Strether) are most nearly duplicating his own most favoured stance.

One or two other settings in the novel should be mentioned. If the balcony was one place of meditation for James, the garden was another, and in this novel we see Strether seated for a long time in the Garden of the Tuileries—sitting and watching as he does so often in the book. In those gardens "the air had a taste as of something mixed with art, something that presented nature as a white-capped master-chef." The image may seem somewhat indecorous; but the point is that in New England Strether has never had the feeling that nature might, literally, cater for the senses, feed them with permissible pleasures. It is worth noting that James is unusually specific about food, drink, even table-settings in this novel. This is not mere circumstantial realism. Strether is learning the attraction of things that appeal to the senses—surfaces, tastes, odours, colours, etc. There is an appetite of the senses which is not grasping and appropriating and cruel. Of course, it is not spiritual or transcendental either. It is the sort of generous delight we associate with Impressionist paintings and their avowed addiction to the wonder of appearances. Strether, among other things, acquires an Impressionist eye.

Of many interiors two may be singled out; the dwellings of Maria Gostrey and Mme de Vionnet. Maria is a collector: better than a gossip, but not quite a true artist. Her dusky crowded chambers have a strong effect on Strether: "the life of the occupant struck him . . . as more charged with possession even than Chad's . . . wide as his glimpse had lately become of the empire of 'things,' what was before him still enlarged it; the lust of the eyes and the pride of life had indeed thus their temple. It was the innermost nook of the shrine—as brown as a pirate's cave." Now Strether, too, learns to appreciate "things," but the evidence piled up here is of some more acquisitive instinct: "the lust of the eyes" suggests something less than the true disinterest to which he aspires. Strether does not become a collector. He learns from Maria, but he also goes far beyond her. He could not marry her at the end because to do so would be to deny the radical difference between them which has emerged. Mme de Vionnet's house has fine things too, though her possessions are not "vulgarly numerous"; there is no sense of the piled-up loot of the pirate's cave here. Such things as there are have the "dim lustre" of legend about them. The house is very old, full of genuine relics which have long had their place there. "They were among the matters that marked Mme de Vionnet's apartment as something quite different from Miss Gostrey's little museum of bargains and from Chad's lovely home; he recognised it as founded much more on old accumulations that had possibly from time to time shrunken than on any contemporary method of acquisition or form of curiosity. Chad and Miss Gostrey had rummaged and purchased and picked up and exchanged, sifting, selecting, comparing; whereas the mistress of the scene before him, beautifully passive under the spell of transmission . . . had only received, accepted and been quiet." Here is the difference between a collector and a true incumbent, between a purchaser and an inheritor. In Mme de Vionnet's house the recession of unfolding rooms becomes a "vista, which he found high melancholy and sweet—full, once more, of dim historic shades, of the faint far-away cannon-roar of the great Empire." Maria Gostrey sits among her own shrewd purchases: Mme de Vionnet sits amidst her heritage—the history of Europe. These are only two of many houses that Strether finds himself in. But at the end he has no house of his own. Unlike Isabel Archer (who, I suggested in a previous article, chooses the wrong home), Strether recognises that with his particular form of consciousness he cannot commit himself to this or that dwelling, just as he finally will not limit himself to any one specific edifice of values.

The title of the novel is plural, and in order to appreciate what happens to Strether we should examine some of the other "ambassadors." (Maria Gostrey, Chad, Strether, Waymarsh, Jim and Sarah Pocock, Little Bilham, Mamie—all are American "ambassadors" of one sort or another—indeed, Mme de Vionnet is almost the only important European figure in the novel.) Waymarsh was originally "Waymark," and, indeed he seems to be a moral signpost of the severest and most obvious type. Strether finds his unrelenting suspicious moralising in turns amusing, then depressing, and then irrelevant as he passes far beyond the mark which Waymarsh so unbendingly stands for. Waymarsh is at first referred to as a Hebrew prophet, then as Moses—the law-giver supreme. He is also like a grim Indian chief who "stands wrapt in his blanket and gives no sign"—a perhaps more ominous comparison. He is always trying to get away from the European atmosphere or shut it out—hiding behind windows, refusing to relax, trying to make his whole European sojourn into one long withdrawing gesture of disapproval. Yet if he represents a bit of the old New England conscience, there is another aspect to his behaviour which we should note. For instance when Strether and Maria are enjoying the view on the Rows in Chester, Waymarsh grows increasingly uncomfortable with their aesthetic delectation and appraisal. He turns for relief to the shop windows and surprises his companions by suddenly dashing into a shop to buy something. It is a subtle touch: in his unease all he can think of doing is to reduce Europe to a place of purchase. And when Sarah Pocock comes over to Europe a sudden change comes over Waymarsh. With his bright clothes and weird compulsive gaiety he now looks, not like Moses, but a Southern plantation owner—not a pleasant transformation. And with Sarah he starts to dash around Paris in search of shops and certain forms of entertainment like the circus. It is not surprising that these two stern moralists should be drawn together for they share a deep suspicion of, and loathing for, Strether's sort of open aesthetic appreciation of things. They refuse to *see* (as Strether realises); they consult their New England moral scheme and then hold their heads too grimly high ever to notice whether the evidence might be more complex. They judge, they condemn: they never try to appreciate. And yet they are enthusiastic purchasers (to buy something is to show your power over the seller; thus to reduce Europe to a shop is to treat it like a contemptuous patron); and if they do not like the art and architecture which is there to be seen, they take great relish in the circus (this again suggests, not only their philistinism but a more brutal instinct—a desire to use Europe as a low spectacle and entertainment, which again implies a sort of defensive contempt). Not only is there a ferocity of judgment in this pair, but also a harsh crudity of self-indulgence and acquisition. James could see deeply into the self-deceptions of this sort of puritan. Jim Pocock is more crudely candid: he wants the crass sort of "good time" traditionally associated with Paris for the Americans. These people are examples of what James elsewhere called "passionless pilgrims," those who regard Europe as a toy to be used and discarded at will and who miss all that is fine and enriching. "A hundred good instances confirmed this tradition that nothing in the new world was held accountable to anything in the old world." This unpleasant mixture of damning Europe morally, whilst using and abusing it for low pleasures and "bargains" is, for James, a typical result of certain aspects of the New England conscience—which, as Maria Gostrey suggests, is really composed of "intensity with ignorance." Always, of course, a formidable combination.

Behind these people is Mrs. Newsome, Chad's mother, and the employer and maintainer of Strether. She is the real moral iceberg (the image is used) from which the coldness of Sarah Pocock seems to derive. "She's all cold thought—which Sarah could serve to us cold without its really losing anything" says Strether: cold thought as opposed to warm life. And here again, James has added a dimension to this image of radiant moral ice who is so wonderfully present throughout the novel in the immensity of her still, silent, deeply disapproving absence. She gets all her money from a vulgar business which, it is implied, won its way to power through corrupt means. The combination of unscrupulous commercial exploitation and moral self-congratulation is clearly established. Jim Pocock's image for his wife and Mrs. Newsome seems aptly sinister. "They don't lash about and shake the cage ... and it's at feeding time that they're quietest. But they always get there." Small wonder that Sarah Pocock liked the circus. The crude incursion of the Pococks represents a challenge to Strether's changing type of vision and his newly developed habit of observation. They of course fail in observation, but Strether has to ask himself—is their world real, is his own false; "had they come to make the work of observation, as *he* had practised observation, crack and crumble?" In not returning when they return, Strether is refusing their attitude to life. They threaten but he stands firm—stands by Mme de

Vionnet, stands by the perceptible, as opposed to the purchasable, values of Europe. But perhaps the worst ambassador will turn out to be Chad. He is of course completely egotistical: as he claims, he has always had his own way. He is a "taker" supreme for he takes and uses and keeps all the love and care which Mme de Vionnet lavishes on him. Her attentions improve him immensely as a "social animal." In manners, taste, behaviour, etc., he now looks marvellously good whereas before he had been a boorish insensitive ass. But there are intimations that the surface improvements are misleading. Little Bilham offers the opinion that "I'm not sure he was meant by nature to be quite so good." This implies that by nature he is not and cannot be as good as his new appearance suggests. Europe has refined the surface but it has not reached the soul. Deep down he is still "old Chad." Strether is initially taken in by the improved appearance, but by the end he can perceive that Chad is really just another one of those Americans who have come to Europe to take and exploit its valuable things before returning to America and the profits of big business. True, Chad's decision to return is not announced in the novel, but Strether, I think, sees it coming. By the end *he* has to work on *Chad* to keep him in Europe (the major ironic reversal in the book—for earlier Chad has to work on Strether to gain his permission to remain in Europe); and he feels it necessary to utter a strong prospective indictment. "You'll be a brute, you know—you'll be guilty of the last infamy—if you ever forsake her." Chad glibly says that he will never get tired of her, but "he spoke of being 'tired' of her almost as he might have spoken of being tired of roast mutton for dinner." A rank selfishness of mere appetite is hinted at here. And after Strether has exhausted himself trying to show Chad how vile it would be to abandon Mme de Vionnet, Chad suddenly switches the conversation to advertising. "It really does the thing, you know." The "thing" being to make a lot of money. Chad is revealing the old instinct of his family to accumulate a lot of fast dollars—despite all the subtler values that have been so liberally showered on him in Europe. He claims his interest in the possibilities of advertising is only theoretic, but his last comment is: "There at any rate the fact is—the fact of the possible. I mean the money in it." Showing this emergent taste for business and such a confusion of values, it is hard to imagine that Chad will remain with Mme de Vionnet much longer. He is drawn to advertising—the art of manipulating the false appearance for profit. After so long in Europe he is still oblivious to intrinsic values. What is for Mme de Vionnet a real and lasting love is for him a passing amusement to be indulged in before going into business. He takes: Mme de Vionnet gives. But she has a sort of wisdom which the egotistical American ambassadors, from Sarah to Chad, could never attain. As when she says: "What I hate is myself—when I think that one has to take so much, to be happy, out of the lives of others, and that one isn't happy even then. . . . The wretched self is always there, always making one somehow a fresh anxiety. What it comes to is that it's not, that it's never, a happiness, any happiness at all, to *take*. The only safe thing is to give." She has given, and, we feel, she alone of all the characters will achieve the dignity and stature of real suffering. But only Strether can really appreciate her for what she is. And he too attempts to transcend "the wretched self" by a refusal to "take" anything that the world seems to offer. For in the Jamesian world, those who consult and pander to the self are capable of cruel obliquities of vision and a ruthless insensitivity of conduct.

The gradual change and development of Strether's consciousness and vision is a complex and subtle process. To simplify it I want to refer to three key moments: Strether meeting Chad at the theatre; Strether at Gloriani's garden-party; and Strether in the French countryside when he finally realises that Chad is conducting an adulterous affair with Mme de Vionnet. It is worth noticing that the progression theatre-garden-countryside suggests the diminishing presence of art, or "artifice," and an increase in "nature"; just as the scenes show Strether first of all reacting to the illusion of appearances but finally having to cope with the undeniability of realities. One of the key words in the novel is "appearances" and the problem is, how will Strether finally respond to them? At the start we read that upon his arrival in Europe Strether felt "launched in something of which the sense would be quite disconnected from the sense of his past," and this something had begun "with a sharper survey of the elements of Appearance than he had for a long time been moved to take." The opposition is clear. His "past" is his life in America where he has taken small notice of the sensory surfaces of things. Over there, we gather, people focus directly on the moral essence of phenomena. But in Europe Strether is to find himself trying to learn the proper way to handle appearances. It is fitting that the first thing that makes him start to doubt the rightness of his quest as rescuer is the noticeable change in Chad's personal appearance; it is even more fitting that this shock should take place in a theatre, the place most dedicated to the deceptive illusion, the putting on of shows and acts. It was in a theatre in London that Strether had experienced a significant premonitory confusion: "he couldn't have said if it were the actors or auditors who were most true." When Chad makes his dazzling entry into the box at the theatre in Paris it seems like a matter of a superb entry, fine acting with consummate staging. Chad is transformed—"Chad had improved in appearance": Strether cannot yet say if the change goes any deeper. Strether does not shy away from the baffling change.

"All one's energy goes to facing it, to tracking it. . . . Call it then life . . . call it poor dear old life simply that springs the surprises." He finds the fact of radically enriched appearances sufficiently engrossing to make him determine to go more deeply into the matter.

In the central scene in Gloriani's garden (at the start of Book Five) we are made to feel that a representative selection of old Europe has congregated under the supervision of the enigmatic artist Gloriani. Here Strether finds himself in the "queer old garden" next to "the house of art": the people, the garden, and the house distill a heady magic for Strether and it is at this point that he "lets himself go" (it is here that he makes his famous speech to little Bilham—"Live all you can; its a mistake not to"—too well known to need requoting here). In this atmosphere he feels "smothered in flowers" but instead of recoiling from the feeling of suffocation he puts it down to his "odious ascetic suspicion of any form of beauty." He wishes to learn to accept it in the proper way. Like other Jamesian pilgrims he feels a sudden "assault of images": "he had the sense of names in the air, of ghosts at the windows, of signs and tokens, a whole range of expression, all about him, too thick for prompt discrimination." But instead of shutting the thick rich confusion out (as some of the other ambassadors do) he opens "the windows of his mind . . . letting this rather grey interior drink in for once the sun of a clime not marked in his old geography." But along with this new venturous hospitality to life Strether also experiences that nervousness and timidity when threatened with too much proximity to experience which I suggested was discernible in James's own *Autobiography*. He is "aware of fearing close quarters": he prefers to sit apart and view it all from a removed point. It is in this mood that he asks little Bilham, tentatively, if the union of Chad and Mme de Vionnet is "virtuous." The latter answers—"it's what they pass for" and goes on: "But isn't that enough? What more than a vain appearance does the wisest of us know? I commend you . . . the vain appearance." This is clearly not a point of view that Strether would be content to adopt uncritically; but, coming from Woollett he has to learn that appearances may have a value, that there is a knowledge to be gained from the surface as well as from the depth. At this point in the garden Strether is really poised between two visions, two attitudes to life. He still half envies Waymarsh's obtuse and condemnatory refusal to have anything to do with the world of appearances. At the same time he is drawn to the warmer life of impressions and sensory stimuli to which he is now exposing himself. It is a question of how open or how shut to keep the windows of the mind. During his inner conflict he makes a comment which really leads to the key question of the book. Speaking of the Europeans in general he says: "You've all of you so much visual sense that you've somehow all 'run' to it. There are moments when it strikes one that you haven't any other." He means the moral sense, as his interlocutors quickly realise. Miss Barrace admits the charge: "I dare say . . . that we all do here, run too much to mere eye. But how can it be helped? We're all looking at each other—and in the light of Paris one sees what things resemble. That's what the light of Paris seems always to show." Of course the eye (the Lockean window to the mind) is the organ supremely committed to appearances, to noting what things resemble, seeing how things "show" (interesting to recall that Cézanne said of Monet—he is all eye, but my God, what an eye! Strether's adventure among sheer appearances coincides very aptly with the age of Impressionism). Miss Barrace continues:

> "Everything, every one shows" . . . .
> "But for what they really are?" Strether asked.
> "Oh I like your Boston 'reallys'! But sometimes—yes."

That is the most important question Strether asks. If one accepts the visible beauty and charm and decorousness of appearances, to what extent might one be blinding oneself to a hidden immoral reality? How much are things and people *really* what they show as being? How much can one stake on the "vain appearance"? Clearly a good deal, since without sensory impressions we could have no knowledge of this present world. Waymarsh's moral response to the world is based on wilful not-seeing and is thus ignorant and thus worse than useless. Yet if one agrees to regard the world with the same aesthetic attitude as one regards a picture, what invisible but real moral problems may one be overlooking?

This, of course, is the point of the last crucial incident in Strether's "process of vision." He has accepted the aesthetic view, he has left Waymarsh and all he stands for far behind him with no regret. He takes a day out in the country where everything reminds him of a small landscape painting by Lambinet (curiously echoing his own name) which he had seen years before. The reality exactly measures up to the art. He thinks in terms of the frame, the composition etc., of the scene: "it was France, it was Lambinet. Moreover he was freely walking about in it." James makes it explicit: Strether is "in the picture." That is to say that in this perfect moment, the world of actual appearances is exactly consonant with the world of art. Strether's new aesthetic sense basks luxuriously in this merged world of art and nature. But then, in the famous scene, Chad and Mme de Vionnet come sailing into the picture. At first they seem to enhance its pictorial quality ("What he saw was exactly the right thing") but then as other evidence (of hints, glimpses, suppressed gestures, prepared attitudes) emerges, Strether realises that under the felicitous pastoral appearance there is a genuine moral dubiety. This moral reality does not appear directly to the eye; it is something inferred and detected by the human interpreting mind. It is impossible to regard the real world as one would a painted canvas—because genuine moral problems obtrude; problems not of aesthetic values, but of the complexities and cruelties of human conduct. This experience—of the moral reality damaging the aesthetic appearance—is the final test for Strether. He spends hours sitting on his bedroom sofa (sedantry musings become the very essence of artistic meditation in James), turning over this crucial undeniable fact: "there had been simply a *lie* in the affair." His theory had been that the facts were "intrinsically beautiful" as well as apparently so. Now he has to reconsider their intrinsic, as opposed to their apparent quality. He has to assimilate "the deep, deep truth of the intimacy revealed." And it is this challenge which brings Strether to his final maturity of vision. He visits Mme de Vionnet; he perceives her fear; and he achieves an ethical sense which goes far beyond a mere disapprobation for the illicit deed. His fine insight, (James calls it his "sharpest perception yet"), is that "it was almost appalling, that a creature so fine could be, by mysterious forces, a creature so exploited." It is the "exploitation" of people that is the cardinal sin in the Jamesian world: evil is the callous manipulation and selfish appropriation of other peoples' lives—of life itself. According to such a moral scheme, Mme de Vionnet is no sinner but all victim. The exploiters include many of the minor ambassadors, but the central one is Chad. Strether has approached very close to a Jamesian view of the world for by the end the values of character and author overlap to a large extent.

To assert that is to bring into prominence one last crucial question. Why does Strether return to America? Mme de Vionnet's question is very relevant here. She asks him: "Where *is* your 'home' moreover now—what has become of it?" This "unhomeing" of Strether is important. I suggested in an earlier article that Isabel Archer was looking for a home, a defining abode for her "self," and made a major error of choice because of her failures of vision. Strether, having attained a wide and comprehensive vision of life has unfitted himself for any one specific "home." For that would be to return to the very partiality, the limited and limiting commitment, which he has transcended. Like other Jamesian artist figures, he renounces all participation. To take up an image from the book, he must drop off the great stage of life and appreciate it from behind the scenes. The paradox is, as is usual in James, that "he had only to be at last well out of it to feel it, oddly enough, still going on." Just as from the balcony the watcher is "well out of it" but most aware of it all "going on." In addition "it was he somehow who finally paid, and it was the others who mainly partook." He seems to become the containing, all-embracing consciousness of the various participants; but he must pay by forfeiting his place on the stage. That is what is behind the final reason he gives to Maria Gostrey for not staying on in Europe. In going back to America he is, it is made very clear, going back to completely nothing—a blank, a nowhere. But that is the whole point, he explains: "But all the same I must go . . . To be right. . . . That, you see, is my only logic. Not, out of the whole affair, to have got anything for myself." This is the Jamesian logic, no matter how perverse it may seem to some people. For Strether to go back to Mrs. Newsome's money and security would, of course, be an impossible reversion, a wilful blinding, an abdication from his newly won perspective on life. To stay in Europe, however, would subtly contaminate his disinterested efforts on behalf of Mme de Vionnet by making it seem that he has become a corrupt defender of old Europe. He must not appear simply to have opted for one world—of appearances—as opposed to the other—of moral essences. It is not simply a matter of changing sides—it is getting beyond sides altogether, and the geographical equivalent of this is his refusal to seek around for a comfortable corner for himself in Europe. To show that Strether's new vision has passed beyond all the demands of the "wretched self," it is important that he must not get any swag or material loot for himself (as, for instance, even Maria Gostrey has her little museum of sharp acquisitions). He must be above all collecting, all purchasing, all possessing. His gain, his treasures, must all be of the imagination; gems of appreciation, understanding, and a generous sympathy. Thus we have our last glimpse of him looking, perhaps, not unlike James himself—alone, homeless, somehow out of life, but full of a priceless vision.

I have isolated, for purposes of emphasis, Strether's stance on the balcony. But one should also note his increasing preference for the posture of seated meditation. This too reflects James's own preference for what he revealingly called "the bench of reverie" in his *Autobiography*; and indeed the bench has an iconographic significance equal to that of the balcony in James's later work—both, of course, suggest the choice, or sentence, of nonparticipation. His last story is called "The Bench of Desolation," and the figure seated on the bench or in the "chair of contemplation" ("Crapy Cornelia") is a recurrent one in his later work. In his later stories one often finds an ageing man sitting in solitude, and often in pensive sorrow, abandoning himself to melancholy musing and waiting for the twilight to close in. He may feel estranged, excluded, unwanted, or unfulfilled. Thus, for instance,

Traffle in "Mora Montravers": "he could now stare but at the prospect of exclusion, and of his walking round it, through the coming years. . . . But he remained staring out at the approach of evening." But as the night comes on he has, like so many of James's spectators and on-lookers, the consolation and company of his private Jamesian consciousness—"exquisite, occult, dangerous and sacred, to which everything ministered and which nothing could take away." And the prototype for all these seated thinkers is surely James himself, who was, of all the "pilgrims" he wrote about, ultimately the most "passionate"—even if the passion was all for appreciation and not participation. There is a lovely sketch of James, written by himself, which seems exactly to define his own chosen relationship to life. It occurs at the very end of a little-known travel book, *A Little Tour in France,* where James, having, like Strether, travelled and seen and appreciated, retires to a "bench of reverie" as if to turn over the significance and value of all his garnered impressions and sensations. It is the end of the tour, a twilight moment in which memory takes over from experience and the journeyings of life give way to the meditations of art. This picture makes a fitting end to this discussion of *The Ambassadors.* James is in a deserted Parc in Dijon:

> I went there late in the afternoon, without meeting a creature. . . .
> At the end of it was a little river that looked like a canal, and on
> the further bank was an old-fashioned villa, close to the water,
> with a little French garden of its own. On the hither side was a
> bench, on which I seated myself, lingering a good while; for this
> was just the sort of place I like. It was the furthermost point of
> my little tour. I thought that over, as I sat there, on the eve of
> taking the express to Paris; and as the light faded in the Parc the
> vision of some of the things I had seen became more distinct.

It is precisely for the sake of that "distinctness of vision" that the watcher on the balcony and the thinker on the bench alike withdraw from the wonderful, fearful life around them.

JULIET McMASTER

"The Full Image of a Repetition" in "The Turn of the Screw"

When the governess in "The Turn of the Screw" has just been terrified by seeing the apparition of Peter Quint looking in at her through the dining-room window at Bly, she tells us,

> It was confusedly present to me that I ought to place myself where he had stood. I did so; I applied my face to the pane and looked, as he had looked, into the room. As if, at this moment, to show me exactly what his range had been, Mrs. Grose, as I had done for himself just before, came in from the hall. With this I had the full image of a repetition of what already occurred. She saw me as I had seen my own visitant.

She watches the effect of her appearance on Mrs. Grose, giving her, indeed, "something of the shock that I had received."

Oscar Cargill has called attention to this scene as an instance of James's "marvelous symbolic irony, perhaps the best example in his fiction"; and the incident certainly seems to have an impact that goes beyond its immediate import in the narrative. However, what appears to have been overlooked is the significance of the fact that this is not the only instance in "The Turn of the Screw" of an ironic reversal of locations; that in fact James consistently replaces the ghosts with the governess to recreate the "full image" of her own perception. She herself feels compelled to act out the image in her mind.

The first time she encounters Peter Quint, as Freudians will recall, it is

From *Studies in Short Fiction* 6, no. 4 (Summer 1969). © 1969 by Newberry College.

while she is wandering in the garden and daydreaming about the master, and she sees him at the top of the tower. On this occasion she does not, as when she next meets him, immediately go to where she saw him; however, on the night when she wakes to see Flora gazing intently out of the window, communicating, as the governess supposes, with Miss Jessel, she determines herself to look out of a different window that faces the same way: "There were empty rooms enough at Bly, and it was only a question of choosing the right one. The right one suddenly presented itself to me as the lower one—though high above the gardens—in the solid corner of the house that I have spoken of as the old tower." From this room high upon the tower, by again applying her face to the pane, she sees Miles looking up. She herself is sure that he is looking higher still, at Peter Quint *on* the tower, but by Miles's own assertion it was she he was looking at. Again, she is appearing to someone else as the ghost had appeared to her.

Sometimes it is only herself that she horrifies by this identification with the ghosts. On one of her nocturnal ramblings, "I once recognized the presence of a woman seated on one of the lower steps with her back presented to me, her body half-bowed and her head, in an attitude of woe, in her hand." Later she adopts the same attitude in the same place: she has just returned alone from her disturbing interview with Miles outside the church: "Tormented, in the hall, with difficulties and obstacles, I remember sinking down at the foot of the staircase—suddenly collapsing there on the lowest step and then, with a revulsion, recalling that it was exactly where, more than a month before, in the darkness of night and just so bowed with evil things, I had seen the spectre of the most horrible of women." She goes up to the schoolroom, only to find her "vile predecessor" usurping her place at the table, and to have "the extraordinary chill of a feeling that it was I who was the intruder."

Miss Jessel's first and definitive appearance, of course, is at the far side of the lake in the grounds of Bly (chap. 7). And it is almost predictable that it should be there that the governess later confronts Flora. The little girl has escaped her vigilance, has taken the boat and rowed herself across the lake. There the governess finds her and now openly accuses her of being aware of Miss Jessel's presence. But as the governess had once seen Miss Jessel there, a horrifying and evil presence, so now Flora sees *her*:

> "I see nobody. I see nothing. I never *have*. I think you're cruel.
> I don't like you" [and she pleads to Mrs. Grose:] "Take me away,
> take me away—oh take me away from *her*!"

"From *me?*" I panted.

"From you—from you!" she cried.

In the same way, in her agonizing and fatal confrontation with Miles, the governess calls his attention to Peter Quint, looking through the dining room window as she had once looked through at Mrs. Grose; but the only "devil" he can see is the governess herself.

Lear's image for the essential identity of the justice and the thief could be appropriately adapted for "The Turn of the Screw": "Change places, and handy-dandy, which is the governess, which is the ghost?"

My point should be sufficiently clear. The occasion on which the governess runs round to look in through the window and terrify Mrs. Grose as the ghost had just looked in and terrified her—this is only the most obvious instance of a consistently maintained pattern in the action, in which the governess takes the place of the ghost. Part of James's purpose in this systematic exchange of locations is no doubt to give us another facet of the governess' complex psychology. She herself is conscious of some appropriateness in her taking the ghosts' places, and it is evidently part of her longing to be "justified" in her perceptions that moves her to endow her mental images with some measure of spatial reality: she becomes the embodiment of her own mental projections.

But there is a further significance in this image. What we have in effect is the symmetrical reversal of an object and its image in a glass (and if there is no actual glass there is usually the possibility of some other kind of projected image—a reflection in water, a shadow, or a trick effect of distance or half-light). And the question that James deliberately raises is whether that glass is a transparent pane, through which Peter Quint can clearly be seen, or whether it is, as it may become at dusk, opaque like a mirror, simply giving back to the governess a reflection of herself. The apparition and the perceiver may be distinct, each with a separate existence, or the one may be only the reflection of the other.

The image of the reflection is a dominant one in the novel. It is not only glass that can receive and reflect an image, but the human mind; and the recurrence of this word *reflection* becomes significant in the governess' communication as well as in her perceptions. Her mental projections are effected not only spatially, but psychologically, and by this means she makes Mrs. Grose "a receptacle of lurid things." When she tells her of Miss Jessel's appearance, "I was conscious as I spoke that I looked prodigious things, for I got the slow reflection of them in my companion's face." The reflexion is sometimes a two-way affair between these two, we find. It is noticeable that we hear about the major encounters with the ghosts not as they appear to the governess but as she relates the matter to Mrs. Grose afterwards. The total creation of the apparition is not immediate, nor singly in her own mind; it is a product partly of Mrs. Grose's mind, too, as the two catch and reflect back and forth the gleams of suspicion and awareness. Harold Goddard pointed out that it is from Mrs. Grose herself that the governess first gets a hint of some evil male presence at Bly. And now, as she is describing the apparition, she could be enlarging on that hint.

At first, looking for confirmation, she suggests that Mrs. Grose has "guessed" the identity of the male apparition. "Ah I haven't guessed!" she said very simply. "How can I if *you* don't imagine?" For the moment the governess is halted and cannot describe him: "What is he? He's a horror. . . . He's—God help me if I know *what* he is!" But after a few blind alleys, a few gleams of communication, their minds are working in concert, and it is now that, "seeing in her face that she already, in this, with a deeper dismay found a touch of picture, I quickly added stroke to stroke." As in running round to look in through the window she has just created a general impression in Mrs. Grose's mind, so through her urgent and intimate communication with her afterwards she fills out the full image of Peter Quint.

The children's minds, on the other hand, are more opaque than Mrs. Grose's, and like untarnished mirrors give back to the governess only the image of her own distraught face. In talking to Miles, she recalls, ". . . to gain time, I tried to laugh, and I seemed to see in the beautiful face with which he watched me how ugly and queer I looked." Similarly, when she has bundled off Mrs. Grose and Flora in the coach, and set the stage for her harrowing solo encounter with Miles, she communicates her own almost hysterical apprehension to the whole household: "I could see in the aspect of others a confused reflexion of the crisis."

Douglas, too, testifies to her power of communicating her experience with an image that is close to that of the reflection: when asked if he took down her narrative, he replies, "Nothing but the impression. I took that *here*"—he tapped his heart. "I've never lost it."

That pane of glass between the human being and the apparition becomes a focus for the total and deliberate ambiguity in the tale. We may take our own choice as to which side of the pane we want to be: with the governess, looking outwards at the baleful stalking ghosts, or on the other side, looking inwards at her and the working of a diseased imagination. Or alternatively, in another operation of the image, we may think of the glass either as a transparent medium through which real ghosts can be seen, or as a mirror in which the governess sees, essentially, only her own reflection.

The choice is with us from the first, in the account of how Douglas prepares his audience for the governess' narrative. Leon Edel, in his careful analysis of the point of view in "The Turn of the Screw," draws no conclusions as to the significance of this rather elaborate introduction. It seems to me, however, that James has in this passage, the first of the twelve instalments, quite carefully defined two kinds of readers for his story. There are two distinct elements in Douglas' audience. One is a group of sensation-hungry women, who want a few chills and terrors to enliven their long winter evenings in the country-house, and so will hear Douglas' reading of the manuscript as another ghost story. For them dreadfulness is in itself "delicious," and the more turns of the screw the better. Subtlety is not their concern: one of them laments that the story is not told "in any literal vulgar way," because "that's the only way I ever understand."

On the other hand Douglas is more particularly addressing the original narrator of the story, whom for convenience we may call [James]. It is for this kind of hearer, for [James] and, one might add, Goddard, Edmund Wilson and their followers, that the fact of the governess' love for her master becomes particularly relevant:

> He continued to fix me. "You'll easily judge," he repeated: "*you* will."
> I fixed him too. "I see. She was in love."
> He laughed for the first time. "You *are* acute. Yes, she was in love. That is she *had* been. That came out—she couldn't tell her story without its coming out."

For this kind of listener the impact of the tale is not so simple as "sheer terror"; and the distinction is carefully made:

> "Nobody but me, till now, has ever heard. It's quite too horrible." This was naturally declared by several voices to give the thing the utmost price, and our friend, with quiet art, prepared his triumph by turning his eyes over the rest of us and going on: "It's beyond everything. Nothing at all that I know touches it."
> "For sheer terror?" I remember asking.
> He seemed to say it wasn't so simple as that; to be really at a loss how to qualify it. He passed his hand over his eyes, made a little wincing grimace. "For dreadful—dreadfulness!"
> "Oh how delicious!" cried one of the women.
> He took no notice of her; he looked at me, but as if, instead of me, he saw what he spoke of. "For general uncanny ugliness and horror and pain."

There we see Douglas' two kinds of hearer. For the general entertainment, he presents another ghost story; for [James], for "me in particular," he presents something more subtle, that demands deeper psychological perception. Douglas' look through [James] at the illusion he is about to present is like the governess' look through the window at the visions she communicates. [James] the narrator and listener, like James the author, is our transparent medium of perception.

According to my contention, there isn't a right way and a wrong way to interpret the tale, but rather *two* ways, which the same reader may enjoy alternately, if he wishes; and James has carefully established this, both through the imagery of the glass and its reversal of locations, and in the narrative set-up of the story. Just as we may choose to look through the glass *with* the governess or *at* her, so we may choose to listen with the ladies, and hear a ghost story, or with [James], and hear a psychological novel. We have "the full image of a repetition," as in a mirror, and we may decide for ourselves what to take for substance and what for shadow.

ELISABETH HANSOT

Imagination and Time
in "The Beast in the Jungle"

In his preface to *Joseph Andrews,* Maynard Mack suggests that the comic artist achieves his effect by subordinating the presentation of life as experience to the presentation of life as a spectacle. In the first instance the relationship between the characters experiencing life and the reader is a primary one, whereas in the second instance the characters remain detached from the events they observe and the primary relationship of reader and characters is that of onlookers.

"The Beast in the Jungle" is not a comedy but its central character, Marcher, can nonetheless be described in Mack's terms. Marcher is a person who chooses to experience life as a spectacle. Consequently, the only relationship that Marcher can offer May is that of an onlooker, albeit a privileged one with access to information withheld from "the amusement of a cold world" (*The Complete Tales of Henry James,* edited by Leon Edel, 12 vols. (New York: J. B. Lippincott, 1964), vol. 11; all references to "The Beast in the Jungle" are from this edition). The reader, to reverse Mack's terms, is invited to figure to himself, through Marcher, the quality of life that can result from holding ordinary experience at arm's length.

Marcher's detachment from ordinary experience, James tells us, comes from his conviction that an extraordinary experience awaits him which, like a supernatural event, is expected to dislocate, supersede, or render meaningless the normal incidents and attitudes which make up a good part of

From *Twentieth Century Interpretations of "The Turn of the Screw" and Other Tales: A Collection of Critical Essays,* edited by Jane P. Tomkins. © 1970 by Prentice-Hall, Inc.

everyday life. In the course of his narrative James describes some of the attitudes and beliefs which enable Marcher to establish and maintain a distance between himself and the everyday experience available to him, and suggests how, in turn, these dispositions come to constitute the substance of Marcher's own character. One of the most noteworthy concomitants of Marcher's detachment is the curiously passive attitude he adopts toward his own past and future. This passivity—whether it be a cause or a consequence of his detachment—has among its effects a gradual and unperceived impoverishment of his own sensibility, for Marcher maintains toward his own past and future the attitude of a spectator viewing events that he cannot influence. He seems to view both these dimensions of time as discrete, self-contained objects, endowed with their own independent value and bearing little or no relationship to himself in the present.

When Marcher does try to conceive of himself as an active agent he chooses the paradigm of the hero. The hero's singularity might be said to consist in his ability to dominate events by his perfectly timed and conceived actions. James describes this kind of abrupt shift in Marcher's concept of himself as a sudden passage from one extreme of consciousness to another. The images James uses to portray Marcher's rapid, almost unconscious transitions from passive spectator to heroic actor offer important clues to Marcher's attitude toward time.

In his opening sentence, James indicates that Marcher is not interested in questions of causality. "What determined the speech that startled him in the course of their encounter scarcely matters, being probably but some words spoken by himself quite without intention." Marcher at this juncture is wondering what had brought May to remind him of a long forgotten intimacy, a confession made to her ten years ago. Both the past confession and the present rediscovery of it appear to be fortunate accidents, explained, if explanation is needed, by some words spoken by Marcher without intent or purpose. Marcher seems to be a man to whom accidents—including accidents of memory—occur easily. As James portrays him, both in his initial setting at Weatherend and subsequently, Marcher does not conceive of himself as an active agent capable of initiating changes or causing events to occur in his everyday world. He is a man who lacks intentions, perhaps because he lacks desires and purposes by which to define himself and furnish his corner of the universe.

When Marcher does look to the past, it is because he desires to find a groundwork strong enough to support further intimacy with May in the future. He had, James remarks, most curiously forgotten the events of their encounter. The explanation may be that for Marcher these events seemed, in the strongest sense of the word, to be mere accidents, episodes which did not mark him, or even annoy or amuse him enough to recollect them in the intervening years. Marcher's past, seen in this light, might be described as a collection of incidents without continuity or form. These incidents appear as finished, somewhat gratuitous episodes, with little relation to the present and fewer implications for the future.

> He was still merely fumbling with the idea that any contact be-tween them in the past would have had no importance. If it had had no importance he scarcely knew why his actual impression of her should so seem to have so much; the answer to which, however, was that in such a life as they all appeared to be leading for the moment one could but take things as they came.

Another way of describing what has happened to Marcher is to say he declines to live in ordinary time—the time in which people fall in love, get married, assume responsibilities, acquire possessions, and, like the visitors to Weatherend, long for others they cannot acquire. Quite to the contrary, Marcher's concern, upon becoming reacquainted with May, is that she show no right or claim to him.

> The vanity of women had long memories, but she was making no claim on him of a compliment or a mistake. With another woman, a totally different one, he might have feared the recall possibly even of some imbecile "offer."

While he does obscurely sense that something will be required of him if the present meeting with May is to contain the germ for the future development, when Marcher reaches out it is only "in imagination—as against time" that he chooses to look for a fresh start.

Why does James speak of "imagination as *against* time"? As James uses the idea of imagination the phrase implies that Marcher still has available to him a choice of roots by which he can try to reestablish his acquaintance with May. Marcher prefers to use his imagination, James suggests, because the humdrum activity, the everyday business of life, encountered on the al-ternative route seems trivial to him. But as Marcher himself ages and the unused and disdained possibilities of experience within ordinary time are withdrawn, Marcher's imagination comes to serve as a weapon to preserve himself against time.

> "Only, you know, it isn't anything I'm to *do*, to achieve in the world, to be distinguished or admired for. I'm not such an ass as *that*."

As the time allotted him diminishes, Marcher's refusal to seriously take in hand and give value to the everyday business of life makes him dangerously dependent upon the existence of his singular fate, the occurrence of which will, presumably, both vindicate his attitude toward ordinary time and redeem the insignificance of his present life. And, as the margin of time shrinks, Marcher's anxiety increases. He becomes aware that "when the possibilities themselves had accordingly turned stale, when the secret of the gods had grown faint, had perhaps even quite evaporated that, and that only, was failure." But even with this awareness, Marcher continues to see his future as an extraordinary one: his fate is to be bankrupt, dishonoured, pilloried, events without any relation to what Marcher is in the present and with an accidental quality that absolves him of any responsibility for bringing them to pass.

Marcher does not appear to use his imagination to enrich the present by exploring the future; he does not know how to investigate the potentialities or select from the possibilities that the future offers to the present. He imagines the future in a way that isolates it from the present—the only quality which Marcher allows it is a strangeness sufficient to drain the present of any value which it may contain. Marcher's own image of the future is of an agency fully shaped in a way that he cannot specify, impinging at some point on his present and radically altering its shape. While the upheaval is to occur in time, its singularity, and its value for Marcher would seem to be in its indiscernibility; it cannot be prepared for and its eruption in time will be so sudden and of so short a duration that it will scarcely be known other than by its effects—the radical transformation it will leave in its wake.

> "It's to be something you're merely to suffer?"
> "Well, say to wait for—to have to meet, to face, to see suddenly break out in my life; possibly destroying all further consciousness, possibly annihilating me; possibly, on the other hand, only altering everything, striking at the root of all my world and leaving me to the consequences, however they shape themselves."

Marcher uses his imagination as a weapon to ward off time, to keep the dangerous beast at bay. He does this by using his imagination to endow the future with independent agency and significance. Perhaps inadvertently, Marcher sets up a signpost prohibiting all exploration of that domain by consigning it to the unimaginable. When he does choose to use his imagination in time, it is, significantly, only to register his dissatisfaction with a meager past, apparently oblivious of any suspicion that the past is as much constituted by choices made in the present as a record of possibilities missed and experiences denied.

A past as insubstantial as Marcher's may be said to invite imaginative reconstruction and Marcher can, with safety, invest it with deeds of considerable dimension. In this vein, he wonders why he could not have saved May from a capsized boat, or at least recovered her dressing bag, filched by a lazzarone with a stiletto. The heroic self-portrayal is congenial to Marcher because the hero may be viewed as not responsible to the workings of everyday time. The hero, conceived as eternally young, can afford to scorn ordinary intimacies and everyday trivialities. If the hero is impervious to everyday time, it may be because his acts are performed to redress an upset, never of his own making, in ordinary time. To rescue someone from the unexpected is to prevent a dislocation of ordinary time and permit it to resume. When it does resume the hero withdraws (or the tale ends), hence his actions remain eternally fresh and vivid. The hero, in this interpretation, requires no past or future and need not be measured by ordinary time in which actions do have causes in the past and consequences in the future. His actions are fully completed when ordinary time resumes and luminously justified by its humdrum resumption.

In a cruel image, James proceeds to deny to the aging Marcher that any such heroic exemption from time exists.

> He had settled to his safety . . . figuring to himself, with some colour, in the likeness of certain little old men he remembered to have seen, of whom, all meagre and wizened as they might look, it was related that they had in their time fought twenty duels or been loved by ten princesses.

In an important passage, James describes Marcher's present as a "simplification of everything but the state of suspense. That remained only by seeming to hang in the void surrounding it." But even a state of suspense must draw from the future, or from the past, to maintain its vitality. And to the extent that Marcher may, at one time, have feared his future fate, or at the very least feared the possibility that others might find his fate ridiculous, the state of suspense could still be distinguished from the void—if James means by the void the devaluation of the past and future which surround Marcher's present.

It may indeed be because of his early fears that May agrees to watch with him, a willingness that Marcher undervalues because, unlike May, it is his future fate and not his present fears which fix and hold his attention. Unlike her companion, May is aware of the passage of time and her subjection to it. Marcher initially perceives her at Weatherend as having visibly aged. "She *was* there on harder terms than anyone; she was there as a consequence of things suffered, one way and another, in the interval of years." Because she is conscious of the passage of time, May is primarily alert to Marcher's condition in the present. When she does consent to share Marcher's watch, it is only after having asked him three times whether he is afraid. The questions indicate that perhaps what most interests May is not the future in which Marcher alone is to meet his unique fate, but the present in which Marcher has needs that May can meet, needs that make him dependent on her for sympathy, understanding, and support. Marcher is baffled by May's questions because he conceives his relationship to May in the present as subordinate to and at the service of his singular destiny. By contrast May, grasping at straws, hazards that Marcher's destiny, with its by-product of fear that can be met and assuaged, may be used to develop and serve their relationship in the present.

When the question is later resumed between them, and Marcher's "original fear, if fear it had been, had lost itself in the desert," May's watch is at an end and the present is indeed barren. There has been no growth in Marcher's awareness of his dependency upon May, and May's need for Marcher remains mute and unexpressed, for want of an answering voice. Without understanding why, Marcher senses that from that point on their discourse bears the mark of something finished and completed.

At Weatherend May's function was to explain to the curious the history of the place and the objects it shelters. These treasures, so full of history and poetry, have been tested by time, and their value once established, they are to be preserved against time. What is striking is Marcher's way of viewing his own destiny as though it were an object of similar worth. The stupid world is to be kept in deliberate ignorance of his singularity, and it is May, with her superior knowledge, who will be allowed "to dispose the concealing veil in the right folds." She is to be both witness and keeper—and the value of that over which she watches is no more open to discussion than the more publicly recognized treasures at Weatherend.

If Marcher refrains, with a fine show of detachment, from the display of greed which causes his associates to all but handle the objects presented to their view at Weatherend, he is much less circumspect in fingering that other treasure, his consciousness of his own unique fate. His carefully cherished image of his future fate resembles in many ways a work of art: it is the result of an imaginative effort, set apart from ordinary incomplete events, and endowed with its own intrinsic significance. But, unlike Marcher's fate, a work of art is specific. By choosing from the range of possibilities, excluding some in the process of giving meaning to others, a work of art is given its concrete characteristics and this is what Marcher, in analogous circumstances, is unable or unwilling to do.

Likewise Marcher thinks himself disinterested, "even a little sublimely—unselfish" in carefully allowing for May's requirements and peculiarities. But his studied consideration, James indicates, is really a mask for the purest egotism, the price Marcher consents to pay for the luxury of May's attention. Between the greed of the visitors at Weatherend and Marcher's more disingenuous selfishness there would appear to be far less difference than Marcher himself is able to perceive.

Whether he wishes it or not, Marcher lives in ordinary time. James describes Marcher's entanglement with ordinary time as involuntary and to a large extent unconscious, "a passage of his consciousness in the suddenest way, from one extreme to another." Marcher's fate is not to understand, until too late, what such sudden passages signify: that Marcher *is* subject to ordinary time, and that what he figures to himself as perfect detachment will be seen, in the end even by Marcher, as perfect selfishness. When the Beast has sprung and Marcher is forced to see the real measure of his past "in the chill of his egotism and the light of her use" it is too late. Unknown to himself he had lived, been measured, and found wanting—by ordinary time.

DAVID HOWARD

The Bostonians

"In any case," he said, "it was just personal."
—F. SCOTT FITZGERALD, *The Great Gatsby*

"Try to be one of the people on whom nothing is lost!"
—HENRY JAMES, "The Art of Fiction"

"I prefer free unions."
—Verena Tarrant

The Bostonians is a novel about union, even "The Union." What becomes unified is not altogether clear, partly because the word in the novel, as in American history, points consistently to battle. The employment of Miss Birdseye's serene, unifying, dying vision is characteristic:

> Three minutes later Miss Birdseye, looking up from her letter, saw them move together through the bristling garden and traverse a gap in the old fence which enclosed the further side of it. They passed into the ancient shipyard which lay beyond, and which was now a mere vague, grass-grown approach to the waterside, bestrewn with a few remnants of the supererogatory timber. She saw them stroll forward to the edge of the bay and stand there, taking the soft breeze in their faces. She watched them a little, and it warmed her heart to see the stiff-necked young Southerner led captive by a daughter of New England trained in the right school, who would impose her opinions in their integrity. Considering how prejudiced he must have been he was certainly be-

From *The Air of Reality: New Essays on Henry James,* edited by John Goode. © 1972 by Methuen and Co., Ltd.

having very well; even at that distance Miss Birdseye dimly made
out that there was something positively humble in the way he
invited Verena Tarrant to seat herself on a low pile of weather-
blacked planks, which constituted the principal furniture of the
place, and something, perhaps, just a trifle too expressive of right-
eous triumph in the manner in which the girl put the suggestion
by and stood where she liked, a little proudly, turning a good
deal away from him. Miss Birdseye could see as much as this,
but she couldn't hear, so that she didn't know what it was that
made Verena turn suddenly back to him, at something he said. If
she had known, perhaps his observation would have struck her
as less singular—under the circumstances in which these two
young persons met—than it may appear to the reader.

"They have accepted one of my articles; I think it's the best."
      [(chap. 36.) All quotations are taken from the Chiltern
      Library edition (London, 1952), which follows the text
      of the first book edition of *The Bostonians* (1886).]

This is explicitly as well as gently an image of the union of North and
South, or more correctly, through these eyes, an image of triumphant reconstruction, the daughter of New England "imposing" her opinions. As we
know, the opposite is true. Ransom, in achieving the publication of his most
reactionary opinions, those already tried out on Verena, now feels qualified
to pursue their marriage, to take Verena on fully, and through her the other
Bostonian, Olive Chancellor. He is the carpetbagger in reverse. The South
wins the war.

Both versions are combative and public. If Miss Birdseye had heard
Ransom's remark she would have been less surprised than the reader at such
an opening for lovers' talk. These are two performers in a performing world.
(There is, of course, an assumption that what is going on in this part of the
novel is some kind of triumph of love, of personal feelings, which I shall look
at later.)

The detail of this scene is important. The superannuated shipbuilding
town fits the superannuated reformer. And both combine to give a sense of
the heroic New England that is gone. But the hints of desolation, of waste
and debris and aftermath (even possibly of Ransom's ruined plantation, the
South wasted by war) go further than this. The "poverty" of the scene is an
American one. The unformed, blurred vision—Miss Birdseye's spectacles are
notoriously ineffective—a vision involving nonetheless a serene complacent
unifying, goes naturally with the casual unformed or decreated "American

scene." But there is more than one attitude to this scene in the novel, just as there is more than one attitude to unions both private and public.

I want first to glance at some of the obvious "American scenes" in the book, to connect the descriptive detail of this Marmion section with the detailed rendering of New York and Boston. There are other elements this scene takes up: the earlier Miss Birdseye of course, although she turns out to be a personification of debris and disarray; at least two other episodes of false serenity—Ransom almost lulled into the acceptance of Mrs Luna as a wife (chap. 24), and Olive giving herself momentarily to Burrage's world of wealth, taste, and collecting, where human life ceased to be a battle (chap. 18). And we must connect this approaching death, of the "heroic" and "sublime" Miss Birdseye, with the central meditation on death and battle in the Harvard Memorial Hall. But the convenient way into the novel is through other explicitly American scenes.

There is a particular view of Boston from Olive Chancellor's windows which comes very early in the novel, and recurs several times. The view of the Back Bay comes first via Ransom, who has little "artistic sense" but finds its combination of spires, factory chimneys, masts, brackish water "too big for a river and too small for a bay," and modern houses, "picturesque" and "almost romantic" (chap. 3). The Bostonians are proud of this view too, always, according to Mrs Luna, "giving you the Back Bay to look at, and then taking credit for it," so that it is not merely a question of Ransom exposing a provincial sensibility in the city of culture. He assists at a typical, in some ways rather mean, American scene, and that response and scene are rather coldly presented.

The sense of a distance between this American view and James's tone is more evident when this same scene reappears through Verena's eyes. There has been a change of season, and there is much more detail, but it is recognizably the same:

> the long, low bridge that crawled, on its staggering posts, across the Charles; the casual patches of ice and snow; the desolate suburban horizons, peeled and made bald by the rigour of the season; the general hard, cold void of the prospect; the extrusion, at Charlestown, at Cambridge, of a few chimneys and steeples, straight, sordid tubes of factories and engine-shops, or spare, heavenward finger of the New England meeting-house. There was something inexorable in the poverty of the scene, shameful in the meanness of its details, which gave a collective impression of boards and tin and frozen earth, sheds and rotting piles, railway-

lines striding flat across a thoroughfare of puddles, and tracks of
the humbler, the universal horse-car, traversing obliquely this path
of danger; loose fences, vacant lots, mounds of refuse, yards be-
strewn with iron pipes, telegraph poles, and bare wooden backs
of places. Verena thought such a view lovely.

(chap. 20)

It is wrong to stop the quotation there of course, but doing so does bring
out this distance I mentioned; leaving it like this makes of it an almost
appalling separation. The passage goes on:

and she was by no means without excuse when, as the afternoon
closed, the ugly picture was tinted with a clear, cold rosiness. The
air, in its windless chill, seemed to tinkle like a crystal, the faintest
gradations of tone were perceptible in the sky, the west became
deep and delicate, everything grew doubly distinct before taking
on the dimness of evening. There were pink flushes on snow,
"tender" reflections in patches of stiffened marsh, sounds of car-
bells, no longer vulgar, but almost silvery, on the long bridge,
lonely outlines of distant dusky undulations against the fading
glow.

The view at sunset does qualify, and this in fact had already been hinted at
in the earlier view of it through Ransom's eyes. But there is a severe discrimination at work here which appears to condemn both Ransom and Verena.
Unlike the "real" Bostonian, Olive, they don't know when to look. They are
really "without excuse," especially because the transformation of ugliness—
"poverty," "meanness," "refuse," etc.—is so great: "car-bells, no longer
vulgar, but almost silvery." The American scene is vulgar, rarely rescued by
silver sound or rosy light. Like Miss Peabody, though, with her "delicate,
dirty, democratic little hand," it fades or dies rather well. Yet a few pages
later there is the most intensely vulgar scene in the novel, the scene of Ransom's New York life. Here there is no fading light to work magical transformations. Instead there is the positive assertion of vigorous ugliness, of
triumphant jumble and debris, of participation in a "rank civilization" (I
quote only a fragment):

The house had a red, rusty face, and faded green shutters, of
which the slats were limp and at variance with each other. In one
of the lower windows was suspended a fly-blown card, with the
words "Table Board" affixed in letter cut (not very neatly) out of

coloured paper, of graduated tints, and surrounded with a small
band of stamped gilt. The two sides of the shop were protected
by an immense pent-house shed, which projected over a greasy
pavement and was supported by wooden posts fixed in the curb-
stone. Beneath it, on the dislocated flags, barrels and baskets were
freely and picturesquely grouped; an open cellarway yawned beneath the feet of those who might pause to gaze too fondly on
the savoury wares displayed in the window; a strong odour of
smoked fish, combined with a fragrance of molasses, hung about
the spot; the pavement, toward the gutter, was fringed with dirty
panniers, heaped with potatoes, carrots, and onions; and a smart,
bright waggon, with the horse detached from the shafts, drawn
up on the edge of the abominable road (it contained holes and
ruts a foot deep, and immemorial accumulations of stagnant
mud), imparted an idle, rural, pastoral air to a scene otherwise
perhaps expressive of rank civilization.

(chap. 21)

In spite of that final cautious note there is real excitement and relish
here, an almost visceral closeness. The word "picturesque" is inadequate:
the scene invites not distance but exploration and discovery, a peering—even
a falling—into one fascinating hole or box or cage after another. The excitement of the response is most clearly indicated later in the passage with
the glimpse of the Elevated Railway "overhanging the transverse longitudinal
street, which it darkened and smothered with the immeasurable spinal col-
umn and myriad clutching paws of an antediluvian monster."

One of the striking things about the whole passage is that James is being
frankly personal and also apparently frankly irrelevant. The Dutch grocery
is mentioned "not on account of any particular influence it may have had on
the life or thoughts of Basil Ransom, but for old acquaintance sake and that
of local colour." Then he adds (with an echo of "The Art of Fiction")
"besides which, a figure is nothing without a setting," and this is immediately set aside by "our young man came and went every day, with rather an
indifferent, unperceiving step, it is true, among the objects I have briefly
designated"—how different from Hyacinth Robinson. This setting seems to
exist not for Ransom but for no purpose at all, or for a novel or part of a
novel which is not going to be written:

If the opportunity were not denied me here, I should like to give
some account of Basil Ransom's interior, of certain curious per-

sons of both sexes, for the most part not favourites of fortune,
who had found an obscure asylum there.

(chap. 21)

However sceptically one takes that "I should like," and one has to bear
in mind the American magazine public, this passage as far as it goes has
great force. One thinks here of course of James's dalliance with naturalism
and the Dickensian, and of the ambitions of *The Princess Casamassima*.
Within this novel one is made very aware of what James won't touch: both
Ransom's bohemian life in New York and that southern setting which includes "something almost African" (chap. 1); and also, the crucial case,
Verena's setting. It is not my intention in this essay to go into the relation
of Verena to the feminist movement in America in the 1870s. Andrew Sin-
clair's suggestion that she is a pale reflection of Victoria Woodhull, however
questionable it may be, sufficiently points to how much of the extraordinary
world of reform in this period is not there. But I think we have to put the
issue of figure and setting in a different way.

The question is whether James wanted to give her any setting at all. "A
figure is nothing without a setting," but we have just seen James refuse to
find Ransom "among the objects I have briefly designated." This may be a
reluctance or inability to explore certain areas of life, comparable with the
failure to find in *The Princess Casamassima* "the real thing." But it begins
to look more than that if we remember that this setting is not a setting at
all in one sense. It is the most powerful of the "American scenes" I have
been quoting. And its power comes from letting the promiscuous detail and
sensation have its head "without excuse," as was implied by Verena. Its
debris is so assertive it doesn't need justification either by a certain slant of
light or a certain kind of hero, or indeed any furtherance of the novel. James
without design is without excuse. It is not simply that this American scene
triumphs over an art of fiction, of "setting": it is almost wilfully irrelevant
and indifferent. Setting and figure and author are liberated. The book, having
turned from Boston, is on holiday.

But if the novel escapes at this point, however briefly, from a certain
kind of discrimination of the ugliness and the "poverty" of the American
scene, it looks relevant, however destructively, to a larger design. For the
visual vulgarity of America is only one part of a general and increasing
American vulgarity. I do not want to dwell on this too long. It is very explicit
in the novel and is brilliantly done. The assurance in the handling of the
New York fashionable world, for example, is remarkable. My enquiry is into
possible complexities of attitude towards this vulgarity. In the same way I

shall neglect the particular reform questions, especially the woman question (as James does himself), for a more general sense of their American character. This should lead us to the elusive Verena, the crucial case as I have suggested for relation of figure to "setting," now in the wider sense of "the age."

The obvious focus for a sense of the age are Ransom's remarks in chapter 34. But although they give one version of contemporary mediocrity, and Ransom sees it as his task to rescue Verena from that mediocrity, he is in no clear way James's spokesman. To call him, as James does immediately afterwards, "poor fellow," and to write of the "ugliness" of his profession of faith, may well be irony at the expense of Verena and the age—"Mr Ransom, I assure you this is an age of conscience." But it is more likely that, given the consistent handling of Ransom, the irony is cutting both ways. Like Miss Birdseye he finds it difficult to recover from earlier severe treatment: for instance, "five thousand, ten thousand, fifteen thousand a year? There was a richness to our panting young man in the smallest of these figures"; and "he was conscious at bottom of a bigger stomach than all the culture of Charles Street could fill." The sardonic handling persists into the New York section of the book: "where should he find the twenty-dollar greenbacks which it was his ambition to transmit from time to time to his female relations, confined so constantly to a farinaceous diet?" His pronounced values are male, martial, antidemocratic, and stoical:

> it's a feminine, a nervous, hysterical, chattering, canting age, an age of hollow phrases and false delicacy and exaggerated solicitudes and coddled sensibilities, which, if we don't look out, will usher in the reign of mediocrity, of the feeblest and flattest and the most pretentious that has even been. The masculine character, the ability to dare and endure, to know and yet not fear reality, to look the world in the face and take it for what it is—a very queer and partly very base mixture—that is what I want to preserve, as I may say, to recover.
>
> (chap. 34)

Now this is not so much argument as oratory. Verena finds herself listening to the eloquence, the man, rather than the ideas. We know that voice, kept back for most of the book, comes from a "large stomach" and a great ambition for success. It has that sincerity. And it is of course typical of the novel that relationships are conducted in this way. Ransom's resentment against women is natural, given his experience since leaving the South. He has found women in control wherever he has gone. The Olive Chancellors, Mrs Farrinders, Mrs Burrages, and Mrs. Lunas, have the wealth or power or both. And their men are non-existent or weak—Olive's brothers, for example, were killed in the war. Like any other "failure" or minority group he needs a conspiracy theory, but this hardly makes that theory the summation of the book's view of "the age."

Rather, given James's generally sardonic handling of him, he himself is part of the age. It's illuminating to compare him to Olive Chancellor in this respect. In terms of his statement *she* is the age, the enemy. But they are in the book the two chief discriminators of the age. They share a sense of how much "trash" there is in it. They regret a lost heroic American past and posit the recovery of nobler human values of daring and suffering. The exactly comparable statement of Olive's views comes earlier in the book:

> Olive had a standing quarrel with the levity, the good-nature, of the judgements of the day; many of them seemed to her weak to imbecility, losing sight of all measures and standards, lavishing superlatives, delighted to be fooled. The age seemed to her to be relaxed and demoralized, and I believe she looked to the influx of the great feminine element to make it feel and speak more sharply.
>
> (chap. 16)

Putting these two passages together most clearly reveals the irony of James's design. There is a very similar diagnosis and sense of the mediocrity of the age, with exactly opposite treatment: "the masculine character," "the great feminine element."

Olive, on this occasion, has been talking to Matthias Pardon, the journalist with hair "precociously white." His "gossip's view of great tendencies" personifies the age for her. And I would have thought that it is to the world of Matthias Pardon, and Selah Tarrant, we have to look for the most consistent portrait of the age. There are two passages on Tarrant and Pardon in chapters 13 and 16 written in the brilliant manner of the first half of the novel which especially have a firm satirical confidence. In the first passage James comments that to Selah Tarrant "human existence . . . was a huge publicity" which combined happily with the need for "receipts" (chap. 13). But it's the description of Pardon which catches "the age" most ambitiously:

> He had small, fair features, remarkably neat, and pretty eyes, and a moustache that he caressed, and an air of juvenility much at variance with his grizzled locks, and the free familiar reference in which he was apt to indulge in his career as a journalist. His friends knew that in spite of his delicacy and his prattle he was

what they called a live man; his appearance was perfectly reconcilable with a large degree of literary enterprise. It should be explained that for the most part they attached to this idea the same meaning as Selah Tarrant—a state of intimacy with the newspapers, the cultivation of the great arts of publicity. For this ingenuous son of his age all distinction between the person and the artist had ceased to exist; the writer was personal, the person food for newsboys, and everything and everyone were every one's business. All things, with him, referred themselves to print, and print meant simply infinite reporting, a promptitude of announcement, abusive when necessary, or even when not, about his fellow-citizens. He poured contumely on their private life, on their personal appearance, with the best conscience in the world. His faith, again, was the faith of Selah Tarrant—that being in the newspapers is a condition of bliss, and that it would be fastidious to question the terms of the privilege. He was an *enfant de la balle,* as the French say; he had begun his career, at the age of fourteen, by going the rounds of the hotels, to cull flowers from the big, greasy registers which lie on the marble counters; and he might flatter himself that he had contributed in his measure, and on behalf of a vigilant public opinion, the pride of a democratic State, to the great end of preventing the American citizen from attempting clandestine journeys. Since then he had ascended other steps of the same ladder; he was the most brilliant young interviewer on the Boston press. He was particularly successful in drawing out the ladies; he had condensed into shorthand many of the most celebrated women of his time—some of these daughters of fame were very voluminous—and he was supposed to have a remarkably insinuating way of waiting upon *prime donne* and actresses the morning after their arrival, or sometimes the very evening, while their luggage was being brought up. He was only twenty-eight years old, and, with his hoary head, was a thoroughly modern young man; he had no idea of not taking advantage of all the modern conveniences. He regarded the mission of mankind upon earth as a perpetual evolution of telegrams; everything to him was very much the same, he had no sense of proportion or quality; but the newest thing was what came nearest exciting in his mind the sentiment of respect.

(chap. 16)

The particularization and the representativeness are superbly managed here, especially in the use of the wise child motif. (The passage does have a slightly different kind of power if we remember the trouble James ran into for being personal about Elizabeth Peabody, the model for Mrs Birdseye, and the way in which the injunction to the novelist to be "one of the people on whom nothing is lost" in "The Art of Fiction" is just as much a reporter's watchword as a novelist's.)

We have to remember then—perhaps James doesn't sufficiently remind us—that Pardon is as important a contender for Verena's hand as anyone else. Ransom and Olive are rivals but they both seek to rescue Verena from Pardon's world, which in many ways is her natural world. But then we come to James's major irony. Both Ransom and Olive have a partial discriminatory intelligence which enables them to see through the world of publicity. But like most other characters in the novel, with the notable exception of Dr Prance who is doing real and quiet work, they both seek a place in it, and in the end both have compromised with it. Olive plans to "launch" Verena finally with Pardon's co-operation. Ransom has had his best article accepted. They both of course distinguish *their* public role from the world of publicity. They will offer the best article. But I don't think the book allows this kind of distinction final weight. Certainly the climax, with its vulgar public squabbling, can't. The point in Ransom's case is most economically made in the brilliant comic scene with Mrs Luna and Pardon before the Music Hall finale. Mrs Luna finds herself unwillingly providing material for the world of publicity—"What Miss Chancellor's Family Think About It":

> "If you have the impertinence to publish a word about me, or to mention my name in print, I will come to your office and make such a scene!"
>
> "Dearest lady, that would be a godsend!" Mr Pardon cried, enthusiastically; but he put his note-book back into his pocket.
>
> "Have you made an exhaustive search for Miss Tarrant?" Basil Ransom asked of him. Mr Pardon, at this inquiry, eyes him with a sudden, familiar archness, expressive of the idea of competition; so that Ransom added: "You needn't be afraid, I'm not a reporter."
>
> "I didn't know but what you had come on from New York."
>
> "So I have—but not as the representative of a newspaper."
>
> "Fancy his taking you"—Mrs Luna murmured, with indignation.
>
> (chap. 40)

We are surely here meant to relish this mistaken identity because it makes a point about Ransom, which is not Mrs Luna's: that he is not so distinguishable. Ransom of course is taken for "one of us" in various ways in the book. Not the least embarrassing is that lady's way, claiming him as part of her own coarse, wealthy, Europeanized conservatism. He is not the reporter from New York, although in a sense he has from the beginning been gathering material; rather, fluid American character that he is, despite his "stiffness," that is one of his possibilities. Certainly at this stage of the novel he feels himself to be on his way in his own part of the world of publicity.

All this will seem to avoid the main question of Ransom and Verena's mutual love, his desire to remove Verena from this "detestable" world, and his influence in giving her—the first one to do so—a private identity, a sense of a self other than the continuously public self of her upbringing and life, a self, predictably, of a genuine domestic and familial vocation. But it seemed best to come at this in the way I have done in order not to confuse Ransom's public role with Verena's. Ransom doesn't stand for contempt of public life, except in so far as he stands for contempt of life in general, the queer and base mixture; but he is against women's involvement in it. "He had always had a desire for public life; to cause one's ideas to be embodied in national conduct appeared to him the highest form of human enjoyment" (chap. 21). Verena is offered the private life of a public man.

Nevertheless it may be argued that Ransom stands for personal values against the world of publicity. The difficulty with a word like "personal," certainly much used by James, is that it can get a blanket endorsement— what could be of value which was not personal?—which can obscure the complexity of what it is pointing to. The use of the word in "The Art of Fiction" for example, or in the essay on Daudet, is ambiguous, probably contradictory. In *The Bostonians* the word usually operates against the vocabulary of public life. The key moment in the development of the love of Ransom and Verena comes when she says his interest in her is not "controversial" but "personal." Again, Olive's disqualification for public life is that—in Ransom's view, like all women—she takes things too personally, too hard.

One of the simplest readings the book offers is as a backstage drama— will the show go on? The anticipation here of *The Tragic Muse* is relevant but can be misleading. In that complex novel the performing art transcends and transforms the meanness of life, especially women's life, and the meanness of lesser arts, including the art of politics. In *The Bostonians* there is no secure world of discrimination and art, the actresses are more likely to be "variety." But there is this powerful element in the novel of a felt need to escape from the confinement of the personal, from private sensation, into contact with "life," especially the life in "the social dusk of that mysterious democracy." "I'm sick of the Back Bay," cries Olive.

It may be objected that, in noting this markedly Hawthorne-like aspect of the novel, I am really generalizing from Olive's particular "problem" as wealthy guilty spinster, and in doing so possibly confusing the private, in terms of isolation, with the personal, with its necessary additional "relationships." Certainly what the novel does and was intended to do is to show "one of those friendships between women which are so common in New England." This relationship is in different ways "life" for both women, and it may be supposed to be a perverse version of the personal, disguised in the language of self-sacrifice and dedication. But this is rather stale ground, that of public activity and reform always being definable in terms of indirect or thwarted "personal" desires.

But are we then to assume that the love of Verena and Ransom is "really" personal in some sense?—heterosexual being better than lesbian, in spite of its grotesque variants in the book such as the Farrinders ("and his name was Amaria"), or Selah Tarrant's "association" with Ada T. P. Foat?

Eventually it comes to the question of the nature of the relationship, the union. And uncertainties and forebodings about that do not spring from the novel's grim last sentence alone: "It is to be feared that with the union, so far from brilliant, into which she was about to enter, these [tears] were not the last she was destined to shed." If this is the most substantial relationship in the book (although one would have to say that the Olive–Verena affair is the more subtle, also involving as it does a rationale of free union), it is because it takes up and confirms what all other "unions" point to: dominance for one partner, defeat for the other. That is the force of sexuality in the novel. Olive's sense, which James delicately guesses at, of Verena exhibiting women's "hideous weakness—their predestined subjection to man's larger and grosser insistence" (chap. 39) agrees with Ransom's attitude toward Verena (beneath his politeness): "she was tremendously open to attack, she was meant for love, she was meant for him" (chap. 36).

But the sexual sense of "personal" in this relationship combines with the public as well as being opposed to it. Over another "queer" American private life, another "fiasco," looms the encompassing fiasco of the Civil War, the war of union, with the lurking irony of Ransom's championship of "minority rights." And it is Ransom's dedication to a cause, his forlorn but powerful hope of public success, that is part of his persuasion of her.

It is typical of the novel's procedure that this persuasion takes place in public (all their courting is done this way, except for those limited hours in

Marmion), in the characteristic American scene of Central Park, under the gaze of the unemployed, "the children of disappointment from across the sea." It's the first time that Ransom lets go his bantering tone and speaks sincerely, from the stomach as it were—he is virtually unemployed himself at this time. She is partly won, as I have already suggested, by oratory, greater public conviction. For her to submit in that way is not surprising—it is not after all so odd a match for a daughter of the lecturing-circuit to make.

James thought of naming the novel after her, but who is Verena? Verena is a great creation, she makes *The Bostonians* plural in its greatness, gives the novel a compensating and complementary generosity along with its sardonic and satirical verve. Sometimes it is the idea of her that is great, rather than the embodiment. James does not always know how far to go with her or how much sceptical qualification to introduce. But even these reservations pick on something almost necessary to her presence.

Who she is is really part of the question of whom she is taken to be, whom she is made to be. She enters the book as the passive instrument of her father, and leaves "enslaved" by Ransom. "She had always done everything that people asked," "it was in her nature to be easily submissive, to like being overborne." Like Priscilla in Hawthorne's *The Blithedale Romance* she waits to be possessed, to be created. But that parallel is immediately disturbing. Hawthorne's "gentle parasite" draws on the energies of other people. Verena's submission, sexual or otherwise, involves her as a source of energy, a capturable vitality.

For Olive she is "life," particularly the life, "the romance of the people." She is that "poor girl" Olive has been looking for, whom she will raise, and who will answer that need "to know everything that lies beneath and out of sight." In her first appearance in the novel she is eager and restless, "not a quiet girl." With her extraordinary red hair and bizarre dress (James shows her interest in dressing up at several points in the novel) she appears "theatrical," but "naturally theatrical." Her performance at Miss Birdseye's is "fresh" and "pure," "an intensely personal exhibition." For Ransom

> the necessity of her nature was not to make converts to a ridiculous cause, but to emit those charming notes of her voice, to stand in those free young attitudes, to shake her braided locks like a naiad rising from the waves, to please everyone who came near her and to be happy that she pleased.
>
> (chap. 8)

"All her desire was to learn" and "she was ever-curious about the world." She had "no particular feeling about herself; she only cared, as yet, for

outside things." As you came to know her "you would have wondered immensely how she came to issue from such a pair" as the Tarrants.

To Olive (in an unusually socialist moment):

> she was so strange, so different from the girls one usually met,
> seemed to belong to some queer gipsy-land or transcendental Bo-
> hemia. With her bright, vulgar clothes, her salient appearance,
> she might have been a rope-dancer or a fortune-teller; and this
> had the immense merit, for Olive, that it appeared to make her
> belong to the "people," threw her into the social dusk of that
> mysterious democracy which Miss Chancellor held that the for-
> tunate classes know so little about, and with which (in a future
> possibly very near) they will have to count.
>
> (chap. 11)

Verena "had moved her as she never had been moved."

She was also "a creature of unlimited generosity" who "never held
back." Her "gift" was a mystery, "dropped straight from heaven"—nothing
to do with her awful parents, her "queer" life and background. She has
survived that "perfectly uncontaminated, and she would never be touched
by evil" in spite of announcements like "I prefer free unions." She smiled at
everyone, she "likes the individual."

There is a "characteristic raciness of speech" in her. She is "the most
extraordinary mixture of eagerness and docility," her success is "simply to
have been made as she was made." Olive welcomes her as an innocent "flower
of the great Democracy," without vulgarity, coming from "the poorest, hum-
blest people," "the very obscure," the only persons "safe" from vulgarity.
Yet she is "miraculous," a "whim of the creative force." "There were people
like that, fresh from the hand of Omnipotence" (chap. 15).

She flirts, or rather this is "the subtle feminine desire to please." "There
were so many things she hadn't yet learned to dislike." She represented "the
consummate innocence of the American girl." "The very stones of the
street—all the dumb things of nature—might find a voice to talk to you"
(chap. 17). She enables both Olive and Ransom to speak. She wants to "intellectually command all life" but she is not "naturally concentrated" like
Olive. She jokes—turns the sacred formulae of feminist success into pleasantries. She is of "many pieces," "irresponsible," but she can "kindle, flame
up . . . resolve herself into a magical voice, become again the pure young
sybil." In entering the partnership with Olive she was attracted by "the vision
of new social horizons, the sense of novelty, and the love of change." She

"put forth a beautiful energy." She lacks pride, she is "free from private self-reference."

> her bright mildness glided over the many traps that life sets for our consistency . . . everything fresh and fair renewed itself in her with extraordinary facility, everything ugly and tiresome evaporated as soon as it touched her.
>
> (chap. 20)

Under Olive's care she "assimilated all delicacies and absorbed all traditions." She could "do anything she tried."

Mrs Luna thinks her a third-rate adventuress, "trash." At his second meeting with her Ransom finds she has a "fantastic fairness," she is an actress making a "scene" of anything. She has a natural oratory and the "air of being a public figure," but in this she is "genial" not "dogmatic." She was "honest and natural" but with "queer, bad lecture-blood in her veins . . . a touching, ingenuous victim, unconscious of the pernicious forces which were hurrying her to her ruin" (chap. 26). She is like an actress or singer, an "improvisatrice . . . a chastened, modern, American version . . . a New England Corinna."

She is "meant for love." She has a great power of enjoyment, she responds in New York to "the infinite possibilities of a great city." She was made to enjoy rather than suffer, there is the "epicurean" in her, the impulse to "live only for the hour." She proves "by the answering, familiar brightness with which she looked out on the lamp-lighted streets that, whatever theory might be entertained as to the genesis of her talent and her personal nature, the blood of the lecture-going, night-walking Tarrants did distinctly flow in her veins" (chap. 31).

She resists protection: "I must take everything that comes. I mustn't be afraid." She is "a good thing" to get hold of, "the latest thing," someone who "might easily have a big career," "an article for which there was more and more demand" (an intellectually third-rate article in Ransom's opinion). Ransom tells her, "I don't know where you come from nor how you came to be what you are, but you are outside and above all vulgarizing influences" (chap. 34).

As the book nears its close James himself takes up her analysis much more, writing of "her peculiar frankness" and "the extraordinary generosity with which she would expose herself, give herself away, turn herself inside out, for the satisfaction of a person who made demands of her" (chap. 37). She was "always passion" (whether in love or for the feminist cause), but without a great capacity for suffering:

> With her light, bright texture, her complacent responsiveness, her
> genial, graceful, ornamental cast, her desire to keep on pleasing
> others at the time when a force she had never felt before was
> pushing her to please herself, poor Verena lived in those days in
> a state of moral tension—with a sense of being strained and
> aching—which she didn't betray more only because it was ab-
> solutely not in her power to look desperate.
>
> (chap. 38).

She had only a "hothouse loyalty" to Olive and her cause, and eventually,
like those other poor girls, there was a "Charlie" to take her off.

James's sceptical note in that last extended quotation has its own complexities. The "*light,* bright texture . . . *complacent* responsiveness" are being
measured against Olive's suffering, her capacity to take things too hard. *Her*
morbidity makes desperation always at her disposal. The irony of a force
"pushing her to please herself" is clearer, especially as that "force" has told
Verena that "what is most agreeable to women is to be agreeable to men."

Given that general sense of Verena, however much "of many pieces" it
is, it becomes clearer still that Verena in love with Ransom is a defeated
Verena. Like Fitzgerald's Gatsby, also a "son of God," her discovery of
personal love is limiting and destructive (far more so than the relationship
with Olive). And what it limits or destroys is what James's lyrical tone in
presenting her so often manifests, something personal in a different sense,
her "gift," what is responsive and vivifying in her nature.

And that love, that separable self, is closely related to the repeated
attempts, very evident in the combined impressions of her I have quoted, to
find her "essence," to separate her from her background, her "setting"—her
parents, her class, the world of publicity, the whole vulgar American scene.
She is both representative of the age and uniquely separable from it, and we
are continually watching her in the novel being taken both ways. The comedy
of these attempts is that they keep reopening the satirically settled question
of the American scene. It gives that scene, the "age," a perpetual second
chance. And that chance can't be defined merely in terms of vulgar car-bells
sounding almost silvery. It's the chance of Verena's indiscriminate vision
itself, that power to make all things, including Ransom and Olive, speak, to
make all things live.

This Orphic role, together with other religious and legendary associa-
tions—Minerva, "fresh from the hand of Omnipotence"—however playful,
give her a mythic potentiality. But her human variousness remains dominant.
Her force is not that of a transcendent presence; not so much a second

coming, more an American second chance, a superhumanized possibility, a Whitmanesque "song of myself" and "democratic vista," a creative innocence like that of Huck Finn's, both close to and separate from the world of the confidence trickster and the adventurer.

Her defeat then is naturally associated with the Civil War. It is in the visit with Ransom to the Harvard Memorial Hall that her self-consciousness begins. At the start of this episode her talk—about her attendance at the Women's Convention—is typically gay and earnest: "We had some tremendously earnest discussions, which it would have been a benefit to you to hear, or any man who doesn't think we can rise to the highest point. Then we had some refreshment—we consumed quantities of ice-cream!" And it is also typically impersonal about her success—"it had no more manner about it than if it concerned the goddess Minerva." In Ransom's imagination of the scene she is "ruined," the victim of a hall "filled with carpet-baggers." And it is the intensity of this concern which shows and provokes her discovery: "See here, Mr Ransom, do you know what strikes me? ... The interest you take in me isn't really controversial—a bit. It's quite personal!" (chap. 25).

This new sense of the personal is interrupted by Ransom's contemplation of the Hall, which draws from James one of his most apparently unequivocal passages in the book:

> The effect of the place is singularly noble and solemn, and it is impossible to feel it without a lifting of the heart. It stands there for duty and honour, it speaks of sacrifice and example, seems a kind of temple to youth, manhood, generosity. Most of them were young, all were in their prime, and all of them had fallen; this simple idea hovers before the visitor and makes him read with tenderness each name and place—names often without other history, and forgotten Southern battles. For Ransom these things were not a challenge nor a taunt; they touched him with respect, with the sentiment of beauty. He was capable of being a generous foeman, and he forgot, now, the whole question of sides and parties; the simple emotion of the old fighting-time came back to him, and the monument around him seemed an embodiment of that memory; it arched over friends as well as enemies, the victims of defeat as well as the sons of triumph.
>
> (chap. 25)

Then as their own discussion intensifies, over the question of whether Verena will tell Olive of their meeting, their relationship fits with this heroic American past:

> "I tell her everything," said the girl; and now as soon as she had spoken, she blushed. He stood before her, tracing a figure on the mosaic pavement with his cane, conscious that in a moment they had become more intimate. They were discussing their affairs, which had nothing to do with the heroic symbols that surrounded them; but their affairs had suddenly grown so serious that there was no want of decency in their lingering there for the purpose.
>
> (chap. 25)

We surely connect Verena with this "temple" to youth and generosity, this dedication and sacrifice, exclusively male as it is; and make the connexion not only in terms of her own cause, and the struggle of men and women, but also in what is becoming more serious to her at this moment, the "intimate" personal battle with Ransom and Olive. The Civil War, the war for the Union, elsewhere described as "one of the biggest failures that history commemorates, an immense national fiasco," is solemnized (as it is from this period on in America) with a transcendental generosity, a slightly hollow effort of reconciliation—"the victims of defeat as well as the sons of triumph."

This solemn reconciliation is the setting for Verena's own kind of reconciliation, her "feminine logic": "It is very beautiful—but I think it is very dreadful, if it wasn't so majestic, I would have it pulled down." She objects to the glorification of bloodshed, the male martial sacrament of sacrifice. But she responds, she partially submits, as she will later to Ransom's intensity. As their own intimate battle starts, her own sacrificial role is prepared. And as the chapter proceeds Ransom begins to assert his newly-felt power, his "man's brutality" over her.

The Hall, then, operates both as a solemn memorial of an heroic American past, a past contrasting with a mediocre modern age, and as an ironic image of union. Here as everywhere in the novel the idea of union, whether private or public, leads to conflict, and either victory or defeat. The escape, "after the battle had ceased," is momentary, rhetorical, and delusory, except as death's "sacrifice."

Yet Verena stands for an alternative, not an escape, within the unmemorialized world. She is not after all a heroine. Her thinking is not like Ransom's or Olive's. She *is* superficial, she *is* absurd. "The truth had changed sides." She changes her mind. She "liked herself better." There is something reassuring in that, and in James's refusal to make her "tragic," to go for the full resonance of the innocent child-victim, as in *What Maisie Knew* or even "Daisy Miller." There is nothing sacred in her defeat. There is something reassuringly mean in it, and in her (and their) prospects. If this is loss of innocence it is not *the* loss of innocence. A girl without a setting, or too many settings, too many changes of mind, cannot be that symbolic. Nothing American can be that symbolic.

The solemn temple appears in a different form at the end of the novel. The Boston Music Hall is the final meeting place for the trains of imagery of battle and religious apotheosis, and where they reach their most dramatic, and in some ways most vulgar, expression. Ransom fights his last daring battle of a campaign which has become increasingly desperate. This includes one carefully placed reference to him imagining himself in the role of Lincoln's assassin (chap. 41). Like Olive he is prepared for martyrdom.

The temple of course is dedicated to the world of publicity, to the launching of "the latest thing" into the mediocre age. But that is more Olive's and Ransom's view of it; both conceive of themselves as defying the mob. But it's Verena again who won't allow the reactionary image of the democracy to cohere:

> "And what will the people do? Listen, listen!"
> "Your father is ceasing to interest them. They'll howl and thump, according to their nature."
> "Ah, their nature's fine!"
>
> (chap. 42)

In the brilliantly rendered final fiasco, the refought battle of North and South, Verena's idea persists in the midst of contending parties. There is nothing final about the ending of the novel—we are not sure what will become of the Ransoms. More immediately, we may not be sure what will happen to Olive. "I am going to be hissed, hooted, and insulted." But the people may give her a voice.

In *The Bostonians* James wanted to write "a very American tale," and in looking back at it towards the end of his life he found he had written a very "curious" one. To search for the representative and come up with the curious is characteristically Jamesian. It could be a shorthand for what goes wrong with *The Princess Casamassima*. But it is the achievement of *The Bostonians* to convince of the curiosity of the very American, and, if Verena is given her full value, to celebrate that curiosity, sardonically but also generously.

D. J. GORDON AND JOHN STOKES

The Two Worlds of The Tragic Muse: A Holiday in Paris

One of James's problems [in *The Tragic Muse*] was how to connect the story of the public or political life, and therefore the story of Julia, with the story of art and the life of art. Those objects at the Salon, sculptures in the sunny air where the English visitors are sitting, or pictures hung indoors, can be made to point to both. The absent Julia can, obtrusively, be connected with objects, beautiful objects, by Lady Agnes and Grace; but Nick rejects this offered link between himself and Julia: the taste, the intelligence that brought those objects together was not Julia's but her dead husband's. The Salon shows not a "collection" but objects made by living artists. Through these we are to be led into generalizations, not so much about the worth of those new things as about the conditions that produced them, the conditions which must be available for the life and work of the artist. Biddy, biddable, innocent, offers a first proposition:

> "The subject doesn't matter; it's the treatment, the treatment!"
> Biddy announced, in a voice like the tinkle of a silver bell.
> [All quotations are taken from the Hart-Davis edition
> (London, 1948), chapters 1–12.]

Falling from Biddy's lips this tinkles like a dropped formula, a stock response to the subject/treatment dilemma, coming as though she had learnt it by heart even in the presumably discreet studios where she was allowed to study

From *The Air of Reality: New Essays on Henry James*, edited by John Goode. © 1972 by Methuen and Co., Ltd.

"modelling." Nick brushes it aside, affectionately. His answer to his mother indicates here, among these tangible signs, responses, presuppositions, phrases that are to conduct us through James's principal enquiry:

> This place is an immense stimulus to me; it refreshes me, excites me, it's such an exhibition of artistic life. It's full of ideas, full of refinements; it gives one such an impression of artistic experience. They try everything, they feel everything. While you were looking at the murders, apparently, I observed an immense deal of curious and interesting work. . . . All art is one—remember that, Biddy dear. . . . It's the same great, many-headed effort, and any ground that's gained by an individual, any spark that's struck in any province, is of use and of suggestion to all the others. We are all in the same boat.

Effort and work are what preoccupy Nick. Biddy, though she would like to, does not understand him; and, strolling among those objects, he transposes her jargon, or their mother's vocabulary, into the context of this effort and of the general conditions that must support it. "Ideas"—what Biddy hopes to find for her modelling, the "capacity for ideas" which she hopes she has— are put alongside *application*; her own *trying* becomes *trying seriously*; and definition of the crucial adverb is put into a paradox that translates Lady Agnes's position into its opposite: art is good, or acceptable to Lady Agnes when it is bad, which means when it is the affair of odd hours, a distraction like a game:

> The only thing that can justify it, the effort to carry it as far as one can (which you can't do without time and singleness of purpose), she regards as just the dangerous, the criminal element.

Biddy translates Nick's meaning into *professional*—that is what her mother doesn't want one to become; and Nick accepts the word. Professional is a social definition of what he meant, and could become (with still other social nuances) *work*, something one spends one's life on and tries to earn one's living by: Biddy immediately introduces "Your own work—your painting." But this is a light sense of *work* which Nick rejects, for himself. Painting has never been his *work*: "if it had . . . I should stick to it." A set of terms has been erected, generated by occasion, by this sort of dialogue based on in-comprehension (though in this case, sympathetic); and these are to persist. That a moment has been reached is marked by closing the dialogue and introducing a summary account of Nick Dormer's long transactions with Paris. His awareness of what the exhibits at the Salon stand for involves now the whole city. What he responds to is a manifold, comprising garden, shadows of summer clouds, the white images, provocative, "hard in their crudity," even the rattle of plates in the restaurant. For this too is part of the contagion of Paris, that has always offered so many suggestions in the way of art; and now especially offers—the earlier phrase is repeated—"a sense of artistic life": studios, companionships, youth, "and a multitudinous newness, forever reviving and the diffusion of a hundred talents, ingenuities, experiments." What the artistic life means as an activity is still his preoccupation. He felt that the exhibition "would help him to settle something"; and he associates "the idea of help" with a man whom he sees approaching. This is Gabriel Nash.

There is a major transposition from Nick's terms, *artistic life* or *life of art* and its glimpsed conditions, to *life as art,* with its proposed terms and conditions. Gabriel Nash offers this. Biddy cannot understand Nash, any more than she can identify or place him, except as a "gentleman," or any more than she can identify even the nationality of the two silent women who were with him as they met. She can only try to understand, by finding some named role or formula that will bring Nash somewhere within a known world. Nick's part is to question, to welcome, neither to accept nor deny. Nash appears, as it were, from nowhere, to Nick who has not seen or heard of him for a long time: that he should move in what seems to others—not to himself—a cloud of uncertainty is essential to his full presentation. Nick's questions permit Nash to talk about himself—not in riddles or evasions, as Biddy may think, but in generalizations; for Nash is his own case, his own text, illustrating a new set of rules to live by.

Nash redefines and revalues accepted kinds of human activity, both art and politics, together with the conditions of their practice: he offers another sort of activity—in his definition as final. His premise is a version of what *experience* is; and this involves both the individual and his social relationships.

Nash's refusal to allow that he lives in the nineteenth century, or in London rather than in Samarkand, is the same as his refusal to allow that he either likes or dislikes English art. He is refusing any *formula* or social definition or *generalization*. And this he does in the name of *feeling*. "They try everything, they feel everything," Nick had said of the French artists; and Nash says "We must feel everything, everything we can. We are here for that." Nick's *feeling* had immediate reference to the artistic experience and the work that comes out of it. Nash's *feeling* is absolute, referring to nothing beyond itself: for there is nothing else that we have. In the one life we know, we have only our *impressions. Impressions* becomes the word for what our consciousness is made up of, and these impressions had better be agreeable ones:

> the happy moments of our consciousness—the multiplication of those moments. We must save as many as possible from the dark gulf.

Generalization loses its normal sense and is only admissible as autobiography (what I do)—"My only generalizations are my actions"—and "my behaviour" (what I do) is my feelings. This is not passive acceptance of anything that may come. If *feeling* modulates into *impressions,* and *impressions* modulate into the restrictive *agreeable impressions* ("happy moments"), these in turn are translatable into *the beautiful.* Our *feelings* are *behaviour* because we are capable of "shades of impression, of appreciation," *appreciation* being a faculty we have, "a special sense" that can be trained and extended so that we can get hold of the *beautiful.* With these words, *consciousness, impressions,* and *appreciation* we have a new vocabulary that connects with Nick's as he reflected on the life of art. Nick's question has to be (we are still among the sculptures): What does all this produce? And Nash's answer is, in his terms an inescapable one: he makes himself: "I am a fine consequence." "Are you an aesthete?" Biddy asks. But that is only another name, a definition operating within the social reference which the "I" denies:

> Ah, there's one of the formulas! That's walking in one's hat! I've *no* profession, my dear young lady. I've no *état civil.* These things are part of the complicated ingenious machinery. . . . Merely to be is such a *métier*; to live is such an art; to feel is such a career!

So the major transposition is effected. Such terms refer back to and reverse Nick's relating of the *serious* and the *professional* in the life of art; and refer also to the conditions of the political life. Biddy had introduced that life as an alternative choice to Nash's: Nick's choice to put right wrongs, abuses and sufferings. This has been dismissed as belonging to the *formulas* or the complicated social machines that are opposed to the free movements of the individual consciousness. Politics—returning to the vocabulary of *function,* and to an application that would horrify Lady Agnes—is

> a trade like any other, and a method of making one's way which society certainly condones.

But the *observer*—and thus Nick assigns a known role to Nash—engaged in distinguishing his *shades* must himself be involved in the world of *naming.* Nash agrees: he has his *terminology* (a set of names), and this is his *style* (a word that goes with *appreciation*); but *style* is wholly individual, which means wholly private. To function for the convenience of others means that the names, or signs or style must become grosser; and the shades, which are what truly distinguish, must go. And here the conditions of the practice of art and politics meet. And so too Nash has given up his own art, writing.

Nash has used, for himself, the vocabulary of the critic of art or literature: the notion that *style* is the man reaches its conclusion that style cannot be a vehicle of social relation. He is both in a role—critic, observer—and is denying it. And he does not observe that he is still as fond of generalizations as Nick says he had been while at Oxford. In the name of the final freedom of the isolate consciousness we are offered generally applicable rules for conduct.

Nash, then, reduces the political life to an affair of words, of Nick's speeches coming, like literature, within the orbit of his word "style," and subject to the same condemnation: "style" being essentially private and individual, both politics and literature must suffer corruption because they have to do with communication, with an audience, and so with the convenience of others, and so with the realm of machinery, both operating through names or formulas which, by identifying, thereby falsify. Politics, like literature, is excluded from the realm of doing, of *action*, of the true *métier*, behaviour being feeling; or from the realm of art, for the true *métier* is to *be*: the true work of art (the fine consequence) being myself. When Nash concludes that politics (meaning, this time, being a "great statesman") is "a trade like any other," and a method of making one's way which society certainly condones, "he is taking up *work*" (which itself went with *professional*), which Nick had used as both a description of an essential condition of the life of art and a social definition of the artist's occupation ("my work"—"my occupation"), refusing, as we saw, to accept the word, in either application for himself, as painter.

There are other ways of defining the conditions of the *public life* (or the political life). What Lady Agnes offers as Nash, Nick and Biddy stroll and talk is a version of these conditions that must (as Nash's do) guide our expectations about how this story is to be presented. What Lady Agnes knows is that the inescapable condition of the political or public life is *money*:

> "It's all very well to say that in public life money isn't necessary, as it used to be. . . . Those who say so don't know anything about it. It's always necessary. . . ."
>
> "I dare say; but there's the fact—isn't there?—that poor papa had so little."

"Yes, and there's the fact that it killed him!"

These words came out with a strange, quick little flare of passion.

If Nick is to have money he has to get it from someone. There are two sources, Julia and Mr Carteret. It is left for the graceless Grace to say outright what Nick's marriage to Julia would be for all of them—"she would be so nice to us"—and to assume that "Mr Carteret will always help him." Lady Agnes knows only uncertainties: that she does not really know what Nick is, that his relationship with Julia is not to be taken for granted; that Mr Carteret's bounty depends on Nick being *serious,* of which his marriage to Julia would be a sign: money goes to money.

If Nick becomes rich, Charles Carteret will make him more so.
If he doesn't, he won't give him a shilling.

Lady Agnes does know that Julia and Mr Carteret have existences of their own, but this is only to know that there are limits to the ways in which they can be used. She accepts without hesitation Julia's function in the impending by-election at Harsh, as does Julia's brother, Peter Sherringham, who takes it for granted when he brings the news to Lady Agnes. Their language dangerously assumes and portends a relation of ownership. Julia "undertakes" to bring Nick in. And to pay the bill: "I think that's her idea." "Delightful Julia!" Lady Agnes ejaculated. Julia will leave Paris "for her man." "Her man?"—Lady Agnes's question means more to us than Peter's answer covers: "the fellow that stands, whoever he is; especially if he's Nick." Neither the naked cash basis, nor the sort of relationship this involves, affects for a moment Lady Agnes's version of the value of the political or public life. For her this value is wholly comprehended in Nick's relationship to his father, which is the relationship to a *name*: "One of the greatest, simply." And Lady Agnes's version will be expanded to become one of the kinds of *tradition* with which the novel is concerned.

"Poor Julia, how you do work her!": this is Nick's recognition that his mother and sister have cast Julia for a specific instrumental role, which would imply that he, in his turn, is to serve Julia's purpose, and demonstrate the conditions of his political life. "'Julia wants me? I'm much obliged to her!' . . . 'Where's the money to come from?' 'The money? Why, from Jul—' Grace began, but immediately caught her mother's eye." *Harsh* as a name is a joke to Gabriel Nash, but its realities are harsh enough for Nick, and for the English system. "It belongs very largely to my cousin, Mrs Dallow." "But I thought we had no more pocket boroughs" is Nash's immediate translation.

Nash, at this luncheon party, playing his part as visitor from Samarkand, can now go on with his devaluation of the political life. Surely a pocket borough fills your pockets? Surely only a bribe would induce a man to go into Parliament? Accused of thinking politics dreadful his answer is "only inferior. . . . Everything is relative."

It is characteristic of Nash's technique that the particular statement should be offered as an application of the wider generalization, and that this supporting generalization should be put forward as aphorism or epigram, and in a manner that assumes general acceptance, as of a commonplace. By now "everything is relative" as a general measure of value was sufficiently commonplace, as Nash knows perfectly well, but he is playing a familiar role at this moment. And also to introduce this cliché is to bring into action his doctrine of experience, of which that phrase is an essential postulate. It helps him to continue his devaluation of politics, for only that application of the phrase is picked up, by Lady Agnes ("Inferior to what?"); but it will pass into and support the ways in which Nash evaluates art.

One of the purposes of the complex game played around this luncheon table is to establish a major theme: the theatre—actor, scene, play—as art, and in connexions with the political life, with other sorts of art, with questions about experience; and from the beginning, to establish the whole question of the theatre in a situation of dispute and controversy.

That the theatre would eventually come was adumbrated when Biddy, attempting to identify Gabriel Nash, saw him as a musician or an actor, and saw the younger of the two women with him as a dancer. The luncheon-table conversation opens formally with a life/theatre comparison from Nash. Tactically, this leads straight to money—"The world isn't got up regardless of expense"; it also introduces a theme in his doctrine of experience: an economical stage procession shows the same figures appearing again and again, and this is an analogue for the "repetition" and "recurrence" that we haven't yet abolished "in the study of how to live." This is another way of talking about "moment" or "moments." The actual theatre comes in through Nash's first account of those unexplained women, and passes immediately from the individual case—the girl wants to go on the stage—into generalizations so extreme that they enclose all the positions that Nash and Peter Sherringham will in due course state and enact. Nash is not helping the girl because he considers the theatre "the lowest of the arts"—although the *Théâtre français* is a greater institution than the House of Commons:

> "I agree with you there!" laughed Sherringham; "all the more
> that I don't consider the dramatic art a low one. On the contrary,
> it seems to me to include all the others."

Those great polemical assertions made—Nash acknowledges them as a "view"—Peter's are kept till later for formal restatement. Lady Agnes seizes on what she understands: it is really better for a gentleman to be an actor?

> Better than being a politician? Ah, comedian for comedian, isn't the actor more honest?

What a gentleman is to do is a question that Julia Dallow is soon to ask Nick. In answer here, Lady Agnes can only invoke Nick's "great father"— for that image is the only value she knows in the realm of political action, the assumptions of class and family being her furthest generalizations. Nick's response is partial and only a *perhaps,* but he accepts Nash's predicated value: his own father was "an honest man," and perhaps that is why he could not endure (or died of) the political life. Actor and politician have this in common, that they can only function in relation to an audience; that to catch this audience both speak and feign "parts" that have been written and devised for them by others—they must be what they are not. *Honesty* is in relationship to "part" and words and audience; the actor sets out to deceive no one (to interpret Nash); the politician's art, if he would succeed, is to deceive, radically. The comedian is the more honest man, yet *comedian for comedian* devalues both activities. Nash allows the actor more grace, certainly, but just a little more, and in this comparison.

Acting and its conditions (the theatre) are to become the central paradigmatic instance of the artist's life, with all those questions about how the actress becomes an actress, what she brings, and what she must acquire; and this must involve enquiry not only into the formation of the actress, but into what James, fascinated by the problem, called elsewhere the *nature d'actrice;* and brings too an enquiry, which James would not have admitted to be either separate or grander, into what the actress *does,* and what her art achieves: into, that is, the nature or meaning of her art, and into those necessary limitations which are imposed by those very conditions—the theatre depending as it does on several fixed relationships under which, as things are, it is practised. Those skirmishes, tentative beginnings, at the luncheon table are to prepare us for the general and special developments of Nick's concern with the life of art and with Nash's rejection of art. Nash has already moved into position about the theatre and so has Peter Sherringham: these topics are to be in their hands.

They turn, these topics, on two women: on the aspirant actress, Miriam Rooth, the younger of those two women who walked with Nash among the sculptures and whom he so rapidly got rid of; and, counterposed to Miriam, the great achieved artist, the aged Carré, of the *Théâtre français,* whose past is legend, whose present is still potent, and who is to be brought together with Miriam when she hears the young woman "say" something, so that she can pronounce judgement on her.

The tale of the Rooths is Gabriel Nash's; and it will serve more than one purpose. There is his report of Mrs Rooth's account of her splendid origins. This is fiction: Mrs Rooth has as much to do with truth as her daughter (who will have a good deal to do with it) will have to do with ruth. If Mrs Rooth's tale were true—it interests Lady Agnes—it would perhaps be less important for the aspiring actress than what Nash has learned or inferred about the facts. These have to do with Miriam's formal education—mostly bits and pieces of languages picked up during mother and daughter's cheap peregrinations through Europe; and we are to take this with Nash's confident claim that Miriam is stupid. And, more importantly, these facts have to do with Miriam's inheritance. Biddy, at first sight, had imagined Miriam as a particularly violent dancer; and Miriam has this of the Old Testament about her (and perhaps, proleptically, more, for Miriam, the sacred dancer, offended the Lord by conspiring to betray his servant, and was smitten by leprosy), that her Christian name indicates her father's faith: his surname had been Roth; and Miriam is half a Jewess. Of her name Peter Sherringham says immediately: "It is as good as Rachel Félix"—and so Rachel, the Tragic Muse of painters and writers, first appears: that child of a Jewish pedlar, trailed across Europe, uneducated, whose legend is to be so powerful a presence, a reference for achievement and a touchstone for theory. With Rooth's Jewishness went a taste for collecting (Julia Dallow's husband had it, on a grander scale), and some skill in music ("like most of his species"); in fact he had the *artistic temperament*; but this phrase is given to Mrs Rooth, which puts its seriousness in doubt, and James uses it very gingerly as an explanation or description of the artist's nature. But there is no doubt that this paternal and racial inheritance was to count for Miriam.

The exchange turning on Carré is explicitly put forward as a rehearsal of currently familiar positions. Thus Nash accuses Sherringham of using the language of the *feuilletons,* and Sherringham accuses Nash of using an attitude and arguments in vogue among the *raffinés.* Sherringham particularly refers to Nash's insistence on the poverty of the modern dramatic form, as compared with the novel.

The older dramatists, Nash argues, had an easier task: to represent a simpler civilization in which man expressed himself directly and violently in action and passion. But today "What can you do with a character, with an idea, with a feeling, between dinner and the suburban trains?" Nash is, in part, defining "modernity" in the sense of what the modern dramatist has to deal with. He is also giving a reason why the achievement even of a Carré must be limited. When Sherringham says that to watch her was

> an education of the taste, an enlargement of one's knowledge

we are certainly to believe him, but we are also to believe Nash's rejoinder:

> She did what she could, poor woman, but in what belittling, coarsening conditions! . . . The dramatist shows us so little, is so hampered by his audience, is restricted to so poor an analysis.

Even a Carré is limited, like the dramatist, by what he calls "the essentially brutal nature of the modern audience." "Theatre" is tending to split into two: here Sherringham's concern is for *acting*, Nash's for what the actor has to work with.

Nash's attack on the actual conditions of theatrical performance (even his reference to the time-tables of the last suburban trains), which mark the infrangible limits of the dramatist's (and therefore of the actor's) art, is anything but new or esoteric. Yet it can serve as a consistent extension of his earlier declarations. The criterion of theatrical representation is *success*: there are not many bad actors because most of them succeed in "that business," "more easily and completely than in anything else." Such success—money or satisfied vanity for the actor, or just money for managers and stage carpenters—depends wholly on giving the gross audience what it wants. The theatre is indeed "a commercial and social convenience." But the repetition of that word *convenience* and this insistence on the theatre's corrupting dependence takes us back to Nash on the art of writing, or the life of politics—which were condemned for precisely this same reason: the inevitable corruption of those other dealers in words, through the audience which they who properly exist as individuals are tied to—and tied therefore to the realm of convenience, formulas, generalizations.

Nash has another, equally consistent, version of why he has to come to reject the theatre, but this position is more radical, for it carries forward Nash's basic doctrine of experience. This step comes in the shape of still another generalization, turned by repetition into a formula. Nash first met the Rooths when Mrs Rooth was selling off her husband's objects. Those included pots, and at that time Nash was collecting pots. "It was a little phase—we have our little phases, haven't we? . . . and I have come out on the other side." And of his earlier enthusiasm for the theatre he says:

> Oh, I used to be of your way of feeling. . . . It's a phase like another. I've been through it.

This connects with "everything is relative"; and *phase* is an extension of *moment* or *moments*. Repetition or recurrence is fatal: happy *moments*, or a *phase*, had their value, but cannot retain it. We must move on: the moments must be multiplied.

Nick's admonition to Biddy that "all the arts are one" had specific reference to the artist's necessary effort to carry his art further, and had involved no direct comparison between what artists *make*, with paint or stone or words. Peter's assertion that the "dramatic art" includes all the others had been left unelaborated except for his justification of Carré; and that rests on a certain assumption about the unity of the arts based, like Nick's, in terms of effort, and on one, but not the only view of what the actor actually does.

> It's not easy . . . to produce, completely, any artistic effect . . . and those that the actor produces are among the most moving we know.

Part of the argument that Sherringham needs he offers to Nick after lunch as they stroll by themselves, aimlessly, through the streets. Nash had first used *represent* about what the dramatist does, and in its general sense of "shewing forth" (drama as "mirror" of its age). This is the word Sherringham uses as the basis of his argument, applying it, however, principally to the actor's art (the dramatist provides material for him to work on):

> I am fond of representation—the representation of life: I like it better, I think, than the real thing. You like it, too, so you have no right to cast the stone. You like it best done one way and I another; and our preference, on either side, has a deep root in us. There is a fascination to me in the way the actor does it, when his talent (ah! he must have that!) has been highly trained (ah! it must *be* that!). The things he can do, in this effort at representation (with the dramatist to give him his lift) seem to me innumerable—he can carry it to a delicacy!—and I take great pleasure in observing them, in recognizing them, and comparing them. It's an amusement like another: I don't pretend to call it by any exalted name; but in this vale of friction it will serve. One can lose one's self in it, and it has this recommendation (in common, I suppose, with the study of the other arts), that the further you go in it, the more you find. So I go rather far, if you will. But is it the principal sign one knows me by?

This is formally set out: the generalizations offer that restricted part of the argument about the unity of the arts that the novel will most require. They insist, again, on the process of *doing,* and introduce terms relative to this (*talent, training*)—which are almost immediately to be picked up in the case of Miriam—and relative to the critic's activity (*observe, recognize, compare*), which Peter claims for himself; and they offer no *justification* for the taste—it is more than this—for one or other kind. The vital suggestion that the "representation" may be preferred to the "real," is informally, almost casually, brought in.

This formal explicit argument is constructed to introduce the first formal explicit statement of Nick's situation:

> The idea of representation fascinates you, but in your case it's representation in oils—or do you practice water-colours too? You even go much further than I, for I study my art of predilection only in the works of others. . . . You're a painter, possibly a great one; but I'm not an actor.

Peter's argument is a piece of self-defence; the accusation he thinks he has to meet, which forces him to the formal statement and to its application to Nick, is an extension of the concern with *naming* or *identification.*

This begins with questions about Gabriel Nash ("He sounds like an Elizabethan dramatist," Peter says) and what he is: an ass, in Peter's version, or a real case for enquiry into what might prevent "the whole man from being as good as his parts," in Nick's. So to the luncheon dispute about the theatre, and Nick's

> the old sign one knew you best by: your permanent stall at the *Français.*

and to Peter's argument, and to his final question, repeating Nick's phrase as a question. In language—used however lightly—that associates him with Nash and the critics ("I ought to discriminate . . . I always want the further distinction, the last analysis"), Nick answers yes. And the dialogue is brought to a conclusion through a return to Nash, which is a return to the problem of defining him (or distinguishing him).

> Most people have a lot of attributes and appendages that dress them up and superscribe them, and what I like him for is that he hasn't any at all.

Sign, superscription: holy writ has been called in to extend the vocabulary available for proofs or tokens of identity. Peter's self-justifying declaration, which is also a way of asking by what sign Nick is best known, leads into brief companion biographies of the two young men, held up till now so that they should go with this revealing formal declaration: from indications we move to statement.

The biography of Nick is not simple. It is a comment on the conditions and values of the political, or public, life, in a specified English setting.

Political life is a function of family and class situation, and in turn guarantees that situation; it can only be exercised through money and can bring safety through money or alliance with money. Lady Agnes has already shown, vividly, that she knows this. Nick's great father—that great name— was a younger son; he had inherited baronetcy and property from his elder brother; Nick himself is the younger son. Bricket, "that moderate property," is in the hands of his elder brother; that "pleasant white house" (no great house of stone, let alone marble) is let, while the heir neglects his family and devotes himself to big-game shooting: an occupation approved of by a society which the narrator—the tone is plain—does not approve of. Lady Agnes's jointure is not "an incitement to grandeur." There is no dower house for her and her daughters, and no proper town house; she has to live in Calcutta Gardens, in a "gabled, latticed house in a creditable quarter, though it was still a little raw, of the temperate zone of London." This, in London, and dated by the speculative builder's name, is the precarious edge of the world; largely dependent on Mr Carteret's "convenient cheques," it is to be "in a general way" his mother's and his sister's "providence," as Mr Carteret is his. Lady Agnes's anxieties are real. The Dormers are in danger.

That the political life is proper to a gentleman is, we know, the limit of Lady Agnes's generalization; the content and value of the activity lie in its connexion with—and this would include the family—Nick's duty to maintain his father's name: which is also a kind of property he would bring to a contest in Harsh, balancing—in his mother's eyes—Julia's gifts. What Nick's father actually *did* to achieve "greatness" we are not quite clear about: to leave us uncertain, and to define the achievement through Mr Carteret, or newspaper allusion or other report, are ways both of reducing the political life and of relating it socially—indirectly to class and directly to the media of publicity.

Mr Carteret's generosity to Nick (but Lady Agnes has already foretold its terms) springs from devotion to the great name: he has nothing more real (except his money).

> He had never married, espousing nothing more reproductive than
> Sir Nicholas's views (he used to write letters to *The Times* in
> favour of them).

That parenthesis suggests, again, that politics is an ephemeral verbal activity, and the summary of Nick's first success also gives this:

the fresh cleverness of his speeches, tinted with young idealism and yet sticking sufficiently to the question (the burning question, it has since burnt out). . . . There had been leaders in the news-papers about it.

The death-bed scene, when father dedicates son to the carrying on of his work, is treated in just the same way. We learn of it indirectly. Lady Agnes knew that Sir Nicholas's charge had been

a solemn communication of ideas on the highest national ques-tions (she had reason to believe he had touched on those of ex-ternal as well as of domestic and of colonial policy). . . . It was work cut out for a lifetime, and that "co-ordinating power in relation to detail," which was one of the great characteristics of Sir Nicholas's high distinction (the most analytic of the weekly papers was always talking about it), had enabled him to rescue the prospect from any shade of vagueness or ambiguity.

The streets of Paris meant Nick's last hours of freedom, he felt. Later, with Julia Dallow, he comes out to the boulevard and to Paris at night: crowds, lights, sounds, "tokens of a great traffic of pleasure, that night-aspect of Paris which represents it as a huge market of sensations." Light and murmur, through the windows of Julia Dallow's sitting-room, accompany Nick's di-alogue with her. But she cannot interest herself except for a moment in all this. She is "awfully tired" of the city; to visit France for her is to transfer a social life from one place to another, and her France is never cut off from London, the true centre of activity, or from Harsh; and these both mean political activity.

When Nick is eventually alone with Julia he has to tell her that he will gratefully accept the chance of standing for Harsh; and their dialogue is part of his enquiry into the gracefulness of her mind, and into the relationship between her imperiousness and her generosity. He will try to find out whether Julia has any more notion of what the political life means than, for example, his mother has; and this will involve the other question.

Julia aligns herself with Mr Carteret in the world that Lady Agnes recognizes. And though Julia does not like Nick to compare her with Lady Agnes, whom from the security of her riches she can patronize and organize, it is there that she belongs; for Lady Agnes, anxious now, dependent in her meagre substance, had shown high competence—"ideas"— in the organization of the public life of a public man. Julia's price for making Lady Agnes's stay in Paris comfortable (carriages and presents) is the silent expectation that the Dormer ladies will do precisely what they are told. In politics *winning* is Julia's concern; and she will expect to be paid for her help, just as much as Mr Carteret will for those cheques that will meet the election expenses. Julia's payment will come as *success*: the success that will make her mistress of a successful political salon. For that, Nick tells her, is what she really wants, because she, no more than Lady Agnes, has "an idea . . . to call an idea." And *serious* and *work,* words that for Julia belong to the business of winning the election, are according to the usage of Lady Agnes, and not according to Nick's reference of them, in that first dialogue with Biddy.

Elections are won by making speeches (and by newspaper reports that degrade even the speeches). Nick is good at this activity:

> "I've got the cursed humbugging trick of it. I speak beautifully. I can turn it on, a fine flood of it, at the shortest notice. The better it is the worse it is, the kind is so inferior. It has nothing to do with the truth or the search for it; nothing to do with intelligence, or candour, or honour. It's an appeal to everything that for one's self one despises," the young man went on—"to stupidity, to ignorance, to density, to the love of names and phrases, the love of hollow, idiotic words, of shutting the eyes tight and making a noise. Do men who respect each other or themselves talk to each other that way?"

Nick himself has been evasive enough, or playful, or oblique, or tangential, about both politics and art; but this speech here is a passionate declaration, not patient of any ambiguous reading. And the verbal art is still further reduced; words are not even *names* and *phrases,* they compose an idiot's tale of what is *hollow,* merely *noise.*

Julia, reaching after "ideas," can only answer with unexamined words that might well come from a speech or an editorial, only to find Nick translating them into the reality or meaning of a situation. Her "the good of the country" turns out to mean keeping the Tories out, and helping to prevent them doing whatever it is they want to do; and this is really what our organized political game is all about, whichever party is playing it. Her "the simple idea that one ought to do something or other for one's country" Nick brings down to the irreducible reality of the individual act: "there is one thing one can always do for his country, which is not to be afraid." Her "when it's for the country . . . for *them*" as justifying the use of other people's money to meet expenses receives the disenchanted answer "when they get it back"—as Mr Carteret and Julia will, in their ways. Realizing that they have been speaking different languages Julia finally asks

Pray, isn't a gentleman to do anything, to be anything?

Doing and *being* are bound together, and the doing defines the being. But the *doing* means for Julia aspiring "to serve the State"—which Nick renders (and we need not avoid the ambiguity of his word) as "to make his political fortune." Lady Agnes would have recognized Julia's words. Nick's parting suggestion that there are other ways of *doing*, that he, for example, is very fond of painting, gets only a gesture refusing to take him seriously. But Gabriel Nash had already raised the question of *being* and *doing*.

Carré has been renowned for half a century: she is Art itself, defined in a certain way, conscious of this, wholly confident that there is no other. Against the questions or innocuities of Mrs Rooth, Carré stands four-square, stable, "classical" or historical as the Maison de Molière (or the Maison Carré). We approach her through history: the walls of her drawing-room are hung, as though it were a theatrical museum, with a lifetime's trophies, letters, or gifts, or wreaths, or diadems. Gabriel Nash wanders round looking at them. Nick sees her early portraits and wonders curiously how she manages to have been alive then, and alive now. Peter knows what this and Carré mean. She is art as tradition, taught and transmitted by master to pupil: Carré's art and her most celebrated parts go back to a great comédienne of the early years of the century. She also, by her survival, testifies to his theory that the actor's art is now in decadence, going down into vulgarity. The narrator, himself, establishes for us the final limits of this art and life and history—the little room is a museum, but there is something missing from it: "clappings which . . . could now only be present as a silence." This version of the life of art at its greatest is "the history of a mask, of a squeak, a record of movements in the air." A skull placed here in the formal composition is to remind us, in the presence of greatness, both of Carré's insistencies on what this art's instruments are, and of its transitoriness. She *is* insistent: she understands perfectly; in her way she is as rigid as Lady Agnes or Julia, as dependent on definition; but this may be—the question will expand—a necessary condition of the life of art.

Nick is almost embarrassed to hear the kind of life that Miriam might lead discussed in the girl's presence, but he reflects that the echoes of such discussions seem to linger "in the egotistical little room." The general questions, that is, are considered by Carré either not at all, or as having been settled once and for all, or as having to do only with the single question of

what the girl's potentialities as an artist are. There is a turning of discussions
we have heard before, but with a new specificity of application. The large
questions come from Mrs Rooth, who cannot separate the notion of her
daughter's becoming an actress (she knows the pressing need) from questions
about "life" and conduct; and these will find a form in that Paris/London
contrast which the very presentation of Carré is also designed to indicate.
On one side is the old artist whose Paris may be going, on the other the
mother, whose age is as indeterminate as her origins, whose London is certainly unreal: lies, fantasy, ambition. Between the two women, the three men
offer attitudes whose differences are also set out through reference to the
cities.

> You mix things up, *chère madame,* and I have it on my heart to
> tell you so.

When Madame Carré says this to Mrs Rooth she is bringing out that
she knows perfectly well what the essential point in their relation is. She
goes on:

> I believe it's rather the case with you other English, and I have
> never been able to learn that either your morality or your talent
> is the gainer by it. To be too respectable to go where things are
> done best is, in my opinion, to be very vicious indeed; and to do
> them badly in order to preserve your virtue is to fall into a gross-
> ness more shocking than any other. To do them well is virtue
> enough, and not to make a mess of it the only respectability.
> That's hard enough to merit Paradise. Everything else is base
> humbug! *Voilà, chère madame,* the answer I have for your scru-
> ples!

What Carré knows is her *métier.* "Morality" works only within the
métier. Mrs Rooth's worries about respectability—"we are very very re-
spectable"—or about the possibility of her daughter having to represent a
bad woman, or the thankfulness with which she can fall back on Shakespeare's purity: all this is not only silly, it is plain irrelevance. If the English
stage can offer all that Mrs Rooth wants, so much the better for England.
But *"je ne connais qu'une scène—la nôtre."* Nash agrees. Peter agrees, but
thinks something might be done for London. Gabriel Nash, who agrees with
Carré anyhow, is quick to indicate the relevance of what she has been saying
to Nick's situation. Nick, agreeing in his turn that Carré has shown "an
intelligence of the question," is annoyed that Nash should think that the
position is new to him, and proceeds to make his own translation for Mrs
Rooth:

In other words, your daughter must find her safeguard in the artistic conscience.

Mrs Rooth understands neither version. This does not prevent her from uttering her own:

Oh, a fine artistic life—what indeed is more beautiful?

This is rather worse than Biddy's chatter about subject and treatment. Nor does Mrs Rooth mean by "earnest" or "serious" what Carré does.

Carré's generalization is sufficiently central. Here it covers her objections to Mrs Rooth's account of the gifts or accomplishments that Miriam has to offer to the stage, which is the immediate question. Miriam is "educated": she knows English, French, Italian, German. Carré's rejoinder is that in that case the girl had better be a governess: only the right education matters, and one language is enough provided Miriam can speak it. She has, her mother claims, a "voice" of rare beauty; Carré replies

Ah, then, if she has intelligence she has every gift.

Mrs Rooth's answer is that Miriam has "a most poetic mind." To that piece of English mixing-things-up Carré does not even reply.

The history of a squeak, the narrator has warned us. At Carré's first words—she is a red-faced woman in a wig with beady eyes—Gabriel Nash exclaims, "*Ah, la voix de Célimène!*" What Carré is listening for, what she will judge on, what Nick is listening to, is Miriam's voice. The scene enforces this from start to finish. Miriam does very badly. Her training—to the French woman—has been grotesque: a few lessons from a retired English actress and from an Italian tragedian. At the moment her voice is impossible. The problem is whether there is something there, a note, an inflection that could be disengaged. Peter is more willing to find this quality than Carré, but, by the end of the scene, she too is willing to find something—from whatever motives, for it may well be that the old woman believes that Miriam's youth and her beauty and the interest of these young men will assure her a future, anyhow.

This beauty is not obvious. At first sight Peter finds that her face expresses no "sentiment," even her obvious terror shows itself only as a kind of stupidity. But at the same moment he sees that the head is good. "The head is very good," Carré repeats a moment later. The eyes are "fine," "deep," "sombre." When Miriam prepares for the first time to speak a part there is an immediate sense of a great physical presence. Her face now appears "pale and regular, with a strange, strong, tragic beauty." Forcing herself to speak:

she frowned portentously; her low forehead overhung her eyes; the eyes themselves, in shadow, stared, splendid and cold, and her hands clinched themselves at her sides. She looked austere and terrible, and during this moment she was an incarnation the vividness of which drew from Sherringham a stifled cry. *"Elle est bien belle—ah, ça!"* murmured the old actress; and in the pause which still preceded the issue of sound from the girl's lips Peter turned to his kinsman and said in a low tone:

"You must paint her just like that."

"Like that?"

"As the Tragic Muse."

Nick has looked at Carré with the painter's observation, he has been alive to Miriam's possibilities as a model, and he will repeat his hope that she may one day sit for him. At this moment he says nothing. Nor does Gabriel Nash (who is going to spend most of the time looking out of the window). This incarnation has its effect only on the old professional, and on the critic who works within the realm of that profession. Yet for Carré that surprised recognition was not necessarily the recognition of a talent for the stage. Here professional and critic—the latter, in spite of his understanding, is an amateur—are almost on different sides. The "plastic quality" is the only sign of a vocation that Peter can find in Miriam; and this is something he has learnt to distrust. It is a "gift" that may lead to nothing. And he knows that it is something that Carré discounts almost completely as an element of the "histrionic nature," unless it is accompanied by more important attributes. At the extreme, Peter and Carré's dispute has been about the respective contributions of "gifts," which he has championed, and "unwearying study," which she has championed. The test case they had both used was Rachel. Peter had cited Rachel as a pre-eminent example of the great artist made by her "natural endowment." Carré had insisted that Rachel, although she had a voice and an eye, was "essentially formed by work, unremitting and ferocious work." But of course Carré had added, "Rachel wasn't a *bête*: that's a gift, if you like!" This means, in the appropriate vocabulary, that Rachel had "intelligence." About Miriam's "intelligence" Carré is doubtful. It is Mrs Rooth who thinks that Miriam has "ideas": "She gets them from you" is Carré's reply. "Ideas" are certainly what is needed, and go with "intelligence" and not being a *bête*: so far it has been Biddy who hoped to find them. Work, work, practise, practise, is the injunction she leaves her with, whatever future she may see for the girl. It is not she but Gabriel Nash who supposes that the voice, when it's worth anything, "comes from the heart."

At Peter's tea-party Miriam is presented to an English audience, whose standards and knowledge are very different from those of Carré, as Peter well knows; and, given that audience—people whom a rising young diplomat might well, though a shade dangerously, invite—Miriam is a success. This is a general misunderstanding, but for some of those present the occasion also serves to bring out other misunderstandings of which they are hardly aware, or it worsens those already established.

Biddy, who is "immensely struck" by the recital, sees Miriam as a phenomenon that she must try (and Biddy always tries) to understand; but their conversation is about Nick:

> "If your brother's an artist, I don't understand how he's in Parliament."
> "Oh, he isn't in Parliament now; we only hope he will be."
> "Oh, I see."
> "And he isn't an artist, either," Biddy felt herself conscientiously bound to subjoin.
> "Then he isn't anything," said Miss Rooth.
> "Well—he's immensely clever."

When Nash is alone with Julia the misunderstanding, on her part, is total. Nash has already involved himself in Nick's problems, although they have yet to be fully expounded to him. Julia's involvement with Nick is of a different order. It is not enquiring, nor does it "extend tolerances to others." Her affection is of the kind that "isolates and simplifies its object." She is "rigidly direct"; her desires for Nick are an expression of what she desires for herself; that rigidity controls her responses to anyone or anything outside of those particular desires, including Nash. His attack on the recent social pretensions of actors, an extended version of earlier remarks, meets no response. Elaborate discussions of the artistic life, as held at Carré's or, as here, of the lives that artists lead, have for Julia no meaning whatsoever, even when Nash obliquely refers them to Nick. And when her belated enquiry (yet another attempt to place the speaker) "Are you an artist?" receives the apparently unhelpful answer "I work in life," Julia turns away.

This is absolute failure. Other failures are recorded by the application of certain words to certain people, when those words have quite different meanings for the speaker and listener. By the company in general, Miriam is thought to be "clever and successful." She is not. Miriam's comment on Nick, "he isn't anything," is met by Biddy's "he's immensely clever," which hangs in the air. Nash is introduced to Julia by Nick as "one of the cleverest men he knew"; she doesn't find him so. When they discuss Julia, Grace misunderstands Nash by apparently agreeing with him:

> "Ah, she's very charming," said Grace.
> "She's very beautiful," Nash rejoined.
> "And very clever," Miss Dormer continued.
> "Very, very intelligent."

To accord "intelligence" does not advance agreement unless it is known what that person is intelligent about, which requires an agreement about what he is or what he does. Ambiguity in epithet or description is part of ambiguity of identity, and can be resolved only by a definition of identity, or of intention and practice.

Nick has arranged to meet Nash late in the evening and the two young men abandon modern Paris, Haussman's Paris of the *grands boulevards,* the *ville lumière,* for the *quartiers sérieux,* that older, dustier city: here they "look, emphasize, compare." Julia Dallow, to Nash, is a "beautiful specimen" of the English garden flower, a "product" of "high cultivation" and "much tending"; she has the "completeness" that is always satisfying; she will never "understand" him. Nor, Nick says, does he. This is precisely the mark or sign of Nash's relationships: the puzzles are made by those others— it is he who is "simple." He has a "little system" which requires he should be "just the same to everyone"; but *they* depend on the newcomer defining himself by knowing the right password, joining their side, their "camp or religion." He claims—in so far as his mode of qualification, of puzzled self-depreciation allows—that he has

> no interest of my own to push, no nostrum to advertise, no power
> to conciliate, no axe to grind. I'm not a savage—ah, far from it—
> but I really think I'm perfectly independent.

"Little system" is *manner,* this treating everyone in the same way (which may, muddled as we are, seem to be impertinence); that it *is* a *system* in fact relates him—he accepts Nick's challenge—to the rest who also work by system; and Nash will also turn this round (to the politician) by claiming that by his consistent application of it he may become "a perceptible force of good." His system involves the making of no concessions whatever to those who expect him to name and align himself (and he had given up literature because that involved concessions and compromises): he will never concede that "we are only here for dreariness": "modern slang," says Nick, which might be applied to virtue, decency, charity, perseverance, courage, honour. Such qualities Nash does not exclude as part of life. On the contrary, they are *subjects* or materials, like any others: *dreariness* is a matter of *treatment* (or lack of it):

> Life consists of the personal experiments of each of us, and the point of an experiment is that it shall succeed.

What we contribute is our treatment of the material, our rendering of the text, our style. Biddy's parroted formula—which Nick had rejected—is picked up, and sophisticated by extension to include the possibilities of that word "style" (which goes with "manner") which had puzzled Biddy. The first application, here, is to literature, and we ourselves become texts: difficult to read, because a sense of "style" is so rare, but that's no reason why we should not try to write our best (be Macaulays, Ruskins, Renans). *That* is contribution, the "great thing" we can offer. "One has one's form"—that word, too, can pass from one reference to another; and Nash "is not afraid of putting all life" into his, including honour, courage, charity—"I'll only do them good" (Nick has told Biddy that this is what Nash would do for them—like the sculptures in the Salon). "Style," which is "a personal manner," belongs to a way of talking about art. So Nick follows Nash. This is his attempt: art is difficult, there is always more to learn, polishing, refining; but his direction is right, "towards the beautiful." Beauty is really present, concrete, certain, against Nash's games of translation; and Nick gestures to Notre-Dame, rising now in front of the young men: instance and focus of their exchanges, forcing explorations of definitions to what is admission of a dilemma. Notre-Dame is a visual fact, like the streets of old Paris. It is, however, a great deliberated artefact, with the qualities of "simplification" (under the night sky) and "large, full composition." Nick's reference is immediately to the artistic life:

> How it straightens things out and blows away one's vapours— anything that's *done*! . . . The great point is to do something.

"Done" is carried out to its necessary appropriate end: he had left Julia asking whether a gentleman wasn't to *do* or *be* (in her synonyms) anything; and Nash turns the word against him, to the very reference of that scene. Nick can't build cathedrals out of words. The poets do, yes—they make cathedrals out of words, Nick has said. But the vocabulary can be seen shifting again within that fluid bound:

> *Their* words are ideas—their words are images, enchanting collocations and unforgettable signs. But the verbiage of parliamentary speeches!

Great "structures"—Nick adds this word—can be made in materials other than stone, timber, painted glass. The great artefact, immobile yet with, it seems, all the movement of some ship, is there for criticism, admiration, discussion; and there is comfort in Nash's "response," his appreciation, exhibited by his own signs, of the "great effect," the freedom of his "feeling" and the utterance of his "impression," his "natural intelligence of everything of that kind." In the great presence Nick can rest, soothed and joyful, "as if it had been the temple of a faith so dear to him that there was peace and security in its precinct." In a small café, away from the work of art, the dialogue continues: the terms are of those relations and signs that society, or the world, recognizes. Nash "goes about his business, like any good citizen." Nick's concerns are with "do," "accomplish," "do anything," "produce," "go for," with "the old false measure of success," as Nash tells him; with "life," yes, but as so signed and marked. It is again a question of transpositions. Nash's "business" is "the spectacle of the world"; and this is not inconsistent with his search for what in this spectacle is "charming."

> Last year I heard of such a delightful little spot: a place where a wild fig tree grows in the south wall, the outer side, of an old Spanish city . . . I lay on the first green grass—I liked it.

This is "doing" and "accomplishment": it is the accomplishment of happiness through "feelings" and "sensations"—"It's rare to have them . . . I go after them—when I judge they won't hurt anyone." He takes his stand on his "nature" or "disposition"; and on "liberty" which, with "spontaneity" and "enjoyment," goes with "being natural." Nick's open disclosure of his crisis or dilemma is being prepared for—Notre-Dame had been a determining sign for him—but he can only come to it through those other signs or definitions of "life" which Nash transposes, or refuses, outright; and Notre-Dame was a thing "done," in more senses than one. He is—he declares—committed to stand again for Parliament. What he wants is to be a painter—"Isn't that the aesthetic life?" But he would want the "aesthetic life," the "little system" to be identified by those signs that mark the other.

> "There will be precious little beauty if I produce nothing but daubs."
> "Ah, you cling to the old false measure of success. I must cure you of that."

The act is its own justification:

> There will be the beauty of having been disinherited and independent; of having taken the world the free, brave, personal way.

A life effort, certainly; but Nick would not now be satisfied without the visible result: he would want to paint "decently." If he were to produce only daubs, Nash would find him a still more interesting "case." As it is, with all that weighs him down and makes him seem, even to himself, so improbable, so freakish—his Philistine family, his traditions, his training, his circumstances, his career, the effect of his giving it up, even his own prejudices—these are enough to make him "a magnificent case." The last words are:

> "It's her place, she'll put me in. . . ."
> "Baleful woman! But I'll pull you out!"

Peter has already confessed his devotion to the particular art of representation practised by the actor, and, in conversation with Nash and Nick, has countered their generalizations with those of his own. His involvement with Miriam is also to provide him with a case, in two ways. Miriam, first of all, may have talent, and Peter will not resist the opportunity to observe and contribute to her development and training. She is also, he becomes convinced, a fine example of the artistic temperament, the *nature d'actrice*. He will now explore the relationship between talent and temperament, and become increasingly trapped between his admiration for the one and his fascination with the other.

Two full chapters describe this involvement, and indicate the kinds of relationship possible between them; these in turn invoke wider implications about the personalities and habits of actors, and their art of representation. The prime revelation comes early on, but is to be repeated again and again:

> It came over him suddenly that so far from there being any question of her having the histrionic nature, she simply had it in such perfection that she was always acting; that her existence was a series of parts assumed for the moment, each changed for the next, before the perpetual mirror of some curiosity or admiration or wonder—some spectatorship that she perceived or imagined in the people about her. Interested as he had ever been in the profession of which she was potentially an ornament, this idea startled him by its novelty and even lent, on the spot, a formidable, a really appalling character to Miriam Rooth.

This perception is a generalized extension to include the whole personality of his even earlier prophetic distaste for what the actress does, a distaste that he had notably failed to communicate to Miriam. That outburst had related to Nash's equation of politician with actor, in terms of what they are both obliged to become for their respective audiences:

> "You're a strange girl."
>
> "*Je crois bien!* Doesn't one have to be, to want to go and exhibit one's self to a loathsome crowd, on a platform, with trumpets and a big drum, for money—to parade one's body and one's soul?"
>
> Sherringham looked at her a moment: her face changed constantly; now there was a little flush and a noble delicacy in it.
>
> "Give it up; you're too good for it," he said, abruptly.
>
> "Never, never—never till I'm pelted!"

His revulsion coexists with a real, if incomplete, understanding of what the actress aspires to, and how she must learn her trade. "If you see the things to do, the art of doing them will come, if you hammer away. The great point is to see them" The contradictions in his own mind are fed by a susceptibility to Miriam's charm, "communicative, persuasive, familiar, egotistical," which he responds to even when disturbed by its apparent inconsistency. Proof of her devotion to, and understanding of, her art, and her desire to "do what's difficult" he can find; what he looks for is "intelligence," and at times recognizes that essential as part of what disturbs him. "All reflection is affectation, and all acting is reflection." There remains the difficulty of finding in her charm, the excellence of her presentation of herself, signs that she has gained from her varied experience anything other than material for representation.

> He made indeed without difficulty the reflection that her life might have taught her the reality of things, at the same time that he could scarcely help thinking it clever of her to have so persistently declined the lesson. She appeared to have put it by with a deprecating, ladylike smile—a plea of being too soft and bland for experience.

These questions are clearly irrelevant to the immediate concerns of Carré or Miriam herself. They lead Peter finally to postulate "something vulgar in the histrionic conscience," that must be reconciled with his first conviction that

> The actor's talent was essentially a gift, a thing by itself, implanted, instinctive, accidental, equally unconnected with intellect and with virtue—Sherringham was completely of that opinion;

but it seemed to him no contradiction to consider at the same time that intellect (leaving virtue, for the moment, out of the question) might be brought into fruitful relation with it.

By flinching from Carré's uncompromising comments on Miriam's talent, Peter has revealed himself as an amateur among professionals:

she has relieved herself, with the rare cynicism of the artist, all the crudity, the irony and intensity of a discussion of esoteric things, of personal mysteries, of methods and secrets.

This world "of mysteries, of methods and secrets," where hard logical passion is applied to the personal, is where Miriam belongs: she is already professional. But at first Peter can safely observe her, "the spectacle of the young lady's genius," without risk either to his career or his emotions. Those dangers will arise when observation becomes involvement, and even then there are kinds of involvement:

Certainly, however, she seemed to belong to him very much indeed, as she sat facing him in the Paris café, in her youth, her beauty and her talkative confidence. This degree of possession was highly agreeable to him.

The object of dispassionate criticism might easily become a protégé, might even become what he possessed, and the possessed might become the used— "she was the instrument, and incontestably a fine one, that had come to his hand"—or, if the revulsion prove too great, the protected—"give it up."

When Peter ponders Miriam's nature, "affected, contradictious," he does so in terms which we already know.

Was this succession of phases a sign that she really possessed the celebrated artistic temperament, the nature that made people provoking and interesting?

This recalls the language of Nash, and, as before, it is applied to the life of the mind, and invokes a doctrine of experience. Significantly the language returns when Peter and Miriam discuss an actor's diction and manner, what is called his style. Peter is very precise about this: "I mean any style that *is* a style, that is a system, an art, that contributes a positive beauty to utterance." Comparisons are made with Nash, whom Peter describes, despite that person's refusal to admit of any audience, as very like an actor, with his "affectations and histrionics."

We come back to the question of the conscious exhibition of the self that it seems the actor must indulge, which Peter both fears and disapproves of, although he does extol a "personal" style that can be so rarely achieved under the conditions of the modern theatre. The "personal style" is that of an actor alone, unencumbered by the stage carpenter and costumier, and is now to be found only in the poor countries, most of all in Italy—"it's a human exhibition, not a mechanical one." But at the same time we are being led inexorably to a paradox. It may be that even the unencumbered human exhibition requires the multiple personality of the actor. If that is so, then the personal, the essential component of style, must also require the "nature," the feigning honesty. The "nature" might be the natural.

Peter's dislike of the modern theatre recalls that of Nash, because both, for reasons of different and varying complexity, resent the public demands that make up conditions for the practice, and are suspicious even of the practice itself.

> you could afford to be vague only if you hadn't a responsibility. He had fine ideas, but she was to do the acting, that is the application of them, and not he; and application was always of necessity a sort of vulgarization, a smaller thing than theory.

Such alignments of opinion reverberate against each other, and are still part of the strategy of the novel. Apparently similar formulas from opposed or dissimilar characters tell us something about both characters and formulas. Miriam's vulgar "I go in for the book of life" echoes disturbingly, but does not repeat, Nash's remark to Julia, "I work in life."

Miriam, too, is both like and not like her mother, as Peter realizes, for both are concerned with fictions. The mother "took everything for the sense, or behaved as if she did, caring above all for the subject and the romance"; the daughter "hungry for the manner and the art of it, the presentation and the vividness." The one makes "the true seem fictive"; the other's "effort was to make the fictive true."

These speculations of Peter's *are* dangerous, but as long as he is able to preserve his role of critic and contribute only his judgement and knowledge he is, in part, protected. Then Miriam "belongs" to him only as a talent and a potential.

> He reflected ingeniously that he owed his escape to a peculiar cause—the fact that they had together a positive outside object. Objective, as it were, was all their communion; not personal and selfish, but a matter of art and business and discussion.

This is "the pure exorcism of art"; but it is not to last long. Once away from

Miriam and the distancing discussions of technique and business, Peter discovers that he has not escaped: "He *was* in love with her: he had been in love with her from the first hour."

Exploring the labyrinth of Miriam's personality and situation, Peter becomes trapped himself.

The return from Paris, the "huge market for sensations," to England means for Nick fresh confrontations with an inheritance whose images and traditions are to be compared with those of Paris, and the next part of the novel is much concerned with those traditions as maintained by persons and place. But there is repetition and extension of previous matter: the subdued but repeated pun on "represent," and the reappearance of words such as "work" and "success" in other contexts. The practical ramifications of money and its relationship to "freedom" which have so far only been asserted by Lady Agnes, now become her desperate and immediate concern: "What freedom *is* there in being poor?"

The political life is to be devalued in terms of its actualities rather than its inherent possibilities; although the actualities are related to traditions of their own, fallen or mechanical as these may have become. Nick's distrust of his own rhetorical skill may or may not express an absolute valuation of the political life. His "double nature" certainly contributes to a further delay of the great decision, but his versatility and imagination obscure and complicate the value of the opposing claim. It is left open whether or not, despite all this, politics might once have, and might still, present a serious alternative. That conclusion is to be delayed, like many others, until, or perhaps beyond, the end of the novel. For the moment the instances that are offered of the political life, personalities and practices, continue a devaluation already suggested by Nash to an attentive Nick in Paris.

Julia, we have been told, is "rigid and singular." There is now a full concentration on Nick's very different ambiguity, his "double personality," his "sympathy" and his ability to participate in the lives of others. But it is these abilities that direct him towards activity and postponement rather than action. Nick's double nature rises to challenges and the chances for activity, and works well with Julia's compulsive organizing. His tactful suppression of dangerous thoughts that might frighten his mother and Julia is, apart from the occasional hint, consistent. Activity and action predicate different kinds of achievement. The work of the politician is singular, continuous and, given its particular terms, automatic; the work of the artist that Nick is drawn to demands an individual appreciation.

Although these sections of the novel lack the density of reference to be found in those dealing with art, the images and characteristics of the political life are offered as a formal counterpoint, whose inadequacies the seemingly neutral narrator alludes to by a re-application of terms already introduced and an unapologetic exploration of Nick's nature. As before, the transposition of terms and images is a way of bringing two worlds together, as well as revealing their differences.

ROBERT L. CASERIO

The Story in It:
The Wings of the Dove

The adventures of innocence have so often been the material of fiction?
Yes. . . . That's exactly what the bored reader complains of. . . . What
is it but . . . a question of interest, or, as people say, of the story?
What's a situation undeveloped but a subject lost? If a relation stops,
where's the story? If it doesn't stop, where's the innocence? It seems
to me you must choose.
—HENRY JAMES, "The Story in It"

The pleasure of handling an action (or, otherwise expressed, of a
"story") is, . . . for a storyteller, immense.
—HENRY JAMES, Preface to The Tragic Muse

The modern sense of plot ignores a crucial step in Melville's development by overlooking and undervaluing the impulse to plot willful political action in *White Jacket* and by canonizing *Moby-Dick* without paying attention to the narrative and moral meaning of Steelkilt. When we come to the case of Henry James, the modern sense of plot makes us overlook and undervalue even more; it excludes both an accurate view of James's work from *The Awkward Age* on and an accurate understanding of James's career as a revolution in moral and formal allegiances. It has been the assumption of modern criticism that James's novels, especially the last ones, contain scarcely any overt or externalized acts, and that they emblematize what *The Sense of the Past* calls "the force of the stillness in which nothing happened." According to modern criticism stillness is informed, of course, by reflection, by

---

From *Plot, Story, and the Novel: From Dickens and Poe to the Modern Period.* ©
1979 by Princeton University Press.

intensely speculative consciousness, by narrative reasonings seeking detachment from concrete practice. Now it is arguable that consciousness is the only "happening" of consequence, that it is the force of the stillness in which everything happens. James certainly gives us reason to claim the relative insignificance of acts in relation to the effective intellectual, imaginative, or moral "picturing" of them; but my contention here is that increasingly with his maturity he gives us powerful reasons to claim otherwise. What happens as sheer act in Jamesian story enlarges in importance as James grows older, and the force of a reflective stillness, of a kind of narrative reason seeking to contain and inhibit action, turns out to be the characteristic mark of James's *earlier work*. Admittedly, the change is obscured not only by the modern sense of plot but by James himself—by the James of the New York edition, whose prefaces attempt to unify more than thirty years of work, to suppress transitions and discontinuities for the sake of an appearance of consistency. It was perhaps odd of James to make so much of consistency; but it has been more odd for criticism to have followed James's endeavor without raising any questions—until, that is, Laurence Holland began to point out the conflicts underneath the appearance. We need to designate and liberate these conflicts even more. What is at issue is the mature James's evergrowing conviction that the featuring of act in story is of positive importance not just to "the novel" but to any civilization worth the name.

The transformation we can see in James's career is both thematic and formal. He shifts his allegiances from subjects and persons who are valuably innocent by virtue of their freedom from plot, understood as intrigue and action, to those who are valuably experienced by commitment to the intriguing and plotting enactments of story. *The Awkward Age* is a turning point in James's career, for it represents a clear break with values and forms best represented by Christopher Newman and *The American*; by 1899 James is ready to begin attaching supreme value and distinction to the strenuous intriguers, not at all like Newman, who will be the heroes and heroines of *The Wings of the Dove* and *The Golden Bowl*. This change of allegiance and evaluation is the essential moral story in James's stories—the story the prefaces leave us to spell out: the story of a change in James's form complementing the change in his thematics and values.

To designate the narrative modes by which he works, James repeatedly uses four terms in the prefaces to the New York edition: *picture, drama, story, plot*. He appears to use these terms interchangeably, favoring each and all by turns, yet usually reserving his highest praise for *picture*, which, as we commonly understand it, means narrative and intellectual reasoning removed from action. But this praise is misleading and also nervous, for the late novels show not only more honor given to the experience and heroism of action but a complementary shift away from James's favoring of the aesthetic and ethical bearing of *picture*. Under the surface of the employment of the terms in the prefaces—and from time to time even on the surface—a battle is going on among the narrative modes; and I argue that ascendancy in the battle belongs finally to *plot* and *story*, understood as founded on action more than on *picture* and on the still, contemplative reflectiveness of pictorial composition.

James matters immensely because of this transformation in his allegiances. The change seems the result of an urgent social judgment to the effect that modern life not only inhibits adequate reflection but inhibits even more crucially the transformation of intelligent consciousness into the form of externalized, adventurous acts. To James the inhibition of goodness as a realizable and realized form of activity is a great human sadness; and by means of a new commitment to plot and story, the late James insists on the necessary conversion of the good glimpsed by him and his characters into a form of active life. As James comes to see them, both American and English social experience have almost broken down even the possibility of such a form. With the exception of Yeats, the contemporaries of James whom we have considered in chapter 6 [of *Plot, Story, and the Novel*] exemplify this breakdown, for they make prestigious a rebellious, amoral quietism, a dissociation of sensibility or human fineness from the creativity of action. The mature James is characterized by a stubborn struggle against this dissociation—one that much of his earlier great work actually honors.

The shift of allegiance occurs most clearly at the thematic level—in what is represented. But in the prefaces we can see clues to the shift in the usage of the terms designating the modes of representation. As James uses the word *picture*, it seems to mean a striking composition of mere appearances that begins (at least) to lend the appearances form and significance, especially by means of their reflection in a personal center of consciousness. A reflective narrative mode, which explains and amplifies both subjectively and objectively what goes on under the surface of appearances, *picture* appears to be analytic and contemplative narrative reasoning rather than dynamic presentation of acts. Unlike *picture*, *drama* (referred to also as the "scenic" mode) seems exclusively objective representation of appearances. If it is reflective or analytic, it presents the immediate surface simultaneous with analysis, it "make[s] the presented occasion tell all its story itself, . . . shut up in its own presence." *Drama* seems to be a middle term between *picture*, *story*, and *plot*, capable of being synonymous with each of the others (except when *picture* is exclusively subjective). What, then, are *story* and *plot*? James uses them to suggest dynamism and development, the unsettling, uncomposed, and very possibly unreflective presence of will and of "headlong," transformative agencies. He calls *story* "action," does not—as the Russian Formalists do—distinguish it from *plot*, and comments on both honorifically by saying that "story *as such* . . . is ever, obviously, the prime and precious thing."

Just how "prime and precious" is it? Such a comment is at odds with how, in the preface to *The Portrait of a Lady*, it is picture that looks prime and precious, although James ends the discussion of Isabel Archer's story by transubstantiating picture into the other modes. Outside of the prefaces, in the novels themselves, this conversion is not typical of James's mature practice of composition; but the play on the terms in regard to the early novel is instructive as a measure of what happens to the use of the modes later. James begins the discussion of *The Portrait of a Lady* with an organic metaphor: he calls the origin of the novel a germ, suggesting that the subject is a seed in life's garden and that its development is a spontaneous blossoming. James seems only to have to gather the blossom, not to make it grow by a plot, by an active, willful construction of relations. The germ is also, James says, a "fictive picture" of the heroine. The picture

> must have consisted not at all in any conceit of a "plot," nefarious name, in any flash upon the fancy, of a set of relations, or in any of those situations, that by a logic of their own, immediately fall, for the fabulist, into movement.

But what would Isabel Archer *do*, her author remembers wondering.

> Without her sense of [her adventures], her sense *for* them, they are next to nothing at all; but isn't the beauty and the difficulty just in showing their mystic conversion by that sense, conversion into the stuff of drama or, even more delightful word still, of "story?"

Difficult as it is to keep hold of a process undergoing mystic conversions, does this mean in effect that the "fictive picture" remains "picture," even though it also becomes "drama" and "story?" Apparently so, if one understands James to mean that Isabel considered as a fictive picture is an intense center of consciousness, a commanding sensibility. Her sensibility converts adventures—the equivalent in external deeds of mere appearances—into intellectually and ethically *significant* actions. In this instance James identifies significant action with drama and drama with story, calls them by the collective term "portrait," and makes them significant by internalizing them.

Yet the interidentity of the terms, their transubstantiation into picture, true as it is for *The Portrait of a Lady,* is not true for all of James. In late James there is more adventure than his characters' *sense for* it. The important question becomes, "What will picture and plot *together* 'do'?" Late Jamesian story can be seen as the effort at a further conversion. It becomes the attempt to turn purely reflective consciousness (merely contemplative narrative reason) back into meaningful activity as a test and a consummation of *all* meaning and significance and not as only a *means* to significance. If plot, the ally of story, is "nefarious," this is because it demands that consciousness act—and activity is threatening and dangerous. It unbalances and may even betray the insights of composed reflection. A *sense* for adventures does not guarantee that the adventurer will act out the story in the reflective narrative picture easily, honestly, cogently—or at all. Yet, for the later James, the enactment is necessary and supremely creative. Of course once the story is worked out and acted, it amounts to a new picture for the reader who contemplates it. And by means of picture, at the end of a tale James too may stand outside action rather than in it, containing activity within his pictorial frame. Yet the movement of story is less lucid than this transcendent stance. We sympathize with pictorial appreciativeness and lucidity, and need it. But would either reader or author be interested or moved if the activity of the characters and the story did not put lucidity and detachment under attack?

I have been arguing in this book that the ultimate test of significance in narrative reasoning is how significance withstands this attack and how it re-forms itself as action in terms of deed as well as of appreciation and thought. Viewed solely as speculative thought or appreciation, narrative intellectual and moral reasoning is a thematizing of experience that separates what happens from perspectives on what happens—a separation that I believe humbles narrative reason and dangerously separates signs from their referents. The young James saw in this separation only intellectual and moral richness, whereas the mature James comes to believe in a union of signs and referents with action, in a closer wedding of theme and plot; hence, in his later years James comes to favor plot and story, to think them more prime and precious than picture, even at the risk of having to allow the narrative modes to be at war with one another. He acknowledges the conflict explicitly: in the preface to *The Wings of the Dove,* he admits "the odd inveteracy with which picture, at almost any turn, is jealous of drama and drama . . . suspicious of picture." It is not only suspicion but open conflict: "Each baffles insidiously the other's ideal and eats round the edges of its position; each is too ready to say 'I can take the thing for "done" only when done in my way.'" Do plot and story also attempt a further insidious baffling of picture and even of drama? The question is important because James is talking about conflicts among presentational techniques, and yet he is also talking about more. Even "drama" can present the absence of action, but the battle James speaks of is ultimately a conflict over what is more privileged: a way of life characterized by reflective consciousness that is not expressed, or is violated, by action; or a way of life that features action, demands the realization of consciousness as act, and may even demand the temporary loss of clear consciousness for the sake of an act. The battle among the narrational modes is a battle between the ways of life on which the modes are ultimately based.

Although the prefaces name the conflict among the modes, they hide the way the conflict increasingly transforms the content of James's work. The James who writes *The Portrait of a Lady* does believe that a sense *for* adventure is greater than adventure; the James who writes *The Awkward Age* and the late novels thinks the adventure of action makes the most significant sense. If we look briefly at *The American, The Awkward Age,* and the stillborn experiment, *The Sense of the Past,* we can see more clearly how the transubstantiating of the terms does not remain possible for James except in the prefaces, how *picture* in his novels themselves gives way to the priority of *story* in thematic as well as in formal terms.

In the young James there is a characteristic identification of virtuous behavior with a denial of action. Indeed in his early work James insists that the creativity appropriate to Americans is located in their ability to keep free of deeds, in their aloofness from any temptation or provocation to enact plot. The American innocence and the American virtue is a sense for adventure that keeps adventure itself outside and at a distance, framed by a personal consciousness that is itself a shy romance, a subjective satisfaction in the intrigues of others. This kind of consciousness is a personification of Jamesian *picture,* and an examination of James's character, Christopher Newman, offers much insight into this particular pictorial mode of narration.

The crisis in *The American* turns on what Newman will make of the Dickensian plot and intrigue revealed to him as the true history of the Bellegardes. How can Newman's picturing consciousness accommodate itself to the dynamic twists and turns of action initiated by the Bellegardes and written down in the narrative of their misdeeds, which their servant Mrs. Bread offers Newman? Newman first wants to expose the story, even if it is not true. He thinks this will force the family to sanction his marriage to Claire Bellegarde, who is being driven into a convent as a result of her older brother's tyrannical opposition to her wedding with the American. The first person to whom Newman decides to tell his story is a noble friend of the family. But as he sits in this duchess's drawing room, he feels more and more confused. He cannot fit his story anywhere into the conversation, and he abandons his intention: "Whether or not the duchess would hear his story, he wouldn't tell it. Was he to sit there another half hour for the sake of exposing the Bellegardes? The Bellegardes be hanged!" He drifts off to England, then back to America, all the while unsure about what he feels or believes. Hearing that Claire has taken her final vows, he rushes back to Paris, looking like a man "with a plot in his head." Yet he does not know what to do, and at last a few moments in Notre Dame resolve him.

> Somewhere in his mind, a tight knot seemed to have loosened. He thought of the Bellegardes; he had almost forgotten them. He remembered them as people he had meant to do something to. He gave a groan as he remembered what he had meant to do; he was annoyed at having meant to do it; the bottom, suddenly, had fallen out of his revenge. Whether it was Christian charity or unregenerate good nature—what it was, in the background of his soul—I don't pretend to say; but Newman's last thought was that of course he would let the Bellegardes go. If he had spoken it aloud he would have said that he didn't want to hurt them. He was ashamed of having wanted to hurt them. They had hurt him, but such things were really not his game.

He burns the narrative Mrs. Bread has given him.

But it is not so much vengeance as the alliance of conscience with elaborate and determined plot that is not Newman's game. His "unregenerate good nature" finally resists his ability to extend the story of the Bellegardes by means of a plot in his own head. He cannot grasp the reality of their history as it has been revealed to him. To Newman all the Bellegardes have the look of adventurers, of characters who inhabit not life but complicated and fabulous tales foreign to American assumptions and experience. Newman cannot comprehend life as literally plotted or storied, and this in the end keeps him from realizing the image of happiness he had projected for himself. And he not only feels that decency and intrigue are incompatible but that even a decency that must be pursued by deliberate, intriguing action is not worth the trouble.

The James who writes *The American* also does not believe in intrigue—either as a fact of life or of novelistic form. Intrigue seems identical with action, and both the innocence of James's hero and the conviction of James himself testify to an incredulity about action: it seems to young James a convention of old-fashioned plot, or it is identical with aggression, deceit, and hurt. Like his character, James admits in his preface to *The American* his disbelief in his own plot, in the way things happen in the novel outside the hero's consciousness. "The way [real] things happen is frankly not the way in which they are represented as having happened, in Paris, to my hero." The novel's interest thus lies both in the consciousness of the hero and in picture—in the portrait of a subjectivity that, like its author's, curiously, appreciatively, and at last antagonistically, pictures action but does not join or participate in it, except in a reflective stillness. For James the lasting value of the book resides in the "more or less convincing image of his hero's center of consciousness":

> The picture of his consistency was all my undertaking. . . . If Newman was attaching enough, I must have argued, his tangle would be sensible enough; for the interest of everything is all that it is *his* vision, *his* conception, *his* interpretation.

In *The American,* as in *The Portrait of a Lady,* story is transubstantiated into the prime and precious thing of picture.

But the man who can picture complex relations and who nevertheless will not enter the frame of the picture keeps James's attention but not his allegiance. Similarly, James retains picture as narrative mode, but commits himself to the primacy of action (or, otherwise expressed, of story). We can see this if we understand that one of Christopher Newman's last emanations is Vanderbank in *The Awkward Age*; considered as the American's heir, Vanderbank is a measure of James's later coldness towards the man who keeps himself puritanically clear of plot and plot's "doings." Now "the awkward age" means not only late adolescence but the era James's novel describes. The modernity of this era is seen in its bad faith about standards and its inhibited and incoherent enactment of its impulses. The novel questions if there is any genuine or significant action or heroism available to the "civilization" of such an era. In this age can young persons realize a decent and fruitful maturity? The vehicles of James's questionings are Longdon, who belongs to an earlier and supposedly better age; Nanda Brookenham, one of the young who feels the need of a life other than that which modern society offers her; and Vanderbank, a young man whose smooth intelligence, self-possession, and glamour have a sinister edge, but who seems to represent the best distillation of the era. Nanda tries to save her friend Mitchett from the indeterminacy of modern values by advising him to marry Aggie, a girl brought up in old-fashioned seclusion and enforced innocence by a modern noblewoman who hardly practices the virtue she preaches to her ward. The marriage is a failure because as a wife the girl shows herself as deceitful as her guardian. Longdon fails in turn to "save" Vanderbank, the young man Nanda loves, by trying to arrange for him a marriage with Nanda free from financial obstacles. In the end Vanderbank rejects Nanda and Longdon's offer, apparently because he does not love the girl enough. But he also may not want to marry her because of the studied humaneness she has adopted from Longdon and has applied with such bad results in the case of Mitchett. The implication of Vanderbank's point of view is that a modern person cannot free himself from all his compromises by returning to expressions of human goodness (Nanda's aid to Mitchett is a kind of outdated Dickensian rescue attempt) that have lost their practicability.

So for Vanderbank there is left finally only a kind of detached, lucid endurance of the age, a lucidity that is modern especially because it is inactive and, in its opposition to the doings of Longdon and Nanda, even opposed to action. The novel begins with Vanderbank comparing a photograph of Lady Julia, symbol of an outmoded form of human goodness, with a photograph of Nanda, symbol of the goodness that must find and enact a modern form for itself. He ends the same way, clinging to the clarity of his pictorial comparisons and appreciations, thematizing experience, having an imaginative sense for it, but making and keeping separate his fullness of speculation and his poverty of deed. Van's development is to only know more certainly, at last, how woefully inept Nanda and Longdon have been in their attempts to put their contemplative images of goodness to work in the world.

Yet unmistakably James admires Longdon and Nanda more than Vanderbank. For James, at this time in his career, it is better to be inept (even if this is the price of "doing") than to be perfect as a reflector. Narrative intellectual and moral reasonings must be attached to active practice. In many of the prefaces James admits his own ineptitude but with a kind of stoic pride, for it is the result of willfully making experience tell as action and as story, not just as picture. By adopting Nanda, Longdon risks an active marriage of past values and a decent—even if compromised—modern humanity. And in so doing he acts to create a community of past and present ways of feeling and acting, even though he recognizes that "everything's different from what it used to be." There is an irony in Vanderbank's refusal to marry Nanda: because Nanda has been exposed to the knowing sophistication and promiscuity of "the age," Vanderbank considers her unacceptably prepared for marriage, but if Vanderbank thinks this way, then he—rather than Longdon—turns out to be puritanical and nostalgic, even sentimental, about the past. And at the same time his appreciative realization that everything has changed is tainted by his refusal to attempt or to execute a further transformation. For the social and historical change that has created "the age" is not humanly satisfying. "What comes out, on reflection" for both Longdon and Nanda is that something must be done about this change, that they must enact a further change; whereas Vanderbank refuses commitment to anything but the reflective comprehension of change.

Vanderbank's commitment is not James's. His withdrawal from action, his appreciativeness of the "doings" of *others*—that quality inherited from Newman—is, as his name keeps telling us, a vanity. In their final alliance Nanda and Longdon are a hope that creative action is not, as Van would have it, "long done." James admires even Nanda's mother, Mrs. Brooken-ham, who in her own insistently willful intriguing is more creative than Vanderbank. And although the other characters call Vanderbank a "sacred terror," his glamour and power may be "the force of stillness in which nothing happens." In Christopher Newman, James had seen the force of stillness as a redemptive human and American virtue; in Vanderbank he sees it as both fine and stagnantly quiescent. But its quiescence cancels its fineness. Such men as Vanderbank leave the social and historical world mired in con-fusion, and they are sadly inactive in the face of its incoherence. In *The American* the intriguing and plotting characters had been the symptoms and agents of social evil, the antagonists of goodness and of passive decency. By the time of *The Awkward Age* James's world is not so neatly divided. He relocates his hope for a new moral and social order in the agents and agency of plot.

Now it is possible that in *The Sense of the Past* (started in 1900 and then not resumed until World War I) James wanted to reverse his new em-phasis and essay a novel in which his narrative modes would once again be personified and interidentified by felicitous mystic conversions as they had been in *The Portrait of a Lady*. But it is also possible that the novel re-mained—and remains—an odd fragment because James could no longer be-lieve in the necessity or value of the transformation. The novel's hero, the historian Ralph Pendrel, loves Aurora Coyne, who is likened to a Renaissance portrait and who refuses Ralph's suit because she wants to marry a man of action. Ralph's success as an historian has arisen from his ability to render intensely the pictorial tone and feel of things past and not from his ability to narrate past deeds, events, and adventures. As he himself says, "I don't know what anyone is who leads the life of action." He then literally slips back into the past by means of becoming the man in a Regency portrait he inherits. What first entranced him in this picture, what "kept him on and on," "was precisely the force of the stillness in which nothing happened."

The projected ending of the novel seems to have been tailored to con-vince both Aurora and the reader that for a modern man "the life of action" finds its equivalent in picture. By becoming the figure in the portrait, Ralph becomes what Aurora wants: a man who has experienced "the prodigy of

... adventure." Story and plot, action and adventure are thus again made synonymous with a picture; moreover, Ralph's moral fineness is projected as the fruit of modernity's denial of the importance of action in Aurora's sense of the word. And yet, even *The Sense of the Past* stirs up contradictions of the formal identities James had especially cultivated in his earlier work and seems to have wanted to cultivate once more. Pendrel was to have been rescued from entrapment in the past by the *strenuous and active doing* of both his Regency sweetheart—a double of Aurora—and Aurora herself. The picture would have been in some way damning, after all; so we can see that in *The Sense of the Past* James's mystic conversions are not working as they used to.

If we turn to a close reading of *The Wings of the Dove*, we can especially observe how the conflict of the narrative modes is both technical and thematic and how the primacy of contemplative picture gives way in later James to the priority of story and action. In this novel of 1902 James makes picture, albeit with one exception, almost synonymous with *unreliable* consciousness, and he dramatizes the moral maturation of his hero as his yielding of reflection to the need for willful action. "Have you seen the picture in the house, the beautiful one that's so like you?" With this question, in the novel's first self-reflexive use of picture, Lord Mark brings Milly Theale face to face with what he thinks of as her double, a Bronzino portrait. Milly bursts into tears. In the picture

> the lady in question . . . was a very great personage—only unaccompanied by a joy. And she was dead, dead, dead. Milly recognized her exactly in words that had nothing to do with her. "I shall never be better than this."

Does Milly recognize the Bronzino "in words that had nothing to do with" its subject because she thinks that she herself will never be better than dead, will always be "unaccompanied by a joy"? What Milly, still facing the portrait, thinks and says after her tears is unclear to the reader and to Milly's interlocuter, Mark. Apparently Milly wants after all to resist recognition that the portrait is her double. Pressed by Mark to clarify her words of "recognition," Milly says she will "never be better" than this particular day has made her feel. She is at a brilliant English house called Matcham, where the entire company has created for Milly "a sort of magnificent maximum, the pink dawn of an apotheosis." The portrait has just become part of the "maximum" for her. But "you're a pair," Lord Mark insists, stubbornly matching (at Matcham) portrait and lady. Surely Milly will admit the identity straightforwardly? But she resists: "I don't know—one never knows one's self." When Kate Croy spots the resemblance and brings other viewers, Milly is doubly uneasy. "Lady Aldershaw . . . looked at Milly quite as if Milly had been the Bronzino and the Bronzino only Milly."

The live creature does not like being mixed up with art. Moreover, she refuses to be identified with what she *appears* to be. Thematically *The Wings of the Dove* worries over a number of problems implicit in the portrait episode. How is life to be made valuable? What is life's best form? How does one really have or hold onto "life" or "self"? But James goes out of his way here to put thematic issues in terms of "picture," and this shows that his feelings about *picture* are as mixed as Milly's. Through the Bronzino scene the pictorial moment is shown to be an unreliable composition of appearances, a misleading still reflection. In its arranged fixity and richness the portrait does not stand for what Milly believes herself to be, nor for what she wants. Already suspicious that she is dying, Milly feels she can never be better than *alive*. The portrait's very lifelikeness is deceptive—its fineness is that of a still life, *hence* unaccompanied by joy.

After Matcham the moments of picture in *The Wings of the Dove* are suspect. Milly herself acts like Lady Aldershaw, mixing up alleged representations and copies of life with truth. One of the reasons the picture of "Milly" at Matcham is false is that it has no story in it: it does not represent its subject by what she does. In the National Gallery scene in Book Fifth, Milly will mistake a picture of Merton for the truth by ignoring how his story, what he is enacting, defines him more truthfully than what he appears to be. Milly is at the gallery to escape truth altogether, of course: at home her doctor is delivering a final diagnosis of her disease. At the museum she feels too weak to look at Titians and Turners, which we are to understand is also a blinking of truth—for she finds herself curious only about the ladies who copy the real pictures. She wants, suddenly, to lose herself, to escape the agony and burden of what she and James call "the personal question." "She should have been a lady-copyist—it met so the case. The case was the case of escape, of living under water."

She feels embarrassed by her interest in the copyists, but instead of turning to the authentic originals, she muses next over the hordes of American tourists in the gallery. When three American women stop in front of her, she watches and listens to their reaction to what she supposes is a portrait "in the English style" (as the women say) hanging at her back. She turns around to see that only Dutch genre paintings are there. The Americans have in fact been looking at Merton Densher. Just returned to England, Merton is at the gallery to meet with Kate, who as suddenly and surprisingly as Merton appears in Milly's line of vision. How, Milly is frightened and anxious to know, is this mysterious composition, this living picture, to be read? Surely the sheer visibility of appearances is all or almost all of the story.

> Little by little indeed, under the vividness of Kate's behavior, the probabilities fell back into their order. Merton Densher was in love, and Kate couldn't help it—could only be sorry and kind: wouldn't that, without wild flurries, cover everything? Milly at all events tried it as a cover, tried it hard.

She asks herself too—the question acting as part of the cover—if Merton will have changed since her meeting with him in America. But the picture is deceptively indefinite; it can be read any way the individual desires. So Milly

> was to see her question itself simply go to pieces. She couldn't tell if he were different or not, and she didn't know nor care if *she* were: these things had ceased to matter in the light of the only thing she did know. This was that she liked him. . . . It was at this point that she saw . . . that all she had to do with was the sense of being there with him.

Merton's pictorial presence (and Kate's behind his) "covers everything." Nevertheless, the questions that go to pieces matter the most. Kate Croy is one of the lady-copyists, forging a substitute picture for the real thing. Milly takes Kate's portrait of Merton for the truth. She passes it on to Lord Mark, and struggles not to recognize her own lie. We see that there is a grave potential of falseness in the privileged pictorial moment. Moreover, whoever works to *fix* his life in the form of privileged picture, of a beatific still composition, is deceived. Meaningful as the pictorial moment is, it either has too many meanings or not enough. The dynamic of story must seize this moment and define and enact its truth. Picture confuses or inhibits the process of active movement and precise definition.

But, we might think, surely action can be no less a forgery, no less a deceiving "act" than the deceptions created by the eye and the mind's eye. However generally true this may be, in late James the act is featured as the means whereby uncertainties are cleared and treacheries are at last routed. In relation to the doubtful and ambiguous authority of picture, action is a superior authority, a final arbiter of truth. Moreover, mature Jamesian picture demands that action realize what consciousness sees, and that consciousness execute vision in the form of act. In Merton Densher, especially, we see the process whereby the truth and action of story—the supplementary execution of vision as deed—overcomes arbitrariness and stillness, even a treacherous passivity, in the purely contemplative or speculative aspect of picture.

At the end of the novel another picture proposes itself—this time to Merton—again as a magnificent maximum. Merton is shown fixating his life upon a final portrait of Milly, a positively sacred icon set up in his imagination. With Mrs. Lowder in attendance, he contemplates himself contemplating Milly:

> He saw a young man, far off, in a relation inconceivable, saw him hushed, passive, staying his breath, but half understanding, yet dimly conscious of something immense and holding himself, not to lose it, painfully together. The young man, at these moments, so seen was too distant and too strange for the right identity; and yet outside, afterwards, it was his own face Densher had known. . . . At present there, with Mrs. Lowder, he knew he had gathered all. . . . He had been, to his recovered sense, forgiven, dedicated, blessed; but this he couldn't coherently express. It would have required an explanation—fatal to Mrs. Lowder's faith in him—of the nature of Milly's wrong. So, as to the wonderful scene, they just stood at the door. They had the sense of the presence within—they felt the charged stillness; after which, with their association deepened by it, they turned together away.

Merton has been mystically converted and possessed by a new version of the Bronzino, but the possession is disconcerting to him and to us. There is again, as at Matcham and the National Gallery, an unsettling arbitrariness in the pictorial phenomenon—and, as this passage emphasizes, an ethical unreliability. The stillness of the picture is charged with implicit demands that stillness be broken, that passivity of awareness be transformed into activity for the sake of a finer utterance of truth. Even Merton's identity, maintained by the force of the stillness in which nothing happens, is deceiving and deceived.

By what grace has Merton become supported and fixed by an image of exemplary human decency? The arbitrariness of pictorial significance—in spite of any tendency to sanctify them as absolutely reliable iconography—is reinforced if we remember that Merton, only a few months before the scene with Mrs. Lowder, had found himself—as the young man he now strains to recognize—experiencing apparently the same phenomenon when the presence and the image had been Kate's:

> What had come to pass within his walls lingered there as an

obsession importunate to all his sense; it lived again, as a cluster of pleasant memories, at every hour and in every subject; it made everything but itself irrelevant and tasteless. It remained, in a word, a conscious, watchful presence, active on its own side, forever to be reckoned with, in face of which the effort at detachment was scarcely less futile than frivolous. Kate had come to him; . . . to stay, as people called it; and what survived of her . . . was something he couldn't have banished if he had wished. Luckily he didn't wish, even though there might be . . . almost a shade of the awful in so unqualified a consequence of his act. It had simply worked, his idea, the idea he had made her accept; and all erect before him, really covering the ground as far as he could see, was the fact of the gained success that this represented. It was, otherwise, but the fact of the idea as directly applied, as converted from a luminous conception into an historic truth.

Merton had presented Kate with the sketch of a plot. When the sketch is realized according to his vision Merton is dazzled by the consonance of his "luminous conception" with "historic truth." Picture, story, and plot here look identical. And yet Merton is deluded. Other forces are turning his historic truth back into an idea, less consequential as fact or act than he realizes. Kate's "conscious, watchful presence, active on its own side" seems to enjoin Merton from further "working"—another Jamesian synonym for plot. Further work may expel the presence filling Merton's room. It is expelled. *Milly*'s "conscious, watchful presence, active on its own side" takes over. But although Milly's icon seems more blessed to Merton because it has not been made in the active, willful way he made Kate's, Merton is again mistaken. He must stop picturing Milly's goodness to himself in a way that keeps him still and passive. The sacred icon, the luminous conception whose values are ethical as well as pictorial, demands conversion once again into a form of action so that it may become a deed, and hence "historic." This is one step further in the articulation of "history" than the one suggested as necessary [elsewhere] when it was argued that Carlyle, for example, could not make history feel actual to us if he did not picture it or frame it in terms of theory. James's Merton suggests that a theoretical formulation provides only the preliminary formulation of an act. The act is greater, that is, more valuable and more truthful and definite than the theory.

Fixed before the icon of Milly in his scene with Mrs. Lowder, Merton is adhering to theory, to *that* "stillness"; but his story will not end until he exchanges contemplation—purely speculative narrative reasoning about

Milly—for an act that supplements speculation and is initiated by himself.
How does Merton at last succeed as an actor, giving up the passivity, quiescence, and arbitrariness of relation with which the picturing consciousness
in late James seems doubtfully intertwined? Merton's success in making Kate
come to him is the first step of his transformation from passive watcher to
active maker of the story that is his, Kate's, and Milly's; but no sooner has
he taken the step, than he returns to passivity. At this point in the novel we
are given a double sense of picture—reminded of its potential for truth as
well as for falsity. By having consummated sexual relations with Kate, Merton makes himself more false to Milly; but "it was only on reflection that
the falseness came out." "Reflection," the characteristic and fruit of picturing
consciousness, is here a touchstone of truth and genuine conscience, and is
being favored by James. But although the deed enacts the truth of Merton's
relation to others, thus defining and mastering what reflection can bring out,
reflective consciousness also resists such mastering definition. Consequently
Merton can use reflection, in spite of what he undeniably does, to picture a
false and happy composition of relations among Kate, Milly, and himself:
Are they not each getting their just deserts? Everything is all right, that is—
if Merton will just *see* it that way. And it helps Merton to see it that way if
he does not commit himself to any further defining action, if he lets his
action sink back into a felicitous composition of appearances.

> Action itself, of any sort, the right as well as the wrong—if the
> difference even survived—had heard . . . a vivid "Hush!" the in-
> junction, from that moment, to keep intensely still. . . . His wis-
> dom reduced itself—to the need again simply to be kind [to
> Milly]. That was the same as being still—as creating, studiously,
> the minimum of vibration. He felt himself, as he smoked, shut
> up to a room, on the wall of which something precious was too
> precariously hung. A false step would bring it down, and it must
> hang as long as possible.

Is not the picture hanging here the falsely composed affair with Milly? Reflection is not bringing out the truth, after all, and the "precious" picture
must be brought down, by the clarifying agency of what Merton will do.

But it is Mark who acts first, pushing Merton out of falsity and quiescence. The picture is brought down the moment Merton sees Mark, the
evangel of truth, sitting behind the plate glass of Florian's café on the Piazza
San Marco with the *Figaro* on his knee, with an unfinished drink on his
table, and staring at a rococo wall. This is, curiously, a replacement of one
picture by another; but now the picture is incontrovertibly "true." The vision

of Mark is the supreme pictorial moment in *The Wings of the Dove,* realizing once more James's old ambition to have a reflective moment tell the entire story for both the fictional character and the reader—a moment reconciling the presentational ideals of the narrative modes and conveying an absolute of truthful perception through the reconciliation. Seeing Mark, Merton takes two turns around the square in order to see him twice more. The terror of this appearance compels him to repeat the sight. Merton literally envisions a reversal of his fortune and his life, for he immediately understands that the truth of his relation to Milly has just been revealed to her. And simultaneously he knows he can no longer cover up from himself the truth of his relation to her. What happens to Merton here echoes James's remark in another preface:

> One never really chooses one's general range of vision: ... this proves ever what it has *had* to be, this is one with the very turn one's life has taken; so that whatever it "gives," ... we regard very much as imposed and inevitable.

In the scene in St. Mark's square, Merton's physical vision is unified with the fatal turn the reality and significance of his life have taken. And picture, drama, plot, and story are also unified because here Merton's apprehension of Mark's appearance does not have to await unfolding and testing by time, by action, or by "work." The image is at once one with definitive historic truth.

Yet it is not enough for the late James—and for Merton—to "see" story this way. In the café window Mark's image is story, imposing itself visually as truth and picture. But story's form of "doing" is not identical with vision, either physical or speculative. What is anyone—what is Merton—to *do* with "one's general range of vision?" Consciousness, pervaded by awareness and "vision," presses for a further conversion, a transformation into action, a making of a novel difference to itself through an externalizing of what it knows, in the form of an overt deed. When Merton hangs his precious picture of *Milly* on his wall, it too must be brought down—and by his own willful agency, not by passive acquiescence. For the revelation produced by Mark in Venice is again a passive reflective experience for Merton; so is his being held by Kate's design, then by Milly's icon, then by Milly's will.

In the last pages Densher struggles against passivity. Milly's will makes her an ally of Kate. It composes the fate of all three persons in—apparently— the happiest terms. But Merton refuses to accept this final composition. For him his internalized pictures of Milly, her will, and his will, do not match. The document from New York is a picturing of herself that Milly hands on

to her survivors. Merton refuses to take this image for the truth: he rejects
it as incompatible with his feelings and with goodness. Milly must be better
than this. Merton says he will marry Kate on condition that they reject
Milly's legacy. This condition subordinates and even annuls Kate's creative
agency; it makes Merton the superior actor and intriguer. Merton will now
do more than recognize he has cherished Milly and has regretted deceiving
her. Recognition could be appreciative of Milly and could still be "covered"
by acceptance of the legacy, but Merton's accession to intrigue is to interpret
his sacred icon of Milly by enacting his sense of its value with a deed that
wipes out Milly's last picture of herself as well as Kate's entire design.
Densher does offer Kate the appearance of a marriage with him, but she
knows as well as he the absolutely defining nature of the act rejecting the
legacy.

What Densher wills and does, not merely what he appreciates, sees, or
feels, makes definite Kate's judgment about his transformation. And Merton's act defining the transformation closes the novel, breaking him and Kate
apart at the moment when Merton has become, as an *enactor* of a perception
of values, most like Kate. His similarity to Kate at this point is of course
easily available to detached pictorial consciousness, but the break with Kate
might be said to underline how action tells more than the identities available
to picture. And for the most proper appreciation of Merton's telling action,
it is necessary to emphasize and reiterate that Merton contravenes Milly as
well as Kate. For this means that Merton himself is picturing goodness without a clear, available, external model (Milly's will is obviously not one) and
insisting that he make himself the model of this goodness by an action
attempting concretely to define and embody the value he "sees." What he
sees may be only awkwardly embodied in action (just as in *The Awkward
Age* Nanda and Longdon are awkward actors), but the vision *must* be followed through with a deed. Merton's final move against Milly and Kate
features Merton as actor by cancelling the heroines' self-picturings and their
speculative designs. The novel ends its narrative reasoning emphatically as
story.

Merton is thus not a Newman or a Vanderbank, withdrawing from
action either for the sake of a superior quiet goodness and intelligence or for
the sake of avoiding something compromising of or frustrating to lucidity in
the form of action in the modern era. Merton's act is a sort of risk of moral
creativity that neither Newman nor Vanderbank could manage. Moreover,
the morality or goodness of Merton's action is complex: his deed does not
simplify experience, nor does it make experience conform to innocence. The
goodness or fineness in Milly to which Merton's act testifies is not Milly's

innocence or kindness. It is as if James identifies Milly's goodness with an integrity of passionate desire in her, with what she wants most: we can assume that Merton feels this integrity betrayed by the self-effacing kindness of the will. Merton's own last willful action testifies to the identity of his self with his transformed *desire*: he has come to love Milly more than Kate. In Merton's case, as in Milly's, James ultimately portrays goodness as fidelity to one's desires and truth to the transformations they create. Merton's action thus does not instance an abstract morality of love or kindness but a goodness that is truth: truth to one's essential reality. Through Merton James is willing to risk the idea that such truth is preeminently moral, no matter what is the object of desire or the nature of the character to which the actor is morally true. Of course, neither the desire nor the essential nature and reality is seen by James as possessing integrity if it is not witnessed by and as action.

In this risky notion of what is good or moral we can see James's imagination of Merton, like his imagination of Kate, looking forward to the achieved apotheosis of intrigue and plot in *The Golden Bowl*, where the morality of action leaps beyond reflective pictorial composition and conventional good and evil, beyond easy discriminations of innocence and betrayal. And, in looking forward to *The Golden Bowl* and its princess, we must not underestimate "princess" Milly's address to goodness and to action. Milly matures by becoming an intriguer. How else can she really *have* her life: when she marches through Regent's Park, fresh with the news of her approaching death, she is as fiercely purposeful and grasping, as committed to an intrigue and action that leave behind conventional good and evil as Kate is. Thus, we have followed James's lead in involving his characters with his technical modes, for as we have seen in citations from *The Wings of the Dove*, the characters are often figured as live symbols of *picture* or of *story*, in such a way as to dramatize the differing weights and values of primarily contemplative or primarily active ways of life. But we must now ask, what is the good of Merton's and James's enactment of their version of good? And what is the good of James's cultivating a battle between ways of life that turns out to disrupt and even sacrifice his aesthetic transubstantiations of picture, drama, plot, and story?

The featuring of act in the late James is the result of his growing conviction that the inhibition of action, either by passive, still, and quiescent life or by a limitation upon action's intellectual and moral diversity and risk, is a blow to civilization, to the fortunes of human community. Since the shift in James's technical and thematic interests is so motivated, it is necessary to consider further what the sense of plot means to James in terms of the fate of society. The young James presents the withdrawal from plot and active intrigue as an American and social virtue, not merely as a private one. And beginning with *The Awkward Age,* the elder James shows the active intrigue of Longdon and Nanda as an honorable attempt to redeem a blighted social state. But in what way are the actions "social" whereby Kate or Merton execute their purposes and values? The fruit of Merton's break with Kate can only be satisfaction with his own will and act. It creates nothing happy or blessed for Kate; it contravenes Milly; it leaves him utterly alone. Kate's activity too has left her penniless and destitute. Is the fruit of action only desolation and solitude? No wonder human happiness and good, even human interrelation, may seem more available to contemplative narrative consciousness than to the consciousness that transforms "picture" into action. The active plotter is true to himself, but appears also to do himself harm and to do no one else any good.

Bleak as this prospect is, James's most valued late characters find that they must embrace it. Merton may create nothing for himself but an isolation, but paradoxically this represents hope for a decent form of human interrelation—even if the form can exist only as an act of hope. Human relation as it already exists is far from happy. Kate once exclaims to Milly with great pathos and envy: "You're an outsider, independent and standing by yourself; you're not hideously relative to tiers and tiers of others." In many of the novels both early and late, James's characters begin their stories without sufficient independence. An excess of relationship, crowded with presences and possibilities of connection, demoralizes and even terrifies them. Kate's activity is finally sadder than Merton's, perhaps because she cannot think of alternatives to the closeness of relation that characterizes her family. She describes her "narrow little family feeling" as a "small stupid-piety." She insists on honoring it, though, when "face to face . . . with the bond of blood," she finds it neither uplifting nor sweet. Unfortunately she reproduces these relations among herself, Merton, Mrs. Lowder, and Milly. Her family feeling becomes a literally bloody bond. But if Milly becomes quickly relative—hideously so—to tiers and tiers of others, it is not just because Kate plots or "works" her into relation. Kate only uses the connection already existing between Milly and Merton.

All the characters of *The Wings of the Dove* are hideously relative to each other, through family ties, love, or financial need. The bonds of connection are almost instantaneous. Lord Mark and Milly agree not to be intimate, but, despite the agreement, Milly feels "a perverse quickening of the relation [with Mark] to which she had been, in spite of herself, appointed." When Mark seems to exchange with Kate looks that comment on Milly, Milly feels the onset of a "relation into which she was sinking." Indeed

Milly's consciousness is "crowded" with "the various signs of a relation," and this is a kind of suffocating terror to her. In the face of relation as crowded, bloody bond and passive sinking, the activity that achieves isolation (such as Merton's last act) is thus an honorable and creative check to the bondage of passive interrelations. In their place, the act puts a hope of interrelations that are freely created. This hope suggests what positive social relations, rather than "sinking" ones, would be.

Here is an interesting difference between James, his predecessors, and his Victorian contemporaries, for in Scott, Dickens, or Eliot the characters are originally isolated, and they plot in order to achieve a final close, even crowded, state of connection. But when the reverse happens in James, it is nevertheless motivated by social intention. Of course we are speaking not of a passive withdrawal of the individual from the crowd of relations but of an active plotted assertion against them. Not surprisingly, in the prefaces James talks of relations constituted by passive sinkings in terms of "pictorial" metaphor, so that it seems plot or story can be actions moving against relations associated with the contemplativeness of picture. For example, when James says that "really, universally, relations stop nowhere," the famous sentence has an ominous side. The expansiveness promises the novelist and his characters unlimited developments, but it simultaneously threatens confusion and entrapment. Just after the famous sentence James says that connections and continuities frighten him. Even as "a young embroiderer of the canvas of life," he "soon began to work in terror, fairly, of the vast expanse" of surface before him. Since James speaks here in terms of a pictorial figure, we may take him to mean that picture's relations stop nowhere. This fecundity is a hazard for James the mature storyteller. The immense quantity of such relations needs to be checked by plot, which for the sake of a significant action must sacrifice some of them. Otherwise, James will find himself in the situation of Milly, for whom, in a moment of picture, relations seem to "stop nowhere" and are a matter of passive sinking. With emotional and moral urgency, James intervenes against the passivity, and shows the characters of his later work doing the same for their lives and for others. Art demands, James says,

> a dire process of selection and comparison, of surrender and sacrifice. The very meaning of expertness is acquired courage to brace one's self for the cruel crisis from the moment one sees it grimly loom.

Story, plot, action: these are other names for the "dire process" that brings the storyteller, his story, and his characters to an emphatic end. The relation stops somewhere, for good and for ill. If this process sacrifices possibilities of picture on the aesthetic and reflective level and passive communities of relationship on the ethical and social level, it is for the sake of "the cruel crisis" of action. For the late James, without active plot or doing, no form of goodness substantiates itself. This means a willful self-bracing, an acquired and even brutal courage on the actor's part. The price and the fruit of this is the radical alteration of the actor's social being, whether he is the novelist or the novelist's fictive agent. The possible or probable isolation that results *may* do the actor harm and may not—in practical and immediate terms—do much good for anyone else. Yet, as James sees it, his braced sacrificial deed can be the hope of any human and aesthetic state in which relation is characterized by only passively received givens or by a consciousness that can reflect upon its discriminations but cannot fulfill its narrative reasonings by enacting them.

There will be advocates of James who will resist this account of him, who will insist that the narrative modes receive no individual featuring or favor earlier or later in the career, and who will find in work as rich as James's numerous exceptions to my argument. But these advocates will sadly have little or no sense of what James believed was at stake in an American storyteller's relation to action at the beginning of this century. In *The American Scene,* we find James once again using the pictorial mode—this time in nonfiction—and we find him simultaneously perplexed and frustrated by "scenic" impressions. James decides that America has devoted itself to something like a parody of Jamesian picture: the country basks in monstrous self-reflections of its economic and physical grandeur; it insistently matches its identity with a portrait James at first assiduously scrutinizes and then rejects as uncreative and probably uncivilized. What damages America for James is that it resists story and history, that it denies the narrative motions of consciousness, especially insofar as those motions feature acts. In one sense, of course, James's America does favor action by the primacy it assigns to the "work" of business, but it inhibits and overlooks action of every other kind. In *The American Scene* James's prescription for American civilization is not contemplation or withdrawal from the action of business but a finer cultivation of will and adventure, a broadening of the possibilities for significant human deeds. Because James's recommendation has obvious bearing on his mature thoughts about story, *The American Scene* deserves attention here. And to focus the sense of plot especially brought out by this last of James's examinations of American culture, it will also be fruitful to take a long look backward at the attitudes towards the relations of picture and story, of contemplative composition or reflection and action in Nathaniel Hawthorne, the novelist who most inspired James's lifelong pictorial technique as well as the type of Jamesian "drama" represented by *The American*. Hawthorne's presence and achievement must inevitably frame a consideration of Jamesian story; and the older James's difference from Hawthorne is one of the best gauges of transformation in James's sense of the value of story and action for American civilization.

Jamesian *picture* seems to have sprung directly from *The House of the Seven Gables,* the drama of which concerns a hero whose photographic pictorial art is identified by Hawthorne with truth and quiescent speculation and with the absence of manipulatory intrigue and will, and whose story-telling art—in direct contrast—is identified with lying and coercion, with mastery of others, with plot and action considered as evil. Through Holgrave Hawthorne gives storytelling a nefarious name, for the photographer plots to put a mesmeric spell on Phoebe Pyncheon by reading her his story of Alice Pyncheon. He all but succeeds, and Hawthorne tells us that "to a disposition like Holgrave's, at once speculative and active, there is no temptation so great as the opportunity of acquiring empire over the human spirit." Holgrave's kind of storytelling is this great temptation to acquire empire over the reader and the listener by spellbinding them with the tale's proximity to reality and by using the tale to incite action rather than reflection. Fortunately, we are made to think, Holgrave cedes his intriguing ambitions for the sake of Phoebe, who represents natural truth free of story's alleged magics and artifices. Hawthorne follows Holgrave's example. He deauthorizes the truth of his novel, insisting that the reader *not* suspend disbelief in the tale. It is not magic or metaphysical evil that *The House of the Seven Gables* attacks but fictive fabling, which according to Hawthorne curses experience by manipulating its shape and calling it truth. The legends of the house are spurious superstructures of plot and will. The novel's authentic story, its only real or important truth, lies in picturings available to natural light or to nonmanipulative reflective light. In a remarkably early instance of the modern sense of plot, Hawthorne juxtaposes his characters in a variety of combinations for the sake of speculative comparisons and contrasts. When these combinations of pictures bring the characters to the threshold of a fable or a plot, Hawthorne lingers and draws back, anxious *not* to fable but to remain on the threshold of story. Indeed what Hawthorne seems to want in *The House of the Seven Gables* is to replace story with Phoebe's "easy and flexible charm of play," with "a succession of kaleidoscopic pictures" like those in Maule's Well, whose water provides "a continually shifting apparition of quaint figures, vanishing too suddenly to be definable." Where plot is concerned, in *The House of the Seven Gables* Hawthorne has the detachment and the innocence of Newman confronting Mrs. Bread. And Hawthorne's emphasis upon Phoebe deauthorizes the life and fact of action: the heroine represents a suspension of will and act, a reproof to the prestige and definiteness of deeds.

Hawthorne's reluctance to master appearances by means of plot and his conversion of story and action into indefinite picture and play are taken up by James and made the essence of much of his career. But *The American Scene,* although it is nonfiction, shows as significantly great a difference from the narrative and moral values of James's master as *The Wings of the Dove* or *The Golden Bowl* show from the narrative and moral values of *Roderick Hudson* and *The American.* In *The American Scene* James's pictorial moments, although he has committed himself to their use, are all questionable: their lack of reliability makes him feel "pricked by thorns," "impotent," and "poisoned." "The lone visionary" finds himself "betrayed and arrested in the very act of vision." He finds some relief from the betrayals of picture, however,

> in that blest general drop of the immediate need for conclusions, or rather in that blest general feeling for the impossibility of them. . . . [The spectator] doesn't *know,* he can't *say,* before the facts, and he doesn't even want to know or say: . . . it is as if the syllables were too numerous to make a legible word. The *il*legible word, accordingly, the great inscrutable answer to questions, hangs in the vast American sky, to his imagination, as something fantastic and *abracadabrant,* belonging to no known language.

But this relief is momentary, and creative initiative passes from reflective composition to willful making of relations. In the face of nonsense James must *make* sense. "The high honour of the painter of life [is] always to *make* a sense," even when he surmises that "the cluster of appearances can *have* no sense. . . . The last thing decently permitted him is to recognize incoherence—to recognize it, that is, as baffling." Does not Hawthorne's narrative playfulness allow experience to be recognized by the storyteller as baffling, even incoherent, in no way that he can correct? As a descendant of Holgrave, James cannot be content with bafflement; he wants "empire" over appearances. By emphasizing his own resistance to passive spectatorship, James shifts the vehicle of his analysis to willful exertion: "the painter of life" remains a visionary, but in response to the scene he becomes a purposefully shaping actor. James thus highlights one of his principal definitions of civilization: it is "the capture of conceived values," and the means of realizing this capture are the enactments that supplement conceptions. Thus, the fa-

mous identification of the "hotel-spirit" as *the* modern American hallmark
is not a condemnation on James's part: by the time he reaches Florida, he
realizes that the American hotel is, after all, a "capture" of the "inordinate
desire for taste." The activity is all to the good, for it transforms the conception of taste into a definite and realized form. The only pathos of this
desire, James explicitly says, is that it will "remain a mere heartbreak to the
historic muse" by not transforming itself into a greater variety of realizations
or enactments—especially by confining its "capture" to a pictorial and visible
form of business activity:

> The human imagination, . . . the collective consciousness, in how-
> ever empty an air, gasps for a relation, as intimate as possible,
> to something superior, something as central as possible, from
> which it may more or less have proceeded and round which its
> life may revolve—and its dim desire is always, I think, to do it
> justice, that this object or presence shall have had as much as
> possible an heroic or romantic association. But the difficulty is
> that in these later times . . . the heroic and romantic elements,
> even under the earliest rude stress, have been all too tragically
> obscure, belonged to smothered, unwritten, almost unconscious
> private history: so that the central something, the social *point de
> repére,* has had to be extemporised rather pitifully after the fact,
> and made to consist of the biggest hotel or the biggest common
> school, the biggest factory, the biggest newspaper office, or, for
> climax of desperation, the house of the biggest billionaire.

The pictorial presences and grandeurs are mere blanks if they are cut
loose from the diverse and complex actions and stories that make them.
James is most shocked to note the national absence of reference to the Civil
War. But although the War's increasing obscurity would be reversed by an
American renewal of consciousness and reflection in relation to its past,
James is also arguing that America has "unmade" the complex ideological
and spiritual activity it represented. If there were room again for a spectrum
of activities other than business and the pursuit of material grandeur, America might be able to imagine the War again, and might become more civilized
by broadening the scope of action whereby values are captured. Now James,
as I have said before, never gives up his pictorial mode; nor does he ever
equate it with vulgar visibilities, as America equates her own self-picturings;
nor does he even suggest that America can dispense with reflective self-
awareness. But he wants to insist on both the value of the narrative realities
that America has made secret and on the value of the stories and actions she

inhibits or hides. What James calls "the great social proposition" is a matter of cultivated and captured diversity of character, and character itself is "developed to visible fineness only by friction and discipline on a large scale, only by its having to reckon with a complexity of forces." True "visible fineness" develops out of the frictions and forces that in America belong to the "smothered, unwritten, almost unconscious" private histories, relations, and acts that it is the storyteller's vocation to designate and express.

James ends his book on modern America with an act of rejection that typifies the late Jamesian sense of plot: reflective consciousness must fulfill itself by a supplementary determined enactment. To collect pictures is not enough; what the pictures show must be matched by a deed. James's definitive deed is the break with America announced at the end of *The American Scene*. This is his proud and willful resolution of the meaning of the illegible word hanging in the vast American sky. Hawthorne, who far more than James is to be associated with ambiguities, would not have pressed the American questions to so definite and active a conclusion; but James *will* show his empire over the "abracadabrants" of experience. He shows his empire by breaking off his relation: "one's supreme relation . . . was one's relation to one's country," but to carry on the hope of community implicit in that relation and to show his own personal capture of conceived values, James resolves the story of his ties by an act of rejection that undoes them. What this act constitutes in the actor is a form of the goodness we have seen in Merton: a complex integrity, discrimination, and enactment of desire. Civilization needs such resolving, constitutive acts, by means of even "nefarious" plots and plotters, since such resolutions create the stories—the testimonies of conceived *and enacted* discriminations—for which humanity hungers. Might I suggest in closing that James's surrender of American citizenship in 1915 is another measure of his final distance from Hawthorne and Christopher Newman, is an instance too of his late favoring of the story in complex intrigue and overt action rather than of the story in picture? In his change of nationality, whatever claims are to be made for its sheer convenience, James designates as his country the one whose novelistic tradition shows, at least in the last century, relatively more trust than America's in plot, story, and the representation of action.

MARTIN PRICE

James: The Logic of Intensity

LUCIDITY AND BEWILDERMENT

In his later novels, Henry James leaves some crucial portion of his action, and of his characters, indeterminate. He does this, in part, by giving us characters' conscious responses—at a somewhat shallow level of awareness—without accounting for their deeper motives or even, in some cases, indicating whether the surface awareness is consistent with what lies below. By a shallow level I mean only that the principal action of his novels takes place close enough to the surface of consciousness to alert us to meanings that are almost evident and therefore the more frustrating for their elusiveness. We are never given a fully determinate account of Vanderbank's feelings about Nanda, or of Lambert Strether's decision to leave Paris and Maria Gostrey behind him, or of Milly Theale's motives for leaving the money to Densher, or even of Densher's final feelings about Kate Croy. In *The Golden Bowl* we are largely kept outside the minds of Adam Verver and, to a lesser degree, of Charlotte Stant. How deeply inside Maggie and the Prince we are taken is less of a question, but even there we find some attitudes given only by implication and open to surmise.

This indeterminacy is, to a degree, a willed vagueness on the part of the characters, the "merciful muddle" or "bewilderment" they cannot do without. But the indeterminacy arises, too, from James's artistic design; the design is, of course, essential to the kind of suspense and intensity he wants

From *Forms of Life: Character and Moral Imagination in the Novel.* © 1983 by Yale University. Yale University Press, 1983.

to give to the experience of reading these novels and of puzzling out the motives and meanings of his characters' words. It is not a trivial suspense; it has all the depth of the search for truth where truth is almost impossibly hard, and yet urgent, to recognize.

"Lucid and ironic, she knew no merciful muddle." So James presents Kate Croy in *The Wings of the Dove*, free both of illusion and of cant. When Merton Densher demands, as the encouragement of his deception of Milly Theale, that Kate come to his rooms, she takes "no refuge in showing herself shocked." As he sees her "stand there for him in all the light of the day and of his admirable, merciless meaning," he feels in some sense already "possessed of what he wanted"—possessed at least "of the fact that she hadn't thrown over his lucidity the horrid shadow of cheap reprobation. Of this he had had so sore a fear that its being dispelled was in itself of the nature of bliss" (chap. 27). [In this (essay) I have used the following editions of James's novels: *The Wings of the Dove*, 1st ed. of 1902; *The Awkward Age*, New York edition of 1907–09; *The Ambassadors*, 1st ed. of 1903; and *The Golden Bowl*, 1st ed. of 1904. All references are given by chapter, except in the case of *The Ambassadors*, where book and chapter numbers are given.] Later, near the close of the novel, when Densher believes that they have lost their "dreadful game," Kate can perceive his "horror, almost, of her lucidity" (chap. 34).

That lucidity returns in the last scene, when Densher has received his inheritance from Milly Theale, the inheritance that will finally allow him and Kate the freedom to marry. Kate asks Densher if he is not now in love with Milly's memory. Nor does she allow him to dismiss the possibility. She would have been so in his place, she claims, and she recognizes his feelings: "Your memory's your love. You *want* no other." When he meets this by offering to marry her at once, she asks, "As we were?" But she turns away from his assent with a final shake of her head. She is beyond the illusions he tries to sustain, and she speaks the moving last sentence of the novel: "We shall never be again as we were!" (chap. 38).

Earlier in the novel, Kate Croy's lucidity has taken on "a kind of heroic ring, a note of character that belittled" Densher's "own capacity for action." And he sees in it "the greatness of knowing so well what one wanted" (chap. 28). Kate has been setting forth a plan for Densher and Milly, but she demands his complicity in its formulation. "Don't think . . . I'll do *all* the work for you. If you want things named, you must name them."

> He had quite, within the minute, been turning names over; and there was only one, which at last stared at him there dreadful, that properly fitted. "Since she's to die I'm to marry her?"

It struck him even at the moment as fine in [Kate] that she met it with no wincing nor mincing. She might, for the grace of silence, for favour to their conditions, have only answered him with her eyes. But her lips bravely moved. "To marry her."

Kate has undergone a long strain of "impatience for all he had to be taught." Now he learns it or at least he emerges from the "merciful muddle" which has allowed him to come so far. "It was before him enough now, and he had nothing more to ask; he had only to turn, on the spot, considerably cold with the thought that all along—to his stupidity, his timidity—it had been, it had been only what she meant." And, while Densher feels the shock of unmitigated clarity, she goes on: "You'll in the natural course have money. We shall in the natural course be free." Kate's use of "the natural course" is ironic enough; but if it underlines the unnatural use they will make of Milly, it is also a recognition that they will not induce her early death but rather console her for it. As for their use of Milly, it can only prosper: Densher will have "a free hand, a clear field, a chance—well, quite ideal." Densher is shocked again by her use of "ideal," by her single-minded concentration upon the efficacy of the plan. He doesn't raise the moral issue that so clearly distresses him. Instead he asks how Kate, if she cares for him, can "like" this procedure. And again her lucidity cuts across his questions with a "heroic ring," almost a stoical severity or a categorical imperative: "I don't like it, but I'm a person, thank goodness, who can do what I don't like" (chap. 28).

Densher accepts her instructions, persuading himself that he is merely "seeing what she would say" and that she will "somewhere break down." But she does not break down, and he finds himself continuing. The prospect is daunting: to propose marriage to a dying girl whom he does not love. But Kate has imagination enough to see the full case: "She isn't for you as if she's dying." Densher recognizes the truth of this. As they look across the room, Milly sends back to them, as if in response, "all the candour of her smile, the lustre of her pearls, the value of her life, the essence of her wealth." How explicit in Kate's or Densher's mind is that interweaving of "candour" and "lustre," of "life" and "wealth," we are not told; but they are made "grave" by "the reality she put into the plan" (chap. 28).

We can see Densher's "merciful muddle" at an earlier stage—a stage where he resembles George Eliot's characters as they find themselves not making, but having made, a decision. Densher is already acting on Kate's instructions but is troubled as to whether Kate "really meant him to succeed quite so much." He is also in frequent danger of giving himself away. When he urges Milly to return to London after her travels, he says, "Try us, at any rate . . . once more" (chap. 21). When she in turn asks whom he means by "us," he is pulled up short and quickly dispels the sense of "an allusion to himself as conjoined with Kate." So a moment later, when Milly speaks of her indebtedness to Mrs. Lowder and to Kate, she concludes, "I'd do anything . . . for Kate." Has she laid a trap for him?

> "Oh, I know what one would do for Kate!"—it had hung for
> him by a hair to break out with that, which he felt he had really
> been kept from by an element in his consciousness stronger still.
> The proof of the truth in question was precisely in his silence;
> resisting the impulse to break out was what he *was* doing for
> Kate.

As he avoids that danger he moves on to others, the dialogue becoming more and more intense with his sense of risk. He avoids displaying too full an acquaintance with Kate's ways; he can remark "with a good intention that had the further merit of representing a truth: 'I don't feel as if I knew her—really to call know.'"

The passage which follows is a brilliant treatment of the flickering of conflict which underlies the few spoken words; it looks forward to such passages as I have cited [elsewhere] from Virginia Woolf and Nathalie Sarraute, a notable instance of *sous-conversation*:

> During a silence that ensued for a minute he had time to recognize
> that his own [words] contained, after all, no element of falsity.
> Strange enough therefore was it that he could go too far—if it
> *was* too far—without being false. His observation was one he
> would perfectly have made to Kate herself. And before he again
> spoke, and before Milly did, he took time for more still—for
> feeling that just here it was that he must break short off if his
> mind was really made up not to go further. It was as if he had
> been at a corner—and fairly put there by his last speech; so that
> it depended on him whether or no to turn it. The silence if pro-
> longed but an instant might even have given him a sense of her
> waiting to see what he would do.
>
> (chap. 21)

They are interrupted by the arrival below of Milly's carriage. Densher can recognize his attraction for her as she first denies that she was going out and then proposes that he ride with her.

Densher's happy response, however, had as yet hung fire, the process we have described in him operating by this time with extreme intensity. The system of not pulling up, not breaking off, had already brought him headlong, he seemed to feel, to where they had actually stood; and just now it was, with a vengeance, that he must do either one thing or the other. He had been waiting for some moments, which probably seemed to him longer than they were; this was because he was anxiously watching himself wait. He couldn't keep that up for ever; and since one thing or the other was what he must do, it was for the other that he presently became conscious of having decided. If he had been drifting it settled itself in the manner of a bump, of considerable violence, against a firm object in the stream. "Oh yes; I'll go with you with pleasure. It's a charming idea."

Densher is touched by "her wishing to oblige him," and, as he waits for Milly to get ready, he recognizes that "she had made him simply wish, in civil acknowledgment, to oblige *her*; which he had not fully done, by turning his corner. He was quite round it, his corner." He has, in effect, begun to deceive Milly under the comforting sense of kindness.

"It seems probable," James wrote in the preface to *The Princess Casamassima*, "that if we were never bewildered there would never be a story to tell about us." The novelist must avoid making his characters "too *interpretative* of the muddle of fate . . . too divinely, too priggishly clever." The "wary reader" urges, "'Give us plenty of bewilderment . . . so long as there is plenty of slashing out in the bewilderment too.'" For too much intelligence precludes "the very slashing, the subject-matter of any self-respecting story." To represent bewilderment, as we have seen in the case of Densher, requires an exploration of characters' feelings with a measure of detachment, an "appreciation," on the part of the novelist. The "doing" of such characters is, "immensely, their feeling." Any "intimacy with a man's specific behaviour, with his given case, is desperately certain to make us see it as a whole. . . . What a man thinks and what he feels are the history and the character of what he does; on all of which things the logic of intensity rests."

The "*quality* of bewilderment" will depend on the nature of the consciousness invented and engaged, and it will range from "vague and crepuscular to sharpest and most critical." Each story requires its fools, who embody "the coarser and less fruitful forms and degrees of moral reaction;" but the leading interest requires a consciousness "subject to fine intensification and wide enlargement." Such a consciousness will expose the deficiencies of the fools; but the problem is to keep it from soaring too high, to "keep it connected, connected intimately, with the general human exposure, and thereby bedimmed and befooled and bewildered, anxious, restless, fallible"—and yet not with such bewilderment as will make the situation and the story "unintelligible." These persons are "intense *perceivers*"—James cites among others Isabel Archer, Lambert Strether, and Merton Densher— "even . . . the divided Vanderbank of *The Awkward Age,* the extreme pinch of whose romance is the vivacity in him, to his positive sorrow and loss, of the state of being aware."

It is to the last of these cases I wish to turn, for Vanderbank displays a consciousness which can embrace two quite different conceptions of life but which cannot finally choose between them; or at least, since inaction is itself a choice, cannot choose actively or with full lucidity. There is a sense in which the very intensity of his perception is disabling, making him not a spectator but a failed participant.

The Awkward Age was an experiment in a new form: "a form all dramatic and scenic," as James wrote to a bewildered friend, "of presented episodes, architecturally combined and each making a piece of the building; with no going behind, no *telling about* the figures save by their own appearance and action and with explanations reduced to the explanation of everything by all the other things *in* the picture." And, for all that indirectness, James feels special pleasure in his central characters. "I think Mrs. Brook the best thing I've ever done—and Nanda much *done*." Mrs. Brookenham and her daughter Nanda are both in love with Vanderbank, who, in his mid-thirties, is younger than Mrs. Brookenham and older than her daughter. Nanda quite frankly and simply loves Vanderbank. Her mother, whose lover he seems to be, and might as well be, but perhaps is not (if we accept the evidence of a not very generous friend), counts on Van as a member of her circle. He is, as James said, "divided," attracted by the decencies and sincerity of another kind of life, but unable to separate himself from Mrs. Brook and the bold, free talk of her circle.

The novel opens with a dramatic presentation of Van's self-division. He has just met at Mrs. Brook's a charming old man, Mr. Longdon, who has known both Mrs. Brook's mother and Van's mother as well. Mr. Longdon once courted each lady, but with no success. Van now finds himself looking at Mrs. Brook's circle through the eyes of Mr. Longdon. They provide him with the occasion—for the feelings are clearly not new—to voice his uneasy dissatisfaction with the circle, with London, with modernity and his own part in it. How deeply Van feels this and how much he merely plays at self-castigation is hard to determine and, as I have suggested earlier, is meant to be indeterminate. But there seems to be something more than amusement or complacency in his attempt to grasp and appropriate Mr. Longdon's attitude.

The older man has lived outside London for years, and Van, whose imagination "liked to place an object, even to the point of losing sight of it in its conditions," conceives what a "nice old nook it must have taken to keep a man of intelligence so fresh while suffering him to remain so fine" (chap. 1). Van can only suppose that the free talk at Mrs. Brook's must have struck Mr. Longdon as "odd." If Van shows "elation" in producing his surmise, it is not, I think, the pleasure of being shocked but the delight of his accuracy in placing Mr. Longdon and in imagining his response. Van is, moreover, almost eager to be caught out in vulgarity: when he speaks of Mrs. Brookenham as Fernanda, he at once accepts Mr. Longdon's "scruple" and admits that he does not use that name in her presence. Van cannot resist a light and rather cheap remark (too often the level of the circle's wit) when he explains how seldom his own Christian name, Gustavus, is used by Mrs. Brook. "Any implication that she consciously avoided it might make you see deeper depths." To this Mr. Longdon replies with pain: "Oh, I'm not so bad as that!" (chap. 1) When they speak of Nanda's age, which is almost nineteen but which her mother vaguely sets at sixteen, Van is amused by Mrs. Brook's vanity. "She has done so, I think, for the last year or two" (since, in fact, she has turned forty). But Van's amusement must now, because of Mr. Longdon's presence, be turned upon himself as he recognizes what he has done: "It was nasty doing that? I see, I see. Yes, yes: I rather gave her away, and you're struck by it—as is most delightful *you* should be— because you're, in every way, of a better tradition." No friendship, Van concludes, of the kind Mr. Longdon has cherished, can survive in "great towns and great crowds." London society must seem to an outsider "an elbowing, pushing, perspiring, chattering mob." But Mr. Longdon sees acutely enough that Van is too quick and glib in mocking self-deprecation. "That shows you really don't care," he says; and he adds, "You ought to, you ought to" (chap. 2).

Mr. Longdon is struck by the resemblance he finds between photographs of Nanda and those of her grandmother, Lady Julia. Van can see an "originality" in his preferring Nanda's beauty to Mrs. Brook's. "London doesn't love the latent or lurking," he explains, and there have been some fears about Nanda's chance for an early marriage (chap. 2). Mr. Longdon cannot yet imagine that Nanda is unwelcome in her mother's drawing room. She has reached the "awkward age" at which she can no longer be hidden in the nursery but is still too young to enter the free talk of her mother's circle. To prevent Nanda's damping the wit of their "temple of analysis," Mrs. Brook allows Nanda great freedom to visit friends, including the unhappily married Tishy Grendon. This is no gesture of trust by Mrs. Brook: it is the laxity of indifference and the pursuit of her own convenience. Nanda becomes in the process exposed to all the scandalous secrets that animate London conversation. She does not regard the scandals with primness or with prurience. She does not take pleasure in others' disadvantage. Her "lucidity" accepts truth with candor and genuine concern.

In contrast to Mrs. Brook, her friend the duchess—the title is Italian, but Jane is English—raises her niece Aggie in protected innocence. She wants Aggie to read only proper books, history "that leaves the horrors out." As a "little rounded and tinted innocence had been aimed at," Mr. Longdon reflects, "the fruit had been grown to the perfection of a peach on a sheltered wall." Little Aggie has been "deliberately prepared for consumption." Nanda, in contrast, is a "northern savage," all the elements of her nature overt and unforced.

> Both the girls struck him as lambs with a great shambles of life
> in their future; but while one, with its neck in a pink ribbon, had
> no consciousness but that of being fed from the hand with the
> sweet biscuit of unobjectionable knowledge, the other struggled
> with instincts and forebodings, with the suspicion of its doom
> and the far-borne scent, in the flowery fields, of blood.
>
> (chap. 18)

This final contrast reveals Mr. Longdon's changing consciousness. He has come to recognize in Nanda, for all her modernity of manners and precocious awareness, a more radical innocence than Aggie possesses. Aggie remains ostentatiously virginal—the ostentation is not hers but her aunt's—until she marries. Then she breaks free with a smash, capturing her aunt's lover (who is also her husband's friend) for herself.

Mr. Longdon comes to see how impossible it would be—for all their physical resemblance—to recreate Lady Julia in Nanda. He has lived through that past from which his manners and his values come, and he relinquishes any thought of preserving it at the cost of doing justice to Nanda's distinctive beauty. Vanderbank, in contrast, is less realistic. He projects into the generation of Mr. Longdon and Lady Julia the beauty by which he measures all he finds ugly in his own age and in himself. It is a more romantic, more fragile, more external, perhaps more inhuman vision of the past. It arises from the division within himself, and it must be protected all the more jealously for the consolation it provides. Vanderbank cannot accept the element of modernity in Nanda, for all its candor. He sees it as defilement.

The division within Vanderbank is central to the novel. I think we must grant him a sincere enough dream of innocence, just as we must recognize the genuine appeal he has for Mr. Longdon as well as for Nanda. Mitchett says of Van at one point that he is "thoroughly straight," at another that he is "formed for a distinctly higher sphere" and that "on our level"—that of Mrs. Brook's circle—he is "positively wasted" (chap. 10). Vanderbank *is* different from Mrs. Brook and most of her circle; it may be the very division within him which accounts for the "sacred terror" others feel in him. If we take him as a man intrinsically flawed with indecisiveness—a Jamesian hollow man, like John Marcher in "The Beast in the Jungle"—we rob the book of much of its intensity. For its dramatic action arises from Mrs. Brook's effort to prevent his marrying Nanda.

One can see the quality of Mrs. Brook's world most succinctly by considering her son Harold. Harold is not made a contrast to his mother as Nanda is. He reduces to a series of comic turns the selfishness that his mother, for the most part, covers with style or wit. His mother encourages Harold to secure invitations to country houses, where, we learn, he cheats at cards. As his mother lightly says, "however Harold plays, he has a way of winning" (chap. 6). At home he pilfers any money that is not locked up, and he duns the men who visit his mother, particularly the amiable Mitchy. Harold's parents feel that they should ask Mitchy if he has been dunned; but, as Mr. Brookenham remarks, it "will be such a beastly bore if he admits it." Brookenham can't easily and doesn't want to pay his son's debts; and, somewhat like the John Dashwoods in *Sense and Sensibility,* the Brookenhams rationalize their comfortable obliviousness: "they ought to tell us, and when they don't it serves them right." (When the question of Vanderbank arises, Mr. Brookenham's reply to his wife is, "I think, Van, you know, is your affair.") Mrs. Brook offers, with no great expectation of being believed, the danger of her husband's outrage as a reason for Mitchy to conceal Harold's guilt. Thereupon she promptly adopts a contrary-to-fact construction: "if you *had* let Harold borrow," she says to Mitchy, "you would have another manner." By the end of the novel, Harold has come far out, savagely impertinent and very much, Van tells us, "the rage." He has become the lover of Lord Petherton's sister and Mr. Cashmore's wife, Lady Fanny, and thus keeps her from running off with a Captain Dent-Douglas—like Anna Karenina, as Mrs. Brook observes, to "one of the smaller Italian towns" (chap. 21). Mrs. Brook remarks of her son, "His success is true. . . . I hold my breath. But I'm bound to say I rather admire."

Mrs. Brook herself is "charmingly pretty," with "lovely, silly eyes" and a "natural, quavering tone" of voice that work together, like a "trick that had never yet been exposed," to give her always "the pure light of youth" (chap. 4). Beneath that charm is an unblinking sense of her advantage, a powerful will, and awesome shrewdness. She is of the strain of Becky Sharp and Trollope's Lizzie Eustace. She sees Mr. Longdon as a possible benefactor because of his devotion to the memory of her mother. "The thing is," she softly wails, "that I don't see how he *can* like Harold." She looks coolly at the facts: "And I don't think he really likes *me*. . . . I mean not utterly *really*. He has to try to." But that, she concludes, won't matter. " 'He'll be just the same.' She saw it steadily and saw it whole. 'On account of mamma.' " The derisive tag from Matthew Arnold helps to fix by contrast the closeness with which Mrs. Brook's vision operates as she chooses her strategy: "He *must* like Nanda" (chap. 6).

Mr. Longdon's wealth, Mrs. Brook thinks, must be immense. "I can see it growing while he sits there," she remarks to Van. "I should really like not to lose him." As she contemplates Mr. Longdon's uses, she asks Van in turn, "What can we make him do for you?" Van's blank, embarrassed response requires a stronger assertion. "How can any one love you . . . without wanting to show it in some way? You know all the ways, dear Van, . . . in which *I* want to show it." His reply returns them to the business at hand: "That, for instance, is the tone not to take with him" (chap. 14). Mrs. Brook is conscious of what attracts Van in Mr. Longdon and gives Van influence in turn. It is an image of goodness that she finds at best boring. And Mrs. Brook clearly sees the danger in Van's divided mind: "It will be him you'll help. If you're to make sacrifices to keep on good terms with him, the first sacrifice will be of me."

There are two measures Mrs. Brook uses to keep Van. One is to insist again and again on how much that is improper Nanda knows, how much she is pursued by Mr. Cashmore (who has tired of his mistress, Tishy Grendon's sister), how free she is at Tishy's to keep her own hours. The other is to insist, with the force of a willed prophecy, that he will not act. We see both of these measures at work in the remarkable twenty-first chapter. Mrs. Brook complains to Van of the cost of Nanda's presence—the reduction of their talk to the "stupid, flat, fourth-rate." She speculates on what Mr. Longdon may do for Nanda, and at last asks Van directly, "Has he given *you* anything?" Mrs. Brook still captivates Van by "the childlike innocence with which her voice could invest the hardest teachings of life." Then "with the air of a man who had suddenly determined on a great blind leap," Van reveals what Mr. Longdon asked him to keep a secret, the offer of a large sum of money to make Van's marriage to Nanda possible. Van has been reluctant to tell Mrs. Brook of this, but he is even more reluctant not to do so. Is it an effort to make her release him or an appeal for her to hold him? She is bold enough to reply: "Do you imagine I want you myself?" She refuses to plead with him and insists upon the chance of success: "Of course you know . . . that she'd jump at you." Van is still locked in uncertainty and tries to read his own motives: "Isn't there rather something in my having thus thought it my duty to warn you that I'm definitely his candidate?" And once more Mrs. Brook takes a high hand: "What kind of monster are you trying to make me out?" And then she introduces the other measure:

> Holding him a minute as with the soft, low voice of his fate, she sadly but firmly shook her head. "You won't do it."
> "Oh!" he almost too loudly protested.
> "You won't do it," she went on.
> "I *say*"—he made a joke of it.
> "You won't do it," she repeated.
> It was as if he could not at last but show himself really struck; yet what he exclaimed on was what might in truth most have impressed him. You *are* magnificent, really!"
>
> (chap. 21)

Mrs. Brookenham's great stroke is to expose Nanda's sophistication—through a sordid French novel Nanda has read and passed on to Tishy Grendon (one, ironically, belonging to Vanderbank, whose name Nanda has inscribed in it). Mrs. Brook does this in such a way as to shock Van, and at the same time she "calls in" Nanda from Mr. Longdon's care. Her purpose is to force upon Mr. Longdon the ugliness of Nanda's life so as to make him save her by adoption and a financial settlement. When Mrs. Brook demands Nanda's return, her husband wanders into the conversation and maladroitly exclaims, "We wouldn't *take* her" (chap. 29). Mrs. Brook's resourcefulness is great. She brilliantly meets the duchess's observation that Brookenham has spoken without his cue:

> "We dressed today in a hurry and hadn't time for our usual rehearsal. Edward, when we dine out, generally brings three pocket-handkerchiefs and six jokes. I leave the management of the handkerchiefs to his own taste, but we mostly try together, in advance, to arrange a career for the other things. It's some charming light thing of my own that's supposed to give him the sign."
>
> (chap. 30)

For all her resourcefulness, Mrs. Brook's plan brings no immediate success. Vanderbank, in spite of Mr. Longdon's support, delays for months.

Nanda has earlier sensed his revulsion from her modernity, as if to say to
him, "I can't help it any more than you can, can I?"

> So she appeared to put it to him, with something in her lucidity
> that would have been infinitely touching; a strange, grave calm
> consciousness of their common doom. . . . [Vanderbank sprang
> up] as if he had been infinitely touched . . . and there was in fact
> on Vanderbank's part quite the look of the man—though it lasted
> but just while we seize it—in suspense about himself.
>
> (chap. 23)

The last book of *The Awkward Age,* the one named for Nanda, is made
up in large part of Nanda's visits from three men: Vanderbank, Mitchy, and
Mr. Longdon. Vanderbank is painfully flustered and uneasy, but Nanda's
purpose is to spare him all she can. She is like Maggie Verver in the second
part of *The Golden Bowl*: "To force upon him an awkwardness was like
forcing a disfigurement or a hurt, so that at the end of a minute . . . she
arrived at the appearance of having changed places with him and of their
being together precisely in order that he—not she—should be let down easily" (chap. 35). That is a good brief account of Maggie's treatment of Charlotte Stant and, to a degree, of the prince. Nanda not only does not reproach
Vanderbank, but she urges him not to desert her mother. "I verily believe
she's in love with you. Not, for that matter, that father would mind—he
wouldn't mind, as he says, a twopenny rap" (chap. 36). And she adds, with
unashamed maturity: "She's so fearfully young." As she tries to reconcile
them, Nanda can say, with an implicit sense of her own life as a daughter,
"You *can't* know how much you are to her. You're more to her, I verily
believe, than any one *ever* was." Van is touched because he is also relieved:
"no one who ever *has* liked her can afford ever again, for any long period,
to do without her. . . . She's a fixed star." Nanda helps him rise to more and
more celebration, almost as if she were reviving his feelings for Mrs. Brook
by making him voice them. At the last, he reverts to an indirect apology,
cast as a message to Mr. Longdon: "Look after my good name. . . . I've
odiously neglected him—by a complication of accidents. There are things I
ought to have done that I haven't. . . . I've been a brute, and I didn't mean
it, and I couldn't help it" (chap. 36).

When Nanda relays his message, Mr. Longdon is struck by her pride.
"Pride's all right," he says, "when it helps one to bear things." But Nanda
will not have it that way. When one wants to take most, rather than least,
from things, she says, "one . . . must rather grovel." When Mr. Longdon
wishes she didn't "so wonderfully love" Van, she bursts into tears. She sees

herself as "the horrible impossible," who *is* what Van thinks her. "We can't help it. It isn't really our fault. . . . Everything's different from what it used to be." She turns to Mr. Longdon, who has come so far. "Oh, he's more old-fashioned than you." But he tried—"he did his best. But he couldn't" (chap. 37).

The "extreme pinch" of Vanderbank's "romance is the vivacity in him, to his positive sorrow and loss, of the state of being aware." Van's awareness only creates division rather than spreads to cover and to embrace. It seems, as Robert Caserio has written, that Van, rather than Longdon, is "puritanical and nostalgic, even sentimental, about the past." This is, I have tried to suggest, a reflex of his dissatisfaction with himself, the expression of that part of him which distrusts and even rebels against Mrs. Brookenham, for all his devotion to and need for her. Is it true (to pursue Caserio's account) that he has "a kind of detached, lucid endurance of the age, a lucidity that is modern because it is inactive"? I should prefer, for reasons I've indicated, to stress Vanderbank's ultimate bewilderment in contrast with Nanda's hard-earned lucidity. He remains bewildered because he can never reconcile the opposed impulses within himself; he seems doomed to a joyless (if not un-pleasant) life in Mrs. Brookenham's circle. "What are parties given for in London," the duchess remarks, "but that enemies may meet?" (chap. 8).

If Vanderbank's inaction remains the crux of the plot, the culmination is the heroic generosity of Nanda in giving him "that refined satisfaction with himself which would proceed from his having dealt with a difficult hour in a gallant and delicate way" (chap. 35). It is for Nanda, in fact, to do so in order to leave Vanderbank with the sense that he has done so. In his preface to *The Spoils of Poynton* James writes of the "free spirit"—in that novel Fleda Vetch, as it is Nanda in this—"always much tormented, and by no means always triumphant . . . heroic, ironic, pathetic . . . 'successful' only through having remained free." That freedom may be earned, in Joseph Conrad's phrase, through "the supreme energy of an act of renunciation." Milly Theale renounces any grievance in leaving the money to Densher; Densher renounces the money for himself. In this novel Nanda Brookenham renounces any claim on Vanderbank's conscience or upon his self-regard. Like Maggie Verver, later, she preserves those who have failed or wronged her, both Van and her mother. Conrad goes on to observe that a "solution by rejection must always present a certain lack of finality, especially startling when contrasted with the usual methods of solution by rewards and punish-ments." One can connect Conrad's observations with James's words in "The Art of Fiction" (1884): the "essence of moral energy is to survey the whole field." James wishes to reject an external, rule-bound conception of morality, and in the process he often celebrates the consciousness which can see around all others and enfold them in its understanding. So with the author: the "moral" sense of a work of art depends on "the amount of felt life concerned in producing it." The artist's sensibility should be a soil in which "any vision of life" can grow "with due freshness and straightness" (Preface to *The Portrait of a Lady*).

James is always ready to put deeper virtues in the balance with conventions and rules. When he writes W. D. Howells about the French novelists he knows, he strikes such a balance: "They do the only kind of work, today, that I respect; and in spite of their ferocious pessimism and their handling of unclean things, they are at least serious and honest." There is a telling contrast drawn between Thackeray and Balzac:

> Balzac loved his Valérie then as Thackeray did not love his Becky, or his Blanche Amory in *Pendennis*. But his prompting was not to expose her; it could only be, on the contrary . . . to cover her up and protect her, in the interest of her special genius and freedom. All his impulse was to *la faire valoir,* to give her all her value, just as Thackeray's attitude was the opposite one, a desire positively to expose and desecrate poor Becky—to follow her up, catch her in the act, and bring her to shame: though with a mitigation, an admiration, an inconsequence, now and then wrested from him by an instinct finer, in his mind, than the so-called "moral" eagerness. The English writer wants to make sure, first of all, of your moral judgment; the French is willing, while it waits a little, to risk, for the sake of his subject and its interest, your spiritual salvation.

Clearly James is distrustful of any moral restrictions set upon the field of consciousness. But he distrusts other restrictions no less. In his early essay on Baudelaire he writes, "to count out the moral element in one's appreciation of an artistic total is exactly as sane as it would be (if the total were a poem) to eliminate all the words in three syllables." Morality "is in reality simply a part of the essential richness of inspiration—it has nothing to do with the artistic process and it has everything to do with the artistic effect. The more a work of art feels it at its source, the richer it is; the less it feels it, the poorer it is." The kind of moral imagination James brings to the case of Vanderbank, or of Densher, is to be seen in a remark he made in an early letter: "We know when we lie, when we kill, when we steal, when we deceive or violate others; but it is hard to know when we deceive or violate ourselves."

"ALMOST SOCRATIC"

As James presents one of Mrs. Brookenham's questions, he calls her "almost Socratic." It is an interesting observation because one feels at times a remote influence upon James of the Platonic dialogues. I have no wish to fix that influence but only to consider the kind of midwifery of ideas, like that which Socrates claims, we can find in some of James's dialogue. One of the forms of intensity James achieves is the dramatization of a process wherein a man's accepted ideas are gradually brought into question and replaced. A good instance is the evening Lambert Strether spends in London with Maria Gostrey, at dinner and at the theater (*The Ambassadors*). It is also a good instance of that principle of which James wrote to H. G. Wells: "It is art that *makes* life, makes interest, makes importance."

In this chapter, the first of book 2, Strether is learning "to find names" for many matters, and on no evening of his life has he tried to supply so many. Maria Gostrey is the "mistress of a hundred cases or categories," and Strether soon feels that she "knew even intimate things about him that he hadn't yet told her and perhaps never would." She is eliciting from him the names or categories by which he has organized experience all of his life in America, and the very process by which she elicits them requires Strether to bring them to full consciousness, and then withdraw from, circumambulate, and question attitudes he has so far taken as natural and necessary. He has not told her these things about himself because he has not known that he knew them. They emerge in consciousness through the art of her questions.

Everything about Strether's evening defines itself in opposition to the world he has known; when he has gone to the theater with his American patron, Mrs. Newsome, he has enjoyed no "little confronted dinner, no pink lights, no whiff of vague sweetness." Nor has Mrs. Newsome ever worn a dress cut so low. Strether finds himself given over to "uncontrolled perception," to a freedom of awareness that Mrs. Newsome's black dress and white ruff have never encouraged. The red velvet band around Maria's throat becomes a "starting-point for fresh backward, fresh forward, fresh lateral flights." If Mrs. Newsome's ruff suggested Queen Elizabeth, Maria Gostrey's band evokes Mary Stuart. Strether finds in himself a "candor of fancy" that takes pleasure in such an antithesis. The texture of all he sees becomes more complex; the English "types" both on the stage and in the audience will prove more varied and distinct than Woollett allowed.

As Maria Gostrey draws Strether out on the subject of his mission, she requires him to attend to those terms he has never before questioned. She often echoes a response, holding a note he has sounded until it becomes the object of their joint perception. And to see with her eyes is to begin to free himself from the limits in which he has unconsciously acquiesced. She has also a tendency to abet his most treasonous thoughts. He begins, at the theater, to feel "kindness" for the young man on the stage who wears perpetual evening dress and weakly succumbs to "a bad woman in a yellow frock." Would Chad Newsome (whom he has come to rescue) wear evening dress, too? Would Strether have to do so himself to meet Chad at a proper level?

As his own thoughts warily approach such questions, Maria Gostrey puts them so directly before him that he can hardly evade them. "You've accepted the mission of separating him from the wicked woman. Are you quite sure she's very bad for him?" Strether is startled by the question: "Of course we are. Wouldn't *you* be?" Maria refuses the comfort of easy judgment. "One can only judge the facts." Might, after all, the woman be charming? Again, Strether is startled:

> "Charming?"—Strether stared before him. "She's base, venal—out of the streets."
> "I see. And *he*—?"
> "Chad, wretched boy?"
> "Of what type and temper is he?" she went on as Strether had lapsed.

We aren't told why he has "lapsed," but presumably he is forced to ask himself whether Chad is merely a virtuous American lad seduced.

> "Well—the obstinate." It was as if for a moment he had been going to say more and had then controlled himself.
> That was scarce what she wanted. "Do you like him?"
> This time he was prompt. "No. How *can* I?"

Once Strether has acknowledged his dislike of Chad Newsome, he wishes to attribute it to the son's treatment of his mother. Mrs. Newsome inspires a rather exalted idiom: "He has darkened her admirable life." Then, as if to bring it down to earth, Strether makes the point less stuffily: "He has worried her half to death." Maria, for reasons of her own, picks up the first and, as it were, the "official" version: "Is her life very admirable?" To this Strether replies with a solemn, perhaps reverent, "Extraordinarily." James indicates the timing of these remarks: "There was so much in the tone that Miss Gostrey had to devote another pause to the appreciation of it." She proceeds to deflate Strether's dictum and perhaps also to uncover the strong managerial role of Mrs. Newsome: "And he has only *her*? I don't mean the bad

woman in Paris . . . for I assure you I shouldn't even at the best be disposed
to allow him more than one. But has he only his mother?"

Strether mentions Chad's sister, Sarah Pocock, and he can imply of her,
as he could not of her mother, that she is not universally beloved. Maria calls
up Strether's earlier "admirable": "But *you* admire her?" And this releases
Strether's critical awareness: "I'm perhaps a little afraid of her." What Maria
is trying to uncover is the kind of will that governs the ladies and Strether
as their ambassador. When he exclaims that they would do "anything in the
world for him," Maria turns that conventional tribute inside out: "And you'd
do anything in the world for them?" Strether is uncomfortable; she "had
made it perhaps just a shade too affirmative for his nerves: 'Oh I don't
know.'" Their generosity begins to turn, under Maria's cool queries, into
something like officiousness. "The 'anything' they'd do is represented by
their *making* you do it."

A comic view of Mrs. Newsome begins to emerge. "She puts so much
of herself into everything—." And Maria nicely picks up the absurdity: "that
she has nothing left for anything else?" Strether begins to let go his admiration. Maria supposes that "if your friend *had* come she would take great
views, and the great views, to put it simply, would be too much for her."
Strether by now is no longer defensive; he is "amused at" Maria's "notion
of the simple," but accepts her terms: "Everything's too much for her."

James catches the conflict of exaltation and vulgarity in the unmention-
able thing whose manufacture is the source of Mrs. Newsome's wealth: "a
small, trivial, rather ridiculous object of the commonest domestic use,"
Strether lamely describes it; "it's rather wanting in—what shall I say? Well,
dignity, or the least approach to distinction." James looks ahead to Maria's
many attempts to have him name it; with their failure she can treat "the
little nameless object as indeed unnameable—she could make their abstention
enormously definite." And behind this suppressed object there are sources
of money even more questionable, not simply vulgar but dishonest. We begin
to see Mrs. Newsome covering these wrongs with a high manner, as a "moral
swell," the patron of the review that Strether edits and that few read. "It's
her tribute to the ideal," Strether explains. Maria puts it otherwise: "You
assist her to expiate—which is rather hard when you've yourself not sinned."

Perhaps the saddest and most significant exchange concerns the plans
for Chad:

> "He stands . . . if you succeed with him, to gain—"
> "Oh a lot of advantages." Strether had them clearly at his
> fingers' ends.

> "By which you mean of course a lot of money."
>
> "Well, not only. I'm acting with a sense for him of other things
> too. Consideration and comfort and security—the general safety
> of being anchored by a strong chain. He wants, as I see him, to
> be protected. Protected I mean from life."
>
> "Ah *voilà*!"—her thought fitted with a click. "From life. What
> you *really* want to get him home for is to marry him."

There is something pitiable in this distrust of "life." Strether has been, as
he now would have Chad be, "anchored by a strong chain." To question
this prepares, of course, for his speech in Gloriani's garden, the rueful "Live
all you can!"

Maria Gostrey has come to recognize the range of awareness that
Strether can, with release, attain. He has modesty, simplicity, good will,
conscience—beneath the conventional attitudes he has come abroad to represent are generosity and imagination. Later, Little Bilham will say to him,
"you're not a person to whom it's easy to tell things you don't want to know.
Though it *is* easy, I admit—it's quite beautiful . . . when you do want to"
(bk. 5, chap. 1). When Maria first asks Strether what, if he should fail, he
stands to lose, he exclaims, "Nothing!" As she leaves him, she asks once
more, "What do you stand to lose?"

> Why the question now affected him as other he couldn't have
> said; he could only this time meet it otherwise. "Everything."
>
> (bk. 2, chap. 1)

Has he come at last to reject the old language-game he has brought from
Woollett, to reverse the meanings of "succeed" and "fail"? Later, in Paris
with his dogged fellow American Waymarsh, the question of when he will
see Chad comes up.

> "Well," said Strether almost gaily, "I guess I don't know any-
> thing!" His gaiety might have been a tribute to the fact that the
> state he had been reduced to did for him again what had been
> done by his talk of the matter with Miss Gostrey at the London
> theatre. It was somehow enlarging.
>
> (bk. 3, chap. 1)

The enlargement will take Strether to a vision of Chad and Mme de
Vionnet, and of Paris itself, so large as to reverse all of his original judgments.
When Strether learns that the "virtuous attachment" he has imagined is not
what he thought, when he discovers that Mme de Vionnet is in fact Chad's

mistress, he has come too far to revert to his earlier moral categories. He has already seen Mrs. Newsome's lack of imagination and force of will. He has not been able to budge her from her preconceptions, and all that is left is "morally and intellectually to get rid of her." He sees her "fine cold thought" as a "particularly large iceberg in a cool blue northern sea." And Maria complements his thought with her own: "There's nothing so magnificent—for making others feel you—as to have no imagination" (bk. 11, chap. 1).

At Strether's final meeting with Mme de Vionnet in her apartment, the aristocratic setting promises support: the "things from far back—tyrannies of history, facts of type, values, as the painters said, of expression—all working for her and giving her the supreme chance, the chance . . . on a great occasion, to be natural and simple." Her lie and Chad's now seem to him "an inevitable tribute to good taste," even as he winces "at the amount of comedy involved" in his own misunderstanding (bk. 12, chap. 1). But what Strether learns is how helpless her passion for Chad has been. As she has put it obliquely, "The wretched self is always there, always making one somehow a fresh anxiety." And while she asserts that the "only safe thing is to give," she seems, after all, in her fear that Chad will leave her, "exploited." She has made Chad better; "but it came to our friend with supreme queerness that he was none the less only Chad." Strether finally exclaims to Mme de Vionnet, "You're afraid for your life!" (bk. 12, chap. 2). Her aristocratic nature will not save her. Strether recalls the fate of Madame Roland, the "smell of revolution, the smell of the public temper—or perhaps simply, the smell of blood" (bk. 12, chap. 1). He sees Mme de Vionnet at once as "the finest and subtlest creature" caught in a passion "mature, abysmal, pitiful."

After two reversals, then, Strether finds himself once more voicing a moral view. To Chad, who shows signs of being ready for Woollett and the "art" of advertising, who seems somewhat tired of Mme de Vionnet and perhaps unfaithful to her, Strether appeals "by all you hold sacred" to remain in Paris (bk. 12, chap. 4). Strether finally sees beneath the charm of his new manners Chad's limited consciousness; Chad has spoken of being tired of Mme de Vionnet "as he might have spoken of being tired of roast mutton for dinner." And Strether calls Chad to moral responsibility as intensely as he might once have done, but the moral vision comes now out of a breadth of consciousness that would have been unimaginable in his early talk with Maria Gostrey. "You owe her everything," he tells Chad, "very much more than she can ever owe you. You've in other words duties to her, of the most positive sort; and I don't see what other duties . . . can be held to go before them" (bk. 12, chap. 4).

As Strether later recounts the meeting to Maria Gostrey, he recognizes the "portentous solemnity" of his moral view, but, he concludes, "I was made so." And he must leave Maria and Paris so as not to get anything for himself: "To be right." Just as the early moral attitudes had to give way to the more inclusive awareness that aesthetic ordering permitted, so now the scope of the aesthetic is in turn enlarged—but in a far different way and with much more at stake—by the concern with conduct. Mme de Vionnet is more and less than she was, Chad's change seems less complete, and even Maria and her "hundred cases and categories" must be surrendered to a final view that is sterner. "It was awkward, it was almost stupid, not to seem to prize" the beauty and knowledge in Maria's life and in her offer of love (bk. 12, chap. 5). But, as James put it in the "project" for the novel, Strether "has come so far through his little experience that he has come out on the other side—on the other side even of a union with Miss Gostrey. He must go back as he came—or rather, really, so quite other that, in comparison, marrying Miss Gostrey would be almost of the same order." The sternness comes of an acceptance of consciousness, with all its privileges and pains, at the expense of all else.

DEBORAH ESCH

A Jamesian About-Face:
Notes on "The Jolly Corner"

And we know how the possible—that ghostly and unreal life of what
might have been, figures with which we have a standing rendezvous—
exerted a dangerous, sometimes almost insane attraction on James,
which perhaps art alone enabled him to explore and exorcise.

         —MAURICE BLANCHOT

The question of unrealized possibilities—of what one might have done, who
one might have become, had circumstances been different—is posed with
notable persistence in James's narratives, the autobiographical and critical as
well as the fictive. Dencombe, the figure for the writer in a tale called "The
Middle Years," is a dying novelist obsessed with the idea of revision (the
reader finds him compulsively correcting the proofs of what turns out to be
his last novel, *The Middle Years*), with the books he might have written and
might still write if he could only get, as he laments, an "extension." When
a number of prominent authors were asked, during a recent symposium on
literary composition, to reflect back on their own careers in order to name
the work they would most like to have produced, at least one participant
recognized a Jamesian note in the question, and responded in kind:

> In a story by Henry James, "The Jolly Corner," a man at night
> looks in an empty house for the ghost of the person he could
> have been if his life had been different. The house is that of his
> youth. In it, thus, are all the possibilities that have not come true.

From *ELH* 50, no. 3 (Fall 1983). © 1983 by the Johns Hopkins University Press
and © 1985 by Deborah Esch.

> At dawn the man sees his ghost, and it frightens him. This is the
> story I would have wanted to write, or that I would have wanted
> to live, or the story in which I identify myself when I try to
> imagine the books that I could have written instead of those I
> have.

With his choice of James's late ghost story, Italo Calvino, himself a raconteur
with a penchant for the fantastic, provides a concise plot summary along
with an appropriate point of departure for a reading of "The Jolly Corner."
Like Spencer Brydon, the tale's protagonist, Calvino is asked to conceive of
"possibilities that have not come true" for him, and he finds the question
itself thematized in the work he would have written. What is more, Calvino
not only identifies the story, but does so several times over, in a process of
revision punctuated by "or" that, in effect, opens two distinct avenues of
interpretation to other readers of the tale.

On the one hand, the story might be read as "the exploration of a
consciousness and the education of a perception"—that is, as a narrative of
self-identification ("the one in which I identify myself") and eventual self-
consciousness on the part of character (Brydon) and reader (here, Calvino).
In this light, altogether familiar in the criticism of James's fiction, "the house
on the jolly corner, like the House of Usher, becomes the emblem of a mind,"
and the tale is understood to enact the painful ordeal of that mind as it
struggles to fuller consciousness of itself. On the other hand, a slight shift
of emphasis in Calvino's assessment would suggest that "The Jolly Corner"
might be read in another light as well: the story he would have wanted to
write, the one that comes to mind when he tries to imagine the books he
could have written, might be approached in terms of reading (and self-read-
ing) and writing (and self-writing). The many attentive interpreters who have
traced and retraced the Jamesian "coming to terms" in the psychological
and the epistemological senses of a character's becoming reconciled to his
or her hard-won self-consciousness tend to overlook the other, rhetorical
significance of the activity of mind indicated by this phrase: namely, that of
finding the "terms" that will turn its experience into a writable, readable
narrative. It is presumably clear, even to the reader for whom language as
such is not an issue in the fiction, that the crucial terms arrived at by the
Jamesian consciousness (whether narrator or character) are invariably terms
of comparison, or metaphors. Yet this observation is generally relegated by
the critics to a discussion of style or technique as categories understood to
subsume this aspect of the prose, rather than serving as a spur to the interpretation of the pervasive figures of speech themselves. This neglect of

James's consistent and explicit appeal to figurative language is particularly perplexing in the case of "The Jolly Corner," a tale that turns upon the consequences, for character, narrator, and reader, of "strange figures" lurking in the text in the guise of familiar idioms. For the reader who acknowledges the force of these metaphors, the suspense attending this ghost story is displaced from the recounted act or event to the narrative's textual surface. The "ordeal of consciousness," in this exemplary Jamesian narrative, is a function of the process of figuration that it thematizes—of the ordeal, that is, of reading and writing.

"The Jolly Corner" was first published in December 1908 in Ford Madox Hueffer's newly-founded *English Review,* after suffering rejection by a number of other editors. In keeping with James's characteristic practice of revision, even this late tale underwent minor modification as it passed from the journal to volume 17 of the New York edition. In most respects, however, the two versions are identical: they recount a critical moment in the history of Spencer Brydon, a middle-aged American expatriate who, after a sojourn of thirty-three years in Europe, returns to New York and his ancestral home. To this extent, the tale has some autobiographical basis, and critics have rightly recognized aspects of the author's career in that of his character. James returned to his birthplace in 1904, following an absence of twenty-two years, on a journey that is documented in the essay "New York Revisited," collected in *The American Scene.* Like Brydon, James finds the city greatly changed, in ways he had not anticipated. He articulates his ambivalence, as a "revisiting spirit," by way of a figure of writing, of inscription: "It was an extraordinary statement on the subject of New York that the space between Fourteenth Street and Washington Square *should* . . . figure as the old ivory of an overscored tablet." The nostalgic narrative of his own history is disrupted by the most drastic alteration James discovers on his homecoming: the "house of his youth" has been razed to make room for "a high, square, impersonal structure" that "so blocks, at the right moment for its own success, the view of the past, that the effect for me, in Washington Place, was of having been amputated of half my history." Having linked the activity of remembering with one of dismembering, he further figures his disenchantment as follows:

> This was the snub, for the complacency of retrospect, that, whereas the inner sense had positively erected there for its private contemplation a commemorative mural tablet, the very wall that should have borne this inscription had been smashed as for demonstration that tablets, in New York, are unthinkable. . . . Where,

in fact, is the point of inserting a mural tablet, at any legible height, in a building certain to be destroyed to make room for a sky-scraper?

Spencer Brydon likewise experiences a mixed response of fascination and dismay on his belated return to New York, and borrows James's figure of the "overscored tablet" when he compares the city to "some vast ledger-page, overgrown, fantastic, of ruled and criss-crossed lines and figures" (this and subsequent references to "The Jolly Corner" and others of James's novels, essays, and tales are to the New York edition). He is repelled by the philistine values everywhere in evidence, judging them "vulgar" and "monstrous" (epithets that will reappear later in the story). But Brydon's perspective is not "blocked," his history is not "amputated," by the unexpected loss of his birthplace sustained by James. He is the possessor of two properties in the city, and has returned in part to inspect them, their rent having financed his life abroad. One of these, the unoccupied house on the site named in the title, is his ancestral home. It is also the house he comes to haunt in pursuit of the character he might have been had he lived those thirty-three years in his native city. Brydon's nightly vigil in the great vacant structure culminates in a stunning scene of recognition, when his *alter ego,* the "I" of his increasingly obsessive "I might have been," finally materializes and confronts him face to face.

Thematically, "The Jolly Corner" broke little new ground for James. Brydon's pilgrimage to New York is in some respects a revision of that of Clement Searle, the protagonist of "A Passionate Pilgrim," a tale written more than thirty years earlier. And the preliminary notes for James's last novel, *The Sense of the Past,* record the use he made of a "scrap" of that unfinished work, which also featured a ghost of sorts, in composing "The Jolly Corner." In the story-line borrowed for the shorter narrative, the

> hero's adventure there takes the form so to speak of his turning the tables, as I think I called it, on a "ghost" or whatever, a visiting or haunting apparition otherwise qualified to appall *him,* and thereby winning a sort of victory, by the appearance, and the evidence, that this personage or presence was more overwhelmingly affected by him than he by *it.*

The language in this excerpt from the notebooks rehearses the earlier account, in the autobiographical volume *A Small Boy and Others,* of a memorable scene of James's childhood—the Galerie d'Apollon in the Louvre, an old haunt of his youth—and the setting it provided for a dream he had later in life. The climax of the dream that James called "the most appalling yet most admirable nightmare" of his life was

> the sudden pursuit, through an open door, along a huge high saloon, of a just dimly-described figure that retreated in terror before my rush and dash . . . out of the room I had a moment before been desperately, and all the more abjectly, defending by the push of my shoulder against hard pressure on the lock and bar from the other side. The lucidity, not to say the sublimity, of the crisis had consisted of the great thought that I, in my appalled state, was probably still more appalling than the awful agent, creature, or presence, whatever he was. . . . The triumph of my impulse, perceived in a flash as I acted on it by myself at a bound, forcing the door outward, was the grand thing, but the great point of the whole was the wonder of my final recognition. Routed, dismayed, the tables turned on him by my so surpassing him for straight aggression and dire intention, my visitant was already but a diminished spot in the long perspective, the tremendous, glorious hall, as I say, over the far-gleaming floor of which . . . he sped for *his* life.

The "final recognition" James alludes to—that he has prevailed over "the awful agent, creature, or presence"—is predicated on a prior *self*-recognition on the part of the dreamer; insofar as James is able to identify himself as the first person in the nightmare, the account can constitute further autobiographical material for the story he would subsequently write. In both of the passages cited, the idiomatic expression "turning the tables" is used to convey the essential affair of the narrative, which in each case is an act of reversal performed by the protagonist. Spencer Brydon credits himself with the same fait accompli in the text of "The Jolly Corner," when he reflects, by way of a rhetorical question, on the turn his situation has taken: "People enough, first and last, had been in terror of apparitions, but who had ever before so turned the tables and become himself, in the apparitional world, an incalculable terror?" "Turning the tables" is a figure of speech based on a meaning of "table" other than that invoked earlier, of a tablet bearing or intended for inscription, a memorial plaque fixed in a wall, or a notice-board (*OED*); the sense of "table" in James's recurrent phrase is that of a game-board, as in chess. The player who does the turning rotates the board so as to reverse the relative positions of the opponents, putting each in the other's former place. In James's dream and in the story, the protagonist's sense of "victory," of "triumph," consists in his having effected such an about-face. On the night following his third absence from the house, calculated to lull his quarry into a false sense of reprieve, Brydon recommences his vigil with a fresh certainty, formulated in terms of another analogy with a bigger game: "'I've hunted him till he has "turned": that, up there, is what has happened—he's the fanged or the antlered animal brought at last to bay.'" The cornered prey, according to the metaphor of the chase, senses that escape is impossible and is obliged to turn and face the hunter.

The "turning" that Brydon attributes to his own cleverness and persistence in keeping pace with his adversary is placed within the quotation marks that appear with remarkable frequency in James's prose—often, but by no means exclusively, around clichés—to indicate that the word or expression quoted signifies in the manner of "so to speak" or "as it were"—that is, figuratively. It is not, then, a literal turning that Brydon is convinced has taken place, but a revolution of another sort. Immediately following his reflection, the narrative first person intrudes, as it will do no more than three times in the course of the tale, to emphasize the decisiveness of Brydon's coming-to-terms: "There came to him, as I say—but determined by an influence beyond my notation!—the acuteness of this certainty." It is an arresting moment in the story, marking an unbidden and seemingly unwarranted confession: it represents, in fact, the intervention of the narrator to call into question the possibility of a sufficient narration. Is the reader, then, to understand this interjection as an expression of undue self-efface-ment on the part of the narrator, who has so far been equal to the twists and turns of Brydon's obsessive pursuit? If so, it is curious that a second such intrusion is made for the express purpose of affirming the adequacy of the narrative notation to what is transpiring:

> Discretion—he jumped at that; and yet not, verily, at such a pitch, because it saved his nerves or his skin, but because, much more valuably, it saved the situation. When I say he "jumped" at it I feel the consonance of this term with the fact that—at the end indeed of I know not how long—he did move again, he crossed straight to the door.

Once again, the quotation marks around "jumped" indicate not only that the narrator is citing himself in a gesture of linguistic reflection, but also that he is using the term figuratively, to signify a moment in Brydon's thought process. In this case, the character's subsequent action, his virtual leap across the room, justifies the narrator's "notation" by literally acting it out. In the earlier instance of intrusion, the operation of an "influence beyond his no-tation" might, of course, rather be understood as a narrative strategy in keeping with the ostensibly uncanny, supernatural elements of the tale. But whether the remark is read ironically or taken at face value, it remains for the reader to pursue the logic and validity of the claims here being made, by character as well as narrator. This entails posing interpretive questions that are, once again, rhetorical: not because they are necessarily asked in order to produce an effect rather than to elicit a reply, but because they can be answered only with respect to the rhetorical structures and strategies in the story. Has Brydon succeeded, as he here persuades himself, in "turning the tables" once and for all to vanquish his *alter ego*? And is there indeed at work in the tale a determining influence that is beyond the narrative's ability to account for it?

The two questions—of the status of Brydon's relation to the figure for his other self, and of the status of narrative notation—are, to a considerable extent, congruent. In fact, Brydon sees his life as a linear history, a time-line along which he can trace actions and events backward and, at a fork in the path marking two incompatible routes, choose (albeit hypothetically) the alternate one. He longs to rewrite the story of his life from the moment of that choice, recover his lost opportunities, and rescue his unfulfilled potential. From the outset, before he is even conscious of its character and scope, Brydon's obsession with his conditional-imperfect past is articulated most forcefully by way of his own explicit metaphors and analogies, notably those already mentioned whose terms involve pursuit and confrontation. Early in the tale, his companion and confidante Alice Staverton observes, with the "slightly greater effect of irony" that distinguishes her version of the matter from Brydon's, that in view of the aptitude for business he has demonstrated in an exchange with a building firm representative, he has clearly neglected a real talent, a genius in fact, and could doubtless have "anticipated the inventor of the sky-scraper" if he had remained in New York. Her words constitute a refrain ("If he had but stayed at home. . . . If he had but stayed at home") and strike a chord that reverberates in Brydon's consciousness long after they are spoken, prompting his own speculation:

> It had begun to be present to him after the first fortnight, it had broken out with the oddest abruptness, this particular wanton wonderment: it met him there—and this was the image under which he himself judged the matter, or at least, not a little, thrilled and flushed with it—very much as he might have been met by some strange figure, some unexpected occupant, at a turn of one of the dim passages of an empty house. The quaint analogy quite hauntingly remained with him, when he didn't indeed rather im-

prove it by a still intenser form: that of his opening a door behind which he would have made sure of finding nothing, a door into a room shuttered and void, and yet so coming, with a great suppressed start, on some quite erect confronting presence, something planted in the middle of the place and facing him through the dusk.

As Brydon's analogy unfolds, his conception of what he might have been, which has itself no phenomenal existence, assumes the shape and substance of this "strange figure" as a result of what the narrator terms "the strangest, the most joyous, possibly the next minute almost the proudest, duplication of consciousness." But the vocabulary of consciousness cannot sufficiently account for the structure of Brydon's reflection and the specificity of the form it generates. What escapes the character, and apparently the narrator as well, is the realization that Brydon's agency (which for him, as avowedly for James, consists in his ritually turning the tables to triumph over his *alter ego*) in fact manifests itself as an ongoing activity of literalization, a turning of the tables on his own figures in an effort to fix their significance once and for all. With his nocturnal vigil on the jolly corner, he grants "all the old baffled forsworn possibilities" of the life he has missed precisely the form that a visiting apparition might have:

> What he did therefore by this appeal of his hushed presence was to wake them into such measure of ghostly life as they might still enjoy ... they had taken the Form he so longed to make them take, the Form he at moments saw himself in the light of fairly hunting on tiptoe ... from room to room and from storey to storey.

If the criticism of consciousness has no precise name for Brydon's "strange figure," for the "Form" with a capital *F* that he grants his imagined past, rhetoric can supply the missing term: *prosopopoeia* designates the figure that makes present to the senses something abstract and not susceptible of phenomenalization. In giving a face (*prosopon*) or the semblance of one (*prosopeion,* a later variant denoting *mask*) to an entity that lacks a literal visage, prosopopoeia serves as a guarantor of its existence. In its stricter sense, prosopopoeia is usually accompanied by personification, and often by apostrophe (it is the conventional figure of address in lyric poetry, and constitutive of the form of the ode). According to Pierre Fontanier in his rhetorical handbook *Les figures du discours,* prosopopoeia consists in

> somehow staging [*mettre en scène*] the absent, the dead, supernatural beings, or even inanimate objects, to make them act,

speak, respond; or at least to take them for confidants, witnesses, guarantors, accusers, avengers, judges; and this, either in jest [*par feint*] or in earnest, depending upon whether one is master of one's imagination.

While his preoccupation is evidently in earnest, whether Spencer Brydon is master of his imagination, and of the images it figures forth, is a pressing question for a reading of "The Jolly Corner." The obsession with his *alter ego* takes on the form, the phenomenality, of the "strange figure" in order to satisfy Brydon's own design; it is thus no longer, to his mind, merely conceptual and so subject to doubt, but can afford him the clarity and distinctness of a perception whose "sense" is perfectly accessible: "He knew what he meant and what he wanted; it was as clear as the figure on a cheque presented in demand for cash. His *alter ego* 'walked'—that was the note of his image of him, while his image of his motive for his own odd pastime was the desire to waylay him and meet him." But Brydon, in his eagerness to confront his other self, gets his figures confused: it seems he cannot tell (or cannot admit) the difference between the figure indicated on a check, a number that represents a fixed amount of money and can be exchanged on demand for that sum, and the "strange figure" of his earlier analogy—the prosopopoeia—to which he is attempting to assign as stable a significance by literalizing it—that is, by turning what he might have turned into into an actual, palpable presence. In other words, Brydon cannot read the word "figure," though he uses it repeatedly, because he cannot tell (or admit) the difference between its literal and figurative senses. He has forgotten, if he ever knew, that the figure of his *alter ego* is a figure by virtue of the linguistic process of figuration. Moreover, he is unable to read the quotation marks that are of his own inscription, unable to tell (or admit) the difference between walked and "walked." His claim to knowing "what he meant and what he wanted" becomes a self-deception based on a refusal *not* to literalize his own figures of speech.

This self-mystification sometimes takes the form of delusions of grandeur—Brydon is convinced that no one before him has ever achieved a frame of mind or forged a set of circumstances comparable to his own. He imagines himself, at one point in his adventure, as a Lancelot figure undergoing a test of courage:

This was before him in truth as a physical image, an image almost worthy of an age of greater romance. That remark indeed glimmered for him only to glow the next instant with a finer light;

since what age of romance, after all, could have matched either
the state of his mind or, "objectively," as they said, the wonder
of his situation? The only difference would have been that, bran-
dishing his dignities over his head as in a parchment scroll, he
might then—that is in the heroic time—have proceeded down-
stairs with a drawn sword in his other grasp.

At present, really, the light he had set down on the mantel
would have to figure his sword; which utensil, in the course of a
minute, he had taken the requisite number of steps to possess
himself of.

In the final sentence in the passage, the narrative voice resumes a description
of the action, and reminds the reader that the instrument Brydon brandishes
is not "really" the imagined sword; he merely gets hold of the closest figural
facsimile, the candle, since there is no literal rapier at hand. But the text
affords Brydon numerous other opportunities to practice his penchant for
literalizing his own figures of speech. In an exchange with Alice Staverton,
he offers an analogy for his "rage of curiosity" about what might have been:

[It] brings back what I remember to have felt, once or twice, after
judging best, for reasons, to burn some important letter un-
opened. I've been sorry, I've hated it—I've never known what
was in the letter. You may say it's a trifle . . . I shouldn't care if
you did! . . . and it's only a figure, at any rate, for the way I now
feel.

The analogy is based, as the reader discovers, on an act Brydon has performed
"once or twice" in the past—a gesture that is of course charged with symbolic significance (the same decisive measure is enacted by Kate Croy in a
pivotal moment near the conclusion of The Wings of the Dove, when she
burns Milly Theale's final letter to Densher before he can open it). In this
instance, Brydon insists on the figurative status of his comparison, as if for
Alice's instruction. Yet in another early dialogue, she catches him, as it were,
in the act. When he takes her to see the house of his youth, he denies having
even the ghost of a reason for holding on to it, rather than capitalizing on
its prime location and sacrificing it for financial gain, as he has the second,
inferior property. Alice replies by asking, elliptically, whether "the 'ghost' of
one doesn't, much rather, serve—?" Her intonational quotation marks themselves serve to indicate that "ghost," in his phrase "ghost of a reason," is a
trope, a catachresis. Brydon masks his uneasiness at her so taking note of
his guilty figure with a literalizing response that tries to make light of her

acuity: "Oh ghosts—of course the place must swarm with them! I should be ashamed of it if it didn't." The narrative is then given over to conjecture about Alice's subsequent thoughts:

> Miss Staverton's gaze again lost itself, and things she didn't utter, it was clear, came and went in her mind. She might even for the minute, off there in the fine room, have imagined some element dimly gathering. Simplified like the death-mask of a handsome face, it perhaps produced for her just then an effect akin to the stir of an expression in the "set" commemorative plaster. Yet whatever her impression may have been she produced instead a vague platitude. "Well, if it were only furnished and lived in—!"

The death mask, the prosopopoeia, produces more than the "stir of an expression," or "a vague platitude": it furnishes the house with the kind of haunting apparition Brydon alludes to in an offhand way when he literalizes the phrase "ghost of a reason." Again, he forgets the rhetorical status of the figure, and seeks to engage it as an opponent in a battle of wits—in the text's phrase, a "concentrated conscious *combat*":

> he had tasted of no pleasure so fine as his actual tension, had been introduced to no sport that demanded at once the patience and the nerve of this stalking of a creature more subtle, yet at bay perhaps more formidable, than any beast of the forest. The terms, the comparisons, the very practices of the chase positively came again into play; there were even moments when passages of his occasional experience as a sportsman, stirred memories, from his younger time, of moor and mountain and desert, revived for him—and to the increase of his keenness—by the tremendous force of analogy.

The analogy of the hunt is one that James himself uses, in his preface to *The Golden Bowl* and elsewhere, to represent the pleasure he takes in writing fiction, which he calls "the entertainment of the great game," and an "inordinate intellectual 'sport.'" In Brydon's reliance on the metaphor of the chase, "the terms, the comparisons," that he brings into play are in effect denied the "play" of possible signification that is the mark of figurative language; they are instead positively put into practice, enacted by the character's literalizing compulsion, in order that their meaning may become one—and only one—with his purpose. In the opening paragraph of the tale, when Brydon finds his belated return to his native city attended by one surprise after another, he reasons that this "might be natural when one had so long and so consistently neglected everything, taken pains to give surprise so much margin for play." He discovers soon enough that "margin for play" is precisely what he has not given, what he cannot afford to give:

> The great fact all the while however had been the incalculability; since he *had* supposed himself, from decade to decade, to be allowing, and in the most liberal and intelligent manner, for brilliancy of change. He actually saw that he had allowed for nothing; he missed what he would have been sure of finding, he found what he never would have imagined.

Later, when his *alter ego* is brought at last to bay, in the logical conclusion to the figural chain set in motion by the metaphor of the hunt, Brydon again finds what he never would have imagined—"it proved, of all the conceivable impressions, the one least suited to his book." He realizes, namely, that his prey has "turned," and is now tracking *him* at a distance, keeping him (as Brydon imagines) in sight while he remains blind to his own position vis à vis his adversary. Indeed, as Brydon reflects, "prey" has become, "by so sharp an irony"—that is, by the sharp about-face of the figure, the turn of the trope—"so little the term now to apply."

His conviction that the tables have been turned on him is, as the narrator intercedes to emphasize, "determined by an influence beyond my notation." But it is only when Brydon comes upon the closed door to the fourth-floor room with no alternate access (recalling the door in his original analogy, and in James's twice-told nightmare)—the door he is certain he has left open, in accordance with his policy—that he experiences "the violent shock of having ceased happily to forget." When he must (involuntarily) remember the rhetorical status of the figure, the possibility of another agent's being at work presents itself: "Another agent?—he had been catching, as he felt, a moment back, the very breath of him; but when had he been so close as in this simple, this logical, this completely personal act? It was so logical, that is, that one might have *taken* it for personal . . . and this time, as much as one would, the question of danger loomed." The act and the agency in question are "so logical" that they might be taken for "personal"—and are mistaken for such by Brydon in the form of the prosopopoeia, the figure that gives phenomenality to his speculation and desire, to the point of their being incarnated in the person of his projected *alter ego*.

Brydon expresses earlier in his adventure an appreciation for the *impersonal*, which he evokes by opening the shutters of the upper rooms out onto the night. He relishes

the sense of the hard silver of the autumn stars through the win-
dow-panes, and scarcely less the flare of the street-lamps below,
the white electric lustre which it would have taken curtains to
keep out. This was human actual social; this was of the world he
had lived in, and he was more at his ease certainly for the countenance, coldly general and impersonal, that all the while and in
spite of his detachment it seemed to give him.

In his anxiety, Brydon takes comfort in the impersonal "countenance"—in
the sense of moral support or encouragement—offered him by the vision of
the world outside his private ordeal. Now, however, as "the question of
danger looms," what he had taken for personal—the operation of the strange
figure in the act of closing the door—proves to be the function of another
countenance, one he mistook for personal, but which, as a linguistic phenomenon, is strictly impersonal: namely, the countenance of the prosopopoeia by which he has given a face, a form, a personality, to a conception.
The potential danger, however, does not arise from any real threat posed by
this "prodigy of a personal presence," odious as it appears to Brydon when
it finally presents itself to block his escape from the house. The hazard stems
from his conceivable loss of mastery over his discourse—from the possibility
that his metaphors are out of his control. The figure refuses to be restricted
to the significance assigned it by Brydon, and lets him know as much, by
way of a sign: "Shut up there, at bay, defiant, and with the prodigy of the
thing palpably proveably *done*; thus giving notice like some stark sign-
board—under that accession of accent the situation itself had turned, and
Brydon at last remarkably made up his mind on what it had turned to."

    When it is no longer merely the tables that have turned, but the situation
itself, the relative positions of the players in this elaborate game are no longer
clear, and neither are the "terms to apply." This includes, to some extent,
the terms that have organized the reading thus far: literal and figurative,
terms that appear, parenthetically, in the text of the tale. Brydon's fear that,
if he returns to check on the door closed by the phantom, he might find it
open again, and the figure at large in the house, takes the "awful specific
form" of the image of throwing himself out the window. It is a chance he
decides not to take, opting instead for "uncertainty"; as he heads for the
staircase to make his getaway, the narrative attests that he is scared speech-
less: "He couldn't have spoken, the tone of his voice would have scared him,
and the common conceit or resource of 'whistling in the dark' (whether
literally or figuratively) have appeared basely vulgar." The quotation marks
and parentheses punctuate a new uncertainty, reflected in the "or" or "lit-

erally or figuratively." The presentation of both possibilities might be read as another instance of the narrator's irresolution about what is passing through Brydon's mind: he is doubtful as to whether the character is contemplating producing an actual sound, or simply pretending to ignore the threat—"whistling in the dark" in the metaphoric sense (the same figure appears in "The Beast in the Jungle" as well as in *The Ambassadors*). But whether the narrator is here master of *his* discourse or not, the point is that the text will not, cannot decide the question posed by the "or." The possibility that the figure resists being confined to one signification or the other sheds a light on the nature of this uncertainty, revealing it as a hesitancy about the adequacy and the ultimate usefulness of a distinction that begins to blur when the language in which it is presented is susceptible to the very indetermination that the distinction tries to prevent.

In this drama—this pantomime—of facts and figures, "the great fact," to allude once more to the second paragraph of the tale, has been and remains "the incalculability," the indeterminacy of the figure—the force that overwhelms Brydon when, in the story's climactic scene, he encounters his *alter ego* in all its identity and difference. The progress of figuration has been thorough; the "ghost, or whatever," is rendered in more concrete sensory detail than any other character, any other figure, in the tale, including Brydon himself:

> Rigid and conscious, spectral yet human, a man of his own substance and stature waited there to measure himself with his power to dismay. This only could it be—this only till he recognized, with his advance, that what made the face dim was a pair of raised hands that covered it and in which, so far from being offered in defiance, it was buried as for dark deprecation.

Every fact of the figure's appearance, from its double eyeglass to its polished shoe, becomes visible, to Brydon's great revulsion:

> That meaning at least, while he gaped, it offered him; for he could but gape at his other self in this other anguish, gape as proof that *he,* standing there for the achieved, the enjoyed, the triumphant life, couldn't be faced in his triumph. Wasn't the proof in the splendid covering hands, strong and completely spread?—so spread and so intentional that, in spite of a special verity that surpassed every other, the fact that one of these hands had lost two fingers, which were reduced to stumps, as if accidentally shot away, the face was effectually guarded and saved.

If James, on finding that his birthplace has been torn down to make room for more progressive structures, characterizes the effect as one of "having been amputated of half my history" in the passage from "New York Revisited," Brydon has a literal amputation on his hands. Though the face seems, initially, to be effectively masked despite the two missing digits, it turns out that it is not "saved" in the end, literally or figuratively. The hands fall away to reveal the monstrous visage, and Brydon is not spared the resulting humiliation:

> the bared identity was too hideous as *his,* and his glare was the passion of his protest. The face, *that* face, Spencer Brydon's?— he searched it still, but looking away from it in dismay and denial, falling straight from his height of sublimity. It was unknown, inconceivable, awful, disconnected from any possibility—! He had been "sold," he inwardly moaned, stalking such game as this: the presence before him was a presence, the horror within him a horror, but the waste of his nights had been only grotesque and the success of his adventure an irony. Such an identity fitted him at *no* point, made its alternative monstrous.

While Calvino can cite "The Jolly Corner" as "the story in which I identify myself when I try to imagine the books I could have written," the tale's protagonist fails to identify himself in the figure he has authored. He finds it disfigured beyond recognition: it is not *his* face, but a hideous mask that fails to fit him, and Brydon denies it, losing face and consciousness. He falls into a dead faint, and it appears that he has given up the ghost.

In the story's epilogue, Brydon awakes after an undetermined lapse of time to see the faces of Mrs. Muldoon and Alice Staverton watching worriedly over him, and finds himself with his head cradled in the latter's lap, stretched out on the black and white squares of the hallway. As he regains consciousness, his nightmare and its aftermath are summed up, not surprisingly, by analogy:

> It had brought him to knowledge, to knowledge—yes, this was the beauty of his state; which came to resemble more and more that of a man who has gone to sleep on some news of a great inheritance, and then, after dreaming it away, after profaning it with matters strange to it, has waked up again to serenity of certitude and has only to lie and watch it grow.

Though Brydon is quick to identify himself with the dreamer in his analogy, there is a confusion in the last pages between waking and sleeping that calls into question his "serenity of certitude" and the status of the entire preceding episode. For if, when one dreams, one invariably dreams that one is awake, the project of distinguishing between waking and sleeping, sensing and dreaming, seeing and hallucinating, is problematized. In thinking (or perhaps in dreaming) that he has (whether literally or figuratively) "waked up again" to knowledge, Brydon may well be deceiving himself once more, and the pursuit of his *alter ego* may have been, like James's appalling and admirable nightmare, only a dream.

Alice Staverton, on the other hand, seems more capable of discriminating between these questionable states. She informs Brydon that she, too, has seen the strange figure, at the same time that it appeared to him—but seen it, as she has twice before, in a dream. To substantiate her claim, she describes the apparition down to the last grisly detail, and her companion has no choice but to believe her: "Brydon winced—whether for his proved identity or for his lost fingers." But whose identity is in fact proved through Alice's testimony? How can either she or Brydon be certain that their respective figures are identical? Alice explains that when the visitant appeared to her she "knew it for a sign," that she was not, like Brydon, horrified by the "poor thing," but could accept him, not "for his proved identity," but "for the interest of his difference." Miss Staverton, to whom the narrator repeatedly attributes a saving sense of irony, allows the figure what Brydon has consistently denied it: a life, and a story, of its own, independent of his authorship and of any attempt to fix the terms of its interpretation. To this extent she is an example for the reader of the tale, who can now turn the tables on its narrator's insistence upon the determining force of an influence beyond his notation, to counter that what is at issue in "The Jolly Corner" is nothing less than a notation—the narrative's system of written signs—that is beyond Brydon's, or Alice's, or the narrator's, or the reader's influence. Notation, the *alter ego* of no one and nothing, is what has finally to be confronted—that is, to be read. Such an alternative reading has, however, its monstrous aspect, for it forces the reader to face his (or her) inability to identify himself (or herself) in the tale that tells the story of what (s)he could have read, and would have read, if reading had been a possibility.

CARREN O. KASTON

Imagination and Desire
in The Spoils of Poynton
and What Maisie Knew

Although James's literary commitments are anchored in social and psychological realism and Emerson, in contrast, is essentially a mystic, Emerson's image of the self as a transparent eyeball provides a clarifying context
for James's work with the character of consciousness. Emerson's eyeball is
an image of self-transcendence; the boundaries that are ordinarily felt to
separate the self from the world, the "I," or eye, from what it sees, are
dissolved when Emerson says, "I am nothing. I see all. The currents of the
Universal Being circulate through me" (*Nature, Addresses, and Lectures*).
The particular self is transcended by taking into itself the world outside of
it. James created a group of characters whose distinctive feature is a similar
ability to transcend the self. He pointed to this achievement, which came to
fruition in *The Spoils of Poynton* in the character of Fleda Vetch, when he
commented on the character of Rowland Mallet in *Roderick Hudson*: "What
happened to him was above all to feel certain things happening to others, to
Roderick, to Christina, to Mary Garland, to Mrs. Hudson, to the Cavaliere,
to the Prince." When what happens to others is felt as happening to the self,
social and psychological realities touch borders with the mystical. But James's
characters transfer the ground of self-transcendence from nature, where
Emerson located it, to society. Consciousness then takes into itself principally
other people: not the natural landscape, but the social one. The ramifications
of this change for the identity and autonomy of the self in James are
enormous.

From *Imagination and Desire in the Novels of Henry James*. © 1984 by Rutgers, The
State University. Rutgers University Press, 1984.

James's characters of consciousness live in a world made vivid by the social and psychological risks implicit in Emersonian Transcendentalism, though Emerson took care to defend consciousness from the consequences of those risks by situating it apart from society, in nature. Quentin Anderson, Richard Poirier, and Tony Tanner, who productively place Emerson at the center of America's literary tradition, present the problems of an American visionary self (Poirier locates it specifically in Emerson's eyeball image) that cannot adequately represent itself in or grapple with the social, material world. Formulating the continuities between Emerson and James, they see James as having attempted to escape from the limitations of this world in his fiction by creating what Anderson calls an "imperial" or "hypertrophied" self, a character who through powers of imaginative expansion seeks to create another world, apart from this one.

The obstacles that threaten such expansiveness have typically been located in forces outside of the self. From Ezra Pound to Stephen Donadio, whose recent study of Nietzsche and James explores, among other things, their common debts to Emerson, the threat has been located in society, most devastatingly in "the pressures and encroachments of other wills." Sallie Sears, formulating the matter in terms of competing authorial visions, proposes this melodramatic paradigm: the "imaginary worlds that the characters create for themselves annihilate each other. They cannot coexist because the victory of one *by definition* means the undoing of the other." The same melodramatic formulation is offered by James himself when he contemplates "that bright hard medal, of so strange an alloy, one face of which is somebody's right and ease and the other somebody's pain and wrong."

Yet James also showed that, external forces aside, the self could be its own worst enemy. In an implicit critique of Emerson, he questioned whether a self that has transcended its particular identity can avoid losing itself. He suggests that the threat or restriction that finally matters most for consciousness comes from points of view and desires that have been incorporated into the self from outside of it and take possession of its center. As we have seen [previously] with Isabel Archer, James's characters of consciousness identify with certain points of view that they contain more compellingly than with any that might be considered their own. Such a process, in which the self evaporates instead of expanding, poisons the roots of artistry for these characters and subverts the concept of the "imperial self."

In grounding my presentation of Jamesian self-transcendence in Emerson, I am not so much trying to establish a line of direct influence, though Emerson was a living presence in both the James family household and the New England culture in which the Jameses grew up. Rather, Emerson is a valuable point of departure for this study because he gave the theme of visionary, or self-transcendent, possession of experience "life and flamboyance; it was he who generated it into [a] literary mythology," which made it available to other American writers "through agencies more mysterious than direct literary influence."

For Emerson, then, in the famous epiphany of chapter 1 in *Nature,*

> Standing on the bare ground,—my head bathed by the blithe air, and uplifted into infinite space,—all mean egotism vanishes. I become a transparent eye-ball. I am nothing. I see all. The currents of the Universal Being circulate through me; I am part or particle of God. The name of the nearest friend sounds then foreign and accidental. To be brothers, to be acquaintances,—master or servant, is then a trifle and a disturbance.

For Emerson, the self was primary, yet its status was precarious. In becoming universalized, the personal self or "mean ego" ceased to exist. Afloat in nature and one with it, an eyeball without a body, incorporeal and in an important sense anonymous, Emerson's image projects what might be called a selfless self.

Emerson conceived of himself as being all the more himself for being continuous with the world, all the more his particular self for being part of a universal identity. He was capable at times of making selfhood and otherness coincide with absolute success: "Spirit, that is, the Supreme Being, does not build up nature around us, but puts it forth through us, as the life of the tree puts forth new branches and leaves through the pores of the old."

Yet overall, there are serious difficulties for Emerson in believing that the particular self can find its essence and meaning through an epiphanic oneness with the universe. According to Roy Harvey Pearce, who brilliantly isolates this problem in American literature and culture, "Emerson's characteristic failures result from his striving so much to universalize the self that it gets lost in the striving." Jonathan Bishop notes that Emerson's way of existing in community was to be there hardly at all, to have others "hear from me what I never spoke." In addressing this paradox of selfless selfhood, however, Bishop tends to dissolve the tensions, as in his discussion of this journal entry: "All that we care for in a man is the tidings he gives us of our own faculty through the new conditions under which he exhibits the Common Soul." Bishop's gloss is "We are, potentially, already in the only point of view from which the whole can be understood." While this is helpful on one level, on another it perpetuates the problem. If all that we care for in a man is what he tells us about ourselves and the universal soul, how can we know him? How can we have a relationship with him? Anderson comments that Emersonian consciousness "denies that our sense of ourselves is based on a reciprocal or dramatic or dialectic awareness of one another." Yet to do away with other is to do dialectical damage to the self.

These difficulties can be summed up in the observation that Emerson lacked a social theory, a theory that could explain how the self is to keep the company of others (a lack that caused him pain and stumbling especially in "Experience"). At the end of the eyeball passage in *Nature,* all relations are disavowed. Friends, brothers, acquaintances, masters, and servants are all dismissed. The Emersonian self is universalized without being socialized. It does not know how to have a conversation or a relationship with another self even though—even perhaps because—self and other are conceived as one. James, however, made central in his work the question of how the self is to keep the company of others in a way that might preserve the integrity of both.

James consciously focused on the tenuousness of the Emersonian personal self in an ambivalent description of Emerson that comes rather close to characterizing his own characters of consciousness: "He had polished his aloofness till it reflected the image of his solicitor [that is, the person asking something of him]. And this was not because he was an 'uncommunicating egotist,' though he amuses himself with saying so to Miss Fuller: egotism is the strongest of passions, and he was altogether passionless. It was because he had no personal, just as he had almost no physical wants." James's characters of consciousness also act as though they have "no personal . . . wants." And the imagery of mirrors and reflectors, used here to describe Emerson, James often employed in the prefaces to describe those characters. One implication of the image is the risk that identity may be constituted largely by what it mirrors, that the self may be defined by what is outside of it. This image of the self as a reflector, of consciousness as a mirror, receiving its identity from outside of itself, closely resembles and helps us to understand the stereotypical feminine self scrutinized by feminists. The image beautifully articulates the paradox that seems to define female identity—that women are more sensitive, more conscious than men, but that these assets often fail to give them an advantage. Because of them, in fact, women are generally less able to bring a personal self into existence.

Some of James's remarks about his mother evoke this image of a mirror-self, a selfless self: "She lived in ourselves so exclusively, with such a want of use for anything in her consciousness that was not about us and for us, that I think we almost contested her being separate enough to be proud of us—it was too like our being proud of ourselves." Even more pointedly:

"She *was* he [the senior James, her husband], *was* each of us." An expert at what one might call selfless or evacuated selfhood, Mrs. James makes real Poulet's image of the Jamesian fictional self as a decentered circle.

By saying the James character of consciousness is lacking a personal self in an important and revealing sense, however, I do not mean to imply that Strether, for example, does not feel a personal sort of pleasure from *dejeuner* with Mme de Vionnet, or that Fleda Vetch lacks a defining context of realistic detail, such as the possession of a father in West Kensington. Fleda may even manifest a perverse sort of self-gratification or egoism in her desire, while getting nothing for herself, to take charge of the affairs of others. Leon Edel sensitively discusses the way Mrs. James could be self-sacrificial, and yet "all-encompassing," even "gubernatorial." What I mean by saying that the James character of consciousness lacks a personal self, then, is that in terms of the novels' psychic flow, the energies of Fleda and Strether's egos are severely disrupted. Though they are personages in their books, Fleda and Strether are also empty centers much of the time. They accumulate experience, but lack what would be thought of as a self.

In creating characters of consciousness like Fleda Vetch and Strether, James in effect socialized or domesticated Emerson's visionary eyeball self. Being visionary now meant floating out over other characters' consciousness, becoming a medium of reception capable of registering what it was like to be them, at the risk, as with Emerson, of making the personal self tenuous. It is precisely here, where the social and the mystical overlap (in mysticism, the self feels that it is in communion with a reality larger than itself), that James touches Emerson. In his 1918 memorial essay, which is still one of the most fertile sources of ideas about James, T. S. Eliot maintained that "The real hero, in any of James's stories, is a social entity of which men and women are constituents. . . . Compared with James's, other novelists' characters seem to be only accidentally in the same book." Eliot was commenting on the profoundly social nature of James's work, but social in this case means that the work shows a concern with the fabric of awareness that constitutes communities of intimacy. On the whole, in James, these communities are woven from the narrative center outward as that character makes a relation with other characters by registering their desires and points of view.

James invokes these ideas about the self in relation to others in the preface to *The Spoils of Poynton* when he calls Fleda Vetch a "free spirit." He means by that term something close to an Emersonian eyeball self. The "free spirit," James says, "almost demonically both sees and feels, while the others [the "fools," who are "the fixed constituents" of the action] but feel without seeing." The others are fixed in the sense that they are trapped

inside of themselves by the very intensity of their feelings, in what might be
called the tyrannous centricity of the self, with all of its purely personal
desires and claims. It was probably in order to get free of this narrow conception of personality posed by an exclusively self-centric way of being in
the world that James invented the novelistic version of transcendental consciousness we know as the James character of consciousness, or the "free
spirit." Fleda is free by virtue of the fact that she can see what is outside of
herself; she can get beyond herself.

James valued empathic imagining so highly because he equated it with
morality. He wrote of "the perfect dependence of the 'moral' sense of a work
of art on the amount of felt life concerned in producing it," and implied the
perfect dependence of a moral sense in people, or in characters that represent
people, on the "amount of felt life" they can feel. To get outside of the self
and imagine what experience feels like to others is to experience greater and
greater amounts of "felt life" oneself. This conception of morality also, I
believe, helps to explain James's preference for the technique of the central
consciousness over the technique of first-person narration. In the preface to
The Ambassadors, James speaks disenchantedly of "the terrible *fluidity* of
self-revelation." The phrase suggests that he viewed first-person narration as
inundatingly self-centric, a way of being in the world in which the self floods
out all others.

The question provoked by James's comments on the free spirit is whether
a commitment to what is ordinarily thought of as the personal self, or personality, need spell the death of freedom. Is it really liberating to be a self
without a center? In dissolving the separation between self and other, and
getting beyond the fixed limits ordinarily imposed by a sense of self, the free
spirit makes a kind of contact with other selves that the Emerson persona
customarily cannot manage. Yet despite the virtually limitless possibilities
for growth perhaps potentially sponsored by self-transcendence in a social
setting, the totally decentered self in James constitutes an invitation to melodrama and repression. For when James's characters escape the potential tyranny of their own personalities by making consciousness an instrument for
encompassing other characters' feelings, they are in danger of being occupied
at their centers by these competitive versions of experience. In Poulet's terms,
"the object of attention [the person being observed] becomes the point of
arrival of a movement of prospection and exploration. . . . So everything
changes, consciousness, from central, becoming peripheral, and the object
contemplated, becoming the central objective." The result, when the "object
of attention" is another character, is that the imagination of the narrative
center is given over to this now "central objective" and subdued to its desires

and the compositions of reality prescribed by these desires. Usually these are compositions that cause the characters of consciousness to disclaim their own desires. Such renunciation is a logical result of self-transcendence, a predictable outcome for characters who regard their own emotions primarily as a form of limitation.

THE SPOILS OF POYNTON

In *The Spoils of Poynton* (1897), James turns his concern with the limits imposed on the imagination by decenteredness into a study of ambassadorial consciousness. The transcendental character of consciousness in James often appears on the social scene as an intermediary or ambassador. *The Ambassadors, In the Cage,* and even *What Maisie Knew* come to mind, in addition to *The Spoils of Poynton*. Ambassadors are persons empowered by others to realize goals and purposes not their own, or only adoptively theirs. Although they may have a measure of freedom to negotiate independently and may even enter, at times, into a kind of working partnership with the bargaining parties, they are still not negotiating for themselves. Even if their employer's purposes and emotions become their own, the spoils will finally go to other parties. Strether's renunciatory ideal at the end of *The Ambassadors,* "not, out of the whole affair, to have got anything for myself," is a kind of manifesto of ambassadorial service. The same ideal governs the labors of Fleda Vetch up until the critical point at which she allows herself, at Owen's invitation, to journey to Poynton to pick an object of personal gain from among the spoils.

Fleda, like Strether, is employed to conduct diplomacy between mother and son. Her life as an ambassador begins when she is pressed to undertake for the widowed Mrs. Gereth and her son Owen the touchy negotiations that have arisen over the possession of Poynton's contents as a result of Owen's upcoming and, as it turns out, contingent marriage to Mona Brigstock. Mrs. Gereth and her son "transmit through" Fleda; she is their "communicator," their "envoy," and virtually leaves herself out as she negotiates on their behalf. She identifies with their picture of her as an ambassador to such a degree that even when they want her to profit personally from the negotiations, she remains committed to ambassadorial consciousness.

The egoless, free-floating quality of the Emersonian eyeball is especially apparent when Owen offers to buy Fleda a token of appreciation for her assistance with his mother. Fleda busies herself "wondering what Mona would think of such proceedings." "What she noticed most was that . . . [Owen] said no word of his intended." When Fleda construes Owen's "un-

sounded words" as an offer to live with her at Ricks, she "could only vainly
wonder how it provided for poor Mona." And when she hears that Mona
jealously suspects her motives in continuing to negotiate between Owen and
his mother, "It was a sudden drop in her great flight, a shock to her attempt
to watch over Mona's interests." The conjunction here of imagery of flight
and vision conjures up a flying eyeball, with, in this case, intentionally comic
effect. The eyeball's unexpected "drop" is a pratfall that subjects the enterprise it implicitly signifies—self-transcendence—to intended scrutiny. (In *The
Wings of the Dove,* Milly watches over the interests of Densher and Kate
Croy in a selfless flight that is subjected to some of the same scrutiny.) Fleda's
effort to "watch over Mona's interests" extends the role of intermediary to
which Owen and his mother first appointed her. The fact that Mona has not
employed her as an ambassador makes even clearer her need to negotiate on
behalf of someone else, on behalf of anyone except herself.

Robert C. McLean questions the self-transcending capacity of Fleda's
imagination, and contends that Fleda is imprisoned in herself and that her
imaginings of others should be taken as delusions and self-projections.
Richard A. Hocks, however, insists that Fleda is genuinely self-transcendent:

> Her ethic is . . . pragmatistically oriented—that is, parallel to Wil-
> liam's own broadening or "radical" aspects of utilitarianism—in
> that Fleda characteristically *creates* a possible other case about
> Mona, projects a version of the other girl as someone for whom
> Owen's earlier proposal is "a tremendous thing," someone who
> "must" love him because Fleda herself does. The saltatory mind
> can immediately say that Fleda is merely creating Mona in her
> own image, and that is so to the extent that she . . . makes Mona's
> feelings coalesce with her own. To the same saltatory mind that
> sounds simply like making others into yourself. In fact it is just
> the reverse: it is conceiving of each person as so distinctively
> individual that you are willing continually to subsume your own
> views into them rather than classify them as Other.

When Fleda attributes feelings to Mona that cannot be verified, however,
there is good reason to think that if she is not creating Mona in her image,
she is externalizing her own feelings by means of Mona. Fleda's displacement
of her own emotion onto Mona is particularly apparent when she argues
with Owen about Mona's reasons for postponing the wedding: "Doesn't it
occur to you . . . that if Mona is, as you say, drawing away, she may have in
doing so a very high motive? She knows the immense value of all the objects
detained by your mother, and to restore the spoils of Poynton she's ready

. . . to make a sacrifice. The sacrifice is that of an engagement she had entered upon with joy." With such reasoning, Fleda injects into Mona's motives her own high-tonedness, tenderness, and inclination to sacrifice. When Fleda greets the prospect of Owen's disengagement from Mona with the question, "Can you take such pleasure in her being finished—a poor girl you've once loved?," it is easier to recognize Fleda herself as the piteous "poor girl" about to be "finished" than it is to recognize the robust Mona. And when Fleda exhorts Owen not to "break faith" with Mona because "She must love you—how can she help it? *I* wouldn't give you up! . . . Never, never, never!," she seems to be saying that Mona must love Owen because she, Fleda, does. Although she claims that she would not give Owen up, the irony, of course, is that she does so, as though she had quite emptied herself of these emotions in attributing them to Mona.

Fleda later imagines the suffering of Ricks' maiden aunt in a flight of consciousness that, like her imagination of Mona, is never verified. In contrast, we accept Maggie Verver's imagination of Charlotte's shriek and Amerigo's pacing as the unquestionable reality of *The Golden Bowl* because Maggie's self is sufficiently present to make what she imagines *become* novelistic reality. Fleda feels her own emotions best by giving them away, however, and as a result she responds to them in a self-defeating way. When she expresses her own love by imagining Mona's love for Owen, for instance, her interests are displaced in her consciousness by Mona's; and Mona's dictate that she, Fleda, shall renounce the young man. Thus Fleda actively labors for this end, as though for some cause of her own.

Mrs. Gereth also serves as an external agent by which Fleda experiences her own emotional life. At first, Mrs. Gereth's disapproval of Mona as Owen's fiancée seems to express an oedipal competitiveness: removing the furnishings from Poynton looks like competing with Mona for them, and for Owen. But in the flow of raw psychic energy beneath the novel's surface, the mother's sexual dimension becomes Fleda's own in dislocation, giving form to Fleda's barely recognized stirrings. She encourages Fleda to compete with Mona on sexual terms: "'I want you to cut in!' . . . She challenged again and again Fleda's picture, as she called it (though the sketch was too slight to deserve the name), of the indifference to which a prior attachment had committed the proprietor of Poynton. . . . 'Only let yourself go, darling— only let yourself go!'" When Fleda returns from a trip to London, in the course of which she has lost track of Owen rather than letting herself go to him, and she tries to calm Mrs. Gereth while submitting to her interrogation, Mrs. Gereth "rose again from where Fleda had kept her down," like Fleda's own impulses. Mrs. Gereth's lecture "affected our young lady as if it had been the shake of a tambourine borne toward her from a gipsy dance; her head seemed to go round and she felt a sudden passion in her feet."

Thus inspired, Fleda sees the situation and herself with Mrs. Gereth's eyes, and consents, in James's metaphor, to dance to her patron's tambourine, with the result that her determination "to lose herself"—as James puts it when she hides from Owen in her father's West Kensington flat—to claim nothing for herself, is for a moment suspended. She temporarily recomposes her sketch of the plot by volunteering to find Owen and marry him without further ado. She takes the extraordinary step, for her, of sending Owen a telegram asking him to come to her, putting her desire for him, until now displaced onto Mrs. Gereth and Mona, into words explicitly from her, hoping thus to disprove Mrs. Gereth's contention that she "could invent nothing better" than to send Owen back to Mona (Fleda's instructions to Owen in London). As a sign of her effort to concentrate her distributed energies into a personal self, Fleda even refuses Mrs. Gereth's offer to pay for the telegram: "To succeed it must be all me!"

Yet the incompleteness of her effort to locate a self—to "be all me"—and to recompose the sketch is evident even as she awaits an answer to the telegram. James evokes her psychic division in terms of a virtually Freudian architecture. "Her trouble occupied some quarter of her soul that had closed its doors for the day and shut out even her own sense of it; she might perhaps have heard something if she had pressed her ear to a partition. Instead of that she sat with her patience in a cold still chamber from which she could look out in quite another direction." Absent from the scene of her trouble, she remains partitioned off from her own emotional life. She sits in less private spaces of the self, unable to inhabit the full residence. Thus when Mrs. Gereth brings her the news that Owen is already married, "All the girl's effort tended for the time to a single aim—that of taking the thing with outward detachment, speaking of it as having happened to Owen and to his mother and not in any degree to herself."

Fleda's way of owning pain is, as it was before, with other emotions, to register it in another self. With Owen married, Fleda prepares for a life of memories and spinsterhood, enhanced in her eyes by qualities she attributes to Ricks' former proprietor, a maiden aunt. From the beginning, her unverified imagination of the aunt's life contains her own feelings of suffering: "The poor lady . . . had been sensitive and ignorant and exquisite. . . . [Fleda] was so sure she had deeply suffered." On her third visit to Ricks, after Mrs. Gereth has sent back the furnishings stolen from Poynton and reinstated the maiden aunt's few effects, Fleda hears these speak with a voice full of her own sense of frailness: "a voice so gentle, so human, so feminine—

a faint far-away voice with the little quaver of a heart-break." It is a voice
that turns deprivation into something romantic and appealing, something
"exquisite." Fleda has the sense of "something dreamed and missed, something reduced, relinquished, resigned: the poetry, as it were, of something
sensibly *gone*." In deriving poetic pleasure from this contemplation, Fleda
can aestheticize such sufferings as might well be her own and, in doing so,
avoid the acknowledgment of her own pain that might enable her to throw
it off.

Even at this late date, she chooses to remain "vague" about the nature
of her pain:

> Then Fleda said: "What I mean is, for this dear one of ours [the
> aunt], that if she had (as I *know* she did: it's in the very touch
> of the air!) a great accepted pain—"
>
> She had paused an instant, and Mrs. Gereth took her up. "Well,
> if she had?"
>
> Fleda still hung fire. "Why, it was worse than yours."
>
> Mrs. Gereth debated. "Very likely." Then she too hesitated.
> "The question is if it was worse than yours."
>
> "Mine?" Fleda looked vague.

Though her consciousness does not register the pain as her own, Fleda herself
has become part of the spoilage of Poynton.

Although Fleda has been employed by Owen and his mother, she betrays
them both, promoting events that probably neither of them wants to occur.
Mona, who never appointed Fleda, is, ironically, the one party whose interests she does not betray. No sooner does she sense that Owen might want
her to help him end his engagement, and that she herself might want to help,
than she fosters a sequence of events leading to the return of the spoils to
Poynton, a move she knows will satisfy Mona and precipitate the marriage.
Mona is the character from whose point of view Fleda essentially operates—
Mona and perhaps the maiden aunt. As a character of consciousness, incor-
porating other selves at the expense of her own sense of self, Fleda necessarily
favors characters whose pictures or fictions of experience commit her to
strategies of personal loss.

Skepticism about Fleda's renunciation is fed by what seems to be a desire
on her part for visible justification and moral simplification. Before the marriage, when Owen seeks Fleda out at her sister's, he hears, "'Ah you see it's
not true that you're free!' She seemed almost to exult. 'It's not true—it's not
true'": a crow of satisfaction rather than, as one might expect, a lament.
To Mrs. Gereth's news that Owen is married Fleda responds, "That he has

done it, that he couldn't *not* do it, shows how right I was." Subsequently her certainty about what is right seduces her into a dead language, a rhetoric suggesting that what she embraces as rightness may be rigidity. When Owen invites her, after his marriage, to take something from him, something from Poynton, the best thing in the collection, or whatever she most loves, she feels compelled to reason out the invitation, straining all the way, as "a token of gratitude for having kept him in the straight path." To a reader, this rhetorical deadness undermines her renunciatory selflessness as much as it undermines Isabel's when Isabel turns, rhetorically and literally, to the rigid rightness of the "straight path" to show her what to do after the confusion of Caspar's kiss.

The tenuousness of Fleda's personal self, her tendency to turn to Mona or the maiden aunt for tidings of her own condition, prevents her from achieving full authorial status in the book and, therefore, from making the prevailing picture of the plot accommodate her own desires. The implications for authorship of Fleda's renunciatory consciousness can be seen best by returning to the figure of Mrs. Gereth. James calls her "the very reverse of a free spirit." "She had no imagination about anybody's life save on the side she bumped against. . . . Mrs. Gereth had really no perception of anybody's nature—had only one question about persons: were they clever or stupid?"— were they, that is, capable of appreciating Poynton? Imprisoned in her narrowly defined particular self, Mrs. Gereth is, in Emersonian terms, a "mean egotist." She lacks the largeness of vision to apprehend others on their own terms—and thus to be a figure of consciousness. For example, when she moves from Poynton to the dowerhouse, redecorating it with furnishings stolen from Poynton, she is at first so devoid of empathic imaginative response to the meager but touching objects left by her predecessor that, Fleda feels, "The maiden-aunt had been exterminated." Nevertheless, once Mrs. Gereth returns the spoils to Poynton, she reinstates the old aunt's few effects at Ricks and makes them grow "indescribably sweet" around her. And despite her incomprehension of Fleda's nature and motives for betraying her, she keeps Fleda with her at the end and cannot help but care for her, even if waspishly.

Mrs. Gereth is thus a complex figure in the allegiances the novel creates in the reader. Even her devotion to the "mean ego," the particular self, generates ambivalence. That James intended this is suggested by the fact that her advice to Fleda to let herself go echoes James's most urgent and moving exhortation to himself in his notebooks, the record he kept of his work in progress for more than thirty years. "I have only to let myself *go*! So I have said to myself all my life. . . . Yet I have never fully done it. The sense of it—

of the need of it—rolls over me. . . . I am in full possession of accumulated resources—I have only to use them. . . . All life is—at my age, with all one's artistic soul the record of it—in one's pocket, as it were. Go on, my boy, and strike hard: have a rich and long St. Martin's Summer."

Here in 1891 James speaks of his art in terms of the energies of Victorian commerce and, implicitly, its ethos of self-fulfillment: "accumulated resources" in "one's pocket" which it is imperative to "use." Composition is analogized not so much to saving (though there is talk in the prefaces about the economy of art) or to paying (which often takes the form in James of punishment and loss), but to having and spending, a difference of emphasis that suggests a generous regard for the resources of the self. Fleda's "imagination of a disaster" as she travels down to Poynton to claim her gift is an aspect of James's own melodramatic vision, as James confessed to A. C. Benson the year before he published *The Spoils*: "I have the imagination of disaster—and see life indeed as ferocious and sinister." Nevertheless, the letting go, which in the notebooks James required of himself for the sake of his art, is allied with the kinds of letting go—both emotional and sexual— by means of which Fleda herself could become authorial and purge the plot of *The Spoils* of its similarities to a genteelly-suffering-maiden-aunt melo-drama. The invitation Mrs. Gereth extends to Fleda to let herself go and imagine herself beyond renunciation is, in effect, James's own.

Although Emerson opposed the values of the genteel tradition, partic-ularly the failure of originality in its indebtedness to the European inheri-tance, and although he periodically, in his essays, issued calls to action in the material world, his image of the self as an incorporeal eyeball floating cleanly above a world of getting and spending has something in common with the disengagement from experience prized by the genteel tradition. This attitude characterizes the genteel tradition even though it reached its vantage of disengagement from a base of compromising material security. In electing to work with the character of consciousness, James departed from both Emerson and the genteel tradition. He showed that to be free of worldly and personal desires, nevertheless, is not to be free—that for the earthbound, integrity and a measure of freedom necessarily come through the personal self and the satisfaction of earthly desires. Although Fleda resists the invi-tation, the pressures of James's material point toward the possibility of a consciousness capable both of possessing itself without becoming self-ab-sorbed and possessing its world instead of losing itself in it.

James wished to evaluate the costs of being a transparent eyeball lodged in a material world. The costs for Fleda are an inability to include much of her world in her composition of it. For example, though Fleda has rendered a sense of Owen's love through her consciousness, she does not know his pain; there is no space for that in the novel as her awareness composes it. The destruction of Poynton and its contents by fire is the ultimate symbol of Fleda's authorial failure, the result and the sign of her inability to imagine for herself an existence and a plot that could incorporate what the spoils in the largest sense include: love, sexuality, and ownership in the physical, material world. The novel suggests that Poynton burns because Fleda's sketch of experience affords no space to those desires of the particular self. To save it would require a self capable of being both eyeball and body.

James creates the impression in several ways that the destruction of Poynton is both symbol and consequence of Fleda's absence from herself and the design she has promoted. It is partly a matter of timing. The house goes up in flames on the precise morning Fleda has picked, after weeks of waiting, for her visit to claim the gift Owen has invited her to take. The accusatory effect is heightened by an eerie sense that the objects of Poynton have suddenly come to life to take revenge on Fleda for abandoning them to Mona's negligent hands. A sense of dislocated energy further relates the fire to Fleda's selflessness: it is as if her desire at last to get something for herself triggers in her a fantasy of guilt and punishment which is projected onto the external world in the destruction of what she loves.

An author in James must ultimately participate in and profit from the design in order to be assured of "*supreme* command" over the fictional arrangements. In Maggie Verver, James did create a character of consciousness capable both of transcending the self and fully occupying its center, being both other and self, eyeball and body, a fusion that enables her to be a fully successful artist of her situation. But Fleda is unable to make the spoils (the objects and the book) her *Spoils* in the way that Osmond can make Isabel his *Portrait* and Maggie can make the bowl (object and book) her *Bowl*. The Spoils resembles *The Wings of the Dove* in that imagination and consciousness acquire a certain degree of control over the plot, but not enough to secure the predominance of their designs. In *The Wings of the Dove*, Milly seeks to compose shapes for the lives around her through her will, the "sacred script" she leaves behind after her death, but in her absence she cannot make the design take hold. Presiding authorially from a distance proves to be an inadequate sort of authorship for Strether too when, in lecturing Chad at the end of *The Ambassadors*, he futilely delegates to the young man his own desire to love and protect Mme de Vionnet. . . .

WHAT MAISIE KNEW

Like Fleda Vetch, Strether, and the young telegraphist, six-year-old Maisie Farange is trapped in ambassadorial service. *What Maisie Knew*

(1897) begins when a divorce court assigns the child to alternating terms with parents who use her as "a messenger of insult." Once she has "puzzled out . . . that everything was bad because she had been employed to make it so" by her parents, she begins to repudiate their ambassadorial "employment," to have her own feelings, and to employ them for her own purposes. At the end of the novel, rejecting the alien designs for her life that confine her in the novel's various parental houses, Maisie grows up. The intricate five-way custody battle that develops over the course of the book concludes for Maisie at the edge of adolescence with what amounts to an act of self-custody, as she struggles to achieve the "imagination in *predominance*" that will enable her to possess the material of her life in a plot of her own design.

Maisie rejects her parents' ambassadorial conception of her life at first through resistance, a refusal to report what one of them has instructed her to say against the other: she begins with "the idea of an inner self or, in other words, of concealment. . . . Her parted lips locked themselves with the determination to be employed no longer." It is clear what she does not want, but not what she does. The merely negative assertion of self involved in her silence perpetuates her helplessness:

> The sharpened sense of spectatorship was the child's main support, the long habit, from the first, of seeing herself in discussion [by other people] and finding in the fury of it—she had a glimpse of the game of football—a sort of compensation for the doom of a peculiar passivity. It gave her often an odd air of being present at her history in as separate a manner as if she could only get at experience by flattening her nose against a pane of glass.

The effect is as though her life existed outside of and apart from her. She is the football, passively taking direction from the will of other people. But her consciousness is not even in the football—it is watching from the other side of the pane of glass.

Yet Maisie's silence, looking forward to Maggie Verver's in *The Golden Bowl*, is ultimately reinventive. Her "idea of an inner self," cultivated in silence, is in part the same idea that comes to Strether with his disobedient determination to see for himself, and to Catherine Sloper in tentative excursions into dissimulation in a few exchanges with her father and Aunt Penniman. But beyond a certain point in Catherine's verbal evasions, as in her silences, and in the silences of Claire de Cintré, Isabel, Fleda, and Strether, feelings are not found but lost. Maisie's "locked lips," however, prepare for her escape from an emotional life melodramatically manipulated in her by others, even though they seem to associate her with a kind of Jamesian consciousness that never explicitly authorizes the expression of anger.

Consciously resisting one kind of parental employment, the transmission of insult, Maisie is then for a long time the unconscious agent of another: she finds herself unintentionally promoting liaisons for her parents' benefit. First she brings together her beautiful governess Miss Overmore and her father Beale, who later marry. Then she brings together the new Mrs. Beale and Sir Claude, the compassionate and romantic figure her mother has recently married. But this unconscious gift for composition is not fully at Maisie's own disposal, for the new parental pairs prove to be as manipulative, perhaps also as derelict, as the old. They use their connection with the child to promote their own designs—to begin and conceal the affairs, or to give them an air of respectability—while Maisie, unable to exert supreme imaginative command, is trapped and neglected in the architecture of multiplying relations that she has invented.

James himself uses Maisie in the novel's preface in some of the same ways that her various parents use her in the novel. For instance, he speaks of her functioning as a tool of his novelistic design: "Instead of simply submitting to the inherited tie and the imposed complication, of suffering from them, our little wonder-working agent would create . . . quite fresh elements of this order." As a "little wonder-working agent" of James's "order," Maisie is converted from a character into what Bersani calls a "technical ingenuity." Another passage also illustrates the way the prefaces often diminish the emotional impact of the novels. "Not less than the chance of misery and of a degraded state, the chance of happiness and of an improved state might be . . . involved for the child, round about whom the complexity of life would thus turn to fineness, to richness—and indeed would have but so to turn for the small creature to be steeped in security and ease." Readers fresh from the novel may have trouble recalling any impression of "the small creature," even at the end, "steeped in security and ease." Both this remade version of the plot and the one that disposes of her as a structural functionary in the novel might be said to constitute parental houses of fiction in which Maisie does not seem to fit.

James's anesthetized tone toward Maisie in the preface resembles the objectifying way society talks or sounds at the beginning of the novel. With the jargonistic and impersonal voices of the law, finance, and gossip, the book's prologue renders what will become the increasingly subjective and intimate world of Maisie's experience from an initially external perspective. It is reported in the prologue's Latinate legal voice, for example, that "the litigation [of the divorce and custody proceedings] had seemed interminable." And when Beale is unable to refund to Ida some money that he owes her, and the court stipulates that each parent support Maisie in turn, it is said that by this "partition of the tutelary office" Beale's debt is "remitted" to him. We hear too of "people . . . looking for appeals in the newspapers for the rescue of the little one," also called "the bone of contention," language whose preciosity is not far removed from the prefatory coyness of "little wonder-working agent." James informs us that Maisie lives in "a society in which for the most part people were occupied only with chatter," a species of talk which, like that in *Washington Square* and *The Awkward Age,* is disconnected from felt emotion. Just as the abstract and technical voice of the prefaces often anesthetizes the experience of the novels, the various voices of society in *Maisie* forge a variety of talk that betrays the sources of feeling James ultimately makes most important. Though *Maisie* begins, in the vein of *Washington Square,* with the brittle ironies generated by remote and su-perficial views of the heroine's experience, it proceeds to shield her from both irony and melodrama by anchoring itself in her deepening sense of self. That is, she escapes from the rhetorically glib versions of her experience presented in the prologue and the preface by locating in herself the felt emotion absent from their styles. In doing so, she is ultimately able to out-grow all of the parental fictions in which the novel threatens to imprison her. She gets away a little even from the house of fiction that James erects for his heroine in his own voice in the preface.

Maisie's release from her parents is managed in scenes that free her from them both physically and emotionally. Ida is relieved that Sir Claude has abducted Maisie from her custody because it saves her the inconvenience of continuing to have the child in her life. But Maisie distills most of the sting from Ida's desire to abandon her when she has a scene with the captain, Ida's latest lover, in which she discovers the measure of sincerely positive feeling that she has for her mother beyond dread, or mystified awe, or pain. The captain reports about Ida: "She's tremendous fun—she can do all sorts of things better than I've ever seen anyone. . . . She has the nerve for a tiger-shoot. . . . Look here, she's *true!*" If the virtues the captain celebrates are scarcely maternal and barely accurate, that hardly matters since

> What it appeared to . . . [Maisie] to come to was that on the subject of her ladyship it was the first real kindness she had heard, so that at the touch of it something strange and deep and pitying surged up within her. . . . She cried, with a pang, straight *at* him. . . . "Oh do you love her?" . . .
> . . . "Of *course* I love her, damn it, you know!"
> . . . "So do *I* then. I do, I do, I do!"

Maisie has a brief opportunity to feel authentically loving toward her father too in a scene in which Beale abandons her by trying to make her say she does not want him. The scene with Ida's captain and the one with Beale are corresponding moments at the heart of the novel in which Maisie is released from her parents in the most profound sense, even from the impression of hurt.

Maisie's scene with her father begins when he abducts her and takes her, oedipally, to his mistress's rooms. Alone with him there,

> Maisie had her sense . . . of her having grown for him. . . . There was a passage during which, on a yellow silk sofa under one of the palms, he had her on his knee, stroking her hair, playfully holding her off while he showed his shining fangs and let her, with a vague affectionate helpless pointless "Dear old girl, dear little daughter," inhale the fragrance of his cherished beard. . . . it needed nothing more than this to make up to her in fact for omissions. The tears came into her eyes again as they had done when in the Park that day the Captain told her so "splendidly" that her mother was good. What was this but splendid too—this still directer goodness of her father . . . out of which everything had dropped but that he was papa and that he was magnificent?

Though Beale, like Ida, does not in fact deserve Maisie's generosity, he nevertheless, however unintentionally, helps release his daughter from the hold of childhood memories of suffering, as Catherine Sloper is never fully released. Nor for all his "shining fangs" does Beale loom in Maisie's imagination with the melodramatic power that Osmond possesses for Pansy and Isabel. Maisie is no longer her parents' victim not only because she escapes them physically but, more profoundly, because she ceases to regard them as damaging.

With her actual parents out of the picture, the last third of the novel shows Maisie reassembling in Boulogne with her stepparents, Sir Claude and Mrs. Beale, and her current governess Mrs. Wix. Her governess favors a living arrangement that excludes Mrs. Beale; she wishes to save Maisie from what she regards as the corrupting effect of daily exposure to adultery. Sir Claude, however, proposes a household composed of Maisie, Mrs. Beale, and himself, minus the didactic Mrs. Wix. Pressed to choose between these alternatives, Maisie is caught between the possibility that the stepparents care about her for herself, and the alternate or perhaps overlapping possibility that they care for her largely because her presence gives their relationship an appearance of respectability.

An earlier exchange between Maisie and Beale about the stepparents has made clear that in the *Maisie* world, the impulses of caring and the architecture of use are hard to tell apart but difficult to combine for any length of time:

> "They're probably the worst people in the world and the very greatest criminals," Beale pleasantly urged. . . .
> "Well, it doesn't prevent them from loving me. They love me tremendously." . . .
> . . . "You're a jolly good pretext . . . for their game." . . .
> The child reflected. "Well then that's all the more reason . . . for their being kind to me."
> . . . "Don't you understand," Beale pursued, "that . . . they'll just simply chuck you? . . . they'll cease to require you." . . .
> . . . "Cease to require me because they won't care?"

The novel's consideration of the authenticity of emotion beneath stylishness boils down to the question of whether Sir Claude is a fraud. It is one of the book's brilliant strokes that this question, like the one of how we are to regard Charlotte and Amerigo's adultery in *The Golden Bowl,* is never conclusively resolved. Sir Claude's desires and motives are so mixed, there are so many feelings that need to be honored, that it is almost as difficult to convict him of actual dishonesty as it is Madame de Vionnet.

Maisie finally grasps "the implication of a kind of natural divergence between lovers and little girls" in a supremely unstable society that makes people choose between being lovers and being parents—a divergence which, paradoxically, exists even though it is she who has brought the lovers together. She realizes that if she were to forsake Mrs. Wix and accept Sir Claude's proposal that she live with him and Mrs. Beale, the cycle of composition and abandonment in which she has been victimized might reassert itself. This realization makes her counter Sir Claude's proposal with one of her own: that they go away together, just the two of them. The importance of her locating a desiring self, and articulating this desire in the form of a design, can hardly be overemphasized. James says, "She knew what she wanted. All her learning and learning had made her at last learn that."

At the train station, she and Sir Claude very nearly do depart by themselves:

> "I wish we could go. Won't you take me?"
> He continued to smile. "Would you really come?"
> "Oh yes, oh yes. Try." . . .
> Sir Claude turned to a porter. "When does the train go?"
> . . . "In two minutes. *Monsieur est placé?* . . . *Et vos billets?*"

... Then after a look at Maisie, *"Monsieur veut-il que je les prenne?"* the man said.

Sir Claude turned back to her. *"Veux-tu bien qu'il en prenne?"*

It was the most extraordinary thing in the world: in the intensity of her excitement she not only by illumination understood all their French, but fell into it with an active perfection. She addressed herself straight to the porter. *"Prenny, prenny. Oh prenny!"*

Although the train departs on her hauntingly plaintive invocation of a new version of the plot and their relationship, Maisie for the first time has found her voice: *"Prenny, prenny. Oh prenny."* The French, just improvised, suggests that there has been no place in the language they customarily speak for the expression of her personally desiring self; until now, indeed, there have been no words for it at all. Yet if Maisie can thus speak her desire, she cannot, like Maggie Verver, impose it. The upshot of Maisie's success at locating a self with hopes and needs of its own and proposing to Sir Claude a design that fulfills these is that, although Sir Claude is tempted, he finds it impossible to accede. He cannot give up Mrs. Beale. To a degree that undermines her imaginative authority, Maisie's material exhibits its own "germinal property and authority."

But although Maisie is unable to enforce the version of the plot she prefers—that is, life with Sir Claude—she can nevertheless place herself beyond melodrama by escaping from his household, *his* fiction. Catherine Sloper, like Maisie, cultivates through silence a desiring self: she pursues a marriage with Morris despite her father's opposition. Once that design proves impossible to realize, however, she collapses back into her father's fiction of her. Morris was in so many ways like her father that desiring him hardly even constituted a new design. Maisie, on the other hand, makes a convincingly complete exit from the novel's oedipal drama.

For Beale, her actual father, when he holds her on his knee, strokes her hair, murmurs in her ear, and offers her the scent of "his cherished beard," Maisie is no longer a mere child. For her stepfather Sir Claude, the growing Maisie is similarly both a woman and a child, a potential sweetheart and a daughter; he shares the confusion of Beale's "Dear old girl, dear little daughter." He even repeats Beale's symbolically sexual abduction with another of his own when he sweeps Maisie off to Boulogne and nearly elopes with her on the train. In bidding for control of the meanings she inadvertently made possible when she brought Mrs. Beale and Sir Claude together, Maisie seeks to secure what she has always yearned for, a measure of emotional safety.

But it does not follow that she is trying to have Sir Claude strictly as a parent when she proposes that they depart together on the train.

The extent of Maisie's sexual maturity has been a major issue in criticism of the novel. F. R. Leavis, for example, contends that Maisie's adoration of Sir Claude is safely "feminine," but not at all sexual. Harris Wilson, however, has read Maisie's feelings for Sir Claude as incestuously sexual: "Her greatest asset opposed to Mrs. Beale's lush worldliness is her virginity, and that she is prepared to offer" to Sir Claude if they go away together. Edward Wasiolek accepts the sexuality implicit in Maisie's proposal to Sir Claude, but does not consider how the collapse of Maisie's projected scenario actually assists her toward sexual maturity. Similarly, Muriel G. Shine, tracing the movement toward maturity in James's fictional children, blames Sir Claude for sticking with Mrs. Beale, and thus overlooks the potential for growth in Maisie's separation from him.

It seems very unlikely that James concerned himself with the question of whether or not Maisie might go to bed with Sir Claude. It does, however, seem likely—especially in the context of Catherine Sloper, Isabel, and Strether's damaging attachment to parental figures and their fictions—that James was concerned in *Maisie* with the obstacles to sexual and imaginative maturity posed by oedipal irresolution. The difference in this respect between *Maisie* and the earlier works is that the oedipal attachment is initially acknowledged as something natural. Commenting on Maisie's early admission to Mrs. Wix that she is in love with her stepfather, James avers that "Everything was as it should be." This both makes a comedy of the confession and underscores its human naturalness. And by expressing the emotion directly, Maisie is able to grow beyond it. Her departure, by the end of the book, from both her fathers seals her release from the ambiguous oedipal embrace.

James's depiction of the oedipal drama adds a lagging affection for her stepmother to Maisie's love for her stepfather. In the book's penultimate scene, while Sir Claude's "hands went up and down gently on her shoulders," Maisie presses Mrs. Beale to give up Sir Claude: "'I love Sir Claude—I love *him,*' Maisie replied with an awkward sense that she appeared to offer it as something that would do as well [as loving Mrs. Beale]. Sir Claude had continued to pat her, and it was really an answer to his pats. 'She hates you— she hates you,' he observed with the oddest quietness to Mrs. Beale." The neatness with which they all take their places here in a Freudian scene might seem oppressive were it not handled so delicately, and with so unerring an instinct for health. Maisie herself terminates the scene when she asks Mrs. Wix, "Shan't we lose the boat?" Her escape is so complete that even when Sir Claude fails to appear on the balcony for her as she turns around for a last look, and Mrs. Wix explains that "He went to *her*," his mistress, Mrs. Beale, Maisie's response is nothing more damaged or deprived than "Oh I know!"

Sir Claude's failure to be on the balcony to receive Maisie's parting look in one way seals the fraudulence of his affection. In another way, though, it signifies the salutary "lapse of a sequence" that enables Maisie "to recognize . . . the proof of an extinction." The extinction is, as much as anything else, the necessary "death of her childhood." Thus, when Maisie and Sir Claude part, "their eyes [meet] as the eyes of those who have done for each other what they can," that is, with a kind of serene acceptance of a natural ending. Such an extinction may seem premature, with Maisie still so young, but it represents a natural process symbolically accelerated.

The elderly, maternal governess Mrs. Wix attributes Maisie's separation from Sir Claude to her own efforts to work in the girl the triumph of what she calls "the moral sense," the last of the alien fictions in which the novel's various parent figures try to make Maisie dwell with them. Mrs. Wix presides over the genre of moral melodrama, and she herself is the melodramatic imagination of the novel personified. She thinks of Mrs. Beale as a "bad" woman, clings to didacticism for assistance in making sense of Maisie's way of bringing the story to a close, and sees all of the novel's events in simplified terms of good and evil. The beleaguered Maisie to her mind, can be saved from evil only by moral instruction. But at sea with Maisie as she is tossed from one alliance to another, the reader who may want to side with Mrs. Wix's impulse to criticize is bound to recognize that her idea of the moral sense is too simple a *vade mecum*. Marius Bewley argues that "if one denies evil in this novel one will be depriving Maisie's triumphant escape of a good deal of its significance." Yet to agree that Maisie's departure from Sir Claude and Mrs. Beale is a triumph of good over evil is to reconsign the girl to a vision that is not the less melodramatic because the victimization it projects is averted. What such a vision fails to recognize is that Maisie outgrows its terms altogether as she outgrows her childhood.

Mrs. Wix's special virtue is that she is the one parental character whose emotion for Maisie is stable. Yet we respond ambivalently to the safety of her absolutely dependable affection because it is the safety of death itself in its resolution of all uncertainties. For Maisie, "she was peculiarly and soothingly safe; safer than anyone in the world, than papa, than mamma . . . safer even, though so much less beautiful, than Miss Overmore [later to become Mrs. Beale]. . . . Mrs. Wix was as safe as Clara Matilda"—Mrs. Wix's dead daughter. That the elderly governess wears "glasses which, in humble reference to a divergent obliquity of vision, she called her straighteners" reveals that she is walleyed, physiologically unreliable when it comes to the visual equivalent of moral rectitude. The repetitions of the word "straighteners" as a substitute for her name suggest that she is someone who strains to define ethical space, to see as straight what perhaps can never conclusively be made out to be so.

The portrait of Mrs. Wix is worth exploring further especially because she thinks and judges so much like the characters of consciousness in James's other novels. Isabel also settles her uncertainty with an allusion to the straight path, and both Fleda and Strether pride themselves on being right. James's own entertainment of uncertainty, however, constitutes one of the most important ways in which he distances himself from his figures of consciousness who are sure of their rightness. Granted that in the *Maisie* preface James employs some of the same language of salvation that he assigns to Mrs. Wix: "For satisfaction of the mind . . . the small expanding consciousness would have to be saved, have to become presentable as a register of impressions." He speaks of Maisie "sowing on barren strands, through the mere fact of presence, the seed of the moral life." But Mrs. Wix and James mean substantially different things by "moral life" and being "saved." As James insisted in the preface to *The Portrait*, "the 'moral' sense" in art, and, by implication, in life or in characters who represent life, depends "on the amount of felt life" experienced. Thus, although he does indeed describe the lovers in *Maisie* as morally "barren," he says that the promise of moral life for the girl comes from her continuing "presence," not from absence, from her "register[ing] . . . impressions"—presumably including sexual impressions—not from her fleeing them.

With a tranquility very much at odds with Mrs. Wix's harried inquiries and pronouncements, Maisie arrives at a perspective on moral knowledge that endorses its importance at the same time as it treats the inclination to absolutes as something comical. The idea of moralizing experience, of seeing it as a series of lessons, is made funny.

> She judged that if her whole history, for Mrs. Wix, had been the successive stages of her knowledge, so the very climax of the concatenation would, in the same view, be the stage at which the knowledge should overflow. As she was condemned to know more and more, how could it logically stop before she should know Most? It came to her in fact . . . that she was distinctly on the road to know Everything. She had not had governesses for nothing. . . . She looked at the pink sky with a placid foreboding that she soon should have learnt All.

Maisie's gropings after the comically capitalized quantities "Most," "Every-thing," and "All" have the effect of making fun of the pretentiousness of moral certitude—knowing everything—at the same time as they convey a feeling for the largeness of moral knowledge.

Mrs. Wix presses Maisie at the end about her knowledge of the moral sense, like a teacher testing a slow learner on fixed, easily specifiable facts.

> Sir Claude and Mrs. Beale stood there like visitors at an "exam."
> She had indeed [for] an instant a whiff of the faint flower [the moral sense] that Mrs. Wix pretended to have plucked. . . . Then it left her, and, as if she were sinking with a slip from a foothold, her arms made a short jerk. What this jerk represented was the spasm within her of something still deeper than a moral sense. . . . she felt the rising of the tears she had kept down at the station. They had nothing—no, distinctly nothing—to do with her moral sense. The only thing was the old flat shameful schoolroom plea. "I don't know—I don't know."

Maisie substitutes for Mrs. Wix's settled convictions a knowledge that, like the early Newman's, is the larger for encompassing doubt. With her loss of a sure foothold, her admission of uncertainty, and her openness to tears, Maisie embodies the largest ethical appeal imagined in the novel: "something still deeper than a moral sense."

The others, including Mrs. Wix, fend off the pain of that moment with various rhetorical flourishes. We hear a veritable operetta of glib voices. Mrs. Wix flares out at Sir Claude with a florid and melodramatic didacticism: "You've nipped it [Maisie's moral sense] in the bud. You've killed it when it had begun to live." Later she is described as having "found another apos-trophe." Sir Claude responds to Mrs. Wix's accusation with a language inflated after its own fashion, with a hushed aestheticism: "I've not killed anything. . . . On the contrary I think I've produced life. I don't know what to call it . . . but, whatever it is, it's the most beautiful thing I've ever met—it's exquisite, it's sacred." About Maisie's offer to give up Mrs. Wix on the condition that he give up Mrs. Beale, Sir Claude speaks "with a relish as intense now as if some lovely work of art or of nature had suddenly been set down among them. He was rapidly recovering himself on this basis of fine appreciation." His ironically described "recovery" in high-tonedness, like Mrs. Wix's immersion in moralizing, floats him away from Maisie's wordless weeping.

Ultimately, Maisie leaves for England in the company of Mrs. Wix. In doing so, she chooses an ending that appears to validate conventional social

values of disapproval and judgment urged upon her by Mrs. Wix. Maisie's
return to England, however, is not an instance of fidelity to anyone else's
imagination of her life, not even Mrs. Wix's vision of her life as moral
melodrama. When the governess informs Maisie that Sir Claude has left the
balcony to keep company with his mistress and Maisie's reply is no more
censorious than "Oh I know!" James notes that Mrs. Wix "still had room
for wonder at what Maisie knew." Mrs. Wix is thus superseded and must
take her place as no more than a midwife to Maisie's determination to give
birth to herself.

As Maisie gets beyond, one after another, her father, her mother, then
Mrs. Beale and Sir Claude, and even, at last, Mrs. Wix, she enacts a farewell
to parents that has no parallel in what James had written until that time. By
showing that Maisie's sense of the life around her has become larger than
any other character's in the book, James was suggesting that although she
goes off with the elderly governess, she is actually spinning out of herself the
dimensions of her experience, becoming her own source, taking custody of
herself. Instead of constituting a "leak" or victimizing dissipation of power,
instead of disabling her or rendering her "sterile," as James says they do
Fleda, consciousness and vision coupled with the desires of the personal self
confer power on Maisie and ready her for fictions of her own. Dubious
though he might have been that we can live out the designs we compose for
our adults lives, James nevertheless felt that it was imperative to try to create
such designs. For him, growing up was quintessentially an authorial act.

MARK SELTZER

The Princess Casamassima: *Realism and the Fantasy of Surveillance*

"We do not suffer from the spy mania here," George R. Sims observes in his monograph on the London underworld, *The Mysteries of Modern London*; in this "free land," he argues, it is "not our custom to take violent measures" against the secret agents of the nether world. The freedom from violence that Sims celebrates, however, carries a rider that he at once suggests and disavows, and the "spy mania" reappears in a somewhat different guise: "The system of observation is as perfect as can be. . . . every foreign anarchist and terrorist known to the police—and I doubt if there is one in our midst who is not—is shadowed." London's "freedom" is guaranteed by the existence of an unlimited policing and by the dissemination of elaborate methods of police surveillance. An intense watchfulness generalizes the spy mania that Sims has discounted, and for the violence of the law is substituted a more subtle and more extensive mode of power and coercion: a power of observation and surveillance, and a seeing that operates as a more effective means of overseeing. Nor is it merely, in Sims's account, the agents of secret societies and criminals of the underworld who are shadowed by this perfect system of observation. London itself is constituted as a secret society, and everyday life is riddled with suggestions of criminality and encompassed by an incriminating surveillance:

In the 'buses and the trams and the trains the silent passengers

From *Henry James and the Art of Power*. © 1984 by Cornell University. Cornell University Press, 1984. This essay originally appeared in *Nineteenth-Century Fiction* 35, no. 4 (1981). © 1981 by the Regents of the University of California.

sit side by side, and no man troubles about his neighbour. But
the mysteries of modern London are represented in the crowded
vehicle and in the packed compartment. The quiet-looking woman
sitting opposite you in the omnibus knows the secret that the
police have been seeking to discover for months. The man who
politely raises his hat because he touches you as he passes from
his seat would, if the truth were known, be standing in the dock
of the Old Bailey to answer a capital charge.

The melodrama of the secret crime and the secret life passes "side by side
with all that is ordinary and humdrum in the monotony of everyday existence." And since there are "no mysteries of modern London more terrible
than its unrecorded ones," "silence" can only imply a more nefarious criminality; and not to have been brought to book by the police can only invoke
a suspicion of mysteries more insidious and of a criminality more threatening
in its apparent innocence and ordinariness.

If Sims's vision of the London streets is marked by a fantastic paranoia,
it is also a remarkable piece of police work, an attempt to "book" London's
unrecorded mysteries and to supplement the official police record through
an unrestricted lay policing. Discovering mysteries everywhere, Sims places
all of London under suspicion and under surveillance. Nor is Sims's vision
untypical of the manner in which London is seen and recorded in the late
nineteenth century. The extensive documentation that accumulates about
London from the mid-century on displays an interesting paradox. On the
one hand, from George W. M. Reynolds's *The Mysteries of London* (1845–
1848) to Sims's *The Mysteries of Modern London* (1906), London was reproduced as an impenetrable region of mystery; on the other, as this prolif-
erating literature itself testifies, London was subjected to an unprecedented
and elaborate scrutiny and surveillance. The sense of the city as an area of
mystery incites an intensive policing, a police work not confined to the institutions of the law (although the expansion of the London police and detective forces was "a landmark in the history of administration") but enacted
also through an "unofficial" literature of detection: by the reports of tourists
from the "upper world" and by the investigations of an exploratory urban
sociology, particularly the work of Henry Mayhew, Charles Booth, and
B. Seebohm Rowntree. It is played out also in the "discovery" of the city,
and its underworld, by the realist and naturalist novelists.

Henry James's eccentric contribution to the literature of London exploration is *The Princess Casamassima*, his vision of the "sinister anarchic
underworld" of London. "Truly, of course," James observes in his preface

to the novel, "there are London mysteries (dense categories of dark arcana) for every spectator." *The Princess Casamassima* is a novel about the mysteries of London, about spies and secret societies, and it is also a novel about spectatorship, about seeing and being seen. James offers an obligingly simple account of the novel's origin: "This fiction proceeded quite directly, during the first year of a long residence in London, from the habit and the interest of walking the streets." "The attentive exploration of London," he suggests, "fully explains a large part" of the novel; one walked "with one's eyes greatly open," and this intense observation provoked "a mystic solicitation, the urgent appeal, on the part of everything, to be interpreted" [New York edition]. It is the insistent continuity between secrecy and spectatorship, between the "mysteries abysmal" of London and the urgent solicitation to interpretation, that I want to focus on in this study of *The Princess Casamassima*. More precisely, I want to explore two questions that this continuity poses. First, what does it mean to walk the streets of London at this time, and how does this street walking function as a metonymy for the ways in which London is seen by James and his contemporaries? Second, how do the content and the techniques of representation in James's novel reproduce the London spy mania and the coercive network of seeing and power that characterize the literature of London mysteries?

Critics of *The Princess Casamassima* have traditionally located its politics in James's representation of London anarchist activities and have largely dismissed the novel's political dimension by pointing to James's lack of knowledge about these activities. The critical impulse has been to rescue the significance of the text by redirecting attention away from its ostensible political subject to its techniques, and these techniques have been seen to be at odds with the novel's political references. Manfred Mackenzie has recently summarized this depoliticization of the text, claiming that James, "because of his prior or primary American association . . . , cannot participate in any conventional modes of European social power, only in 'seeing,' or 'knowledge,' or 'consciousness.'"

But can "seeing" and "power" be so easily opposed in this literature, and are the politics of *The Princess Casamassima* separable from its techniques, from its ways of seeing and ways of knowing? What I hope to demonstrate is that *The Princess Casamassima* is a distinctly political novel but that James's analysis of anarchist politics is less significant than the power play that the narrative technique itself enacts. This is not to say that the politics of the novel are confined to its techniques: the institutions of the law and its auxiliaries, primarily the prison and the police, function as explicit topics in the text. But beyond these explicit and local representations of policing power, there is a more discreet kind of policing that the novel engages, a police work articulated precisely along the novel's line of sight.

II

If a relation between seeing and power becomes evident in the literature of the London underworld, it asserts itself not because the writer acknowledges the relation but, rather, because he works so carefully to disavow it. Sims, for instance, denies the existence of a "spy mania" on two counts: first, by separating police surveillance from an exercise of power, and second, by attempting to draw a line between his own acts of espionage and those of the police. Sims insists that he does not require a police escort in his wanderings through the London streets: "I have never asked for their assistance in my journeyings into dark places." Nevertheless, he is uneasily aware of the incriminating cast of his prowling and publication of the London netherworld. In his earlier *How the Poor Live and Horrible London* (1883), he notes that "it is unpleasant to be mistaken, in underground cellars where the vilest outcasts hide from the light of day, for detectives in search of their prey." Techniques of "disinterested" information gathering are unpleasantly mistaken for exercises of social control.

Additionally, Sims attempts to defend himself from another kind of "mistake," a misreading that would similarly put his motives in question. He introduces his text with a series of disclaimers: "It is not my object in these pages to bring out the sensational features of police romance"; my task "has for its object not the gratifying of a morbid curiosity, but the better understanding of things as they are." But if Sims seeks to tell "only the truth . . . , a plain unvarnished tale," his account, again, everywhere takes the form of what he protests against. If he will reveal only the truth, it is because the "truth is stranger than any written tale could ever hope to be"; and he proceeds to detail the underworld of East London as "the romances of the 'Mysterious East.'" His motives and, by implication, the motives of his audience cannot be separated from a morbid curiosity-mongering.

Sims's works sensationalize the mysteries beneath the humdrum surface and posit lurid secrets to be detected; they incite and cultivate a fascination with the underworld that converts it into a bizarre species of entertainment. On the one side, putting the underworld into discourse takes the form of a certain detective work, on the other, the purveying of a sensational entertainment. It is between these two poles—policing and entertainment—that Sims wishes to situate his texts, disclaiming both his (mis)identification as a detective and his exploitation of an intrusive voyeurism. Sims tries to open up a narrow space—called "things as they are"—to evade the charge of violating what he sees and reports. But this space is eroded from both sides: watching cannot be freed from an act of violation, from a conversion of the objects of his investigation into, as he expresses it, the "victims of my curiosity."

The double bind in which Sims finds himself, and the alibis he offers to extricate himself, recur frequently in other representations of the London underworld. This literature is always, in effect, playing on the twin senses of "bringing to book," making it difficult to disentangle publication from incrimination, and foregrounding the police work always latent in the retailing of London mysteries. James Greenwood, in his *Low-Life Deeps: An Account of the Strange Fish to be Found There* (1881), feels compelled, like Sims, to offer apologies for his intrusions into the underworld: "The extraordinary endurance of popular interest in the 'Orton imposture' . . . will perhaps be regarded as sufficient justification for here reproducing what was perhaps the most conclusive evidence of the man's guilt at the time, or since brought to light." Greenwood, however, does more than reproduce the evidence and respond, after the fact, to popular demand. His own investigations have in fact produced the confession and its accompanying popularity. Greenwood has brought Orton to book in the double sense that I have indicated: "I am glad to acknowledge that the confession of 'brother Charles' was obtained by me, the more so when I reflect on the vast amount of patience and perseverance it was found necessary to exercise in order to bring the individual in question to book." The impostor Orton is turned over, in a single gesture, to the reading public and to the police. And what follows Greenwood's self-congratulatory acknowledgement of his agency is Orton's signed confession—the signature juridically reproduced at the close of Greenwood's chapter—serving both as an entertainment in the popular interest and as an instrument of indictment.

Greenwood's gesture toward justification is a momentary confession on his own part of the "power of writing" that he exercises; his documentation of London mysteries, in *Low-Life Deeps* and in his earlier *The Wilds of London* (1874), is also a kind of victimization. More often, however, the victimization is less explicit; the function of supplying an entertainment is more obvious than any overt police action. James, we recall, speaks of "mysteries . . . for every spectator," and it is as a spectacle that the underworld is most frequently represented. Furthermore, James's formulation—"mysteries . . . for every spectator" rather than "spectators for every mystery"—

points to the constitutive power that the spectator exerts. The watcher produces, and not merely reproduces, what he sees and puts the underworld on stage as a theatrical entertainment.

The "staging" of the underworld is evident in Daniel Joseph Kirwan's *Palace and Hovel* (1870). Kirwan is an unselfconscious curiosity seeker and desires simply "to see something interesting." Presenting a series of underworld "scenes," he records, for example, a visit to a thieves' den, and his account is typical in the way it manages to convert a potentially threatening encounter into a moment of theater. His desire to be entertained is immediately gratified: each of the thieves Kirwan interrogates presents himself as an out-of-work entertainer, and each in turn performs for Kirwan's amusement. Crude and prefaced with excuses, the performances are clearly extemporized; the criminals have readily adopted the roles that Kirwan has implicitly assigned and have cooperated to produce the spectacle he wants to see. The underworld, quite literally, appears as a sort of underground theater. And the play is a power play in another sense as well. Kirwan, like most tourists of the nether regions, is accompanied and protected by a police detective, and the detective has supplied the cue for the performance that results. Before admitting the visitors, the "master of the mansion" has asked whether it is "bizness or pleasure," adding that "hif hits business you must 'elp yourself." "O, pleasure by all means," the detective replies. The displacement of poverty and crime into theater, of business into pleasure, is clearly marked, and the performers are willing to confine themselves to the roles of a beggars' opera in order to escape a more definitive confinement.

The metaphor of the theater also pervades Sims's *The Mysteries of Modern London*. His intent is to take the reader "behind the scenes": "When the interior of a house is set upon the stage, the fourth wall is always down in order that the audience may see what is going on. In real life the dramas within the domestic interior are played with the fourth wall up. . . . care is taken that no passer-by shall have a free entertainment. I am going to take the fourth wall down to-day." Indeed, this is not "free entertainment" but the basis of a literary industry; poverty, conspiracy, criminality are purchasable spectacles, at once opened to the public and reduced and distanced as theater. "'Do show me some cases of unmitigated misery,' is a request said to have been made by a young lady in search of sensation," Mrs. Bernard Bosanquet records in *Rich and Poor* (1896), her study of the slums. The request might easily be that of James's Princess, who "liked seeing queer types and exploring out-of-the-way social corners."

But if Sims's fantasy of disclosure—his taking down of the fourth wall—has an immediate theatrical reference, it refers also to another sort of fantasy.

The source of Sims's passage might well be the familiar passage in Dickens's *Dombey and Son* in which the author imagines "a good spirit who would take the housetops off . . . and show a Christian people what dark shapes issue from amidst their homes." There is, however, a more immediate source than this fantasy of a providential supervision, a possible source that makes unmistakable the nexus of policing and entertainment I have been tracing: "If we could fly out of that window hand in hand, hover over this great city, gently remove the roofs, and peep in at the queer things which are going on, the strange coincidences, the plannings, the cross-purposes, the wonderful chain of events . . . , it would make all fiction, with its conventionalities and foreseen conclusions, most stale and unprofitable." The speaker is Sherlock Holmes, in A. Conan Doyle's tale "A Case of Identity," precisely the "police romance" that Sims begins by disavowing and precisely the form that most insistently manifests the twin operations of vision and supervision, of spectatorship and incrimination, that the literature of the underworld engages. The impulse to explore and disclose the underworld in detective fiction becomes indistinguishable from a fantasy of surveillance; in the figure of the detective, seeing becomes the mode of power par excellence.

In "The Adventure of the Copper Beeches," Watson confesses to an uneasiness about sensationalizing the netherworld similar to that found in Sims and Greenwood. Holmes's alibi is exemplary: "You can hardly be open to a charge of sensationalism," he maintains, "for out of these cases . . . , a fair proportion do not treat of crime, in its legal sense, at all." Holmes, as everyone knows, repeatedly acts to mark a separation between his own activities and those of the police detective, and he claims repeatedly that his interest is in those matters "outside the pale of the law." But his investigations appear less to stand "outside" the law than to operate as a more efficient extension of the law. If Holmes's policing is extralegal, it registers an expansion and dissemination of policing techniques and of the apparatus of incrimination: an extension that places even what is avowedly legal within the boundaries of a generalized power of surveillance. Crime, in Holmes's sense, has been redefined to include an expanding range of activities, a shift that moves toward the placing of every aspect of everyday life under suspicion and under investigation.

Such a dream of absolute surveillance and supervision is enacted by the literature that the sensational accounts of London mysteries popularize and supplement: the sociological studies of the underworld that began accumulating in the mid-century with the work of the local statistical societies, Thomas Beames's *The Rookeries of London* (1850) and Henry Mayhew's *London Labour and the London Poor* (1851–1861) and culminating in Charles Booth's vast *Life and Labour of the People of London* (1889–1903).

The sociologist also represents London as a region of mystery to be deciphered, as a largely unexplored and unknown territory; the intent is to "map" the nether world, to place it within the confines of the "known world." As Asa Briggs suggests, "there was a dominating emphasis on 'exploration.' The 'dark city' and the 'dark continent' were alike mysterious, and it is remarkable how often the exploration of the unknown city was compared with the exploration of Africa and Asia." William Booth's *In Darkest England* (1890), for instance, opens with an extended analogy between the exploration for the sources of the Nile in Africa and the exploration for the sources of poverty and criminality in London. Similarly, Jack London, in his study of the London slums, *The People of the Abyss* (1903), equates investigating London and colonial exploration: "But O Cook, O Thomas Cook & Son, pathfinders and trail-clearers . . . , unhesitatingly and instantly, with ease and celerity, could you send me to Darkest Africa or Innermost Thibet, but to the East End of London . . . you know not the way."

As the reference to Cook indicates, exploration of the city appears as a specialized and exotic species of tourism even as it displays a "colonial" attitude toward the underworld. The secretary of a London Workman's Association, H. J. Pettifer, articulated in 1884 one form that this colonial tourism was taking: the urban sociologists, who in the absence of institutional funding required substantial personal wealth to undertake their studies, "had been talking of the working classes as though they were some new-found race, or extinct animal." Reduced to the status of the colonized primitive or "natural curiosity," the "strange fish" of London's "low-life deeps" are collected as exotic "specimens." Muniment, for instance, in *The Princess Casamassima*, compares Captain Sholto to a "deep-sea fisherman. . . . He throws his nets and hauls in the little fishes—the pretty little shining, wriggling fishes. They are all for [the Princess]; she swallows 'em down." Hyacinth and Muniment are spoken of as if they were "a sample out of your shop or a little dog you had for sale." "You see you do regard me as a curious animal," Hyacinth complains to the Princess. Sholto and the Princess share a "taste for exploration" and an appetite for queer types; Sholto hunts the slums as he does the imperial territories, bringing back trophies and specimens for the Princess.

There is a more than metaphoric resemblance between this colonial attitude toward the slums and the larger movements of colonization in the period. William Booth, the founder of the Salvation Army, worked to establish "missions" in darkest England. The larger program he proposed called for the establishment of a series of colonies—"the City Colony, the Farm

Colony, and the Over-Sea Colony"—to deal with the social question. And the colonizing of the underworld appears also in a somewhat different, and more comprehensive, form. Booth complains that the "colonies of heathens and savages in the heart of our capital . . . attract so little attention," but in fact they were drawing unprecedented attention. The secret world of London has become, as Booth later admits, an "open secret," and even as the city continues to be spoken of as an impenetrable enigma, the enigma has been systematically penetrated.

The statistical inscription and mapping of the city in the later nineteenth century have been well documented and are part of what might be called a professionalization of the problem of the city. From the formation of the Statistical Society in 1834 to Charles Booth's *Life and Labour*, London was meticulously explored, documented, and systematized. The intent, as Philip Abrams has observed, was, in part, to put on record "the mode of existence of different families—meals and menus, clothing and furniture, household routines and division of tasks, religious practices and recreation": in short, a scrutiny and recording in detail of the everyday life of the under classes. There is a preoccupation with statistical and enumerative grids, with the laborious accumulation of detail, with the deployment of a comprehensive system of averages and norms. The investigator constructs an interpretive matrix covering virtually every area and activity in the city, from the average traffic on the London streets and the cubic feet of air circulated in the London tenements to a detailed classification of criminals, delinquents, and other deviants from the specified norm. For the sociologist, as for James's Hoffendahl, "moving ever in a dry statistical and scientific air" "humanity, in his scheme, was classified and subdivided with a truly German thoroughness."

In the "amateur" investigations of Sims and in the fictive detective work of Holmes, the potential significance of the most trivial detail instigates a thorough scrutiny and surveillance; in the sociological study, we perceive a more discreet and more comprehensive surveillance, leaving no area of the city uncharted. The professionalization of the city proceeds as a tactful and tactical colonization of the territory, enabling an elaborate regularizing and policing of the city. Crucially, the sociological discourse establishes a normative scenario, a system of norms and deviations that effectively "impose[s] a highly specific grid on the common perception of delinquents." A regulative vision of the city is imposed, "subordinating in its universality all petty irregularities" and holding forth the possibility of that "one glorious principle of universal and undeviating regularity" that the sociologists envisioned. As the British sociologist Frederic J. Mouat observed in 1885,

statistics have passed from a merely descriptive stage and have become pre-
scriptive: "statistics have become parliamentary . . . and administrative."

The articulation of the sociological discourse of the city is coextensive
with, and opens the way for, the emergence and dispersal of agencies of
social training and social control: the multiplication of workhouses and
reformatories, of vocational institutions and of institutions for delinquents,
the expansion of the metropolitan police and the penal apparatus. The nominal function of these institutions is to train, to educate, to correct, to reform;
but clearly, their effect is to impose a general disciplinary and supervisory
authority over areas of urban life that have heretofore evaded scrutiny and
control. There is an insistent continuity between the theoretical preoccupation with normative scenarios and the institutionalization of that normative
vision. And it is not surprising that when the sociologist proposes a model
for urban reform, the model is that of the most highly regulated and super-
vised institution, the prison and reformatory: "In a well-regulated reformatory may be seen the effect of moral and religious discipline, combined
with good sanitary conditions, and a proper union of industrial and intellectual education, upon wayward, ignorant and hardened natures. Such an
institution is a type of the great work before us, for there is nothing done
in a reformatory which might not, with proper appliances, be effected for
society at large." The prison, with its routines and timetables, with its all-
encompassing control and supervision, serves as the ideal model for the city.
The regulative vision of the city institutionalizes a regulative supervision.

III

The most evident feature of the discourses of the city that I have been
tracing is an insistent watchfulness, a "spy mania," which appears at once
as a form of entertainment and as a police action. The twin sites of this
obsessive surveillance are the theater and the prison. *The Princess Casamassima* invokes this discursive scenario. James recalled his initial sense of
the novel as a self-implicating network of watchers: "To find [Hyacinth's]
possible adventure interesting I had only to conceive his watching the same
public show, the same innumerable appearances, I had watched myself, and
of his watching very much as I had watched." This specular relation is
reproduced throughout the novel, explicitly in the figures of the police spy
and secret agent, whose disguised presence is always suspected, but also in
the more ordinary exchanges of sight in the novel. In *The Princess Casamassima,* seeing and being seen always implicitly involve an actual or potential power play. Hyacinth, typically, promises "himself to watch his playmate

[Millicent] as he had never done before. She let him know, as may well be supposed, that she had her eye on *him,* and it must be confessed that as regards the exercise of a right of supervision he had felt himself at a disadvantage ever since the night at the theatre." Seeing makes for a "right of supervision" and a power of coercion; it is the nexus of seeing and power that I now want to examine in *The Princess Casamassima.*

Hyacinth dates his "disadvantage" from the "night at the theatre," and it does not take much interpretive pressure to see that a pervasive theatricality runs through the novel. The governing mode of interaction between characters involves a series of performances: the characters engage in the "entertainment of watching" as they are alternately recruited "for supplying such entertainment." Muniment commandeers Hyacinth "for Rosy's entertainment" as Hyacinth is brought to Medley by the Princess because his "*naïveté* would entertain her." The Princess especially is repeatedly referred to in theatrical terms as an "actress" performing on the "*mise-en-scène* of life," and her imitation of a small bourgeoise provides Hyacinth with "the most finished entertainment she had yet offered him."

The insistent theatricality of the novel refers less to any "dramatic analogy" than to the reciprocal watchfulness that invests every relation in the novel. The theater scenes in the novel enact an indifferent interchange of audience and play as objects of observation. The theater is the privileged point of vantage for an "observation of the London world," and if, as Hyacinth notes, "one's own situation seem[ed] a play within the play," it is because one is both spectator and spectacle. It is in the theater that Hyacinth discovers that he is being watched, that he has been spotted by Sholto and the Princess, herself "overshadowed by the curtain of the box, drawn forward with the intention of shielding her from the observation of the house." Hyacinth, in the balcony and not in the box, is not shielded from observation, and his vulnerable position indicates that, despite the exchanges of performance between characters, there is a certain asymmetry in this "entertainment of watching."

Hyacinth, "lacking all social dimensions was scarcely a perceptible person," and he is gratified that Sholto should "recognise and notice him" in the theater "because even so small a fact as this was an extension of his social existence." The under classes "exist" only when they have become the object of regard of the upper classes. But there is a counterside to this visibility. For if to be seen is to exist, it is also to be objectified, fixed, and imprisoned in the gaze of the other. It is to be reduced to the status of a "favourable specimen," to "studies of the people—the lower orders." In the largest sense, to be seen is to be encompassed by a right of supervision.

To escape supervision, characters cultivate a style of secrecy, adopt disguises in order to see without being seen; and, indeed, seeing without being seen becomes the measure of power in the novel. Hyacinth insistently promotes the secret life, at times with a certain absurdity: "I don't understand everything you say, but I understand everything you hide," Millicent tells Hyacinth. "Then I shall soon become a mystery to you, for I mean from this time forth to cease to seek safety in concealment. You'll know nothing about me then—for it will be all under your nose." If seeing is power, secrecy assumes a paramount value, and if beneath every surface a secret truth is suspected, to allow the "truth" to appear is consummately to disguise it.

The relation between a theatrical secrecy and power is most evident in James's representation of the secret society. Invoking Sims's paranoid vision of London conspiracies, the secret society appears as an almost providential power because it is both pervasively present and invisible:

> The forces secretly arrayed against the present social order were pervasive and universal, in the air one breathed, in the ground one trod, in the hand of an acquaintance that one might touch or the eye of a stranger that might rest a moment on one's own. They were above, below, within, without, in every contact and combination of life; and it was no disproof of them to say it was too odd they should lurk in a particular improbable form. To lurk in improbable forms was precisely their strength.

The spy mania is universal; the secret society, arrayed in improbable disguises, exercises a potentially unlimited surveillance, a potentially unlimited supervision.

There is another species of theater in *The Princess Casamassima* that makes even more explicit the nexus of seeing and power: the scene of the prison. Hyacinth's meeting with his mother in Millbank prison appears as another instance of reciprocal watchfulness: "They had too much the air of having been brought together simply to look at each other." Mrs. Bowerbank, the jailer, scripts the encounter, staging a confrontation "scene" and managing the action as an entertainment, expressing "a desire to make the interview more lively." She works to direct an occasion "wanting in brilliancy" and finally moves to "abbreviate the scene." The prison is a theater of power. Further, the jailer's visit to Pinnie sets the novel in motion; the novel opens under the shadow and gaze of the prison, "in the eye of the law" and under "the steady orb of justice." And most striking about Mrs. Bowerbank is not merely her representation of "the cold light of the penal system" and her "official pessimism" but the way in which her unrelenting observation of Pinnie and Hyacinth is experienced as an accusation of guilt and as an arrest by the law. This "emissary of the law" imprisons Pinnie in her gaze, and the dressmaker is "unable to rid herself of the impression that it was somehow the arm of the law that was stretched out to touch her." When Hyacinth is produced for the jailer's "inspection," he asks: "Do you want to see me only to look at me?" But "only" to be seen is already to be inscribed within a coercive power relation, to be placed under surveillance and under arrest. Mrs. Bowerbank's presence transforms the dressmaker's house into a prison house. The jailer appears as an "overruling providence"; her tone "seemed to refer itself to an iron discipline," and Pinnie can only respond "guiltily" to her questioning. Pinnie debates taking the "innocent child" to the prison and "defended herself as earnestly as if her inconsistency had been of a criminal cast." Indicted by Mrs. Bowerbank's observation, she attempts to shield herself, imagining the "comfort to escape from observation," and distracts herself from the "case" "as a fugitive takes to by-paths."

Pinnie, however, is not merely victimized and incriminated by the turnkey's legal eye. The jailer's visit disseminates an array of inquisitorial looks, recriminations, and betrayals, as the law stretches to include each character. But the characters are not merely victims; they in turn become "carriers" of the law. The more discreet and more insidious power of the law that Mrs. Bowerbank represents is the power to reproduce and extend the apparatus of surveillance and incrimination into situations that seem radically remote from crime, in the legal sense. The distribution of mechanisms of incrimination works not only to victimize those it stretches out to touch but more significantly to make its victims also its disseminators.

The opening scene of the novel is a concise instance of this "spreading" of the law, and a summary of the plot of the opening section is a summary of the displacement and extension of the techniques of penality that Mrs. Bowerbank incarnates. Pinnie, for instance, is not only incriminated by this emissary of the law: she herself becomes Mrs. Bowerbank's emissary. The jailer "would like to see" Hyacinth, and Pinnie undertakes to "look for the little boy," realizing at the same time that to make Hyacinth "visible" is also to bring him to judgment: as she expresses it, "if you could only wait to see the child I'm sure it would help you to judge."

To produce Hyacinth is to bring him to the law, and Pinnie both undertakes to produce him and proceeds to exercise a disciplinary authority of her own. As she obeys Mrs. Bowerbank's injunction to supply Hyacinth, she displaces the injunction onto his playmate, Millicent. She simultaneously places Millicent under the discipline of her observation—waiting "to see if her injunction would be obeyed"—and links this injunction with an appropriately reduced attribution of guilt—"you naughty little girl." Millie, in turn, replies with a "gaze of deliberation" and with a refusal to "betray" Hyacinth to this extended arm of the law: "Law no, Miss Pynsent, I never see him." When Hyacinth appears, Pinnie repeats her accusation of Millicent; "Millicent 'Enning's a very bad little girl; she'll come to no good." Hyacinth protests and tries to exculpate his friend from a betrayal in which he is implicated; his reply further suggests the displacements of guilt and responsibility that obsessively proliferate in this opening scene: "It came over him," he observes, "that he had too hastily shifted to her shoulders the responsibility of his unseemly appearance, and he wished to make up to her for this betrayal."

These shifts and displacements of criminality and incrimination indicate a generalized extension of the power of watching and policing in the novel. In *The Princess Casamassima,* police work is contagious, a contagion that James images as the transmission of a certain "dinginess" from one character to another: Hyacinth "hated people with too few fair interspaces, too many smutches and streaks. Millicent Henning generally had two or three of these at least, which she borrowed from her doll, into whom she was always rubbing her nose and whose dinginess was contagious. It was quite inevitable she should have left her mark under his own nose when she claimed her reward for coming to tell him about the lady who wanted him." If Hyacinth has shifted onto Millicent the blame for his "unseemly appearance," leading to Pinnie's accusations of her, the shifting of blame and guilt corresponds to the shifting of a mark of "dinginess," the stigma of the slums.

The opening scene plays out, in an anticipatory and understated fashion, the diffusion of penality that traverses *The Princess Casamassima.* It is the prison that provides the model for the contagion. The first principle of the prison is isolation, confinement, but within the novel Millbank prison stands as the central and centering instance of this spread of criminality; the prison

> looked very sinister and wicked, to Miss Pynsent's eyes, and she wondered why a prison should have such an evil air if it was erected in the interest of justice and order—a builded protest, precisely, against vice and villainy. This particular penitentiary struck her as about as bad and wrong as those who were in it; it threw a blight on the face of day, making the river seem foul and poisonous and the opposite bank, with a protrusion of long-necked chimneys, unsightly gasometers and deposits of rubbish, wear the aspect of a region at whose expense the jail had been populated.

Vice and villainy are not confined by the *cordon sanitaire* of the prison; rather, the prison infects the surrounding area, disperses its "evil air," and blights the city. The prison spreads what it ostensibly protests against and is erected to delimit. The atmosphere of the prison extends from the local site of the prison into every area of the novel, and there is no escape from the contagion of criminality; as Pinnie notes, every "effort of mitigation . . . only involved her more deeply." "He had not done himself justice"; "she seemed to plead guilty to having been absurd"; "Hyacinth's terrible cross-questioning"; "he went bail for my sincerity": one might multiply these quotations indefinitely, and I abstract them from their local contexts because it is the multiplication of these references, in the most banal and "innocent" exchanges in the novel, that establishes a general context of policing and incrimination in *The Princess Casamassima*. The very ordinariness of the allusions indicates the extent to which a fantasy of supervision and police work infiltrates the novel.

"What do you mean, to watch me?" Hyacinth asks Mr. Vetch, and the question alludes to more than the fiddler's paternal overseeing of Hyacinth. The possibility that Mr. Vetch is a police spy has earlier been considered; the manner in which the possibility is dismissed extends rather than limits the spy mania that the novel reproduces: Hyacinth

> never suspected Mr. Vetch of being a governmental agent, though Eustache Poupin had told him that there were a great many who looked a good deal like that: not of course with any purpose of incriminating the fiddler. . . . The governmental agent in extraordinary disguises . . . became a very familiar type to Hyacinth, and though he had never caught one of the infamous brotherhood in the act there were plenty of persons to whom, on the very face of the matter, he had no hesitation in attributing the character.

The secret agent lurks in improbable forms, and as in Sims's fantasies of the anarchic underworld, apparent innocence invites a suspicion of concealed criminality. This passage denies suspicion and the purpose of incrimination even as it attributes the character of the police spy indiscriminately. The attribution attaches, at one time or another, to virtually every character in the novel. To Captain Sholto, for instance: "Perhaps you think he's a spy, an *agent provocateur* or something of the sort." But Sholto's form is not improbable enough, a spy "would disguise himself more." It attaches also to the Princess, who is suspected of being "an agent on the wrong side."

The Princess, Madame Grandoni tells the Prince, is "much entangled. She has relations with people who are watched by the police." "And is *she* watched by the police?" "I can't tell you; it's very possible—except that the police here isn't like that of other countries." Indeed, the police here are not like they are elsewhere—they are everywhere. Just prior to this discussion, the Princess and Paul Muniment have left the house at Madeira Crescent on a conspiratorial mission that remains a narrative secret. The spies are themselves spied upon, as the narrative observer comments: "Meanwhile, it should be recorded, they had been followed, at an interval, by a cautious figure, a person who, in Madeira Crescent, when they came out of the house, was stationed on the other side of the street, at a considerable distance. On their appearing he had retreated a little, still however keeping them in sight." James initially withholds the identity of the observer who has placed the conspirators under surveillance. His revelation of that identity takes a curious form: "The reader scarce need be informed, nevertheless, that his design was but to satisfy himself as to the kind of person his wife was walking with." The disavowal of any need to inform the reader of the figure's identity only points to the reader's initial misidentification. The passage invites a "confusion" of domestic suspicions and police surveillance and indicates the extent to which all actions in the novel have come to resemble a police action. All characters in the novel are "in danger of playing the spy."

There is no space free from the spy mania, from the infection of penality. Medley, the Princess's country-house retreat, provides no escape. The Princess there informs Hyacinth that "I've been watching you. I'm frank enough to tell you that. I want to see more—more—more!" And if Hyacinth ceases "to be insignificant from the moment" the Princess sees him, he experiences his accession to significance as a subjection to "cross-examination." A dispersed surveillance shadows Hyacinth, both in the Princess's watchfulness and in the supervision of his conduct "under the eye of the butler." Medley is, for Hyacinth, the "real country," real nature, but nature itself participates in the general police action: "Never had the old oaks and beeches . . . witnessed such an extraordinary series of confidences since the first pair that sought isolation wandered over the grassy slopes and ferny dells beneath them."

The witnessing eye of nature and the allusion to the providential supervision of the Garden indicate the thorough "naturalization" of mechanisms of surveillance and policing in *The Princess Casamassima*: nature itself appears to supplement the policing function. Mrs. Bowerbank early comments on Florentine's impending death by asserting that "if she lived a month [she] would violate (as Mrs. Bowerbank might express herself) every established law of nature." James's parenthetical interpolation calls attention to the jailer's characteristic mode of expression, her linking of "nature" and the "law," her naturalizing of the penal apparatus. In *The Princess Casamassima,* the power of vision and supervision is not confined to the nominal agencies of the police: it is enforced by the "eyes of the world." It is finally impossible to distinguish between the "eye of day and the observation of the police."

IV

The spy mania and the incriminating techniques of policing and surveillance are not confined but contagious in *The Princess Casamassima*; the prison and the supervision and discipline it implies reappear at every turn in the novel. I have indicated the proposal of the prison as a model for the city at large in the work of the London sociologists, and I now want to take up the significance of this equation from a somewhat different perspective. Michel Foucault, in *Surveiller et punir,* his recent history of the rise of disciplinary practices, describes the extension of social mechanisms of surveillance and discipline into all areas of modern society. More specifically, he traces the reorganization of Western society around the model of the "punitive city": "Near at hand, sometimes even at the very centre of cities of the nineteenth century [stands] the monotonous figure, at once material and symbolic, of the power to punish"—the prison. The architectural figure of this social reorganization is Jeremy Bentham's Panopticon, a circular building, divided into cells, surrounding a central observation tower. The Panopticon operates through a controlling network of seeing and being seen: the inmate "is seen, but he does not see"; "in the central tower, one sees everything without ever being seen." The inmate is trapped in a "seeing machine," trapped in a state of conscious and constant visibility; as a result, he "inscribes in himself the power relation" in which he is caught up and "becomes the principle of his own subjection."

London's Millbank prison was derived from Bentham's panopticon scheme. Convicts were accommodated in six pentagonal ranges that surrounded a central watchtower—the locus of a providential supervision that doubled also, and appropriately, as the prison chapel. James visited Millbank on a December morning in 1884 to collect notes for *The Princess Casamassima*. His description of the prison in the novel emphasizes the power of watching that the Panopticon employs. He records the "circular shafts of cells" ranged about a central observatory and, further, the "opportunity of looking at captives through grated peepholes," at the women with "fixed eyes" that Pinnie is "afraid to glance at"; the inmates are dressed in "perfect frights of hoods." This last detail recalls the practice at Pentonville, where "all contact with other human beings, except the prison staff, was forbidden, and when convicts left their cells . . . , they wore masks with narrow eye-slits in order to prevent identification by their fellows."

The Panopticon effects an exemplary conjunction of seeing and power, the conjunction that extends from the prison throughout *The Princess Casamassima*. "The panoptic schema," Foucault details, ". . . was destined to spread throughout the social body." Foucault discusses the dispersal of this schema in nineteenth-century society, its penetration into the factory, the workhouse, the reformatory, the school—into, in fact, all those institutions that, as we have seen, the urban colonizers deployed and cultivated. And further, the panoptic technique infiltrates "tiny, everyday" social practices, traverses and embraces those "minute social disciplines" apparently remote from the scene of the prison. Confiscating and absorbing "things of every moment," an everyday panopticism is finally universalized: "Police power must bear 'over everything.'"

One final institutionalization of the panoptic technology remains to be considered. It has recently been suggested that Foucault's history might underwrite a radical revision of our sense of the "politics" of the novel, and the problem that I want now to take up, and which has been implicit all along, concerns the relation between these disciplinary techniques and the techniques of the novel, and more particularly of the realist and naturalist novel, which appears on the scene at the same time that the disciplinary society takes power. Foucault suggests that the novel "forms part of that great system of constraint by which the West compelled the everyday to bring itself into discourse." In what way may the realist novel be seen to participate in, and even to promote, a system of constraint?

It has been observed that "excellence of *vision* is the distinguishing mark of realism." "To see" is the dominant verb in the realist text—"la gastronomie de l'oeil," as Balzac expressed it—and realist fiction is preeminently concerned with seeing, with a seeing in detail. The proximity of this realist "seeing" to the overseeing and police work of detection becomes explicitly problematic and is most evident, of course, in the subgenre of realism that we have already glanced at, the fiction of detection. In detective fiction, the relation between seeing and policing is taken for granted; literally, the range of the detective's vision is the range of his power. That power operates by placing the entire world of the text under scrutiny and under surveillance and invokes the possibility of an absolute supervision, in which everything may be comprehended and "policed" and in which the most trifling detail becomes potentially incriminating. Realistic fiction, in a more discreet and, for that reason, more comprehensive manner, deploys a similar tactic of detection; the techniques of surveillance and detection traverse the techniques of the realistic novel. Emerson, instancing Swift, notes "how realistic or materialistic in treatment of his subject" the novelist is: "He describes his fictitious persons as if for the police." Indeed, detective fiction merely literalizes the realist representational scrutiny, its fascination with seeing and with the telling significance of detail, and lays bare *the policing of the real* that is the realist project. "We novelists," writes Zola, "are the examining magistrates of men and their passions."

The juridical expression of the aims of the realist novelist recurs frequently. There is, for instance, George Eliot's statement in *Adam Bede* (chapter 17) of the novelist's obligation to write "as if I were in the witness-box narrating my experience on oath" and Guy de Maupassant's avowal, in his preface to *Pierre et Jean,* to tell "la vérité, rien que la vérité, et toute la vérité." And earlier, there is Lamb's comment that reading Defoe "is like reading evidence in a court of Justice" or Hazlitt's observation that Richardson "sets about describing every object and transaction, as if the whole had been given in on evidence by an eyewitness." The convergence of the literary and the legal recurs also in attacks on the alleged illicitness and "illegality" of the realistic novel; thus W. S. Lilly, writing in 1885, asserts that, in the realist and naturalist novel, "everywhere at the bottom there is filth" (*l'ordure*). Those proceedings in the courts of justice which from time to time bring it to the surface—like an abscess—are merely an experimental novel unfolding itself, chapter after chapter, before the public." The realist novel is seen to proceed as a legal action. The realist novelist is the examining magistrate of everyday life.

There is a complementary movement in realistic fiction: toward a documentation of phenomena in precise detail, and toward a supervision of these phenomena. As Zola concisely expresses it, "the goal of the experimental method . . . is to study phenomena in order to control them." The realists share, with other colonizers of the urban scene, a passion to see and document "things as they are," and this passion takes the form of a fantasy of surveillance, a placing of the tiniest details of everyday life under scrutiny. Is it not possible to discover in this fantasy of surveillance a point of intersection between the realist text and a society increasingly dominated by institutions of discipline, regularization, and supervision—by the dispersed networks of the "police"?

There are a number of ways in which the relation between the novel and the law can be explored. There is, for instance, an intriguing resemblance between the realist typologies of character and the typologies proposed by the late nineteenth-century criminologists, chiefly Cesare Lombroso, a resemblance that Conrad exploits in *The Secret Agent,* another novel of the London spy mania. More generally, one might note the encompassing control

over character and action that the realist and naturalist doctrine of "deter-
minism" secures. As Leo Bersani has recently suggested, the realist's method
works to reduce "the events of fiction to a parade of sameness. For example,
it would not be wholly absurd to suggest that a Balzac novel becomes unnecessary as soon as its exposition is over. The entire work is already contained in the presentation of the work, and the characters merely repeat in
dialogue and action what has already been established about them in narrative summaries. Their lives mirror the expository portraits made of them
at the beginning of the novel."

The linear order and progression of the realistic novel enable the novel
to "progress" only in a direction always preestablished. Indeed, it is as a
"repetition" that Hyacinth experiences his every attempt to break with his
origins and "antecedents," to break with his "naturalist" determinants of
environment and heredity. His recruitment to assassinate the duke presents
itself as "the idea of a *repetition*," as the "horror of the public reappearance,
in his person, of the imbrued hands of his mother." This "young man in a
book" expresses an interest in the "advanced and consistent realists," but
this "consistency," a key word in the novel, becomes another name for an
entrapment in a (narrative) repetition.

In its fixing of consistent "types," and in its predictive control over
narrative possibility, the realistic text gains a thorough mastery over its characters and their actions—a twin mastery of intelligibility and supervision.
The Princess Casamassima has been regarded as James's primary excursion
into the realistic or naturalistic mode. The novel, in its choice of subjects
and in its descriptive method, displays an affinity with the consistent realists,
and certainly, it everywhere displays the fantasy of surveillance which, I have
been suggesting, lies at the heart of the realist project. But we notice that
this surveillance becomes in many ways the subject and not merely the mode
of the novel, and such a foregrounding of the novel's tactics of supervision
indicates, within limits that I will attempt to describe, James's exposure and
demystification of the realist mania for surveillance and his attempt to disown the policing that it implies.

Perhaps the most powerful tactic of supervision achieved by the traditional realist novel inheres in its dominant technique of narration—the style
of "omniscient narration" that grants the narrative voice an unlimited authority over the novel's "world," a world thoroughly known and thoroughly
mastered by the panoptic "eye" of the narration. The technique of omniscient
narration, as is frequently noted, gives to the narrator a providential vision
of the characters and action. It is the fantasy of such an absolute panopticism
that we have previously traced in Sims's lifting of the fourth wall, and in

Dickens's and Doyle's fantasy of "removing the roofs" and viewing the "queer things which are going on." In *The Princess Casamassima,* such omniscient vision is attributed to the master revolutionaries: "They know everything—everything. They're like the great God of the believers: they're searchers of hearts; and not only of hearts, but of all a man's life—his days, his nights, his spoken, his unspoken words. Oh they go deep and they go straight!" Hoffendahl's God-like power is also the power of the omniscient narrator, a power of unlimited overseeing.

But if James inscribes in his text an image of comprehensive and prov-idential supervision, the narrative method of the novel departs from this panoptic technique. As a number of critics have shown, and as James asserts in his preface to the novel, *The Princess Casamassima* marks a technical turning point in James's career: a turning away from the style of omniscient narration toward the technique of the "central recording consciousness" or "central intelligence." That technique displaces the authority of the narrative voice and disavows any direct interpretive authority over the action. It can be said that in *The Princess Casamassima,* omniscient authority is held up to scrutiny, and indicted, in being transferred to, or displaced upon, the masters of the revolution.

Can this supervisory power, however, be so easily disowned? In his preface, James imagines his observation of the underworld as a form of espionage: his vision of London is that of "the habitual observer . . . the pedestrian prowler." But at the same time, he disclaims any violation or manipulation of the figures he "merely" observes: "I recall pulling no wires, knocking at no closed doors, applying for no 'authentic' information." It is Hoffendahl, in the novel, who is the arch wire puller: "He had in his hand innumerable other threads." And it is this puppeteering that James disavows. But having denied such a manipulative power, James proceeds to reclaim what he has dismissed: "To haunt the great city and by this habit to penetrate it, imaginatively, in as many places as possible—*that* was to be informed, *that* was to pull wires, *that* was to open doors."

James distinguishes his "imaginative" penetration of the city from the manipulative vision and supervision of the conspiratorial plotters. The im-plication is clear: James would claim that his imaginative wire pulling is not an act of supervision, that his deep searching of hearts, of spoken and un-spoken words, that his seeing and "haunting" of the city can be distinguished from the policing and spy mania that this haunting of the great city so closely resembles. It is just such a separation between "mere" seeing, consciousness, and knowledge and an exercise of power that I have been questioning. James offers the alibi of a "powerless" imagination to extricate himself from the charge of participating in the spy mania that the novel everywhere engages. But James would have no need to insist on the distinction if it were not already jeopardized, already threatened by the compelling resemblance between his haunting and perpetual prowling and the surveillance and policing from which he would disengage himself.

It becomes clear that the attempt on the part of the writers we have examined to disown the policing that they exercise can be seen as a "cover" for a more discreet and comprehensive policy of supervision, and it is as such a ruse that I think James's displacing of power and authority works. The recession of narrative supervision in *The Princess Casamassima* appears as one further "shifting of the shame," a displacing of responsibility, culpability, and, in the terms which the novel provides, criminality. The shifting of narrative authority makes reference to an uneasiness concerning the shame of power. If James's novel is systematically the story of a criminal continuity between seeing and power, this continuity is finally disowned. If James works toward a demystifying of the realist policing of the real, this police work is finally remystified, recuperated as the "innocent" work of the imagination.

From one point of view, the incompatibility of the novel and the subject of power is the "message" of *The Princess Casamassima*: the incompatibility of aesthetic and political claims leads to Hyacinth's suicide. Critics of the novel have restated this message, insisting, with approval or disapprobation, that the novel sacrifices its political references to technical preoccupations. In his preface, James himself observes that the underworld of London "lay heavy on one's consciousness." The phrase invites us to read "conscience" for "consciousness," and the substitution registers in miniature what has been seen as James's substitution in *The Princess Casamassima* of the ordeal of consciousness (that is, the work's technique) for matters of social conscience (its political subject). Thus it has been argued that "Hyacinth Robinson's sensitive consciousness is the mirror which controls the shape" of the novel, that James's "ignorance in the face of the reality, the great grey Babylon, which was nearest to him," compelled him to distort that reality by circumscribing it with a "controlling and bizarre consciousness," and that, finally, this technical preoccupation means that *The Princess Casamassima's* "theme is not political at all." As Leo Bersani points out, "it has been decided by 'politically conscious' Anglo-American critics that James is a nonpolitical novelist."

Critics of *The Princess Casamassima,* and of James's work generally, have restated the discontinuity that James himself proposed, enforcing a break between technique and subject, between ways of seeing and the subject of power. It is maintained that "in his quest for a quintessential social reality that was also an alien reality, James must necessarily have found himself recoiling upon the merely psychological and even epistemological, the merely imaginative—upon fantasy." But if James's only "political novel" advertises a radical conflict between politics and the novel, there is, working against this simple polarization, a criminal continuity between the techniques of the novel and the social technologies of power that inhere in these techniques. It is in this rigorous continuity established in James's novels between seeing, knowing, and exercising power that the politics of the Jamesian text appears, and it is this continuity that I have been tracing in *The Princess Casamassima.*

James closes his preface to *The Princess Casamassima* by acknowledging an apparently disqualifying lack of knowledge about his ostensible subject. The setting of the novel is the anarchic underworld of London, but the scene of writing is far removed from the scene of the action: "I remember at any rate feeling myself all in possession of little Hyacinth's consistency, as I have called it, down at Dover during certain weeks that were none too remotely precedent to the autumn of 1885 and the appearance, in 'The Atlantic Monthly' again, of the first chapters of the story." Like the Princess, James appears to have "retired to a private paradise to think out the problem of the slums." But even here James obliquely acknowledges a continuity between this scene of light and culture and the policed underworld of London. The law reappears even in the midst of this private paradise: "There were certain sunny, breezy balconied rooms at the quieter end of the Esplanade of that cheerful castle-crested little town—now infinitely perturbed by gigantic 'harbour works,' but then only faded and over-soldiered and all pleasantly and humbly submissive to the law that snubs in due course the presumption of flourishing resorts." "Over-soldiered" and "humbly submissive to the law," in the diffused and extended sense that the novel has promoted, the scene of writing is a muted repetition of the scene of the novel. Re-inscribed in the ordinary and everyday, the "police" are everywhere.

MARIA IRENE RAMALHO DE SOUSA SANTOS

Isabel's Freedom:
The Portrait of a Lady

Das Gesetz hat noch keinen grossen Mann gebildet, aber die Freiheit brütet Kolosse und Extremitäten aus.
—Karl Moor in *Die Räuber*

No, it is awful. She will be nobody's wife; she will be lost!
—Darya Alexandrovna Oblonsky speaking of Anna Arkadyevna Karenin

The idea of the whole thing is that the poor girl, who has dreamed of freedom and nobleness ... finds herself in reality ground in the very mill of the conventional.
—HENRY JAMES speaking of Isabel Archer Osmond

In an article that he very aptly called "The Moment of *The Portrait of a Lady*," Charles Feidelson shows how this novel represents not only a transitional point in James's work and thinking, but also a basic shift of fictional attitude in the nineteenth-century novel, moving towards the twentieth century novel-of-consciousness. By placing "The centre of the subject in the young woman's own consciousness," [as James claimed in the Preface to the New York edition to have done] James begins to reverse the whole idea of fictional narrative. While, for example, in *Bleak House* the social world around Esther Summerson defines her and even conditions her own narrative of herself, in *The Portrait of a Lady* it is Isabel's consciousness that *seems* to define and shape the world about her. Where before the novel had presented the characters in terms of the world—either in harmony with society

From *Biblos* 56. © 1980 by Maria Irene Ramalho de Sousa Santos.

or in opposition to it—now the novel begins to sketch the idea of a character that shapes the fictional form itself: the character-as-consciousness. From now on the world of fiction will depend more and more on the shaping power of this imagining consciousness. The main technical change is, then, a change of voice, or point of view. The so-called omniscient author—"the muffled majesty of authorship" James speaks of—no longer plays his former role. If the character's consciousness holds the center of interest, then the character's consciousness must "tell" the "story," and "the artist, like the God of the creation, remains within or behind or beyond or above his handiwork, invisible, refined out of existence, indifferent, paring his fingernails" [James Joyce, *The Portrait of the Artist as a Young Man*]. Although in *The Portrait*, and for that matter in James's work as a whole, we are still far from Joyce's radical stance of narrative absence, Henry James's novels must be read as transitional in this regard, and *The Portrait* as a clear turning point. Indeed, before we get to the hardly audible authorial voice in *The Golden Bowl*, we witness a process of gradual slowing down of the authoritative, supposedly knowledgeable narrative voice in *The Portrait*, until in chapter 42, "the best thing in the book," the reader is left alone with the contemplation of Isabel, finally almost completely "translated" into the "formula" of her own consciousness.

Thus, from Dickens (or Jane Austen), where we have the individual concerned with society, to the extent that he or she depends on society for his or her own definition, we turn to James, where the individual becomes more and more preoccupied with his or her consciousness, to the extent that his or her alienation from society becomes the gauge of his or her identity. The Jamesian character, by his or her own introspective movement, begins seriously to question previous societal definitions and to assert the right to a separate identity. In this sense also, James's *Portrait* may still be said to be a social novel. For it depicts precisely this changing social context, or world system, in which an individual consciousness has lost its sense of an individual's defined place in the world, a sense of roots growing deeply in a solid soil, however menacing. If it is possible to say that James's demericanized Americans are vivid dramatizations of this sense of displacement, the problem must not be seen merely in the light of James's International Theme. Lord Warburton, the preposterous radical aristocrat, is also definitely unable to reconcile his liberal ideology with the rigid form and the heavy weight of the English tradition in which he finds himself misplaced.

Isabel Archer seems to find her lack of place (or definition) the more interesting and appealing. She believes herself completely free to choose the absence of form that appears most congenial to her, thus typically neglecting the complex network of relationships in which individual facts or events are rooted. Her love for an all-embracing (individual) consciousness equals her love of freedom. This is what is implied in Chase's view that "Isabel has higher ideals than any she thinks can be realized by a life with Lord Warburton." Her higher ideals are the liberal ideals of a "completed consciousness" and of individual freedom, whereas Lord Warburton, even if in spite of himself, has to offer only the "system" her "instinct" tells her to "resist." It is clear right from the beginning of the novel that Isabel Archer dreads the kind of definition implied in a commitment to what Lord Warburton represents, and that is why she cannot "think of [his] various homes as the settled seat of [her] residence." She will have to remain completely disengaged to pursue the "free exploration of life" that her imagination dreams of.

This is exactly what she thinks she will begin to achieve when she decides to marry Gilbert Osmond, the man who presents himself to her seemingly without a system. In justifying her marital decision to Ralph, Isabel says: "He [Osmond] wants me to know everything; that is what I like him for"; and later on, still failing to see the intricate web of relationships, and resolutely ignoring Ralph's socializing warning that "one ought to feel one's relation to things—to others," she refuses to see Osmond but in the light of noble individuality and independence she bestows on him: "He knows everything, he understands everything, he has the kindest, gentlest, highest spirit." Thus, as she had rejected the social commitment implicit in Lord Warburton's proposal, she now accepts the offer that seems to her most uncommitted socially and that she believes to be the total fulfilment of the freedom she needs to expand her imagination limitlessly: "His being so independent, so individual, is what *I* most see in him."

Isabel believes, then, that her marriage to Osmond opens up for her the broad road towards the complete fulfilment of her consciousness. Out of that late Nineteenth century, pre-war idealism that she, too, embodies, Isabel cherishes the kind of individual freedom (i.e. disengagement, separateness, independence) which she believes to be the essence of human consciousness. So, in freedom as she thinks, she chooses to marry the man that had seemed to her most uncommitted, most unconcerned, most disinterested, most independent, most free. Thus, Isabel will truly find herself, as a woman, in her marriage, which is no less than the symbolic reconciliation of her notion of freedom with society's (and her own) as yet unquestioned definition of woman as somebody's wife.

Up to this point we have the social novel about how bad or how good a marriage a certain intelligent and idealistic, but rather presumptuously independent young girl will make. *The Portrait of a Lady* begins overtly like a comedy of manners, with its beautiful Gardencourt setting of English amenities and afternoon tea. Like Jane Austen's heroines, Isabel Archer is also mainly concerned with the difficult problem of marriage. The main issue in the first part of the book seems to be how Isabel will fit in the events that surround her, or rather, how she will attain that important goal of all Austen's heroines: appropriate *location* in a surrounding society by means of a suitable marriage. For in this society, as in Tolstoy's tzarist Russia, to be nobody's wife is to be lost indeed. However, little by little the reader begins to realize that, unlike what happens in Austen's novels, the interesting thing about Isabel is not how she will eventually fit in the surrounding events, but rather if and how the events fit *her*. Since we shall find out in the end that the events in the novel do not fit its heroine at all, that she will rather have to re-invent her freedom in order to force herself to fit them, the *moment* of *The Portrait of a Lady* turns out to be more telling than a mere technical change of fictional stances. While in earlier novels of manners and social comedy the center of interest lay mainly on the full definition of womanhood within society by a woman's right (or wrong) choice of marriage, in *The Portrait* the center of interest is gradually shifting from social events to the main character's consciousness; and marriage, rightly or wrongly assumed, is being quietly, perhaps inadvertently, put into question as a woman's defining principle.

For Feidelson's argument it is indeed important to emphasize the word *consciousness* in James's much quoted piece of self-advice, "Place the center of the subject in the young woman's consciousness;" but the fact that the consciousness is that of a young *woman's* must never slip out of one's mind. Like Hawthorne's *The Scarlet Letter* or George Eliot's *Middlemarch,* two obvious predecessors of *The Portrait,* or James's own short novel "Daisy Miller," *The Portrait of a Lady* reflects its author's latent social preoccupations, or his sensitivity to the changing times, precisely in his heroine's quest for freedom, i.e. in her control, or lack of control, of her own destiny. Whether James actually wanted it so or not, by implicitly siding with many other nineteenth-century authors in their concern for the woman's place in society, James made of Isabel's consciousness not just the growing consciousness of a presumptuous girl, around whom an ado is organized, but the very arena upon which the structure of society is questioned through the young woman's "searching [self] criticism."

The novel-of-consciousness in *The Portrait* begins, therefore, when Isabel sits down to *think* of what has happened to her consciousness and to her freedom; it begins when Isabel learns how to make connections and relate events; it begins when her thoughtful self-criticism enlightens her as to the calculated intrigues that had necessitated her marriage. Isabel's discoveries about her freedom or lack of freedom, as well as her final stubborn attempt to mend the broken image of her illusion of self-control, must then also be read as an implicit comment on the shifting values of late nineteenth century, such as individualism and individual freedom, integrity and dignity of mind and consciousness, inner authenticity and coherence in absolute terms (i.e. regardless of external, social circumstances). Isabel's self-probing consciousness, as well as the subtle gradual translation of social comedy into the novel-of-consciousness, are already clear signs of the crisis in western thinking and ideals that Fredric Jameson has called "the bankruptcy of the liberal tradition."* In James's world, independent young women either die, like Daisy Miller, or, like Isabel Archer/Osmond, are mercilessly crushed by a conventional form. In the following attempt to explain once again why Isabel Archer returns to Rome and to her husband at the end of the novel, I suggest that James's heroine is desperately trying to preserve a lost ideal of individual freedom as the basis for a woman's social identity.

II

> Isabel sat there looking up at her, without rising; her face almost a prayer to be enlightened. But the light of this woman's eyes seemed only a darkness. "O misery!" she murmured at last; and she fell back, covering her face with her hands. It had come over her like a high surging wave that Mrs. Touchett was right. Madame Merle had married her. Before she uncovered her face again that lady had left the room.

In his Notebook entry on *The Portrait of a Lady*, Henry James was still debating whether he should have Mme Merle or the Countess Gemini break the news to Isabel about Mme Merle's relationship to Pansy and Osmond. He thinks that it would be "better on many grounds" that it should be the Countess, and yet he regrets to have, in that case, to lose "the 'great scene' between Madame Merle and Isabel." The passage I quoted above shows how James was able to have the Countess be messenger of bad news and still save one "great scene" between Mme Merle and Isabel. The scene is indeed great. It is a crucial scene in the whole novel, particularly important for our understanding of Isabel's sense of freedom, and her subsequent attempts to preserve it. Isabel Osmond—trapped by the calculated machinations of her husband and of Mme Merle—begins to realize how far away she is now from Isabel Archer, the independent young woman at the beginning of the novel, a symbol in herself of unlimited freedom in her latent potentialities.

After this momentous interview with Mme Merle, Isabel has to go out into the open air: "she wished to be far away, under the sky, where she could descend from her carriage and tread upon the daisies." Of course, this had already become a habit with her. The weariness accumulated in "the house of darkness, the house of dumbness, the house of suffocation" she would rest "upon things that had crumbled for centuries and yet still were upright." It was relieving and refreshing to identify her own sense of wreckage and desolation with the dismal, pain-echoing ruins of the grandeur that Rome had been. The image of a glorious decadence around her worked like a balsamic consolation on her battered, and yet still dignified soul. This time, however, it seems that Isabel's impulse to run into the open space of the Roman landscape comes mainly as a result of her sudden confrontation with the overwhelming revelation: the most important decision of her life had been determined, not by her own free choice, but by someone else's deliberate calculations. In freedom she had wanted to be enlightened, and in bondage she had received only the most terrifying darkness. She had wished her consciousness to expand itself into the realm of beauty in its completeness, and finds out, abjectly, that what she believes to be the basic presupposition for human consciousness itself—freedom—had been lacking in her all the time. The openness of space between the daisies and the sky will help create around her, outside her, the illusion of the liberty she is miserably missing inside her.

We shall have to recapitulate what things like freedom, and liberty, and independence, and self-confidence had always meant to Isabel to understand all the implications of such a discovery. Our first glimpse of Isabel is that telegraphic "quite independent," which Mrs. Touchett had considered an important piece of information to include in her scanty message to her family. When Isabel herself appears on the lawn of Gardencourt, she strikes Ralph as having "a great deal of confidence, both in herself and in others." A little later, she will be appalled at the very idea of being considered "a candidate for adoption": "I'm very fond of my liberty," she says. Liberty means to know everything, including all the possibilities ahead in order to choose freely, confidently, responsibly; as when she tells her aunt that she always likes to know the things one shouldn't do, "so as to choose." A few pages later, we find Isabel afraid of becoming "a mere sheep in the flock"; she wants to be the sole free master of her own fate. In other words, Isabel declines to be a puppet; she wants to act always within the limits of human dignity, which she measures by the freedom of human consciousness.

These are, of course, some of the romantic "theories" of "the mere slim shade of an intelligent but presumptuous girl." When she apparently becomes really free to "meet the requirements of [her] imagination," Isabel is intui-

tively afraid. Unaware of the liberal fallacy of her notion of individual freedom, regardless of the complex interactions at work in human society, Isabel
is, however, perceptive enough to sense the trap she may be walking into:
"A large fortune means freedom, and I'm afraid of that." Isabel is right to
be afraid, for indeed her desire for total freedom will eventually have to be
translated into freedom-as-accepted-necessity. I shall come back to this.
Meanwhile, Isabel's new fortune brings her an enlarged freedom, however
problematic. She believes herself now to be freer than ever before, and she
thinks that, from now on, she will have to cope with a boundless imagination. She is scared of the burden of tremendous responsibility involved in
complete, unquestionable freedom, but she is also exhilarated at the thought
of her consciousness opening up, infinitely, towards the fulfilment of its own
potentialities. That her love of freedom equals her fear of freedom is only an
indication of changing values and conceptions in James's own world: liberal
individualism, all too questionably presented in Isabel's portrait—she is anxious about the use she will make of her freedom, but she never doubts its
reality; she believes herself to be in complete control of her destiny. She is
free—she thinks—to choose her own fate. And so she believes she does when
she fulfils her "one ambition—to be free to follow out a good feeling." For
a person like Isabel, to whom this kind of liberty had always been the dearest,
most cherished value of human life, how dreadful and how crushing and
how destructive Mme Merle's revelation must have been! No wonder Isabel
had to go out into the open air to try to rescue herself from total suffocation.

In marrying Osmond, as she thinks, in freedom, Isabel had wanted "to
transfer the weight [of her money] to some other conscience, to some more
prepared receptacle." That is, she had wanted to share her liberty with a
freer, unprejudiced consciousness, which she hoped to be the fulfilment of
her own. Her marriage had then been for her the symbol of her total freedom.
When Isabel becomes gradually aware of her error of perception concerning
Osmond's character—that though she had married *in* freedom, she had *not*
married freedom—all her strength and sense of dignity come to her through
her still, and now even more, cherished ideal of freedom as opposed to her
husband's strict conformity to standard traditions or sterile forms:

> Her notion of the aristocratic life was simply the union of great
> knowledge with great liberty. . . . But for Osmond it was alto-
> gether a thing of forms, a conscious calculated attitude. He was
> fond of the old, the consecrated, the transmitted; so was she, but
> she pretended to do what she chose with it.

The belief that she is free, has always been, and still is, in spite of the rigid system that Osmond wants to close about her, saves Isabel somehow from irrevocable spiritual death. She had made a mistake, she knows; but she believes she had been free to make it, and that belief saves her self-respect for her. Her sense of freedom is now the only glimmering light in the darkness of her habitation, a quiet, obstinate preservation of integrity, that reflects itself fundamentally in her passive-resistance-like attitude towards Ralph.

Up to the famous scene between Isabel and Mme Merle in chapter 49, two forceful motives have been keeping Isabel faithful to the sacred ideal of her marriage. First, she had been free when she had decided to marry Gilbert Osmond, and therefore she feels she must accept the consequences of her acts, however painful: "one must accept one's deeds. I married him before all the world; I was perfectly free; it was impossible to do anything more deliberate." Secondly, as Henrietta rightly points out in this passage, Isabel's pride determines her unwillingness to admit that she has made a mistake. She knows that she has made a mistake, but she cannot publish it: "I don't think that's decent. I'd much rather die." Isabel's attitude need not, indeed must not be understood merely as the vain stubbornness of a foolish presumptuous girl who stupidly refuses to admit that she has made a mistake; it is rather, in a way, a privilege of her sense of freedom; she is still free to choose the face she wants to show, and she chooses *not* to acknowledge *publicly* such a gross error of perception on her part concerning Osmond. As she tells Henrietta, she owes that much to her own respect for such liberal, Emersonian values as she was taught to love: individual freedom, self-reliance, self-responsibility.

However, there is surely a certain naivety and immaturity in Isabel's desperate need "to feel that her unhappiness should not have come to her through her own fault." In the very first draft of Isabel's portrait, we learn that "she had an infinite hope that she should never do anything wrong," we learn how much she dreads "inconsistency" and "hollowness," and how much she would like "to find herself some day in a difficult position, so that she should have the pleasure of being as heroic as the occasion demanded." In other words, Isabel Archer had always been anxious about the use she would ever make of her freedom, which she never doubts or questions, and her deepest wish had always been ever *to do right*. So that, when she finds herself, as Ralph had foreseen, "in trouble," her first thought goes to a justification of herself. The "need to right herself" that worries Isabel at the beginning of the novel has now gained a deeper meaning for her. In accepting the consequences of what she believes to have been her free acts, Isabel is again in possession of the satisfaction of "doing herself justice," of doing herself the justice of being considerate of herself, of being after all as heroic as the difficulty of the situation demanded. Once, as she thinks, "the sole source of her mistake had been within herself," in order to keep the sense of her dignity in her own eyes, Isabel has to assume the burden of her initial error. This is justification before herself; before others, her pride prevents her from even admitting her mistake. She is free; she may therefore choose to go on showing the world the *image* of her freedom. Thus, while she knows that "the place has surrendered," she wants her flag to be seen waving high up in the sky.

And yet, suddenly, Isabel lets her flag drop. She has to. When she finds out how little free she had been in the most important decision of her life, how much she had been made a convenience of, Isabel is wretchedly confronted with her own collapsing dignity as a human being. Freedom is the highest value, the sum of all human dignity. The discovery of Mme Merle's and Osmond's interference in her marriage forces Isabel to see herself as a mere instrument, a useful tool in other people's hands, a mere puppet. This might have been a comfortable discovery for someone who had wished ever to do right. But Isabel's subsequent behavior indicates that she loves individual freedom more than she loves self-righteousness. If Isabel's discovery washes white the guilt and responsibility of her misery, it also deprives her, to her mind, of human dignity and tragic stature. There is only one gesture left for Isabel: *to invest with freedom,* retrospectively, her initially determined, conditioned choice. This she does by returning to Rome and to her husband in the end. Thus, in sanctioning her first act, in turning it, retroactively, into a free act, Isabel finally *creates* (or invents?) her real freedom, the liberty of a fully expanded consciousness, backwards and forwards, in a complete, calculating control of itself. That the gesture is merely a symbolic one, and that Isabel's *willed* freedom—ominously reminiscent of Emerson's "terrible freedom" inside—is now unequivocally an *image* of freedom, again points to the novel's subtle problematization of late nineteenth-century values.

The interpreter might argue that Isabel would not have been less free or responsible if she had decided to turn away from Osmond and Rome; but Isabel's idealistic humanism had taught her a different lesson. Her notion of human freedom, dignity, and responsibility, as well as her ideal of marriage and her conception of a woman's place in society, inexorably trace for her, paradoxically, her freely chosen path. To be free, then, is to be master of one's destiny. That Isabel achieves by her retrospective act; but she is nonetheless trapped in her disengaged ideals and, as a woman, doubly trapped. As she confides to Ralph right before he dies, her final decision will be dictated by what "seems right." To ratify retroactively her initial choice of fate had meant to choose her destiny again, to redefine her marriage as freedom fulfilled, to assume her identity as Mrs. Osmond, without which she would now be lost. Thus, although the interpreter might say that, in wanting to ascend towards the realm of ends, Isabel is most vilely trapped in the world of means, Isabel herself, by her ratifying act, finds herself finally soaring above a world of necessity and dependence. Seemingly returning to the darkness and dumbness of her suffocating habitation, she is indeed at last enjoying for the first time the meaning of a free, responsible consciousness. How heroic and noble this is will depend, of course, on the value one attributes to Isabel's idea of freedom and responsibility. What I mean is that it may still be difficult for many of us in this day and age to see Oedipus as a mere plaything in the hands of the gods of iron necessity. We demand some sense of freedom, guilt, and responsibility in order to grasp the magnificent dignity of the king's tragedy. This may seem too much of an ado about Isabel Archer; but wasn't exactly that James's idea, that of "organising an ado about Isabel Archer"?

I therefore suggest that Isabel's final decision to go back to her husband, in *enfranchising* her first choice, endows her with the responsibility one demands of all free human beings. When in the end she rejects Caspar Goodwood's proposal, though of course the motive of sexual fear is very obvious, Isabel is above all aware that Caspar's idea of freedom is at odds with her own, that it would indeed nullify her very conception of herself. For Goodwood, freedom means "that a woman deliberately made to suffer is justified in anything in life"; for Isabel, freedom means that a woman that has made herself responsible for her own suffering has only "one straight path" to follow: the wide, but painful, path of authenticity. For the first time in her life, Isabel may be said to be truly, knowingly consistent. Or, as the observant Ralph [James?] might have said, she is once and for all "dismally consistent."

A brief digression will help me put James's novel and its ideals and values, particularly its problematized conception of freedom, in the broader context of Western Literature. At the beginning of Schiller's *Die Räuber*, young Karl Moor expresses his titanic, Promethean longing for glorious deeds that are only to be achieved in freedom: "Das Gesetz hat noch keinen grossen Mann gebildet, aber die Freiheit brütet Kolosse und Extremitäten aus." A deep loathing for the sickly, corrupt laws of mankind turns Moor into an outcast and a robber. When later he finds out that his is not the task, nor the right, to chastise mankind in the name of a higher moral order, it is too late to retrieve. Moor has now lost Schiller's highest values: his freedom and the purity of his conscience. The oath sworn among the robbers and their leader binds Karl Moor helplessly to the iron chain of his band, necessity drags him down forcefully, step by step, towards destruction and self-annihilation. Only when in the end Moor recognizes the higher value of divine and human law does he become free again. Moor had dared to assume as a right of his own the task of purifying a polluted mankind, failing to realize that in breaking the law he was shaking the very moral grounds of the world. When finally he is horrified to think that "zwei Menschen wie ich den ganzen Bau der sittlichen Welt zugrund richten würden," Karl Moor understands that man's freedom lies deep within the boundaries of law. He therefore shuns the pseudo-freedom of suicide, as he had just rejected the pseudo-freedom of lawlessness. Liberty is wilful acceptance of law itself, as the only safeguard of the world's and man's order. This is the only freedom, Schiller suggests, that makes giants of men.

In drawing the parallel between *Die Räuber* and *The Portrait of a Lady*, one has, of course, to be discriminating. Karl Moor is deeply concerned with the destiny of mankind, whereas Isabel is mainly concerned with what happens to her own consciousness. The difference lies surely on the different social and cultural contexts that helped create both works, and it may also be seen as an indication of the growing fictional concern with the human consciousness as a subject. Karl Moor's attitude in the end shows how much the order of the world depends on the freedom of human consciousness to accept legal restraint. In *The Portrait of a Lady* the process is somehow reversed: the integrity (or order) of Isabel's consciousness depends entirely on her free acceptance of the "mill of the conventional," in order to secure her threatened liberty. But while Karl Moor, in accepting *Gesetz* as a higher *Freiheit*, is admitting how conditioned by necessity his past life had been, Isabel's return to Rome, as I read it, is a choice of freedom *in the past*: her gesture ratifies her first decision to marry Osmond, which now becomes truly a free decision. In returning to Rome, Isabel sets herself free, retrospectively, and she is thus as responsible for her deeds as becomes a tragic figure. On the other hand, at the very bottom of both Isabel's and Moor's motivation, we may discern an unconfessed desire for self-glorification. After all, if Isabel Archer had always been longing for some heroic deed in her life, perhaps the accusation of Karl Moor's fellow-robber in the end is not entirely false either: "Lasst ihn hinfahren! Es ist die Grossmannsucht. Er will sein Leben an eitle Bewunderung setzen." So that Isabel is as much the author of her "*tragedy* of consciousness" as Karl Moor is the victim of his own tragedy of freedom.

I would not assert, *positively*, that James wanted to give Isabel a tragic dimension; but I do wish to suggest that he wanted *her* to give *herself* a tragic dimension. In so constructing a new sense of freedom, Isabel was indeed acting as heroically, or as tragically, as the occasion demanded. We are not only beholding "a kind of inverted triumph" instead of "the waste and degradation of a splendid spirit," as Arnold Kettle says; we are also looking at the last masterly touch on Isabel's ideal portrait of herself as a wholly liberated consciousness. That the symbol of her liberation is her sterile marriage must be understood, I think, as an indication of James's implied criticism of her ideals.

I do not want to turn Isabel's conquest of freedom into the sole motive for her return to Rome. She has plenty of reasons to take that decision, as a perfunctory glimpse at the secondary literature would assure us. There is, to name but a few, Isabel's conception of marriage as "sacred"; her fear of sexual passion as offered by Goodwood's alternative; Isabel's promise to Pansy not to "desert" her; her dread of public exposure; her respect for "certain obligations . . . involved in the very fact of marriage." However, the reader is made to sense, in the course of the last chapters of the novel, that none of these reasons is sufficient. Isabel seems all too anxious to find a new reason to return to Rome when the previous one proves no longer valid. Her fear of Goodwood's aggressive manhood at the very end doesn't seem to be enough good reason, either, for, after all, she not only escapes from him but also *does* return to Rome. The last scene between these two characters strikes me rather as one more symbolic aspect of Isabel's desperate quest for freedom. "Why should you go through that ghastly form?" Goodwood asks her; and Isabel replies, "to get away from *you*." If Caspar may be said to stand here for the world that considers Isabel guiltless of her mistake, it is in his eyes that Isabel must more than ever justify herself as a free human being, always in command of her fate, always responsible for her life. If she should for a moment allow herself to suspect that her marriage—i.e. that which alone gives her (social) identity—is at odds with her ideal of freedom, she would be lost indeed.

To conclude I should like to go back to James's *Preface* and then comment a little on the novel's inconclusive closure. Says James:

> The obvious criticism of course will be that it is not finished—
> that I have not seen the heroine to the end of her situation—that
> I have left her *en l'air*—this is both true and false. The *whole* of
> anything is never told; you can only take what groups together.
> What I have done has that unity—it groups together. It is com-
> plete in itself—and the rest may be taken up or not, later.

James is here clearly toying with the idea that *The Portrait of a Lady* is not the end of Isabel's story and I will knowingly bite the bait and rather commit the crime of meaningful speculation than that of sterile synchronicity. Isabel's story is not only the story of a woman's changing place in society, but also the very chronicle of society itself. That the only noble and dignified way that Isabel has of refusing to be "ground in the . . . mill of the conventional" is to accept the "ghastly form" knowingly and freely, is a telling comment on the kind of society presented in James's world; and a comment, too, on the kind of (American) literary tradition this international novelist feeds on: Isabel Archer/Osmond is undoubtedly a lesser Hester Prynne, but still a potential "rebel" who willingly accepts the role of an "agent of socialization." The time has obviously not yet come for the fulfilment of Hester Prynne's ambiguous prophecy at the end of *The Scarlet Letter*:

> at some brighter period, when the world should have grown ripe for it, in Heaven's own time, a new truth would be revealed, in order to establish the whole relation between man and woman on a surer ground of mutual happiness.

However, the choice of a woman's growing consciousness for the portrayal of a changing awareness of society's inconsistencies and incongruities is surely an indication that James, in questioning isolated conceptions and values and in drawing attention to their interrelation and interdependence in their large societal context, is indeed formulating at a newer light Hester Prynne's implied conviction that a critique of society must begin with a searching critique of the relation between man and woman, not in "Heaven's own time," but right *now*, in the time of undeniable social reality—a deep reaching critique of "the bottomless idiocy of the world."

Chronology

1843   Henry James born April 15 in New York City to Henry James, a gentleman-scholar, and Mary Walsh James. Family moves to London.

1844–45   James's father suffers nervous breakdown, becomes a Swedenborgian. Family lives in London and Paris.

1845–55   Family lives in New York, chiefly New York City, where senior James's friends such as Ralph Waldo Emerson, Bronson Alcott, Horace Greeley, and William Cullen Bryant frequently visit. Henry James, Jr., attends various schools in the city, until father decides he and siblings should have European educations.

1855–59   Family lives in Europe—children educated by tutor and private school in several countries. James contracts typhoid. In 1858, family returns and settles in Newport, Rhode Island. James makes friends with Thomas Sergeant Perry, who attends Berkeley Institute with him, and with John La Farge.

1859–60   James family returns to Europe, where Henry attends Institution Rochette, a pre-engineering school in Geneva. Soon withdraws and enrolls in Academy (later University of Geneva) with brother William to study literature. Studies German in Bonn.

1860–62   Family returns to Newport. William studies under William Morris Hunt and Henry sits in. They both attend Frank Sanborn's experimental school in Concord, Massachusetts, favored by the Transcendentalists.

1861   Orphaned Temple cousins come to live with family in Newport. Henry becomes close to Minnie Temple. William leaves study of art, takes up science. Henry suffers back injury during a fire.

1862–63   Attends Harvard Law School. Brothers Gareth Wilkinson James and Robertson James join black Union regiments during Civil War; Wilkinson badly wounded.

1864   Family moves to Boston. James publishes first (unsigned) story, "A Tragedy of Error," in *Continental Monthly*. Begins writing reviews for *North American Review*.

1865   Publishes signed story, "The Story of a Year," in the *Atlantic Monthly*. Begins to write reviews for the *Nation*.

1866–68   Family moves to Cambridge, Massachusetts; James continues to publish reviews and stories. Friendship with William Dean Howells.

1869–70   James returns to Europe for Grand Tour; meets several Pre-Raphaelites, Darwin, and George Eliot while in England. Minnie Temple dies of tuberculosis a month before James returns to America.

1871   *Watch and Ward* and "A Passionate Pilgrim" published in the *Atlantic Monthly*. Tours northeastern United States to write travel sketches for the *Nation*.

1872–74   Returns to Europe, accompanying sister Alice and Aunt Kate on tour. Continues writing stories and travel sketches for the *Nation,* this time of Europe through American eyes, from which he now earns enough to support himself. Friendship with James Russell Lowell, Fanny Kemble, and William Wetmore Story. Travels around Italy with William; returns to America with nearly complete manuscript of *Roderick Hudson*.

1875   *Roderick Hudson* appears, first serially in the *Atlantic Monthly,* then as book. Publishes *A Passionate Pilgrim and Other Tales*; *Transatlantic Sketches*. Moves to Paris, where he will write European letters for the *New York Tribune*.

1876   Turgenev introduces James to Flaubert, who introduces him to Zola, Daudet, de Maupassant, Doré, de Goncourt, and other French intellectuals. Resigns from the *Tribune* job because editor wants too much gossip. Moves to London, where he will live for the next ten years. Serialization of *The American* in the *Atlantic Monthly* (book published 1877).

1878   *French Poets and Novelists* published in England; *The Europeans* serialized in the *Atlantic Monthly*. "Daisy Miller" appears in Leslie Stephen's *Cornhill Magazine*—the foreign publication costs James his American rights and it is pirated in the United States. Elected to Reform Club.

1879   *Confidence* serialized in *Scribner's* (book published 1880); *Hawthorne* published in English Men of Letters series. Friendships with Edmund Gosse, Robert Louis Stevenson, and the Henry Adamses.

1880–81   Winters in Florence. *Washington Square* serialized in *Cornhill Magazine* and *Harper's* (book published 1880). *The Portrait of a Lady* serialized in *Macmillan's* and the *Atlantic Monthly* (book published 1881).

1881–83   Returns to America; visits family in Boston, meets President Arthur in Washington. Mother dies in early 1882 before he can reach her deathbed. Returns to Europe, until he hears father is dying; arrives in America after father's death in late 1882. Quarrels with William over father's estate, of which he is executor. Wilkinson dies in late 1883. Returns to London. Publishes 14-volume collected edition of works, *The Siege of London*; and *Portraits of Places*.

1884   Visits Paris; renews friendships with French intellectuals. Meets John Singer Sargent; persuades him to take up residence in London. Publishes *Tales of Three Cities*, "The Art of Fiction," and *A Little Tour in France*.

1885   Lives with sister Alice in England. Publishes *The Author of "Beltraffio"* and *Stories Revived*. *The Bostonians* serialized in *Century* (book published 1886); *The Princess Casamassima* serialized in the *Atlantic Monthly* (book published 1886).

1886–87   Lives in Italy; friendship with James Fenimore Cooper's grandniece, Constance Fenimore Woolson. Writes "The Aspern Papers," other short stories; begins *The Tragic Muse*.

1888   Publishes *The Reverberator*, "The Aspern Papers," "Louisa
            Pallant," "The Modern Warning," and *Partial Portraits*.

1889–90   James travels around Europe. Dramatizes *The American*.
            Friendships with William Morton Fullerton and Wolcott Bal-
            estier. *The Tragic Muse* serialized in the *Atlantic Monthly*
            (book published 1890), which rejects story "The Pupil" (story
            published in England). Publishes *A London Life*.

1891   Dramatic version of *The American* reasonably popular; James
            concentrates on drama, which meets with indifferent success.
            Writes favorably of Ibsen's *Hedda Gabler*.

1892–93   Death of Alice. Travels around Europe; visits with William.
            Play, *Mrs. Jasper*, produced, but most of the other dramas
            James writes in these years go unproduced. Publishes *The Les-
            son of the Master* (1892) and *The Real Thing and Other Tales*
            (1893).

1894   Constance Fenimore Woolson commits suicide. James receives
            one of four privately printed copies of Alice's diary; burns it.
            Publishes *Two Comedies* and *Theatricals*.

1895   Disastrous opening of play *Guy Domville*. Dramatizes some
            of his fiction. Publishes *Terminations*.

1896–97   *The Spoils of Poynton* serialized in the *Atlantic Monthly* as
            The Old Things (book published 1897). Publishes *Embarrass-
            ments*. Friendship with Joseph Conrad. Hires stenographer
            and buys typewriter. Leases Lamb House in Rye. Publishes
            What Maisie Knew.

1898   "The Turn of the Screw" serialized in *Collier's* (published with
            "Covering End" as *The Two Magics*). Publishes *In the Cage*.
            Receives celebrities at Lamb House, including neighbors Ste-
            phen Crane and H. G. Wells.

1899   *The Awkward Age* serialized in *Harper's* (book published
            1899).

1900   Publishes *The Soft Side*. Lives in Rye and London.

1901		Completes *The Ambassadors*. Publishes *The Sacred Fount*. Obtains permanent room at the Reform Club as London residence.

1902		Publishes *The Wings of the Dove*. Writes "The Beast in the Jungle" and "The Birthplace." Suffers gout and stomach disorders.

1903		Publishes *The Ambassadors, The Better Sort,* and *William Wetmore Story and His Friends*. Friendships with Dudley Jocelyn Persse and Edith Wharton.

1904–05		Publishes *The Golden Bowl* (1904). Returns to America for a visit. Travels around country visiting friends and giving lectures. Elected with William to newly founded American Academy of Arts and Letters; William declines. Returns to England and begins revising his works for the New York edition.

1906–08		Publishes *The American Scene* (1907); writes "The Jolly Corner." The New York edition of James's works is published 1907–09, with eighteen new prefaces by him. Travels around Europe, often with Edith Wharton. Works a little on dramatizations of "Covering End."

1909		Friendship with Bloomsbury Group. Illnesses. Burns correspondence and papers at Rye. Publishes *Italian Hours*.

1910		Ill much of the year; decides it may be form of nervous breakdown. William joins him in traveling to Europe for cure; they learn Robertson has died. James brothers return to America, where William dies. Henry publishes *The Finer Grain* and *The Outcry*.

1911		Receives honorary degree from Harvard. Returns to England, staying in London while working on autobiography.

1913		Publishes *A Small Boy and Others* (autobiography). Friends and admirers subscribe for seventieth-birthday portrait by Sargent; present him with silver-gilt porringer and dish (a "golden bowl"). Visits Lamb House with niece.

1914		Publishes *Notes of a Son and Brother* and *Notes on Novelists*. World War I begins; James does volunteer hospital work, and is elected chairman of the American Volunteer Motor Ambulance Corps in France.

1915–16   Continues war work; becomes English citizen in 1915. Suffers stroke December 1915; awarded Order of Merit on New Year's Day; dies on February 28. His body is cremated and the ashes buried in the family plot in Cambridge, Massachusetts.

Contributors

HAROLD BLOOM, Sterling Professor of the Humanities at Yale University, is the author of *The Anxiety of Influence, Poetry and Repression,* and many other volumes of literary criticism. His forthcoming study, *Freud: Transference and Authority,* attempts a full-scale reading of all of Freud's major writings. A MacArthur Prize Fellow, he is general editor of five series of literary criticism published by Chelsea House.

FRANCIS FERGUSSON is Professor of Comparative Literature Emeritus at both Princeton and Rutgers Universities. His books include *Shakespeare: The Pattern in His Carpet, Dante,* and *Trope and Allegory: Themes Common to Dante and Shakespeare,* as well as his most influential study, *The Idea of a Theater.*

RICHARD POIRIER is one of the editors of *Raritan,* and of the Library of America. He is Professor of English at Rutgers University, and his books include studies of James, Mailer, and Robert Frost, as well as *A World Elsewhere* and *The Performing Self.*

LAURENCE BEDWELL HOLLAND was Professor of English and American Literature at The Johns Hopkins University. He is the author of *The Expense of Vision: Essays on the Craft of Henry James* and editor of *Design in America.*

CAROL OHMANN is Professor of English Literature at Wesleyan University. She is the author of *Ford Madox Ford: From Apprentice to Craftsman.*

TONY TANNER is a Fellow of King's College, Cambridge. His books include *The Reign of Wonder: Naivety and Reality in American Literature, City of Words, Saul Bellow,* and *Adultery in the Novel.*

JULIET McMASTER is Professor of English Literature at the University of

Alberta. She is the author of *Jane Austen on Love, Thackeray: The Major Novels,* and *Trollope's Palliser Novels: Theme and Pattern,* and editor of *Jane Austen's Achievement.*

ELISABETH HANSOT is Professor of Political Science at the University of Nevada. Her publications include *Perfection and Progress: Two Modes of Utopian Thought* and *Managers of Virtue: Public School Leadership in America,* which she edited with David Tyack.

DAVID HOWARD teaches English and American literature at the University of York and is the editor, with others, of *Tradition and Tolerance in Nineteenth Century Fiction.*

D. J. GORDON was Professor of English Literature at Reading University. He is the author of *W. B. Yeats: Images of a Poet* and *The Renaissance Imagination* (published posthumously) and editor of *Fritz Saxl, 1890–1948: A Volume of Memorial Essays.*

JOHN STOKES is Professor of English and American Literature at the University of North Carolina. He is the author of *Oscar Wilde* and *Resistable Theatres: Enterprise and Experiment in the Late Nineteenth Century.*

ROBERT L. CASERIO is Professor of English at Oberlin College and the author of *Plot, Story, and the Novel.*

MARTIN PRICE is Sterling Professor of English at Yale University. His books include *Swift's Rhetorical Art: A Study in Structure and Meaning, To the Palace of Wisdom: Studies in Order and Energy from Dryden to Blake,* and *Forms of Life: Character and Imagination in the Novel.*

DEBORAH ESCH is Assistant Professor of English at Princeton University and is the author of a forthcoming book on James.

CARREN O. KASTON, Professor of English and American Literature at Washington and Lee University, is the author of *Imagination and Desire in the Novels of Henry James* and quandom president of the Henry James Society.

MARK SELTZER is Associate Professor of English at Cornell University and the author of *Henry James and the Art of Power.*

MARIA IRENE RAMALHO DE SOUSA SANTOS is Chairman of the Department of Comparative Literature and Professor of American Studies at the University of Coimbra, Portugal. She has written on Wallace Stevens, Henry James, and modern Portuguese poetry.

Bibliography

Agnew, Jean-Christophe. "The Consuming Vision of Henry James." In *The Culture of Consumption: Critical Essays in American History, 1880–1980,* edited by Richard Wightman Fox and T. J. Jackson Lears. New York: Pantheon, 1983.

Allen, Elizabeth. *A Woman's Place in the Novels of Henry James.* London: Macmillan, 1984.

Allott, Miriam. "Form Versus Substance in Henry James." *Review of English Literature* 3, no. 1 (1962): 53–66.

Anderson, Charles. *Person, Place, and Thing in Henry James's Novels.* Durham, N.C.: Duke University Press, 1977.

Anderson, Quentin. *The American Henry James.* New Brunswick, N.J.: Rutgers University Press, 1957.

———. *The Imperial Self: An Essay in American Literary and Cultural History.* New York: Knopf, 1971.

Andreach, Robert J. "Henry James's *The Sacred Fount*: The Existential Predicament." *Nineteenth-Century Fiction* 17 (1962): 197–216.

Andreas, Osborne. *Henry James and the Expanding Horizon: A Study of Meaning and Basic Themes of James's Fiction.* Seattle: University of Washington Press, 1948.

Appignanesi, Lisa. *Femininity and the Creative Imagination: A Study of Henry James, Robert Musil, and Marcel Proust.* London: Vision, 1973.

Arvin, Newton. "Henry James and the Almighty Dollar." *Hound and Horn* 7 (April–June 1934): 434–43.

Auchincloss, Louis. *Reading Henry James.* Minneapolis: University of Minnesota Press, 1975.

Badger, Reid. "The Character and Myth of Hyacinth: A Key to *The Princess Casamassima*." *Arizona Quarterly* 32 (1976): 316–26.

Banta, Martha. *Henry James and the Occult: The Great Extension.* Bloomington: Indiana University Press, 1972.

Barnett, Louise K. "Jamesian Feminism: Women in *Daisy Miller*." *Studies in Short Fiction* 16 (1978): 281–87.

Barstow, James Missner. "Originality and Conventionality in *The Princess Casamassima*." *Genre* 11 (1978): 445–50.

Barzun, Jacques. "Henry James, Melodramatist." *The Kenyon Review* 5, no. 4 (Autumn 1943): 508–21.

Bayley, John. *The Characters of Love.* New York: Basic Books, 1960.

Baym, Nina. "Revision and Thematic Change in *The Portrait of a Lady.*" *Modern Fiction Studies* 22 (1976): 183–200.

Beach, Joseph Warren. *The Method of Henry James.* Philadelphia: Saifer, 1954.

Beams, David W. "Consciousness in James's *The Sense of the Past.*" *Criticism* 5 (1963): 148–72.

Bell, Millicent. "Style as Subject: *Washington Square.*" *The Sewanee Review* 83 (1975): 19–38.

Bennett, Joan. "The Art of Henry James: *The Ambassadors.*" *Chicago Review* 9, no. 1 (1956): 12–26.

Berland, Alwyn. *Culture and Conduct in the Novels of Henry James.* Cambridge: Cambridge University Press, 1981.

Bersani, Leo. *A Future for Astyanax: Character and Desire in Literature.* Boston: Little, Brown, 1976.

———. "The Narrator as Center in *The Wings of the Dove.*" *Modern Fiction Studies* 6 (Summer 1960): 131–44.

Bewley, Marius. *The Complex Fate.* London: Chatto & Windus, 1952.

———. *The Eccentric Design: Form in the Classic American Novel.* New York: Columbia University Press, 1963.

———. *Masks and Mirrors: Essays in Criticism.* New York: Atheneum, 1970.

Blackmur, R. P. *Studies in Henry James.* New York: New Directions, 1983.

Bloom, Harold, ed. *Modern Critical Interpretations: Henry James's* The Portrait of a Lady. New Haven: Chelsea House, 1987.

Booth, Bradford A. "Henry James and the Economic Motif." *Nineteenth-Century Fiction* 8 (1953): 141–50.

Booth, Wayne C. *The Rhetoric of Fiction.* Chicago: University of Chicago Press, 1961.

Bowden, Edwin T. *The Themes of Henry James: A System of Observation through the Visual Arts.* New Haven: Yale University Press, 1956.

Bradbury, Nicola. *Henry James: The Later Novels.* Oxford: Clarendon, 1979.

Broderick, John C. "Nature, Art, and Imagination in *The Spoils of Poynton.*" *Nineteenth-Century Fiction* 13 (1959): 295–313.

Brooks, Peter. *The Melodramatic Imagination: Balzac, Henry James, Melodrama, and the Mode of Excess.* New York: Columbia University Press, 1985.

Brooks, Van Wyck. *The Pilgrimage of Henry James.* New York: Dutton, 1925.

Buitenhuis, Peter. *The Grasping Imagination: The American Writings of Henry James.* Toronto: University of Toronto Press, 1970.

———, ed. *Twentieth Century Interpretations of* The Portrait of a Lady: A Collection of Critical Essays. Englewood Cliffs, N.J.: Prentice-Hall, 1968.

Cargill, Oscar. *The Novels of Henry James.* New York: Macmillan, 1961.

Chase, Richard. *The American Novel and Its Tradition.* Garden City, N.Y.: Doubleday, 1957.

Chatman, Seymour. *The Later Style of Henry James.* New York: Oxford University Press, 1972.

Clair, John A. *The Ironic Dimension in the Fiction of Henry James.* Pittsburgh: Duquesne University Press, 1965.

Collins, Martha. "Narrator, the Satellites, and Isabel Archer: Point of View in *The Portrait of a Lady*." *Studies in the Novel* 8 (1976): 142–56.

Conrad, Joseph. "Henry James: An Appreciation." In Walter F. Wright, *Joseph Conrad on Fiction*. Lincoln: University of Nebraska Press, 1964.

Cook, David A., and Timothy J. Corrigan. "Narrative Structure in *The Turn of the Screw*." *Studies in Short Fiction* 17 (1980): 55–65.

Cranfill, T. M., and R. L. Clark, Jr. *An Anatomy of "The Turn of the Screw."* Austin: University of Texas Press, 1965.

Crews, Frederick C. *The Tragedy of Manners*. New Haven: Yale University Press, 1957.

Culver, Stuart. "Censorship and Intimacy: Awkwardness in *The Awkward Age*." *ELH* 48, no. 3 (1981): 368–86.

Daugherty, Sarah B. *The Literary Criticism of Henry James*. Athens: Ohio University Press, 1981.

Davis, Sara deSaussure. "*The Bostonians* Reconsidered." *Tulane Studies in English* 23, no. 1 (1978): 39–60.

Donadio, Stephen. *Nietzsche, Henry James, and the Artistic Will*. New York: Oxford University Press, 1978.

Dunbar, Viola R. "The Revision of *Daisy Miller*," *MLN* 65 (May 1950): 311–17.

Dupee, F. W. *Henry James*. New York: Sloane, 1951.

———, ed. *The Question of Henry James: A Collection of Critical Essays*. New York: Holt, 1945.

Edel, Leon. *Henry James*. 5 vols. Philadelphia: Lippincott, 1953–72.

———, ed. *Henry James: A Collection of Critical Essays*. Englewood Cliffs, N.J.: Prentice-Hall, 1963.

Feidelson, Charles. "James and the 'Man of Imagination.'" In *Literary Theory and Structures: Essays in Honor of William K. Wimsatt*, edited by Frank Brady, John Palmer, and Martin Price. New Haven: Yale University Press, 1973.

———. "The Moment of *Portrait of a Lady*." *Ventures* 8, no. 2 (1968): 47–55.

Felman, Shoshana. "Turning the Screw of Interpretation." *Yale French Studies* 55/56 (1977): 94–207.

Fogel, Daniel Mark. *Henry James and the Structure of the Romantic Imagination*. Baton Rouge: Louisiana State University Press, 1981.

Fowler, Virginia C. *Henry James's American Girl: The Embroidery on the Canvas*. Madison: University of Wisconsin Press, 1984.

Funston, Judith E. "'All Art Is One': Narrative Technique in Henry James's *The Tragic Muse*." *Studies in the Novel* 15 (1983): 344–55.

Furth, David L. *The Visionary Betrayed: Aesthetic Discontinuity in Henry James's The American Scene*. Cambridge: Harvard University Press, 1979.

Gale, Robert L. *The Caught Image: Figurative Language in the Fiction of Henry James*. Chapel Hill: University of North Carolina Press, 1964.

Gard, Roger, ed. *Henry James: The Critical Heritage*. London: Routledge & Kegan Paul, 1968.

Gervais, David. *Flaubert and Henry James: A Study in Contrasts*. London: Macmillan, 1978.

Goddard, Harold. "A Pre-Freudian Reading of *The Turn of the Screw*." *Nineteenth-Century Fiction* 12 (June 1957): 1–36.

Goode, John, ed. *The Air of Reality: New Essays on Henry James*. London: Methuen, 1972.

Graham, Kenneth. *Henry James: The Drama of Fulfilment*. Oxford: Clarendon, 1975.

Grover, Philip. *Henry James and the French Novel: A Study in Inspiration*. New York: Barnes & Noble, 1973.

Hartsock, Mildred. "The Exposed Mind: A View of *The Awkward Age*." *Critical Quarterly* 9, no. 1 (1967): 49–59.

Hinchcliffe, Arnold P. "James's *The Sacred Fount*." *Texas Studies in Literature and Language* 2 (1960): 88–94.

Hirsch, David H. "Henry James and the Seal of Love." *Modern Language Studies* 13, no. 4 (1983): 39–60.

Hocks, Richard A. *Henry James and Pragmatistic Thought: A Study of the Relation between the Philosophy of William James and the Literary Art of Henry James*. Chapel Hill: University of North Carolina Press, 1974.

Hoffman, Charles G. "The Art of Reflection in James's *The Sacred Fount*." *MLN* 69 (November 1954): 507–8.

———. *The Short Novels of Henry James*. New York: Bookman, 1957.

Hoffman, Frederick J. "Freedom and Conscious Form: Henry James and the American Self." *Virginia Quarterly Review* 37 (1961): 269–85.

Holland, Laurence Bedwell. *The Expense of Vision: Essays on the Craft of Henry James*. Rev. ed. Baltimore: Johns Hopkins University Press, 1982.

Hopkins, Viola. "Visual Art Devices and Parallels in the Fiction of Henry James." *PMLA* 76 (1961): 561–74.

Hutchinson, Stuart. *Henry James: American as Modernist*. New York: Barnes & Noble, 1982.

Ian, Marcia. "The Elaboration of Privacy in *The Wings of the Dove*." *ELH* 51, no. 1 (1984): 107–36.

Isle, Walter. *Experiments in Form: Henry James's Novels, 1896–1901*. Cambridge: Harvard University Press, 1968.

Jefferson, D. W. *Henry James and the Modern Reader*. Edinburgh: Oliver & Boyd, 1964.

Jones, Granville H. *Henry James's Psychology of Experience: Innocence, Responsibility, and Renunciation in the Fiction of Henry James*. The Hague: Mouton, 1975.

Kappeler, Suzanne. *Writing and Reading in Henry James*. New York: Columbia University Press, 1980.

Kaston, Carren O. *Imagination and Desire in the Novels of Henry James*. New Brunswick, N.J.: Rutgers University Press, 1984.

Kelley, Cornelia Pulsifer. *The Early Development of Henry James*. Urbana: University of Illinois Press, 1965.

Kimball, Jean. "The Abyss and the Wings of the Dove: The Image as a Revelation." *Nineteenth-Century Fiction* 10 (1956): 281–300.

Kirsche, James J. *Henry James and Impressionism*. Troy, N.Y.: Whitston, 1981.

Knights, L. C. "Henry James and the Trapped Spectator." *Explorations: Essays in Criticism*. London: Chatto & Windus, 1946.

Kraft, James. *The Early Tales of Henry James*. Carbondale: Southern Illinois University Press, 1969.

Krier, William. "The 'Latent Extravagance' of *The Portrait of a Lady.*" *Mosaic* 9, no. 3 (1976): 57–65.

Krook, Dorothea. *The Ordeal of Consciousness in Henry James*. Cambridge: Cambridge University Press, 1962.

Labrie, Ross. "Henry James's Idea of Consciousness." *American Literature* 39 (1968): 517–29.

Lang, Hans-Joachim. "The Making of Henry James's *The American*: The Contribution of Four Literatures." *Amerikastudien* 20, no. 1 (1975): 55–71.

Leavis, F. R. *The Great Tradition*. New York: Stewart, 1949.

———. "Henry James and the Function of Criticism." In *The Common Pursuit*, 223–32. London: Penguin, 1962.

Lebowitz, Naomi. *The Imagination of Loving: Henry James's Legacy to the Novel*. Detroit: Wayne State University Press, 1965.

Levy, Leo B. *Versions of Melodrama*. Berkeley: University of California Press, 1957.

Lewis, R. W. B. *Trials of the Word*. New Haven: Yale University Press, 1965.

Leyburn, Ellen Douglas. *Strange Alloy: The Relation of Comedy to Tragedy in the Fiction of Henry James*. Chapel Hill: University of North Carolina Press, 1968.

Long, Robert Emmett. *The Great Succession: Henry James and the Legacy of Hawthorne*. Pittsburgh: University of Pittsburgh Press, 1979.

Lubbock, Percy. *The Craft of Fiction*. New York: Cape & Smith, 1929.

Lubin, David M. *Act of Portrayal: Eakins, Sargent, James*. New Haven: Yale University Press, 1985.

Lukacher, Ned. "'Hanging Fire': The Primal Scene of *The Turn of the Screw.*" In *Primal Scenes: Literature, Philosophy, Psychoanalysis*. Ithaca, N.Y.: Cornell University Press, 1986.

McCarthy, Harold T. *Henry James: The Creative Process*. Rutherford, N.J.: Fairleigh Dickinson University Press, 1958.

Mackenzie, Manfred. *Communities of Honor and Love in Henry James*. Cambridge: Harvard University Press, 1976.

McLean, Robert C. "The Subjective Adventure of Fleda Vetch." *American Literature* 36 (1964–65): 12–30.

McMaster, Juliet. "The Portrait of Isabel Archer." *American Literature* 45 (1973): 50–66.

Marks, Robert. *James's Later Novels: An Interpretation*. New York: William-Frederick, 1960.

Matthiessen, F. O. *Henry James: The Major Phase*. New York: Oxford University Press, 1963.

Maves, Carl. *Sensuous Pessimism: Italy in the Works of Henry James*. Bloomington: Indiana University Press, 1973.

Melchiori, Giorgio. "Cups of Gold for *The Sacred Fount*: Aspects of James's Symbolism." *Critical Quarterly* 7, no. 4 (1965): 301–16.

———. *The Tightrope Walkers: Studies of Mannerism in Modern English Literature*. London: Routledge & Kegan Paul, 1956.

Miller, James E., Jr. "Henry James: A Theory of Fiction." *The Prairie Schooner* 45, no. 4 (1971): 330–56.

———. "James in Reality." *Critical Inquiry* 2, no. 3 (1976): 585–604.

Miner, Earl R. "Henry James's Metaphysical Romances." *Nineteenth-Century Fiction* 9 (1954): 1–21.

Moon, Heath. "More Royalist than the King: The Governess, the Telegraphist, and Mrs. Gracedew." *Criticism* 24 (1982): 16–35.

Mull, Donald K. *Henry James's "Sublime Economy."* Middletown, Conn.: Wesleyan University Press, 1973.

Nettels, Elsa. *James and Conrad.* Athens: University of Georgia Press, 1977.

Norman, Ralf. *The Insecure World of Henry James's Fiction: Intensity and Ambiguity.* New York: St. Martin's, 1982.

O'Neill, John P. *Workable Design: Action and Situation in the Fiction of Henry James.* Port Washington, N.Y.: Kennikat, 1973.

Ozick, Cynthia. "The Jamesian Parable: *The Sacred Fount.*" *Bucknell Review* 11, no. 3 (May 1963): 55–70.

Perlongo, Robert A. "*The Sacred Fount*: Labyrinth or Parable." *The Kenyon Review* 22, no. 4 (1960): 635–47.

Perosa, Sergio. *Henry James and the Experimental Novel.* Charlottesville: University Press of Virginia, 1978.

Peterson, Dale E. *The Clement Vision: Poetic Realism in Turgenev and James.* Port Washington, N.Y.: Kennikat, 1975.

Poirier, Richard. *The Comic Sense of Henry James: A Study of the Early Novels.* New York: Oxford University Press, 1960.

———. *A World Elsewhere: The Place of Style in American Literature.* New York: Oxford University Press, 1966.

Porter, Carolyn. *Seeing and Being: The Plight of the Participant Observer in Emerson, James, Adams, and Faulkner.* Middletown, Conn.: Wesleyan University Press, 1981.

Poulet, Georges. *The Metamorphosis of the Circle.* Baltimore: Johns Hopkins University Press, 1973.

Powers, Lyall H. *Henry James and the Naturalist Movement.* East Lansing: Michigan State University Press, 1971.

———, ed. *Henry James's Major Novels: Essays in Criticism.* East Lansing: Michigan State University Press, 1973.

Przybylowicz, Donna. *Desire and Repression: The Dialectic of Self and Other in the Late Works of Henry James.* University: University of Alabama Press, 1986.

Purdy, Strother B. *The Hole in the Fabric: Science, Contemporary Literature, and Henry James.* Pittsburgh: University of Pittsburgh Press, 1977.

Raeth, Claire. "Henry James's Rejection of *The Sacred Fount.*" *ELH* 16, no. 4 (1949): 308–24.

Rahv, Philip. "Henry James and His Cult." *The New York Review of Books* 19 (February 1982): 18–22.

Raleigh, John Henry. "Henry James: The Poetics of Empiricism." *PMLA* 66 (1951): 107–23.

Rimmon, Shlomith. *The Concept of Ambiguity—The Example of James.* Chicago: University of Chicago Press, 1977.

Roberts, Morris. *Henry James's Criticism.* New York: Octagon, 1970.

Ronald, Ralph A. "*The Sacred Fount*: James's Portrait of the Artist Manqué." *Nineteenth-Century Fiction* 15 (1960): 239–48.

Rowe, John Carlos. *Henry Adams and Henry James: The Emergence of a Modern Consciousness*. Ithaca, N.Y.: Cornell University Press, 1976.

———. "The Symbolization of Milly Theale." *ELH* 40, no. 1 (1973): 131–64.

———. *The Theoretical Dimensions of Henry James*. Madison: University of Wisconsin Press, 1984.

———. *Through the Customhouse: Nineteenth-Century American Fiction and Modern Theory*. Baltimore: Johns Hopkins University Press, 1982.

Salmon, Rachel. "Naming and Knowing in Henry James's 'The Beast in the Jungle.'" *Orbis Litterarum* 36 (1981): 302–22.

Samuels, Charles Thomas. *The Ambiguity of Henry James*. Urbana: University of Illinois Press, 1971.

Schneider, Daniel J. *The Crystal Cage: Adventures of the Imagination in the Fiction of Henry James*. Lawrence: Regents Press of Kansas, 1978.

———. *Symbolism: The Manichean Vision, A Study of James, Conrad, Woolf, and Stevens*. Lincoln: University of Nebraska Press, 1975.

Sears, Sally. *The Negative Imagination: Form and Perspective in the Novels of Henry James*. Ithaca, N.Y.: Cornell University Press, 1968.

Segal, Ora. *The Lucid Reflector: The Observer in Henry James's Fiction*. New Haven: Yale University Press, 1969.

Seltzer, Mark. *Henry James and the Art of Power*. Ithaca, N.Y.: Cornell University Press, 1984.

Sharp, Sister M. Corona. *The "Confidante" in Henry James: Evolution and Moral Value of a Fictive Character*. Notre Dame, Ind.: University of Notre Dame Press, 1963.

Shine, Muriel G. *The Fictional Children of Henry James*. Chapel Hill: University of North Carolina Press, 1969.

Shriber, Michael. "Cognitive Apparatus in *Daisy Miller, The Ambassadors* and Two Works by Howells: A Comparative Study of the Epistemology of Henry James." *Language and Style* 2 (1969): 207–25.

Sicker, Philip. *Love and the Quest for Identity in the Fiction of Henry James*. Princeton, N.J.: Princeton University Press, 1980.

Springer, Mary Doyle. *A Rhetoric of Literary Character: Some Women of Henry James*. Chicago: University of Chicago Press, 1978.

Stallman, Robert Wooster. *The Houses that James Built, and Other Literary Studies*. East Lansing: Michigan State University Press, 1961.

Stanzel, Franz. *Narrative Situations in the Novel: Tom Jones, Moby-Dick, The Ambassadors, Ulysses*. Bloomington: Indiana University Press, 1971.

Stevenson, Elizabeth. *The Crooked Corridor: A Study of Henry James*. New York: Macmillan, 1949.

Stowe, William W. *Balzac, James, and the Realistic Novel*. Princeton, N.J.: Princeton University Press, 1983.

Stowell, Peter H. *Literary Impressionism: James and Chekhov*. Athens: University of Georgia Press, 1980.

Tanner, Tony, ed. *Henry James: Selections of Critical Essays*. London: Macmillan, 1968.

————, ed. *Modern Judgments: Henry James.* London: Macmillan, 1968.

Tillotson, Geoffrey. "Henry James and His Limitation." In *Criticism and the Nineteenth Century,* 244–69. New York: Barnes & Noble, 1952.

Todorov, Tzvetan. "The Ghosts of Henry James." In *The Poetics of Prose,* translated by Richard Howard, 179–89. Ithaca, N.Y.: Cornell University Press, 1977.

————. "The Structural Analysis of Literature: The Tales of Henry James." In *Structuralism: An Introduction,* edited by David Robey, 73–103. Oxford: Clarendon Press, 1973.

————. "The Verbal Age." *Critical Inquiry* 4 (1977): 351–71.

Tompkins, Jane P., ed. *Twentieth Century Interpretations of* The Turn of the Screw *and Other Tales: A Collection of Critical Essays.* Englewood Cliffs, N.J.: Prentice-Hall, 1970.

Tuveson, Ernest. "*The Turn of the Screw*: A Palimpsest." *Studies in English Literature* 12 (1972): 783–800.

Vaid, Krishna Baldev. *Technique in the Tales of Henry James.* Cambridge: Harvard University Press, 1964.

Veeder, William. *Henry James: The Lessons of the Master: Popular Fiction and Personal Style in the Nineteenth Century.* Chicago: University of Chicago Press, 1975.

Volpe, Edmond L. "James's Theory of Sex in Fiction." *Nineteenth-Century Fiction* 13 (1958): 36–47.

Wagenknecht, Edward. *Eve and Henry James: Portraits of Women and Girls in His Fiction.* Norman: University of Oklahoma Press, 1978.

Wallace, Ronald. *Henry James and the Comic Form.* Ann Arbor: University of Michigan Press, 1975.

Wantanabe, Hisayoshi. "Past Perfect Retrospection in the Style of Henry James." *American Literature* 34 (1962): 165–81.

Ward, J. A. *The Imagination of Disaster: Evil in the Fiction of Henry James.* Lincoln: University of Nebraska Press, 1961.

————. *The Search for Form: Studies in the Structure of James's Fiction.* Chapel Hill: University of North Carolina Press, 1967.

Warren, Austin. "Henry James, Symbolic Imagery in the Later Novels." In *Rage for Order: Essays in Criticism,* 142–61. Chicago: University of Chicago Press, 1948.

Wasiolek, Edward. "Maisie: Pure or Corrupt?" *College English* 22 (1960): 167–72.

Watt, Ian. "The First Paragraph of *The Ambassadors*: An Explication." In *Henry James's The Ambassadors,* edited by S. P. Rosenbaum, 465–84. New York: Norton, 1964.

Wegelin, Christof. *The Image of Europe in Henry James.* Dallas: Southern Methodist University Press, 1958.

Weinstein, Philip M. *Henry James and the Requirements of the Imagination.* Cambridge: Harvard University Press, 1971.

Weisenfarth, Joseph. *Henry James and the Dramatic Analogy.* New York: Fordham University Press, 1963.

Wellek, René. "Henry James's Literary Theory and Criticism." *American Literature* 30 (1958): 293–321.

Willen, Gerald, ed. *A Casebook on Henry James's* The Turn of the Screw. New York: Crowell, 1960.

Wilson, Edmund. "The Ambiguity of Henry James." In *The Triple Thinkers,* 88–132. New York: Oxford University Press, 1963.

Wilson, Harris W. "What *Did* Maisie Know?" *College English* 17 (1955–56): 279–82.

Winner, Viola Hopkins. *Henry James and the Visual Arts.* Charlottesville: University Press of Virginia, 1970.

Wright, Walter F. *The Madness of Art: A Study of Henry James.* Lincoln: University of Nebraska Press, 1962.

Yeazell, Ruth Bernard. *Language and Knowledge in the Late Novels of Henry James.* Chicago: University of Chicago Press, 1976.

Zabel, Morton D. "Henry James, the Act of Life." In *Craft and Character in Modern Fiction,* 114–43. New York: Viking, 1957.

Acknowledgments

"James's Idea of Dramatic Form" by Francis Fergusson from *The Kenyon Review* 5, no. 1 (Autumn 1943), © 1943 by Kenyon College. Reprinted by permission of the author and the *Kenyon Review.*

"*The American* and *Washington Square:* The Comic Sense" (originally entitled "*The American; Confidence* and *Washington Square* by Richard Poirier from *The Comic Sense of Henry James: A Study of the Early Novels* by Richard Poirier, © 1960, 1967 by Richard Poirier. Reprinted by permission.

"The Crisis of Transformation: *The Golden Bowl*" (originally entitled "The Crisis of Transformation") by Laurence Bedwell Holland from *The Expense of Vision: Essays on the Craft of Henry James* by Laurence Bedwell Holland, © 1964, 1982 by Faith Mackey Holland. Reprinted by permission.

" 'Daisy Miller': A Study of Changing Intentions" by Carol Ohmann from *American Literature* 36, no. 1 (March 1964), © 1964 by Duke University Press. Reprinted by permission.

"The Watcher from the Balcony: *The Ambassadors*" (originally entitled "The Watcher from the Balcony: Henry James's *The Ambassadors*") by Tony Tanner from *Critical Quarterly* 8, no. 1, (Spring 1966), © 1966 by Tony Tanner. Reprinted by permission.

" 'The Full Image of Repetition' in 'The Turn of the Screw' " by Juliet McMaster from *Studies in Short Fiction* 6, no. 4 (Summer 1969), © 1969 by Newberry College. Reprinted by permission.

"Imagination and Time in 'The Beast in the Jungle' " by Elisabeth Hansot from *Twentieth Century Interpretations of "The Turn of the Screw" and Other Tales: A Collection of Critical Essays,* edited by Jane P. Tomkins, © 1970 by Prentice-Hall, Inc., Englewood Cliffs, New Jersey. Reprinted by permission of the publisher, Prentice-Hall, Inc.

"*The Bostonians*" by David Howard from *The Air of Reality: New Essays on Henry James,* edited by John Goode, © 1972 by Methuen & Co. Ltd. Reprinted by permission.

"The Two Worlds of *The Tragic Muse:* A Holiday in Paris" (originally entitled "The

Reference of *The Tragic Muse*") by D. J. Gordon and John Stokes from *The Air of Reality: New Essays on Henry James,* edited by John Goode, © 1972 by Methuen & Co. Ltd. Reprinted by permission.

"The Story in It: *The Wings of the Dove*" (originally entitled "The Story in It: James") by Robert L. Caserio from *Plot, Story and the Novel: From Dickens and Poe to the Modern Period* by Robert L. Caserio, © 1979 by Princeton University Press. Reprinted by permission.

"James: The Logic of Intensity" by Martin Price from *Forms of Life: Character and Moral Imagination in the Novel* by Martin Price, © 1983 by Yale University. Reprinted by permission of Yale University Press.

"A Jamesian About-Face: Notes on 'The Jolly Corner'" by Deborah Esch from *ELH* 50, no. 3 (Fall 1983), © 1983 by the Johns Hopkins University Press, Baltimore/ London. © 1985 by Deborah Esch. Reprinted by permission of the author and the Johns Hopkins University Press.

"Imagination and Desire in *The Spoils of Poynton* and *What Maisie Knew*" (originally entitled "Ambassadorial Consciousness" and "Imagination in *Predominance*") by Carren O. Kaston from *Imagination and Desire in the Novels of Henry James* by Carren O. Kaston, © 1984 by Rutgers, The State University. Reprinted by permission of Rutgers University Press.

"*The Princess Casamassima:* Realism and the Fantasy of Surveillance" by Mark Seltzer from *Henry James and the Art of Power* by Mark Seltzer, © 1984 by Cornell University. Reprinted by permission of Cornell University Press. This essay originally appeared in *Nineteenth-Century Fiction* 35, no. 4 (1981), © 1981 by the Regents of the University of California. Reprinted by permission of the University of California Press.

"Isabel's Freedom: *The Portrait of a Lady*" (originally entitled "Isabel's Freedom: Henry James's *The Portrait of a Lady*") by Maria Irene Ramalho de Sousa Santos from *Biblos 56,* © 1980 by Irene Ramalho Santos. Reprinted by permission of the author.

Index

335